OPTUM™

RENEW TODAY

SAVE UP TO 25%

when you renew your coding essentials.

- Buy 1–2 items, save 15%
- Buy 3–5 items, save 20%
- Buy 6+ items, save 25%

ITEM #	TITLE INDICATE THE ITEMS YOU WISH TO PURCHASE	QUANTITY	PRICE PER PRODUCT	TOTAL
			Subtotal	
	(AK, DE, HI, MT, NH & OR are exempt)		Sales Tax	
	1 item $10.95 • 2–4 items $12.95 • 5+ CALL		Shipping & Handling	
			TOTAL AMOUNT ENCLOSED	

Save up to 25% when you renew.

Visit **www.optumcoding.com** and enter your promo code.

Call **1.800.464.3649, option 1,** and mention the promo code.

Fax this order form with purchase order to **801.982.4033.** *Optum no longer accepts credit cards by fax.*

PROMO CODE
FOBA13C

Mail this order form with payment and/or purchase order to:
OptumInsight, PO Box 88050, Chicago, IL 60680-9920.

Name

Address

Customer Number Contact Number

○ CHECK ENCLOSED (PAYABLE TO OPTUMINSIGHT)

CHARGE MY: ○ MCard ○ Visa ○ AMEX ○ Discover

Card Number Exp. mm / yr

Signature

○ BILL ME ○ P.O.#

( )
Telephone

( )
Fax

@
E-mail

Optum respects your right to privacy. We will not sell or rent your email address or fax number to anyone outside Optum and its business partners. If you would like to remove your name from Optum promotions, please call 1.800.464.3649, option 1.

INGENIX.

Ingenix is now Optum
—a leading health services business.

OPTUM™

Insurance Directory

Largest and most complete listing of insurers

2014

Publishers Notice

2014 Insurance Directory is designed to be an accurate and authoritative source regarding coding and every reasonable effort has been made to ensure accuracy and completeness of the content. However, Optum makes no guarantee, warranty, or representation that this publication is accurate, complete, or without errors. It is understood that Optum is not rendering any legal or other professional services or advice in this publication and that Optum bears no liability for any results or consequences that may arise from the use of this book. Please e-mail all correspondence to the Optum customer service department at customerservice@optum.com or call 1.800.464.3649, option 1.

Acknowledgments

Mike Grambo, *Product Manager*
Karen Schmidt, BSN, *Technical Director*
Stacy Perry, *Manager, Desktop Publishing*
Lisa Singley, *Project Manager*
Karen M. Adkins, CMM, CPC, CPC-I, CCS-P
Clinical/Technical Editor
Deborah C. Hall, *Clinical/Technical Editor*
Tracy Betzler, *Senior Desktop Publishing Specialist*
Hope M. Dunn, *Senior Desktop Publishing Specialist*
Katie Russell, *Desktop Publishing Specialist*
Jean Parkinson, *Editor*
Shawn Holcomb, *Data Verification Specialist*
Travis Christofferson, *Data Verification Specialist*
Clint Ash, *Data Verification Specialist*
Jason Demke, *Data Verification Specialist*

Copyright

Made in the USA.

ISBN 978-1-60151-748-7

Our Commitment to Accuracy

Optum is committed to producing accurate and reliable materials. To report corrections, please visit www.optumcoding.com/accuracy or email accuracy@optum.com. You can also reach customer service by calling 1.800.464.3649, option 1.

Technical Editors

Karen M. Prescott Adkins, CPC, CPC-I, CCS-P

Ms. Adkins has more than 18 years of experience in the health care profession. She has an extensive background in professional component coding and billing. Her prior experience includes establishing and maintaining a coding and billing service, directing physician practice start ups, functioning as director of physician credentialing, negotiating insurance contracts, and functioning as a health care consultant. Her areas of expertise include coding and reimbursement, documentation education, compliance, practice management, and revenue cycle management. Ms. Adkins is a member of the AAPC, and the American Health Information Management Association (AHIMA).

Deborah C. Hall

Ms. Hall is a new product subject matter expert for Optum. She has more than 25 years of experience in the health care field. Ms. Hall's experience includes 10 years as practice administrator for large multi-specialty medical practices. She has written several multi-specialty newsletters and coding and reimbursement manuals, and served as a health care consultant. She has taught seminars on CPT/HCPCS and ICD-9-CM coding and physician fee schedules.

Contents

Introduction

Introduction

The *2014 Insurance Directory* is a comprehensive reference of listings for the United States, Puerto Rico, Virgin Islands, American Samoa, and Guam insurance companies that process claims. Optum has structured this publication to offer providers, payers, and employers a ready reference of insurance companies' addresses, telephone numbers, web addresses and the payer identification numbers, if available. Furthermore, Optum makes every effort to assure the validity and accuracy of listings in the *2014 Insurance Directory* by personally calling each insurance company listed to verify and update the information published.

In addition to specific company information, the *2014 Insurance Directory* contains an extensive introduction explaining insurance billing policies and procedures. For example, the *2014 Insurance Directory* outlines the appropriate steps necessary to complete the CMS-1500 form required by Medicare Part B and non-Medicare payers for reimbursement. A copy of the standard Electronic Data Interchange (EDI) enrollment form that must be completed prior to submitting electronic media claims to Medicare is also included.

The *2014 Insurance Directory* enhances popular standard features such as the state-by-state listing of private payers, the addresses and phone numbers of individual state insurance commissioners, and contact information for governmental payers such as Medicare, Medicaid, and workers' compensation.

Insurance Directory 2014

Places of Operation

Whether it's a private payer claim, workers' compensation claim, or other government claim, the *2014 Insurance Directory* provides the information necessary to submit your claims to the right place. The *2014 Insurance Directory* also directs you to an insurance company's web address for quick online assistance with your claims questions.

Place of Service (POS) Codes

The *2014 Insurance Directory* contains the CMS Place of Service (POS) listing in appendix B for quick and easy reference.

Electronic Claims Capability

HIPAA requires that payers have the capability to receive claims electronically to reduce the costs and administrative functions of health care tracking and reimbursement. The Administrative Simplification Provisions of HIPAA apply to payers and providers and affect all health claims and equivalent encounter information (professional, institutional, and dental). Some entities are not required to comply with the electronic claims mandate including those with no means of electronic claim submission capability, facilities with 25 or fewer full-time employees, and physician practices with 10 or fewer full-time employees.

Because the majority of claims are filed in an electronic format, the *2014 Insurance Directory* continues to provide more detailed information on electronic claims media. This information, as well as the standard information required at a minimum in each contractor, MAC, and fiscal intermediary (FI) Electronic Data Interchange (EDI) Enrollment Form, can be found in the Claims Processing chapter.

History of Creating a National Health Plan Identifier

The Centers for Medicare and Medicaid Services (CMS) was instrumental in the development of a unique numbering system for health plans to improve the administration of the Medicare and Medicaid programs. Initially, the goal was to create a program that would permit the cost effective identification of health plans which in turn would make routing health care transactions to the appropriate health plan responsible for payment significantly easier and more expeditious.

Prior to the Health Insurance Portability and Accountability Act of 1996 (HIPAA), CMS and others proposed that the PAYERID, a nine-digit numeric identifier, be adopted as the national standard identifier for health plans. Subsequently, the Department of Health and Human Services (HHS) opted to refer to this HIPAA-required identifier as the *plan* ID. The Administrative Simplification Provisions of HIPAA mandated the adoption of standard unique identifiers for health care providers and health plans. The purpose of these provisions is to improve the efficiency and effectiveness of the electronic transmission of health information. CMS has developed the National Plan and Provider Enumeration System (NPPES) to assign these unique identifiers. The National Provider Identifier (NPI) was created for providers and the Employer Identification Number (EIN) was selected as the identifier for employers.

On August 24, 2012, the HHS announced in a final rule the establishment of a unique health plan identifier (HPID) designed to save time and money for physicians and other health care providers. This rule is one in a series of changes, and the fourth administrative simplification regulation issued by HHS, legislated under the Affordable Care Act to reduce the amount of red tape in the health care system. It is estimated that the HPID will save approximately $6 billion over the next decade.

Presently, there is no single comprehensive system to enumerate health plans and as such, providers billing to health plans often are required to use a variety of different identifiers depending on the plan with no established standard format. This can create any number of time consuming issues, including but not limited to, claims rejections resulting from insurance identification errors, misrouting of transactions and the inability to determine patient eligibility.

In addition, HHS will also adopt a data element that will serve as an "other entity" identifier (OEID) that will be used to identify entities that are not health plans, health care providers, or individuals but still need to be identified in standard transactions.

The Office of E-Health Standards and Services (OESS) developed this rule in its role to adopt standards for electronic health care transactions under HIPAA and has indicated that future administrative simplification rules will address the adoption of a claims attachments standard, operating rules for claims attachments requirements to certify health plans' compliance with all HIPAA standards.

The main goal of the HPID and OEID is to increase standardization within HIPAA standard transactions. Issues exist with the current standard unique health care provider identifier referred to as the NPI. The final rule regarding the creation of the HPID and OEID will help eradicate problems, primarily with Medicare Part D, that have occurred where the NPI of a prescribing health care provider is needed for processing of a pharmacy claim but the provider does not have an NPI or has not disclosed it. The HPID and OEID have been adopted in addition to the current NPI requirements and HHS has indicated that these additions are expected to have little to no impact on health care providers or the health care industry at large since there are very few health care providers who do not already have an NPI and applying for an NPI is free and requires little time to obtain.

According to the rule, all health plans, except small health plans, will be required to obtain an HPID by the effective date of November 5, 2014 with small plans having to comply by November 5, 2015. All covered entities will be required to use HPIDs in standard transactions by the November 7, 2016 effective date.

Applications to obtain an HPID or OEID are available through the Health Plan and Other Entity Enumeration System (HPOES) as of the end of the first quarter in 2013.

The *2014 Insurance Directory* provides you with the plan—or payer ID—for each insurance company, when available. Information will be provided on changes to plan identifiers in future updates to the *Insurance Directory* as it becomes available.

Glossary

The *2014 Insurance Directory* features a comprehensive glossary with terms that are often used in the health care insurance industry and can be located in appendix C at the back of this publication.

Payer Landmark Initiative

The Blue Cross and Blue Shield Association (BCBSA), in conjunction with America's Health Insurance Plans (AHIP) are sponsoring regional and statewide plans to evaluate options that would allow physicians access to multiple insurers through one universal information channel (i.e., web portal) in a specific area of the country for the purpose of performing key administrative medical tasks. Specifically, this initiative spotlights the need for centralizing and standardizing service in electronic transactions that physicians have been requesting. Additionally, it is a key step in achieving significant monetary savings by replacing cumbersome and time consuming activities that physician office and hospital staff must deal with as a result of having to access varied and multiple processes in order to complete basic administrative requirements such as eligibility verification, making or obtaining referrals, and billing. Savings are estimated to be worth hundreds of billions of dollars as the health care industry seeks to achieve greater efficiencies through similar moves to automation and consistency in business practices. This program offers the opportunity to streamline and simplify the day-to-day work associated with patient visits and provide physicians and hospitals with "real time" information. Benefits to this include:

- Allows staff to quickly and efficiently determine eligibility and benefit information while minimizing the amount of time and money normally needed to perform such tasks
- Provides access to current and accurate information for physician office staff regarding claims status; thereby eliminating the need for follow-up calls, faxes or letters, and claims resubmissions which ultimately serve to delay rather than expedite reimbursement
- Provides online submission of health care claims
- Tests real time referrals
- Ensures timely preauthorization of services

Benefits of this ground-breaking initiative are not only monetary but clearly represent time savings by reducing the amount of time currently spent on paperwork and administrative duties as well as increase and improve patient care.

The initial initiative was conducted in New Jersey, with a concurrent initiative launching in Ohio, and led by local health plans that represent more than 95 percent of state residents covered under private health plans. The following is a list of the health plans participating in the program:

- Aetna
- AmeriHealth New Jersey
- CIGNA
- Horizon BC/BS of New Jersey
- UnitedHealthcare

Note: Insurance information changes rapidly, and while Optum attempts to provide the latest information possible, there will be new information Optum must hold until the next printing or edition of the *Insurance Directory.*

Health Plan Internet Directory

The 2014 edition of the Insurance Directory includes a new feature designed to help you quickly find a wide range of payer information for more than 400 insurers.

For each health plan we have gathered the following information. Note that access to some health plan web pages may be limited.

- Home page
- Provider page
- Medical policies
- Credentialing
- Formulary
- Claims

To access the Health Plan Internet Directory you must first download a copy to your computer. Got to this internet address:

http://www.optumcoding.com/Product/Updates/ID14

Password **Insdir2014**

Follow the directions posted on this webpage and click on the link to open the file, then save to your computer. Updates to this file will be posted periodically and you will be notified by email when an updated file is available. Please be sure your email address on file with Optum will allow contact by email about product subscriptions. If you have questions, please contact our customer service department at 1-800-464-3649.

Claims Processing

Claims processing describes the course of submitting a claim to the payer and the subsequent adjudication by the payer. Understanding how this process works allows providers and staff members to file claims properly and leads to maximum and timely reimbursement. In addition, this knowledge will allow you and your staff to serve as a invaluable resource to patients in understanding this process.

Patient Information

In order to properly complete the CMS-1500 claim form, it is necessary to obtain accurate and current demographic and billing information from the patient. A key method of collecting this information is through the use of a patient information (PI) form. A standard medical patient information form will request complete demographic information such as the patient's full and legal name; mailing and residential address, city, state, and ZIP code; telephone numbers, including home, work, and cell; as well as date of birth. In addition, it is necessary to request information on the patient's insurance plan and the name of the subscriber or insured, if the coverage is offered through another person other than the patient. This information would consist of the insured's full and legal name and date of birth as well as the policy identification and group number. It should be noted that with the rise in identify theft, a social security number is *not* a requirement in order to submit a claim for most third-party payers. Many non-Medicare payers no longer use a patient's social security number as the insurance identification number. However, Medicare still requires the social security number. Obtaining the necessary information in advance of the patient visit allows for verification of insurance, determining the patient's eligibility and financial responsibility which can then be collected at the time of service. This information is discussed in more detail below.

You may also wish to preregister new patients over the phone, Internet or, if time permits, through the mail. Having a shortened version of your PI form for phone registrations could prove helpful.

Patient information must be updated regularly. Most offices verify the information at each visit. If you work in a multi-physician office or clinic, establishing a uniform information policy makes everyone accountable for current and correct patient data.

Patient information forms follow the same basic format, but each differs by the type of patient your office caters to. Each form is titled with the targeted group's name. If your office has some special information needs or you wish to include additional instructions, consider using the back of the form. If your practice has a high volume of Medicare patients, you may want to consider two separate forms—one for Medicare patients and another for non-Medicare patients. These forms could be printed on different colored paper for easy identification.

Determining Coverage

Ideally, a patient's insurance coverage should be verified before any nonemergent service is rendered. This policy shouldn't apply exclusively to new patients. Established patients may have changed employers, married, divorced, or may no longer be covered by the policy that was in effect during their last visit.

When a patient appointment is made, remind the patient to bring a current insurance identification card. However, a copy of the card does not guarantee eligibility. You may want to take the pertinent information over the phone to verify benefits before the patient arrives. Many payers now allow you to check eligibility online, making it easier for you to validate coverage and eligibility. The law requires Medicaid patients to provide current proof of eligibility with each visit, and requesting this information from all patients can be done in a pleasant manner without alienating anyone.

During the visit, photocopy insurance cards and place the copies in the patient's record. Always check and highlight the eligibility dates as well as coverage information. Many offices have a policy that the first visit is always paid at the time of service, with the exception of Medicare, Medicaid, and any contractual arrangements your office may have with an individual payer. Payment for the first service allows you time to verify coverage prior to additional treatment.

Assignment of Benefits and Release of Information

If you haven't already done so, consider adding an assignment of benefits statement to your patient information form. It should state that the patient has agreed to have insurance payments sent directly to the physician and that medical information can be released to the patient's insurance company. A signed copy of this assignment submitted with a claim helps ensure at least partial payment from most commercial insurers. Assignments also reduce collection expenses. An alternative, lifetime assignment of benefits should nearly eliminate the need to obtain a signature after each date of service; however, there are a few payers who require a current signature with each claim.

If your office participates with Medicare, remember that an assignment of benefits and a release of billing are still necessary. To avoid any difficulty in obtaining updated signatures, you may want to secure lifetime assignment agreements and a commercial insurer's yearly signature agreement. Most commercial payers accept the yearly signature agreement form; however, it is not applicable to the Medicare patient.

The Claim

The most important document for correct reimbursement is the insurance claim form. Other information, such as operative reports, chart notes, and cover letters may establish medical necessity, but the claim itself sets the stage.

There are two types of claims media, paper and electronic. Legislation has been in effect for several years that requires claim submission of HIPAA compliant electronic format for facilities with more than 25 full-time employees and physician practices with more than 10 full-time employees. The legislation also requires that all payers, including small health plans, have the capability of accepting claims in HIPAA compliant electronic format.

With commercial insurance companies, you may submit the claim directly to the payer or provide your patient with the necessary information to submit the claim. If you've signed an agreement with Blue Cross/Blue Shield or with an HMO or PPO, you are probably required to send the claim directly to them. Medicare now requires that all Medicare claims be submitted directly to the carrier, whether you participate or not.

If patients pay at the time of service, you may wish to provide an itemized statement or superbill attached to a claim form that they can submit to their insurance company. This arrangement works well for office services, but surgical services are usually more accurately reimbursed if you bill your hospital and surgical services directly to the payer.

For electronic media claims, all health care providers and health plans are required to use the ASC X12 837, which is the standard HIPAA format. An overview of the ASC X12 837 is described in the Electronic Claims section of this chapter.

Standardized Claims Processing

The Administrative Simplification Provisions of the Health Insurance Portability and Accountability Act (HIPAA) (Title II) require the Department of Health and Human Services (HHS) to establish national standards for electronic health care transactions and national identifiers for providers, health plans, and employers. It also addresses the security and privacy of health data. Implementation of these standards and encouraging the use of electronic data interchange (EDI) in health care will improve the efficiency of the nation's health care system, reduce the administrative burden on providers and health care plans, and save more than $30 billion over the next decade.

Under HIPAA, every health care provider will be able to use EDI standards for billing and other health care transactions, such as referrals and diagnosis reports. All health plans will be required to accept these standard electronic claims and all health care providers using electronic transmittals will be required to use the EDI standards. Providers that submit information by paper will not be affected by the rules. However, the health plans they bill are not prohibited from independently requiring the EDI standards for paper transactions as well.

Guidelines specify that transactions involving the following types of information exchanges between health care plans, clearinghouses, and providers are subject to EDI standards:

- Health care claims and equivalent encounter information
- Health care payment and remittance advice
- Coordination of benefits
- Health care claim status
- Enrollment or disenrollment in a health plan
- Eligibility for a health plan
- Referral certification and authorization
- Health insurance plan premiums

Since October 16, 2003, the majority of health plans, providers, and other entities have been required by law to be in compliance with the HIPAA electronic transactions standards. The only exceptions being certain types of claims, such as those related to demonstration projects and roster billing of Medicare covered vaccinations, and providers with no capability for electronic claim submission and those with less than 25 full-time employees (facilities) and 10 full-time employees (physician practices). This legislation further stipulated that, electronic claims were no longer to be processed if they were in a format other than the HIPAA format. In October 2003 Medicare implemented a contingency plan permitting some providers that bill electronically to continue sending pre-HIPAA format electronic claims. This contingency plan ended October 1, 2005. Effective October 1, 2005, all claims submitted to CMS must be HIPAA compliant. Noncompliant claims will be returned unprocessed.

Standards and Code Sets

CMS has adopted the following standard medical data code sets:

National Drug Codes (NDC): required for reporting drugs and biologicals. (In the *Federal Register* on May 31, 2002 a rule was proposed that would retract the adoption of NDC codes for reporting drugs and biologicals with the exception of retail pharmacy transactions that already use them)

CDT: Current Dental Terminology (CDT®): required for reporting dental services

American Medical Association's CPT®: required for reporting physician and other health care services

HCPCS Level II: required for reporting not only physician and other health care services, but also for supplies, equipment, substances, and other items used for health care services

ICD-9-CM Volumes 1 and 2: required for reporting the following conditions: diseases, injuries, impairments, other health problems and their manifestations, and causes

ICD-9-CM Volume 3: required for reporting diagnostic, preventive, therapeutic, or management procedures or actions provided by hospitals

CMS notes that the CDT and CPT code sets are proprietary and that there are royalties for electronic use of them.

On January 16, 2009, HHS published a final rule in the *Federal Register*, HIPAA Administrative Simplification: "Modifications to the Medical Data Code Set Standards, to Adopt ICD-10-CM and ICD-10-PCS". This rule mandates the adoption of ICD-10-CM and ICD-10-PCS for all covered entities beginning October 1, 2013. However, in February 2012 HHS announced that it was delaying ICD-10-CM implementation to give health care providers more time to prepare for implementation. The new effective date has been set for October 1, 2014.

National Privacy Standards

With publication of a final rule in December 2000, HHS established regulations that protect the privacy of an individual's health information. The regulations are applicable to all medical records and health information that can be individually identified—that is, transmitted in any form. The regulations also grant individuals the right to control the disclosure of their health information and how it is used. Any improper use or disclosure of this information is subject to criminal and civil sanctions including civil monetary penalties, fines, and prison. All covered entities were required to be in compliance with the privacy standards as of April 14, 2004.

In general, the HIPAA regulations for the privacy of personal health information (PHI) require that an individual has the right to be notified as to the uses and disclosures of PHI that may be made by the covered entity. Legislation requires that a written notice of privacy practices be provided to patients. The notice must also explain the individual's rights and the covered entity's legal duties with respect to PHI. Covered entities should make every effort to obtain the patient's written acknowledgement that he/she received or received a copy of the privacy notice.

On February 17, 2012, the American Recovery and Reinvestment Act of 2009 (ARRA) was enacted. Included in the economic stimulus package were federal tax cuts, expansion of unemployment benefits as well as other social welfare provisions and domestic spending in the areas of education, health care, and infrastructure.

However, within this legislation, there was a section titled the Health Information Technology for Economic and Clinical Health Act (HITECH) which talks about the development and implementation of nationwide interoperable privacy protected health information technology infrastructure. HITECH was deemed effective on February 18, 2010 though HHS did acknowledge that it would be difficult for organizations to comply with the regulations for a period of time after they were finalized; therefore, HHS provided organizations with 180 additional days past the effective date to enforce compliance. Further, HHS proposed a period of transition that would allow organizations to modify their business associate (BA) agreements. One significant component of this section provided that eligible professionals (EPs) who could demonstrate "meaningful use" of a "certified" electronic health record may qualify to receive incentive payments of up to $44,000 from Medicare and $65,000 from Medicaid per individual physician to assist in offsetting costs associated with adopting an EHR over a five year period beginning in 2011.

It should be noted that the Health Information Technology Policy Committee has made its first attempt to create a standard definition for "meaningful use" as the term relates to EHRs in June 2011. The committee has stated in its recommendations that the ultimate goal of meaningful use with an EHR is to enable significant and measureable improvements in population health via a transformed delivery system. Further, the committee has indicated that requirements for meaningful use should be staggered and become more complex with each year between 2011 and 2015 with penalties for noncompliance with the standards.

Between 2007 and 2009, a number of major steps were taken in regard to the regulatory structure of HIPAA, most notably the implementation of ICD-10. But, another area of change that took place within this time period involved breach notification. In August 2009, the Office for Civil Rights issued an interim final rule regarding breach notification of privacy breaches when they involve protected health information (PHI); however, this was subsequently withdrawn due to controversy in the health information management community.

Other changes included shifting responsibility for enforcement of security rules to the Office of Civil Rights as well as a congressional mandate for increased enforcement of the privacy and security rules in the 2009 HITECH provisions of ARRA.

On July 14, 2010, HHS posted proposed regulations that would again modify the privacy, security, and enforcement rules under HIPAA. Upon being finalized, the new regulations will in essence implement the legal amendments made to HIPAA under the HITECH Act.

In March 2012, the HHS Office for Civil Rights submitted the final HIPAA Omnibus Rule to the Office of Management and Budget to review; this action constitutes one of the remaining steps needed in order for the rule to be published in the *Federal Register*. The Office of Management and Budget is permitted 90 days to review the rule.

The omnibus rule will bring together four distinct rule makings:

- Changes to HIPAA privacy and security rules implemented by the HITECH Act
- The latest in penalties and breach enforcement regulations
- Final regulations pertaining to the breach notification rule
- Modifications to HIPAA that will include the Genetic Information Nondiscrimination Act

There are some additional stipulations with the new rule that could translate to:

- Regulations around the use of patient information in marketing materials
- Cease the sale of patient data without first obtaining prior authorization
- Eradicate the "harm threshold" that at the present time permits a covered entity from reporting a data breach that is considered to be minor or not harmful
- Implement data encryption for all electronic systems that contain PHI

On January 25, 2013 the HHS released a final omnibus rule strengthening the privacy and security provisions. The omnibus rule:

- Expands business associates requirements that receive protected health information, including contractors and subcontractors
- Increases noncompliance penalties with a maximum penalty of $1.5 million per violation. Penalties are based upon the severity of the negligence
- Revised breach notification requirements
- Modifies the individual authorization and other requirements used for research as well as proof of immunization to schools
- Enables access to expired patient information under specific requirements
- Adopts provisions addressing enforcement of HIPAA noncompliance due to willful neglect found in the HITECH Act
- Expands patients' abilities to receive electronic copies of the health information and to restrict disclosures to health plans concerning treatment for which the patient paid out-of-pocket

Security Standards

HHS proposed security standards for the protection of electronic health information systems on August 12, 1998. The final HIPAA security rules were released to the health care industry on February 20, 2003, but due to the 60-day period mandated by the Congressional Review Act and the 24 months mandated by the HIPAA statute, the security rules did not become effective until April 2005. Small health plans had until April 2006 to comply.

Understanding section 164.306 of the security rules is crucial. This section is the heart of the new security rules and tracks the part of the HIPAA statute that governs security standards and safeguards. Covered entities must meet the four following security requirements specified in section 164.306(a):

- Ensure the confidentiality, integrity, and availability of all electronic PHI the covered entity creates, receives, maintains, or transmits
- Protect against any reasonably anticipated threats or hazards to the security or integrity of such information
- Protect against any reasonably anticipated uses or disclosures of such information that are not permitted or required under the security rules
- Ensure compliance by its workforce

Additional Requirements for Health Plans

Health plans must permit the use of EDI standard transactions when requested to do so. They may not delay or reject a transaction because it is an EDI standard transaction. They may not reject a standard transaction on the basis that it contains data elements not needed or used by the health plan. They may not offer incentives to steer providers toward direct data entry transactions.

A health plan that operates a health care clearinghouse or requires a provider to use a health care clearinghouse to receive, process, or transmit a standard transaction may not charge fees or costs in excess of the fees or costs for normal telecommunications that the provider incurs when it directly transmits or receives a standard transaction to or from a health plan.

National Provider Identifier Overview

On January 23, 2004, HHS published the final rule for the adoption and distribution of national provider identifiers (NPI).

Published in the *Federal Register* and authorized under the Health Insurance Portability and Accountability Act (HIPAA) of 1996, the rule is available at http://www.gpoaccess.gov/fr/index.html. The rule covers providers, individuals, and provider organizations that submit standardized electronic transactions under HIPAA's transactions and code sets rule. However, the rule enables other types of providers to apply for and receive an identifier. This includes providers who do not necessarily submit HIPAA transactions, such as registered nurses, dental hygienists, and technicians.

Health insurers and claims clearinghouses must accept the standard provider identifier. The NPI final rule was effective on May 23, 2005, which was the date when providers began to apply for an ID. Providers, payers, and clearinghouses were required to use the standard identifiers effective May 23, 2007 though small payers had until May 23, 2008 to comply. Since then, the NPI is the required identifier for all claims, paper and electronic. The NPI is a 10-digit, intelligence-free numeric identifier for covered health care providers. The number does not carry other information about the providers, such as the state they live in or their medical specialty. This number must be used in lieu of other provider identifiers in HIPAA standard transactions.

Other provisions of the final national provider identifier rule enumerates providers in two categories. The final rule states that national provider identifiers (NPI) with an "Entity type code" of 1 will be issued to health care providers who are individual human beings and NPIs with an "Entity type code" of 2 will be issued to health care providers other than individual human beings, that is, organizations. These include hospitals, home health agencies, clinics, nursing homes, residential treatment centers, laboratories, ambulance companies, group practices, health maintenance organizations, durable medical equipment suppliers, other suppliers related to health care, prosthetics, and pharmacies, among others.

In April 2012, the Department of Health and Human Services announced a proposal that would establish a unique health plan identifier under the Health Insurance Portability and Accountability Act of 1996 (HIPAA).

Presently, when health plans and other entities such as third-party administrators bill providers, they are identified with varying ranges of different types of identifiers without any regard to consistency such as standard length or even format. Naturally, this creates a number of problems for health providers such as misrouting of transactions, rejection of transactions due to insurance identification errors, difficulty determining patient eligibility not to mention significant time lost.

This rule aims to simplify the administrative process by requiring health care plans to establish a unique identifier of a standard length and format to ease routine use in computer systems. Additionally, this would permit provider offices to automate and streamline their own internal processes especially those related to processing bills as well as other transactions. It is anticipated to generate a savings to health care providers and health plans of $4.6 billion over ten years while simultaneously reducing red tape and increasing efficiency.

This same rule postponed required compliance for implementation of ICD-10-CM and PCS from October 1, 2013 to October 1, 2014. This was decided upon after a number of provider organizations expressed concern over their ability to meet the original October 1, 2013 deadline. Delaying the implementation date for ICD-10 allows providers and other covered entities additional time to prepare and test their systems and assure a smoother and more coordinated transition.

This rule is the third in a series of administrative simplification rules in the new health care law. Plans to announce more will take place in the upcoming months. The first rule was released in July 2011 and the second in January 2012.

On September 5, 2012, a final rule announcing the establishment of a unique health plan identifier (HPID) was posted. This rule is one in a series of changes, and the fourth administrative simplification regulation issued by HHS as directed by the Affordable Care Act and is intended to streamline processes while saving an estimated $6 billion over the next ten years.

The rule also indicates that HHS will also adopt a data element to function as an "other entity" identifier (OEID) to identify entities other than health plans, health care providers, or individuals that need to be identified in standard transactions.

As earlier discussed, the primary objective of creating the HPID and OEID is to provide greater uniformity within HIPAA standard transactions and help eliminate currently existing issues associated with the standard unique health care provider identifier referred to as the NPI.

All health plans, except small health plans, will have to secure an HPID by the effective date of November 5, 2014 while small plans have until November 5, 2015. All covered entities will be required to use HPIDs in standard transactions by the November 7, 2016 effective date. For more information, including how to apply for an HPID or OEID, visit: http://www.cms.gov/Regulations-and-Guidance/HIPAA-Administrative-Simplification/Affordable-Care-Act/Health-Plan-Identifier.html

Electronic Claims

The percentage of electronic claims submitted in HIPAA compliant format to CMS has steadily increased in recent years and now exceeds 99 percent for physician claims and 98 percent for hospital and lab claims. There are a number of advantages to electronic claim submission. These are detailed on the CMS website and include:

- Faster payment is made on HIPAA compliant electronic claims. HIPAA compliant electronic claims can be paid after 13 days while paper claims and electronic claims that are not HIPAA compliant cannot be paid for at least 27 days.
- Electronic transactions are cost effective, and reduce the opportunity for error.
- Electronic claims lower administrative, postage, and handling costs associated with paper claim submissions.
- Online receipt or acknowledgment is provided eliminating delays due to "lost" claims.
- Standardized formats reduce administrative costs since one format will meet all current billing requirements and is accepted by all Medicare contractors as well as many third-party billers.
- Standardized electronic claims submission and COB exchange and remittance receipt reduce system costs.
- Remittances are sent to a provider-preferred location.
- Claim status and eligibility information is available in 24 hours or less.
- Electronic funds transfer (EFT) can have accounts receivable revenue in the provider's bank, drawing interest, in two working days after payment. Paper checks can take as long as one week to process.

Administrative Simplification Compliance Act (ASCA)
The Administrative Simplification Compliance Act (ASCA) prohibits payment of services or supplies that a provider did not bill to Medicare electronically. The term "providers" refers to physicians, suppliers, and other health care providers. Providers are required to self-assess in order to determine whether they meet certain permitted exceptions to this electronic billing requirement.

Examples of exceptions:

- Small Provider Claims—The word "provider" is being used generically here to refer to physicians, suppliers, and other providers of health care services. Providers that have fewer than 25 full-time equivalent employees (FTEs) and that are required to bill a Part A Medicare administrative contractor (MAC) are considered to be small. Physicians and suppliers with fewer than 10 FTEs and that are required to bill a Part B Medicare administrative contractor (MAC) or durable medical equipment Medicare administrative contractor (DME MAC) are classified as small. See section 90.1 of chapter 24 of the *Medicare Claims Processing Manual* (Pub. 100-04) for more detailed information on calculation of FTE employees and this ASCA requirement in general.
- Roster billing of inoculations covered by Medicare, except for those companies that agreed to submit these claims electronically as a condition for submission of flu shots administered in multiple states to a single carrier.
- Claims for payment under a Medicare demonstration project that specifies claims be submitted on paper.
- Medicare Secondary Payer claims when there is more than one primary payer and one or more of those payers made an "Obligated to accept as payment in Full" (OTAF) adjustment.
- Claims submitted by Medicare beneficiaries or Medicare Managed Care plans.
- Dental claims.
- Claims for services or supplies furnished outside of the U.S. by non-U.S. providers.
- Disruption in electricity or communication connections outside of a provider's control expected to last more than two business days.
- Claims from providers that submit fewer than 10 claims per month on average during a calendar year.

In some cases, providers are required to submit a written request to their Medicare contractor to receive permission to submit some or all of their claims on paper. Medicare contractors are required to contact providers that appear to be submitting high numbers of paper claims to verify that those providers meet one or more of the exception criteria for continued submission of their claims on paper. Providers are not to submit that information unless requested as part of an enforcement review. Providers are selected for review based upon the number of paper claims filed in the previous quarter.

If a provider is selected for review and fails to meet one or more exception criteria, or fails to respond to a request for the applicable information, the submitted paper claims will be denied effective on the 91st day after the date of the first letter requesting that documentation. One follow-up notice is issued 45-days after the initial request when a response has not been received. For providers that submit information to substantiate the continued submission of certain types of, or all, paper claims, notification will be provided as to whether the information is acceptable and they have been approved for submission of paper claims. All decisions are final and cannot be appealed.

Electronic Claim Submission Using ASC X12 837
The Administrative Simplification Provisions of the Health Insurance Portability and Accountability Act (HIPAA) of 1996 mandated that the Secretary of Health and Human Services (HHS) establish uniform standards for electronic health care transactions that would reduce the administrative costs in the health care industry. HIPAA focused on the following five areas:

Electronic Data Interchange (EDI): the electronic transfer of information in a standardized format including enrollment, eligibility, payment and remittance advice, claims, health plan premium payments, health claim status, and referral certification and authorization

Code Sets: the data elements used to document the reason a patient is seen and the services and supplies provided

Identifiers: used to identify health care providers, health plans, employers, and patients

Security: standards developed for all health plans, clearinghouses, and providers to protect the confidentiality and integrity of all medical information during all stages before, during, and after the transmission

Privacy: standards that protect the patient's personal health information and define when and how it is appropriate to disclose this information

All claims submitted to CMS must be HIPAA compliant. Noncompliant claims are returned unprocessed.

A final rule published in the August 17, 2000 *Federal Register* acted on the standards of electronic health care transactions, as well as established the medical data sets (code sets) that are suitable for electronic transaction. All health care providers and health plans are required to use the ASC X12 837 for submitting electronic health care claims (hospital, physician/supplier, and dental), and have the option of using a health care clearinghouse to satisfy the HIPAA standard requirements. The ASC X12 837 was also selected as the standard for the institutional claims (hospital, nursing facilities, and similar inpatient institutions) and replaces the UB-92 format developed by CMS for Medicare claims. UB-04 is the paper equivalent of the 837i, electronic format for institutional claims. Likewise, the CMS-1500 is the paper equivalent of the 837p, electronic format for provider claims.

At first glance the ASC X12 837 format may appear daunting because the format has hundreds of fields and hundreds of pages of instructions. However, there are two things to keep in mind when familiarizing oneself with this format. First, the five level hierarchical looping format has been designed to maximize efficiency. The five levels include: billing provider, subscriber, patient, claim level, and line item. When claims data is sorted using this structure, providers only need to complete those lower levels of the claim that differ. Often this will include only the claim level and line item data. Second, upon review of the usage field it should be noted that not all fields are required (R).

The majority of fields have been designated for situational (S) and optional (O) data. While some claim types may require completion of the situational fields and some payers may require completion of some of the optional fields, not all of these fields will need to be completed for all claim types or for all payers.

The implementation guides and formats for the ASC X12 837 standards are not included in this book. They can be obtained from the Washington Publishing Company, 747 177th Lane NE, Bellevue, WA 98008. The guides are also available through the Washington Publishing Company on the Internet at http://www.wpc-edi.com.

HIPAA 5010

The Department of Health and Human Services (HHS) Secretary adopted version 5010 as a replacement to the current version of the X12 standard, which all covered entities must use when conducting electronic transactions. Transactions include professional, institutional and dental claims, claims status requests and responses, enrollment and disenrollment in a health plan, coordination of benefits, and premium payments.

Current versions of the standards (the Accredited Standards Committee X12 version 4010/4010A1 for health care transactions and the NCPDP version 5.1 for pharmacy transactions) have failed to provide certain functionality needed by the health care industry. On January 16, 2009, HHS announced a final ruling that replaced the aforementioned current versions with versions 5010 and D.O. respectively.

Version 5010 includes a number of improvements in structural, front matter, technical, and data content, including improved eligibility response and search options. This version is also more specific in acquiring needed data, collecting and transmitting transactions in misunderstood areas like corrections and reversals, refund processing, and recoupments. This claims transaction standard has significant improvements for reporting clinical data and allows for the reporting of both ICD-10-CM diagnosis codes and ICD-10-PCS procedure codes. Furthermore, it distinguishes between principal and admitting diagnoses, external causes of injury, and reasons for patient visits. These distinctions improve understanding of clinical data, permit better monitoring of mortality rates for certain illnesses, outcomes for specific treatment options and hospital length of stay (LOS) for certain conditions, as well as clinical reasons for why a patient sought hospital care.

Lastly, version 5010 addresses a myriad of business needs that are currently unmet, including an indicator on institutional claims for conditions that were "present on admission" (POA) and accommodates the use of the ICD-10 code sets that are not supported with current version 4010/4010A1.

All covered entities had until January 1, 2012 to be fully compliant. The Office of E-Health Standards and Services (OESS) at CMS acknowledges that a number of outstanding issues and challenges may still exist and will continue to work with health care industry groups as well as Medicare FFS and

Medicaid to increase technical assistance opportunities and eliminate any remaining issues for providers.

It should be noted that the ASC X12 version 5010 standards are national standards and are applicable to all payers, not just Medicare fee-for-service (FFS).

Electronic Data Interchange (EDI) Enrollment Form
Electronic Data Interchange (EDI) forms are available from your local CMS contractor. The agreement is required from each provider of health care services, physician, or supplier that intends to submit electronic media claims (EMC). In addition, a separate EDI form is required for each CMS contractor that is billed. So, if claims are submitted to both a Part B physician contractor and a MAC, a separate EDI enrollment form will be required for each. New EMC billers must obtain a form from each contractor to be billed, complete and sign the form, and submit it to the designated local contractor. The *2014 Insurance Directory* contains a copy of the standard information required at a minimum, in each carrier, MAC, and FI EDI enrollment form. Additional information is available in the *Medicare Claims Processing Manual* (Pub 100-04), chapter 24, section 20.

CMS Federal Program
Contractor's
Logo Here

Electronic Data Interchange (EDI) Enrollment Form

This Agreement notifies (fill in contractor name here) of the provider's consent to participate in Electronic Data Interchange (EDI). EDI may include claims and claims attachments, remittances, eligibility/benefits, claim status, and any other electronic information for Centers for Medicare and Medicaid Services (CMS) federal program data (including but not limited to Title XVIII of the Social Security Act (Medicare), and/or Section 1011 of the Medicare Modernization Act) covered under Health Insurance Portability and Accountability Act (HIPAA) Transactions and Code Sets or Section 1011 of the Medicare Modernization Act (MMA) legislation.

A. The provider agrees:

1. That it will establish and maintain procedures and controls so that information concerning Medicare and/or Section 1011 beneficiaries, or any information obtained from CMS or its contractors, shall not be used by agents, officers, or employees of a business associate except as provided by the contractor (in accordance with §1106(a) of the Social Security Act (the Act));
2. That it will use sufficient security procedures (including compliance with all provisions of the HIPAA security regulations) to ensure that all electronic transmissions are authorized and protect all beneficiary-specific data from improper access;
3. That it will notify the contractor or CMS within two business days if any transmitted data are received in an unintelligible or garbled form.
4. The provider agrees to the following provisions for submitting and retrieving/receiving Medicare and/or Section 1011 information electronically to/from CMS or CMS contractors:

   a) That it will be responsible for all Medicare and/or Section 1011 transactions submitted to CMS by the provider, its employees, or its business associates;

   b) That it will not disclose any information concerning a Medicare and/or Section 1011 beneficiary to any other person or organization, except CMS and/or its contractors, without the express written permission of the Medicare/Section 1011 beneficiary or his/her parent or legal guardian, or where required for the care and treatment of a beneficiary who is unable to provide written consent, or to bill insurance primary or supplementary to Medicare and/or Section 1011, or as required by State or Federal law;

   c) That it will submit claims only on behalf of those Medicare and/or Section 1011 beneficiaries who have given their written permission to do so, and to certify that required beneficiary signatures, or legally authorized signatures on behalf of beneficiaries, are on file;

   d) That it will submit/request electronic transactions on only those beneficiaries with whom the provider has a professional relationship;

   e) That the CMS-assigned unique identifier number (submitter identifier) constitutes the provider's legal electronic signature and when used for claims submission, it constitutes an assurance by the provider that services were performed as billed;

   f) That it will ensure that every electronic claim can be readily associated and identified with an original source document. Each source document must reflect the following information (except if not required for Section 1011):

- Beneficiary's name;
- Beneficiary's health insurance claim number;
- Date(s) of service;
- Diagnosis/nature of illness; and
- Procedure/service performed;

5. That the Secretary of Health and Human Services or his/her designee and/or the CMS contractor has the right to audit and confirm information submitted by the provider and shall have access to all original source documents and medical records related to the provider's submissions, including the beneficiary's signature. All incorrect payments that are discovered as a result of such an audit shall be adjusted according to the applicable provisions of the Social Security Act, Federal regulations, and CMS guidelines;
6. That it will ensure that all claims for Medicare or Section 1011 primary payment have been developed for other insurance involvement and that Medicare/Section 1011 is indeed the primary payer;
7. That it will submit claims that are accurate, complete, and truthful;
8. That it will retain all original source documentation and medical records pertaining to any such particular Medicare claim for a period of at least six years, three months after the bill is paid, or, for Section 1011 beneficiaries, in accordance with the Section 1011 Final Policy Notice;
9. That it will research and correct claim discrepancies;
10. That it will affix the CMS-assigned unique identifier number (submitter identifier) of the provider on each claim electronically transmitted to the CMS contractor;
11. That it will acknowledge that all claims will be paid from Federal funds, that the submission of such claims is a claim for payment under the Medicare or Section 1011 program, and that anyone who misrepresents or falsifies or causes to be misrepresented or falsified any record or other information relating to that claim that is required pursuant to this Agreement may, upon conviction, be subject to a fine and/or imprisonment under applicable Federal law;
12. That if it chooses to participate in electronic remittance transactions it will notify the CMS contractor of any changes in third-party services that it has authorized to access this information on their behalf via the EDI Enrollment form;
13. That if it chooses to use a Network Service vendor for eligibility verification transactions it will notify the CMS contractor of any changes in third-party service arrangements via the EDI Enrollment form;

B. The Centers for Medicare & Medicaid Services (CMS) agrees to:

1. Transmit to the provider an acknowledgment of claim receipt;
2. Affix the CMS contractor number, as its electronic signature, on each remittance advice sent to the provider;
3. Ensure that payments to providers are timely in accordance with CMS' policies;
4. Ensure that no CMS contractor may require the provider to purchase any or all electronic services from the CMS contractor or from any subsidiary of the CMS contractor or from any company for which the CMS contractor has an interest. The carrier or FI will make alternative means available to any electronic biller to obtain such services;
5. Ensure that all Medicare electronic billers have equal access to any services that CMS requires Medicare contractors to make available to providers or their billing services, regardless of the electronic billing technique or service they choose. Equal access will be granted to any services the CMS contractor sells directly, or indirectly, or by arrangement;
6. Notify the provider within two business days if any transmitted data are received in an unintelligible or garbled form.

NOTICE: *Federal law shall govern both the interpretation of this document and the appropriate jurisdiction and venue for appealing any final decision made by CMS under this document. This document shall become effective when signed*

According to the Paperwork Reduction Act of 1995, no persons are required to respond to a collection of information unless it displays a valid OMB control number. The valid OMB control number for this information collection is 0938-0983. The time required to complete this information collection is estimated to average (hours) (minutes) per response, including the time to review instructions, search existing data resources, gather the data needed, and complete and review the information collection. If you have comments concerning the accuracy of the time estimate(s) or suggestions for improving this form, please write to: CMS, 7500 Security Boulevard, Attn: PRA Reports Clearance Officer, Baltimore, Maryland 21244-1850

by the provider. The responsibilities and obligations contained in this document will remain in effect as long as Medicare/Section 1011 claims or any other EDI transactions are submitted to CMS or the CMS contractor. Either party may terminate this arrangement by giving the other party thirty (30) days written notice of its intent to terminate. In the event that the notice is mailed, the written notice of termination shall be deemed to have been given upon the date of mailing, as established by the postmark or other appropriate evidence of transmittal.

C. Signature
I am authorized to sign this document on behalf of the indicated party and I have read and agree to the foregoing provisions and acknowledge same by signing below.

Provider's Name
Title
Address
City/State/Zip
Medicare provider number:
Submitter number (if applicable):
Signed By:
Printed Name:
Title
Date

According to the Paperwork Reduction Act of 1995, no persons are required to respond to a collection of information unless it displays a valid OMB control number. The valid OMB control number for this information collection is 0938-0983. The time required to complete this information collection is estimated to average (hours) (minutes) per response, including the time to review instructions, search existing data resources, gather the data needed, and complete and review the information collection. If you have comments concerning the accuracy of the time estimate(s) or suggestions for improving this form, please write to: CMS, 7500 Security Boulevard, Attn: PRA Reports Clearance Officer, Baltimore, Maryland 21244-1850

Note: Any provider using the services of a billing agent/clearinghouse/network services vendor to submit/receive transactions electronically is required to have an agreement signed by that third party in which the third party has agreed to meet the same Medicare security and privacy requirements that apply to the provider in regards to viewing or use of Medicare beneficiary data (not to be submitted to the carrier but are to be retained by the provider).

CMS instructions allow release of eligibility data to provders or their authorized billing agents for the purpose of preparing an accurate claim. Such information may not be disclosed to anyone other than the provider, supplier, or beneficiary for whom the claim was filed.

National Uniform Claim Committee

The National Uniform Claim Committee (NUCC) is the organization that developed and oversees the standardized data set used by professionals within the health care community for the purposes of transmitting claim and encounter information to and from all third-party payers, replacing the Uniform Claim Form Task Force. The organization encompasses an array of representatives from various health care entities including providers, payers, designated standards maintenance organizations, public health organizations and vendors; the American Medical Association (AMA) functions as chair of the Committee in conjunction with the Centers for Medicare & Medicaid Services (CMS) serving as a critical partner.

NUCC responsibilities include maintaining the physical layout and uniformity of the CMS-1500 claim form as well as the integrity of a set of data element specifications for professional claims submission via the CMS-1500 claim form, the Professional EMC NSF, and the X12 837. Furthermore, the organization also maintains the provider taxonomy codes and has a formal consultative role under HIPAA for all transactions affecting nondental, noninstitutional professional health care services.

This is vitally important because providers have emphasized that delays in billing and processing claims as well as rejections are increased as a result of inconsistent data elements. Payers also voice frustration that without standard claims formats, an increase in resubmitted claims is greater; thus, leading to higher costs in terms of labor and money for both sides.

As part of the organization's responsibilities, NUCC created an instruction manual that provides detailed information on how to complete the CMS-1500 claim form. The purpose being to assist in maintaining the consistency and uniformity in which the form is to be completed across the country. Each year, usually in July, the NUCC releases a new version of the 1500 Claim Form Reference Instruction Manual with an accompanying change log that identifies the changes that have occurred since the last update.

On January 18, 2012, the NUCC released another update to the current CMS 1500 Health Insurance Claim Form Reference Manual, Version 7.0 (07/11). The minor revision was added to clarify reporting of the Service Facility Location NPI (Item number 32a) and was effective immediately.

Instructions for item number 32a now reads as follows: 5010A1:

> Only report a Service Facility Location NPI when the NPI is different from the Billing Provider NPI.

CMS-1500 (08-05)

The following section provides the most current instructions for completing the CMS-1500 (08-05) form. A sample of the form can be found following this section.

Items 1-13
Patient and Insured Information

5010A1 Instruction: If a unique Member Identification Number has been assigned to the patient for purposes of identification, the patient is considered to be the "insured". The patient is reported as the insured in the insured data fields and not in the patient fields.

Item 1
Indicate the type of health insurance coverage applicable to this claim by checking the appropriate box (e.g., if a Medicare claim is being filed, check the Medicare box).

Item 1a
This is a required item. Enter the insured's health insurance claim number (HICN) or policy identification number, if applicable, as shown on the patient's ID card. When the patient has been assigned a unique Member Identification Number by the payer, report that number in this field. For workers' compensation claims, enter the employee ID number. For other property and casualty claims, enter the Federal Tax ID or SSN of the insured person or entity.

Item 2
Enter the patient's complete last name, first name, and middle initial. If the patient has a last name suffix (e.g., Jr, Sr), enter it after the last name, but before the first name. Titles (e.g., Sister, Capt., Dr.) and professional suffixes (e.g., PhD, MD, Esq) should not be used. Commas should be used to separate the last name, first name, and middle initial. A hyphen may be used for hyphenated names. Do not use periods within the name.

If the patient is the insured, it is not necessary to report the patient's name separately in this field.

Alert: Be certain the name appears as it does on the patient's card, as some patients go by their middle name or a nickname. Also, check the spelling; a simple transposition of letters can result in denial or suspension of the claim.

Item 3
Enter the patient's eight-digit birth date (MM | DD | CCYY). Place an X in the appropriate box indicating the patient's sex. If the gender is unknown, leave blank.

Item 4
Enter the insured's full last name, first name, and middle initial. If the insured has a last name suffix (e.g., Jr, Sr), enter it after the last name, but before the first name. Titles (e.g., Sister, Capt., Dr.) and professional suffixes (e.g., PhD, MD, Esq.) should not be used. Use commas to separate the last name, first name, and middle initial. A hyphen can be used for hyphenated names. Do not use periods within the name.

If the patient or their spouse has an insurance plan primary to Medicare, list the name of that insured here. When the insured and the patient are the same, enter the word SAME. Leave blank if Medicare is primary.

For workers' compensation claims, enter the employer's name.

For other property and casualty claims, enter the name of the insured person or entity.

Item 5
Enter the patient's mailing address and telephone number. On the first line enter the street address; the second line, the city and state; the third line, the ZIP code and phone number.

Do not use commas, periods, or other punctuation in the address (e.g., 123 N Main Street 101 instead of 123 N. Main Street, #101). When entering a nine-digit ZIP code, include the hyphen. Do not use a hyphen or space as a separator within the telephone number.

837p Alert: The telephone field does not exist in the electronic 837 Professional 4010A1 or 5010A1. NUCC recommends this field be left blank.

For Workers' Compensation and Other Property and Casualty Claims: If required by a payer to report a telephone number, do not use a hyphen or space as a separator within the telephone number.

Alert: Temporary home or school addresses should not be used.

Alert: If this is a foreign address, contact the payer for specific reporting instructions.

Item 6
Check the appropriate box for patient's relationship to insured when item 4 is completed. The patient's relationship to the insured is not always "self." Spouse indicates that the patient is the husband or wife or qualified partner as defined by the health plan. Child indicates the patient is a minor dependent as defined by the health plan. Other indicates that patient is someone other than self, spouse, or child and may include an employee, ward of the state, or dependent as defined by the health plan.

5010A1 Alert: If the patient is a dependent, but has a unique Member Identification Number and the payer requires the identification number be reported on the claim, then report "Self", since the patient is reported as the insured.

Item 7
Enter the insured's address and telephone number. When item 4 is completed, then this field should also be completed. The first line is for the address; the second line, the city and state; the third line, the ZIP code and phone number.

Do not use commas, periods, or other punctuation in the address (e.g., 123 N Main Street 101 instead of 123 N. Main Street, #101). When entering a nine-digit ZIP code, include the hyphen. Do not use a hyphen or space as a separator within the telephone number.

For workers' compensation claims, enter the employer's address.

For other property and casualty claims, enter the address of the insured noted in item number 4.

837p Alert: The telephone field does not exist in the electronic 837 Professional 4010A1 or 5010A1. The NUCC recommends not reporting this field.

For Medicare claims, When the address is the same as the patient's, enter the word SAME. Complete this item only if items 4, 6, and 11 have been completed.

Alert: The NUCC recommends not reporting this field.

Item 8
Check the appropriate box for the patient's marital status and whether the patient is employed or a student. Only one box on each line can be checked.

837p Alert: Patient status does not exist in the electronic 837 Professional 4010A1 or 5010A1. The NUCC recommends not reporting this field.

Item 9
If item number 11d is marked, complete fields 9 and 9a–d, otherwise leave blank. When additional group health coverage exists, enter other insured's full last name, first name, and middle initial of the enrollee in another health plan if it is different from that shown in item number 2.

If the insured uses a last name suffix (e.g., Jr, Sr), enter it after the last name and before the first name. Titles (e.g., Sister, Capt., Dr.) and professional suffixes (e.g., PhD, MD, Esq) should not be included with the name. Use commas to separate the last name, first name, and middle initial. A hyphen can be used for hyphenated names. Do not use periods within the name.

For Medicare claims: Enter the last name, first name, and middle initial of the enrollee in a Medigap policy if it is different from that shown in item 2. Otherwise, enter the word SAME. If no Medigap benefits are assigned, leave blank. This field may be used in the future for supplemental insurance plans.

Note: Only participating physicians and suppliers must complete item 9 and its subdivisions if requested by the beneficiary. Participating physicians/suppliers sign an agreement with Medicare to accept assignment of Medicare benefits for all Medicare patients. A claim for which a beneficiary elects to assign his/her benefits under a Medigap policy to a participating physician/supplier is called a mandated Medigap transfer.

Do not list other supplemental coverage in item 9 and its subdivisions at the time a Medicare claim is filed. Other supplemental claims are forwarded automatically to the private insurer if the private insurer contracts with the carrier to send Medicare claim information electronically. If there is no such contract, the patient must file his or her own supplemental claim.

Item 9a
Enter the policy or group number of the other insured.

For Medicare claims, enter the policy and/or group number of the Medigap insured preceded by MEDIGAP, MG, or MGAP. Item 9d must be completed, even when the provider enters a policy and/or group number in item 9a.

Item 9b
5010A1 Alert: The "Other Insured's Date of Birth, Sex" does not exist in the 4010A1 or 5010A1 format. The NUCC recommends that this field be left blank.

Enter the eight-digit date of birth (MM | DD | CCYY) of the other insured and an X to indicate the sex of the other insured. Only one box can be marked. If gender is unknown, leave blank.

For Medicare claims, enter the Medigap insured's eight-digit birth date (MM | DD | CCYY) and sex.

Item 9c
5010A1 Alert: The "Employer's Name or School Name" field does not exist in the 4010A1 or 5010A1 format. The NUCC recommends that this field be left blank.

Enter the employer's name or school name. This field identifies the employer or school name attended by the other insured as indicated in item 9, if required by a payer.

For Medicare claims, leave blank if the Medigap PayerID is entered in item 9d. Otherwise, enter the claims processing address for the Medigap insurer. Use an abbreviated street address, two-letter postal code, and ZIP code as shown on the insured's Medigap ID card.

837p Alert: Employer's name or school name do not exist in the electronic 837 Professional 4010A1.

Item 9d
Enter the other insured's insurance plan or program name. Enter the employer's name or school name. This field identifies the name of the plan or program of the other insured as indicated in item 9.

For Medicare claims, enter the nine-digit PayerID number of the Medigap insurer. When no PayerID exists, enter the Medigap insurance program or plan name.

In order for Medicare payment data to be forwarded to a Medigap insurer via the claim-based crossover process, the participating provider of service or supplier must accurately complete all of the requested information in items 9, 9a, 9b and 9d.

Medicare participating providers and suppliers should only enter the COBA Medigap claim-based ID in item 9d when they wish to have the beneficiary's claim cross over to a Medigap insurer. If the provider or supplier does NOT provide this information, Part B contractor or DMAC will not be able to forward the claim information to the Medigap insurer prior to October 1, 2007 or to the Coordination of Benefits Contractor (COBC) for transfer to the Medicare insurer on or after October 1, 2007.

Item 10a–10c
Enter an X in the correct box to indicate whether one or more of the services described in item number 24 are for a condition or injury that occurred on the job or as a result of an automobile or other accident. Only one box on each line can be marked.

Check "YES" or "NO" to indicate whether the encounter is due to an illness or injury that is related to an auto accident. The state postal code where the accident took place must be shown if "YES" is marked in 10b for "Auto Accident." Any item marked "YES" indicates there may be other applicable insurance coverage that would be primary, such as automobile liability insurance. Primary insurance information must then be shown in item number 11.

Item 10d

Refer to the most current instructions from the applicable public or private payer regarding the use of this field as this item is reserved for local use.

When required by payers to provide a sub-set of Condition Codes approved by the NUCC, enter the condition code in this field. Use qualifier BG to indicate that the code reported is a Condition Code. Enter the Condition Code in the following order: qualifier, Condition Code (e.g., BGAD or BGW2).

The condition codes approved for use on the CMS-1500 are located under Code Sets at www.nucc.org.

For workers' compensation claims, condition codes are required when submitting a duplicate claim or an appeal. The original reference number must be indicated in item 22. Condition codes should **not** be used when submitting a revised or corrected claim.

For Medicaid claims, use this field exclusively for Medicaid (MCD) information. If the patient is entitled to Medicaid, enter their Medicaid number preceded by the letters MCD.

Item 11

Enter the insured's policy, group or FECA number as it appears on the insured's health care identification card. If item number 4 is completed, then this field should be also be completed. Do not use a hyphen or space as a separator in the insurer's group number.

For workers compensation and other property and casualty claims, this information is required, if known. Enter workers' compensation or property & casualty claim number assigned by the payer.

For Medicare claims, this item is a required field. In completing this item, the physician/supplier is acknowledging that a good faith effort has been made to determine whether Medicare is the primary or secondary payer.

If there is insurance primary to Medicare, enter the insured's policy or group number and proceed to items 11a–11c as well as items 4, 6, and 7. Enter the appropriate information in item 11c if insurance primary to Medicare is indicated in item 11. When there is no other insurance primary to Medicare, enter the word NONE in this field and proceed to item 12. If the insured reports a terminating event with regard to insurance which had been primary to Medicare (e.g., insured retired), enter the word NONE and proceed to item 11b.

In the event that a lab has MSP information that was previously collected and retained, that information may be used for billing non-face-to-face lab services. However, if the laboratory does not have MSP information for the patient, then the word NONE should be indicated in item 11. When the lab provides a face-to-face encounter with the patient, it is expected that the lab will collect the necessary MSP information and bill accordingly.

The insured's policy, group, or FECA number describes an alphanumeric identifier for the health, auto, or other insurance plan coverage. The FECA number is a nine-digit alphanumeric identifier assigned to a patient claiming work-related condition(s) under the Federal Employees Compensation Act 5 USC 8101.

Circumstances under which Medicare payment may be secondary to other insurance include:

- Group health plan coverage
  - Working aged
  - Disability (large group health plan)
  - End-stage renal disease (ESRD)
- No fault and/or other liability
- Work-related illness/injury
  - Workers' compensation
  - Black lung
  - Veterans' benefits

For workers' compensation claims, the workers' compensation claim number as assigned by the payer should be entered and is required, if known.

Item 11a

Enter the insured's eight-digit birth date (MM | DD | CCYY) and an "X" to indicate the sex of the insured. Only one box may be marked. If the gender is unknown, leave blank.

Item 11b

Enter the insured's employer's or school name.

For Medicare claims, If there is a change in the insured's insurance status (e.g., retired), enter a six-digit (MM | DD | YY) or eight-digit (MM | DD | CCYY) retirement date preceded by the word RETIRED.

The employer's or school name indicates the name of the employer or school attended by the insured as shown per item 1a.

837p Alert:. Employer's name and school name do not exist in the electronic 837 Professional 4010A1 or 5010A1. The NUCC recommends not reporting this field.

Item 11c
Enter the insurance plan or program name of the insured. Some payers may require an identification number of the primary insurer rather than the name in this field.

The insurance plan or program name indicates the name of the plan or program of the insured as shown per item 1a.

For Medicare claims, enter the nine-digit PayerID number of the primary insurer. If there is no PayerID number, enter the complete primary payer's program or plan name. This is required field if there is insurance primary to Medicare that is indicated in item 11.

Item 11d
"Is there another health benefit plan" indicates that the patient has insurance coverage other than the plan indicated in item number 1. When appropriate, enter an X in the correct box. If marked "YES," complete 9 and 9a–d. Only one box can be marked.

This item is not required by Medicare and should be left blank for Medicare claims.

Item 12
Enter "SIGNATURE ON FILE", "SOF", or legal signature in this item. When legal signature is used, enter date signed in six- or eight-digit format. If there is no signature on file, leave blank or enter "NO SIGNATURE ON FILE."

For Medicare claims, The patient or authorized representative must sign and enter a six-digit date (MM | DD | YY) or eight-digit date (MM | DD | CCYY) format, or an alphanumeric date (e.g., January 1, 1998) unless the signature is on file In lieu of signing the claim, the patient may sign a statement to be retained by the provider, physician, or supplier. If the patient is physically or mentally unable to sign, a representative may sign on the patient's behalf. In this event, the statement's signature line must indicate the patient's name followed by the word BY and the representative's name, address, and relationship to the patient, as well as stating the reason the patient cannot sign. The authorization is effective indefinitely unless the patient or the patient's representative revokes this arrangement.

The patient's signature authorizes release of medical information necessary to process the claim. It also authorizes payment of benefits to the provider of service or supplier when the provider of service or supplier accepts assignment on the claim.

Signature on File
This can be "SIGNATURE ON FILE" and/or a computer generated signature.

Signature by Mark (X)
When an illiterate or physically handicapped enrollee signs by mark, a witness must enter his or her name and address next to the mark.

Item 13
Enter "SIGNATURE ON FILE," "SOF," or legal signature. If there is no signature on file, leave this item blank or enter "NO SIGNATURE ON FILE."

For Medicare claims, the patient's signature or the statement "SIGNATURE ON FILE" authorizes payment of medical benefits to the provider. The patient or his/her authorized representative signs this item or the signature must be on file as a separate authorization. However, note that when payment under the Act can only be made on an assignment-related basis or when payment is for services furnished by a participating physician or supplier, a patient's signature or a "SIGNATURE ON FILE" is not required in order for Medicare payment to be made directly to the physician or supplier.

The presence of or a lack of a signature or "SIGNATURE ON FILE" in this field will be forwarded to the Coordination of Benefits trading partners (supplemental insurers) with whom CMS has a payer-to-payer coordination of benefits relationship.

A signature in this item authorizes payment of mandated Medigap benefits to the participating provider if required Medigap information is included in item 9 and its subdivisions. The patient or authorized representative must sign this item or the signature must be on file as a separate Medigap authorization and must be insurer specific. It may state that the authorization applies to all service dates until it is revoked. This can be "SIGNATURE ON FILE" signature and/or a computer generated signature.

Item 14
Enter a six-digit (MM | DD | YY) or eight-digit (MM | DD | CCYY) date of current illness, injury, or pregnancy. For pregnancy, use the date of the last menstrual period (LMP) as the first date for pregnancy.

For chiropractic services, an eight-digit (MM | DD | CCYY) or six-digit (MM | DD | YY) date of the initiation of the course of treatment be entered, and an eight-digit (MM | DD | CCYY) or six-digit (MM | DD | YY) service date be entered in item 19.

Item 15
Enter the first date the patient had the same or a similar illness. Enter the date in the six-digit (MM | DD | YY) or eight-digit format (MM | DD | CCYY). Previous pregnancies are not a similar illness. Leave blank if unknown.

5010A1 Alert: "If Patient Has Had Same or Similar Illness" does not exist in the 5010A1 format. The NUCC recommends that this field be left blank.

This item is not required by Medicare and should be left blank for Medicare claims.

Item 16
If the patient is employed and is unable to work in his or her current occupation, enter a six-digit (MM | DD | YY) or eight-digit (MM | DD | CCYY) date format for the "from-to" dates that the patient is unable to work.

Alert: . An entry in this item may indicate employment-related insurance coverage.

Item 17
Enter the first name, middle initial, last name, and credentials of the professional who referred, ordered, or supervised the service(s) or supply(s) on the claim.

In the event that multiple providers are involved, enter one provider using the following priority order:

1 Referring Provider

2 Ordering Provider

3 Supervising Provider

Periods or commas should not be used within a name; however, a hyphen can be used for hyphenated names.

For Medicare, all physicians who order services or refer beneficiaries must report this data. In addition, when a claim involves multiple referring and/or ordering physicians, a separate CMS-1500 form must be used for each referring/ordering physician.

Medicare defines "referring" and "ordering" as shown below:

> A **referring physician** is a physician who requests an item or service for the patient for which payment may be made under the Medicare program.
>
> An **ordering physician** is a physician or, when appropriate, a nonphysician practitioner who orders nonphysician services for the patient such as diagnostic laboratory tests, clinical laboratory tests, pharmaceutical services, durable medical equipment, and services incident to a physician's or nonphysician practitioner's service.

Medicare claims that are the result of a physician's order or referral must contain the ordering/referring physician's national provider identifier (NPI).

Claims for the following services must contain the ordering/referring provider information:

- Parenteral and enteral nutrition
- Immunosuppressive drug claims
- Diagnostic laboratory services
- Diagnostic radiology services
- Portable x-ray services
- Consultative services
- Durable medical equipment
- Medicare covered services and items that are the result of a physician's order or referral
- Hepatitis B claims
- When the ordering physician is also the performing physician (as often is the case with in-office clinical laboratory tests)
- When a service is incident to the service of a physician or nonphysician practitioner, the name of the physician or nonphysician practitioner who performs the initial service and orders the nonphysician service must appear in item 17
- When a physician extender or other limited licensed practitioner refers a patient for consultative service, submit the name of the physician who is supervising the limited licensed practitioner

Item 17a
Report the other ID number of the referring, ordering, or supervising provider in the shaded area of this field. The qualifier indicating what the number represents should be reported to the immediate right of 17a.

The NUCC defines the following qualifiers, since they are the same as those used in the electronic 837 Professional 4010A1 and 5101A1:

0B State License Number

1B Blue Shield Provider Number

1C Medicare Provider Number

1D Medicaid Provider Number

1G Provider UPIN Number

1H CHAMPUS Identification Number

EI Employer's Identification Number

G2 Provider Commercial Number

Claims Processing

LU Location Number

N5 Provider Plan Network Identification Number

SY Social Security Number (the social security number may not be used for Medicare)

X5 State Industrial Accident Provider Number

ZZ Provider Taxonomy

5010A1 Alert: The NUCC defines the following qualifiers since they are used in the 5010A1 format:

0B State License Number

1G Provider UPIN Number

G2 Provider Commercial Number

LU Location Number (This qualifier is used for Supervising Provider only.)

For Medicare claims, this field is not reported; however, 17b must be reported when services are ordered or referred by a physician.

Item 17b
Enter the NPI of the referring/ordering/supervising provider listed in item 17.

For Medicare claims, all physicians who order services or refer beneficiaries must report this data.

Item 18
Enter a six-digit (MM | DD | YY) or an eight-digit (MM | DD | CCYY) hospital admission date followed by the discharge date (if discharge has occurred). If the patient has not been discharged, leave the discharge date blank. This date is when a medical service is furnished as a result of, or subsequent to, a related hospitalization.

Item 19
This item is reserved for local use. Refer to the most current instructions from the applicable public or private payer regarding the use of this field. Some payers ask for certain identifiers in this field.

The NUCC defines the following qualifiers, since they are the same as those used in the electronic 837 Professional 4010A1 and 5010A1.

4010A1	
0B	State License Number
1B	Blue Shield Provider Number
1C	Medicare Provider Number
1D	Medicaid Provider Number
1G	Provider UPIN Number
1H	CHAMPUS Identification Number
EI	Employer's Identification Number
G2	Provider Commercial Number
LU	Location number
N5	Provider Plan Network Identification Number
SY	Social Security Number (The Social Security number may not be used for Medicare.)
X5	State Industrial Accident Provider number
ZZ	Provider Taxonomy

5010A1	
0B	State License Number
1G	Provider UPIN Number
G2	Provider Commercial Number
LU	Location Number (This qualifier is used for Supervising provider only)
N5	Provider Plan Network Identification Number
SY	Social Security Number (The social security number may not be used for Medicare)
X5	State Industrial Accident Provider Number
ZZ	Provider Taxonomy (The qualifier in the 5010A1 for Provider Taxonomy is PXC, but ZZ will remain the qualifier for the 1500 Claim form)

When reporting a second item of data, enter three blank spaces and the next qualifier and number/code/information.

For Workers' Compensation: This information is required based on Jurisdictional Workers' Compensation guidelines.

When reporting Supplemental Claim Information, use the qualifier PWK for data, followed by the appropriate Report Type Code, the appropriate Transmission Type Code, and then the Attachment Control Number. No spaces should be entered between the qualifiers and the data.

The NUCC defines the following qualifiers, since they are the same as those used in the electronic 837 Professional 4010A1 and 5010A1.

Report Type Code

4010A1	
77	Support Data for Verification (REFERRAL — Use this code to indicate a completed referral form.)
AS	Admission Summary
B2	Prescription
B3	Physician Order
B4	Referral Form
CT	Certification
DA	Dental Models
DG	Diagnostic Report
DS	Discharge Summary
EB	Explanation of Benefits (Coordination of Benefits or Medicare Secondary Payor)
MT	Models
NN	Nursing Notes
OB	Operative Note
OZ	Support Data for Claim
PN	Physical Therapy Notes
PO	Prosthetics or Orthotic Certification
PZ	Physical Therapy Certification
RB	Radiology Films
RR	Radiology Reports
RT	Report of Tests and Analysis Report

5010A1	
03	Report Justifying Treatment Beyond Utilization
04	Drugs Administered
05	Treatment Diagnosis
06	Initial Assessment
07	Functional Goals
08	Plan of Treatment
09	Progress Report
10	Continued Treatment
11	Chemical Analysis
13	Certified Test Report
15	Justification for Admission

5010A1	
21	Recovery Plan
A3	Allergies/Sensitivities Document
A4	Autopsy Report
AM	Ambulance Certification
AS	Admission Summary
B2	Prescription
B3	Physician Order
B4	Referral Form
BR	Benchmark Testing Results
BS	Baseline
BT	Blanket Test Results
CB	Chiropractic Justification
CK	Consent Form(s)
CT	Certification
D2	Drug Profile Document
DA	Dental Models
DB	Durable Medical Equipment Prescription
DG	Diagnostic Report
DJ	Discharge Monitoring Report
DS	Discharge Summary
EB	Explanation of Benefits (Coordination of Benefits or Medicare Secondary Payor)
HC	Health Certificate
HR	Health Clinic Reports
I5	Immunization Record
IR	State School Immunization Records
LA	Laboratory Results
M1	Medical Record Attachment
MT	Models
NN	Nursing Notes
OB	Operative Note
OC	Oxygen Content Averaging Report
OD	Orders and Treatments Document
OE	Objective Physical Examination (including vital signs) Document
OX	Oxygen Therapy Certification
OZ	Support Data for Claim
P4	Pathology Report
P5	Patient Medical History Document
PE	Parenteral or Enteral Certification

5010A1	
PN	Physical Therapy Notes
PO	Prosthetics or Orthotic Certification
PQ	Paramedical Results
PY	Physician's Report
PPZ	Physical Therapy Certification
RB	Radiology Films
RR	Radiology Reports
RT	Report of Tests and Analysis Report
RX	Renewable Oxygen Content Averaging Report
SG	Symptoms Document
V5	Death Notification
XP	Photographs

Transmission Type Code

AA Available on Request at Provider Site

BM By Mail

Example: PWK03AA12363545465

For Medicare claims, the following guidelines apply: enter a six- or eight-digit date when the patient was last seen and the NPI of the attending physician when a physician providing routine foot care submits claims.

For physical therapy, occupational therapy, or speech-language pathology services, effective for claims with dates of service on or after June 6, 2005, the date the patient was last seen and the NPI of the ordering/referring/attending/certifying physician or provider is NOT required. However, should this information be submitted voluntarily, it is imperative that it be correct or it will cause a rejection or denial of the claim. Those therapy services provided incident to the services of a physician or nonphysician provider are still subject to the normal "incident to" policies.

For chiropractor services, enter a six- or eight-digit x-ray date if an x-ray rather than a physical exam was the method used to demonstrate the subluxation. In entering this date and the initiation date for the chiropractic course of treatment in item 14, the chiropractor is certifying that all of the relevant information requirements (Pub. 100-02, chapter 15) are on file and available for carrier review.

A drug name and dosage is required in this field when submitting a claim for drugs categorized as Not Otherwise Classified (NOC). Provide a concise description for unlisted procedure codes or an NOC code when it is feasible to do within the confines of the space provided. Otherwise, supporting documentation should be attached.

When reporting modifier 99 to indicate "multiple modifiers" in item 24d, enter all applicable modifiers. For multiple line items with modifier 99, identify as follows: 1=(mod) where one (1) is the line item and "mod" would be the applicable modifier.

When an independent lab renders an EKG tracing or obtains a specimen from a homebound or institutionalized patient, enter the word HOMEBOUND in this field.

In the event a beneficiary refuses to assign benefits to a nonparticipating physician or supplier who accepts assignment on a claim, enter the statement "Patient refuses to assign benefits." In this case, payment can only be made to the beneficiary directly.

For those services involving the testing of a hearing aid(s), enter the statement "Testing for hearing aid" in order to obtain an intentional denial when other payers are involved.

Enter the specific surgery for which the exam is being performed when billing for dental examinations.

When billing for low osmolar contrast material, enter the specific name and dosage amount if HCPCS codes do not.

When provider's share post operative care for a global surgery claim, enter a six- or eight-digit date for the assumed and/or relinquished date when sharing started.

A demonstration ID number of "30" should be entered for all national emphysema treatment trial claims.

A demonstration ID number of "56" should be entered for all National Laboratory Affordable Care Act Section 3113 Demonstration claims.

Enter the NPI of the physician performing a purchased interpretation of a diagnostic test.

Method II suppliers should report the most recent HCT value for the injection of Aranesp for ESRD beneficiaries on dialysis. (For more information, see Pub 100-04, chapter 8, section 60.7.2).

Individuals and entities who bill carriers of A/B MACS for administrations of ESAs or Part B antianemia drugs not self administered (other than ESAs) in the treatment of cancer must enter the most current hemoglobin or hematocrit test results. Test results should be entered as follows: TR=test results (backslash), R1=hemoglobin, or R2=hematocrit (backslash), and the most current numeric test result figure up to 3 numerics and a decimal point (xx.x). Example: TR/R1/9.0 or TR/R2/27.0.

Item 20

Complete this item when billing for purchased services entering an X in "YES". A "YES" check indicates that the service performed was by an entity other than the billing provider (e.g., services subject to Medicare's antimarkup rule). A "NO" check or blank field indicates that no purchased services are included on the claim. When "YES" is annotated, enter the purchase price in item 32.

When entering the charge amount, enter the dollar amount to the left of the vertical line. Enter number right justified to the left of the vertical line. Enter 00 for cents when the amount is a whole number. Do not use commas or decimal points when reporting dollar amounts. Negative dollar amounts are not allowed. Dollar signs should not be entered. Enter 00 in the cents area if the amount is a whole number.

For Medicare claims, this item should be completed when billing for diagnostic tests subject to purchase price limitations. Enter the purchase price under charges when "YES" is checked. A "YES" check indicates that an entity other than the entity billing for the service performed the diagnostic test. A "NO" indicates "no purchased tests are included on the claim." Complete item 32 when "YES" is checked. Billing for multiple purchased diagnostic tests requires each test to be submitted on a separate CMS-1500. Multiple purchased tests may be submitted on the ASC X12 837 electronic format as long as appropriate line-level information is submitted when services are rendered at different service facility locations.

Item 21

Enter the patient's diagnosis/condition. No more than four ICD-9-CM codes should be listed. The highest level of code specificity should be used, and when reported, do not enter a space, hyphen, or other separator between the qualifier and the identifier. Relate codes to item 24e by line number.

According to official outpatient reporting guidelines, list first the ICD-9-CM code for the diagnosis, condition, problem, or other reason for the encounter/visit shown in the medical record. It is important to note that in some cases, the first-listed diagnosis may be symptoms when a diagnosis has not be confirmed by the provider.

When entering the number, include a space (accommodated by the period) between the two sets of numbers. If entering a code with more than three beginning digits (e.g., E codes), enter the fourth digit above the period.

For Medicare claims, all physician and nonphysician specialties (i.e., PA, NP, CNS, CRNA) must use an ICD-9-CM code number and code to the highest level of specificity for the date of service with the exception of claims submitted by ambulance suppliers (specialty type 59). Enter up to four codes in priority order (primary, secondary condition). All narrative diagnoses for nonphysician specialties should be submitted on an attachment.

Item 22

List the original reference number for resubmitted claims. Please refer to the most current instructions from the applicable public or private payer regarding the use of this field (e.g., code).

When resubmitting a claim, the appropriate bill frequency code should be entered justified left in the left-hand side of the field.

7—Replacement of prior claim

8—Void/cancel of prior claim

For Medicare claims, leave blank as this field is not required by Medicare.

Item 23

Enter any of the following:

- prior authorization number
- referral number as assigned by the payer for the current service
- mammography precertification number
- Clinical Laboratory Improvement Amendments (CLIA) number. Do not enter hyphens or spaces within the number

This field is required when submitting workers' compensation or other property and casualty claims that have been assigned a prior authorization, referral, concurrent review or voluntary certification.

For Medicare claims, enter any of the following as applicable:

- A Quality Improvement Organization (QIO) prior authorization number for any procedure that requires QIO prior approval should be entered in this field.
- Enter an Investigational Device Exemption (IDE) number when an investigational device is used in an FDA-approved clinical trial. In addition, a Post Market Approval number should be reported here when applicable.
- For those physicians who perform care plan oversight services, the six-digit Medicare provider number or NPI of the home health agency or hospice should be entered here when billing HCPCS code G0181 (HH) or G0182 (Hospice).
- A 10-digit CLIA certification number should be entered in this field for laboratory services billed by any entity performed CLIA covered services.

Alert: Item 23 can contain only one condition. Report any additional conditions on a separate CMS-1500.

Section 24

The six service lines in section 24 of the CMS-1500 (08/05) have been divided horizontally so that both the NPI and another/proprietary identifier may be submitted to accommodate the submission of supplemental information to support the billed service. The top portion in each of the six service lines is shaded and is the location for reporting supplemental information. It is not intended to allow the billing of 12 service lines. Supplemental information must be placed in the shaded section of 24a through 24g as described for each item number.

Supplemental information should only be entered with a corresponding, completed service line.

Alert: Providers must verify requirements for supplemental information with the payer.

For Medicare claims, the six service lines in section 24 of the CMS-1500 (08/05) have been divided horizontally so that both the NPI and the legacy identifier may be submitted during the NPI transition and to accommodate the submission of supplemental information to support the billed service. The top portion in each of the six service lines is shaded and is the location for reporting supplemental information. It is not intended to allow the billing of 12 service lines.

When required to submit NDC drug and quantity information for Medicaid rebates, submit the NDC drug in the red shaded portion of the detail line item in positions 01–13. The NDC should be preceded with the qualifier N4 and immediately followed by the 11 digit NDC code. NDC quantities are to be entered in positions 17–24 of the same red shaded area. Quantities entered will be preceded by the appropriate qualifier UN (units), F2 (international units), GR (gram), or ML (milliliter). Six bytes are available for quantity but for quantities less than six bytes, left justify and space fill the remaining positions.

Item 24a

Enter date(s) of service, from and to. If there is only one date of service, enter the date under "FROM" and leave "TO" blank or re-enter "FROM" date. If grouping services, the place of service, procedure code, charges, and individual provider for each line must be identical for that service line. Grouping is only allowed for services on consecutive days. The number of days must correspond to the number of units in 24g.

When required by payers to provide additional anesthesia services information (e.g., beginning and end times), narrative description of an unspecified code, NDC, VP—HIBCC codes, OZ—GTIN codes, contract rate, or tooth numbers and areas of the oral cavity, enter the applicable qualifier and number/code/information starting with the first space in the shaded line of this field.

Do not enter a space, hyphen, or other separator between the qualifier and the number/code/information. The information may extend to 24g.

For Medicare claims this is a required field. A six- or eight-digit date for each procedure, service, or supply should be entered for this item. When a series of identical services are reported with "FROM" and "TO" dates shown, enter the total number of days or units in column G.

Claims with a date of service extending more than 1 day but missing a valid "TO" date will be returned as unprocessable.

Item 24b

Enter the appropriate place-of-service code(s) from the list in appendix B. Identify the location, using a place-of-service code, for each item used or service performed. (see appendix B for the POS codes available at the time of printing). These codes may also be found at www.cms.gov/physicianfeesched/downloads/Website_POS_database.pdf

Item 24c

Check with the trading partner to determine if this element (emergency indicator) is necessary. If required, enter Y for "YES" or leave blank if "NO" in the bottom, unshaded portion of the field. The definition of emergency would be defined by federal or state regulations or programs, payer contracts or as defined in the electronic 837 Professional 4010A1 or 5010A1..

For Medicare claims, leave blank as this field is not required to be completed by Medicare providers.

Item 24d

Enter the procedures, services, or supplies using a CPT or HCPCS Level II code. When applicable, include modifiers with the code.

Enter the specific procedure code without a narrative description. Up to four two-digit modifiers may be indicated on the claim.

For Medicare claims with an "unlisted procedure code" or a "not otherwise classified (NOC)" code, include a narrative description in item 19 if a coherent description can be provided within the confines of the box; if not, an attachment must be submitted with the claim. Claims will be returned as unprocessable if an unlisted procedure code is indicated in item 24d but an accompanying narrative is not present in item 19 or on an attachment.

Item 24e

Enter the diagnosis code reference number (pointer) as shown in item 21 to relate the date of service and the procedures performed to the primary diagnosis. When multiple diagnoses are related to one service, the reference number for the primary diagnosis should be listed first; other applicable diagnosis reference numbers should follow. The reference number(s) should be a 1, 2, 3, 4, or multiple numbers as explained. ICD-9-CM diagnosis codes must be entered in item 21 only. Do not enter them in 24e.

For Medicare claims, providers should reference only one of the diagnoses in item 21 in those situations in which two or more diagnoses are required for a procedure code (e.g., pap smears).

Item 24f
Enter the charge for each listed service.

Enter number right justified in the dollar area of the field. Do not use commas when reporting dollar amounts. Negative dollar amounts are not permitted. Dollars signs should not be entered. Enter 00 in the cents area if the amount is a whole number. Enter 0.00 to indicate a zero dollar amount.

Item 24g
Enter the number of days or units. This field is most commonly used for multiple visits, units of supplies, anesthesia units or minutes, or oxygen volume. If only one service is performed, the numeral 1 must be entered.

Enter numbers right justified in the field. No leading zeros are required. If reporting a fraction of a unit, use the decimal point.

5010A1 Alert: According to NUCC instructions, the total time of the anesthesia provided must be reported as minutes. Units may only be reported for anesthesia services when the code description includes a time period (such as "daily management").

For Medicare claims it should be noted that some services require that the actual number or quantity billed be clearly indicated on the claim form (e.g., multiple ostomy or urinary supplies, medication dosages, or allergy testing procedures). When multiple services are provided, enter the actual number provided.

Anesthesia should be reported showing the elapsed time (minutes) in 24g. Convert hours into minutes and enter the total number of minutes required for the procedure.

See Pub. 100-04 Claims Processing Manual, chapter 20, section 130.6 for instructions on submitting oxygen units.

Medicare requires this field to contain at least 1 day or unit.

Item 24h
For Early & Periodic Screening, Diagnosis, and Treatment (EPSDT) related services, enter the response in the shaded area of the field as shown below:

If there is no requirement (e.g., state requirement) to report a reason code for EPSDT, enter Y for "YES" or N for "NO" only.

If there is a requirement to report a reason code for EPDST, enter the appropriate reason code from the list below. (A Y or N response is not entered with the code.) The two character reason code is right justified in the shaded portion of the field.

The following codes for EPSDT are used in the electronic 837 Professional 4010A1 and 5010A1:

AV Available—Not Used (Patient refused referral)

NU Not Used (Used when no EPSDT patient referral was given)

S2 Under Treatment (Patient is currently under treatment for referred diagnostic or corrective health problem)

ST New Service Requested (Referral to another provider for diagnostic or corrective treatment or scheduled for another appointment with screening provider for diagnostic or corrective treatment for at least one health problem identified during an initial or periodic screening service, not including dental referrals)

If the service is for Family Planning, enter Y ("YES") or N ("NO") in the bottom, unshaded portion of the field.

For Medicare claims, leave blank as this field is not required by Medicare.

Item 24i
Enter the qualifier identifying if the number is a non-NPI in the shaded area of this field. The other ID # of the rendering provider is reported in the shaded area of 24j.

The NUCC defines the following qualifiers, since they are the same as those used in the electronic 837 Professional 4010A1 and 5010A1.

4010A1	
0B	State License number
1B	Blue Shield Provider number
1C	Medicare Provider number
1D	Medicaid Provider number
1G	Provider UPIN number
1H	CHAMPUS Identification Number
EI	Employer's Identification Number
G2	Provider Commercial Number
LU	Location Number
N5	Provider Plan Network Identification Number

4010A1	
SY	Social Security Number (The Social Security number may not be used for Medicare.)
X5	State Industrial Accident Provider Number
G2	Provider Commercial Number

5010A1	
0B	State License number
1G	Provider UPIN number
G2	Provider Commercial number
LU	Location number
ZZ	Provider Taxonomy (The qualifier in the 5010A1 for Provider Taxonomy is PXC, but ZZ will remain the qualifier for the 1500 Claim form. Note: This identifier is not included in this data element in 5010A1)

The aforementioned list contains provider identifiers and provider taxonomy codes. The provider identifiers are assigned to the provider by a specific payer or by a third party in order to uniquely identify the provider. Taxonomy codes are designated by the provider to identify his/her provider type, classification, and/or area of specialization. Both provider identifiers and provider taxonomy codes may be used in this field.

The rendering provider is the person or company (laboratory or other facility) who rendered or supervised the care. In the case where a substitute provider (locum tenens) was used, enter that provider's information here. Report the identification number in items 24i and 24j only when different from data recorded in items 33a and 33b.

For Medicare claims, enter the ID qualifier 1C in the shaded portion of this item.

Item 24j
The individual rendering the service is reported in 24j.The original fields for 24j and 24k have been combined and re-numbered as 24j. Enter the non-NPI ID number in the shaded area of the field. Enter the NPI number in the unshaded area of the field.

The rendering provider is the person or company (laboratory or other facility) who rendered or supervised the care. In the case where a substitute provider (locum tenens) was used, enter that provider's information here. Report the identification number in items 24i and 24j only when different from data recorded in items 33a and 33b.

For Medicare claims, enter the rendering provider's NPI in the lower, unshaded area. In the case of a service provided incident to the service of a physician or non-physician provider, when the person who ordered the service is not supervising, enter the NPI of the supervisor in the lower, unshaded area.

This unprocessable instruction does not apply to influenza virus or pneumococcal vaccine claims submitted on roster bills because they do not require a rendering provider NPI.

Instructions and Examples of Supplemental Information in Item Number 24
Below are types of supplemental information that may be entered in the shaded areas of Item 24:

- Anesthesia duration in hours and/or minutes with start and end times

5010A1 Alert: Anesthesia duration time reporting does not exist in 5010A1. NUCC recommends this field be left blank.

- Narrative description of unspecified codes
- National Drug Codes (NDC) for drugs
- Vendor Product Number – Health Industry Business Communications Council (HIBCC)
- Product Number Health Care Uniform Code Council – Global Trade Item Number (GTIN) previously referred to as the Universal Product Code (UPC) for products
- Contract rate
- Tooth numbers and areas of the oral cavity

NUCC defines the following qualifiers for use when reporting these services.

7 Anesthesia information

5010A1 Alert: Anesthesia duration time reporting does not exist in 5010A1. NUCC recommends this field be left blank.

ZZ Narrative description of unspecified code

N4 National Drug Codes (NDC)

VP Vendor Product Number Health Industry Business Communications Council (HIBCC) Labeling Standard

OZ Product Number Health Care Uniform Code Council – Global Trade Item Number (GTIN)

CTR Contract rate

JP Universal/National Tooth Designation System

JO ANSI/ADA/ISO Specification No. 3950-1984 Dentistry Designation System for Tooth and Areas of the Oral Cavity

When other supplemental information not listed above is required for reporting, refer to payer instructions for the appropriate use of a qualifier for the information being reported. For reporting a service without a qualifier, enter two blank spaces before entering the information

Enter supplemental information at 24A by entering the qualifier and then the information. Do not enter a space between the qualifier and the number/code/information. Do not enter hyphens or spaces within the number/code.

More than one supplemental item can be reported in the shaded lines of Item 24. First, enter the qualifier and number/code/information at 24A; then, enter three blank spaces and the next qualifier and number/code/information.

When reporting dollar amounts in the shaded area, always enter dollar amount, a decimal point, and cents.

Use 00 for the cents if the amount is a whole number. Do not use commas. Do not enter dollar signs.

Examples: 1000.00
123.45

Additional Information for Reporting NDC

When entering supplemental information for NDC, add in the following order: qualifier, NDC code, one space, unit/basis of measurement qualifier, quantity. The number of digits for the quantity is limited to eight digits before the decimal and three digits after the decimal. If entering a whole number, do not use a decimal. Do not use commas.

Examples: 1234.56
2
99999999.999

When a dollar amount is being reported, enter the following after the quantity: one space, dollar amount. Do not enter a dollar sign.

The following qualifiers are to be used when reporting NDC unit/basis of measurement:

F2 International Unit

ML Milliliter

GR Gram

UN Unit

ME Milligram

The following qualifiers are to be used when regulations mandate the use of the Universal Product Number (UPN) for reporting medical and surgical supplies:

EN EAN/UCC - 13

EO EAN/UCC - 8

HI HIBC (Health Care Industry Bar Code)

Supplier Labeling Standard Primary Data Message

UK GTIM 14 - digit data structure

UP UCC - 12

The following additional Information is applicable when reporting tooth numbers and areas within the oral cavity:

To report tooth numbers, add the following, in order: qualifier, tooth number, e.g., JP16.

To report an area of the oral cavity, enter the following, in order: qualifier, area of oral cavity code, e.g., JO10.

To report multiple tooth numbers for one procedure, add the following, in order: qualifier, tooth number, blank space, tooth number, blank space, tooth number, etc., e.g., JP1 16 17 32.

To report multiple tooth numbers per a single procedure, enter the number of units in 24G as the number of teeth involved in the procedure.

To report multiple areas of the oral cavity per a single procedure, enter the following items, in order: qualifier, oral cavity code, blank space, oral cavity code, etc., e.g., JO10 20.

To report multiple areas of the oral cavity per a single procedure, enter the number of units in 24G as the number of areas within the oral cavity involved in the procedure.

The following are the codes for tooth numbers, reported with the JP qualifier:

1–32 Permanent dentition

51–82 Permanent supernumerary dentition

A–T Primary dentition

AS–TS Primary supernumerary dentition

The following codes are for areas of the oral cavity that are reported with the JO qualifier:

00 Entire oral cavity

01 Maxillary arch

02 Mandibular arch

10 Upper right quadrant

20 Upper left quadrant

30 Lower left quadrant

40 Lower right quadrant

For more information regarding these codes, see the most recent edition of the Current Dental Terminology (CDT) Manual available from the American Dental Association.

Below are examples of how to enter the various types of supplemental information for Item 24.

Note: The following examples are for demonstration purposes only to show how the data should be entered into the fields and is not intended to serve as direction on how to code for certain services.

Anesthesia Services, when payment based on 15 minute units:

24. A. DATE(S) OF SERVICE From MM	DD	YY	To MM	DD	YY	B. PLACE OF SERVICE	C. EMG	D. PROCEDURES, SERVICES, OR SUPPLIES (Explain Unusual Circumstances) CPT/HCPCS	MODIFIER	E. DIAGNOSIS POINTER	F. $ CHARGES	G. DAYS OR UNITS	H. EPSDT Family Plan	I. ID. QUAL.	J. RENDERING PROVIDER ID. #
7Begin 1245 End 1415 Time 90 minutes													N	G2	12345678901
10	01	05	10	01	05	22		00770	P2	134	875 00	6	N	NPI	0123456789

Anesthesia Services, when payment based on minutes as units:

24. A. DATE(S) OF SERVICE From MM	DD	YY	To MM	DD	YY	B. PLACE OF SERVICE	C. EMG	D. PROCEDURES, SERVICES, OR SUPPLIES (Explain Unusual Circumstances) CPT/HCPCS	MODIFIER	E. DIAGNOSIS POINTER	F. $ CHARGES	G. DAYS OR UNITS	H. EPSDT Family Plan	I. ID. QUAL.	J. RENDERING PROVIDER ID. #
7Begin 1245 End 1415													N	G2	12345678901
10	01	05	10	01	05	22		00770	P2	134	875 00	90	N	NPI	0123456789

Unspecified Code:

24. A. DATE(S) OF SERVICE From MM	DD	YY	To MM	DD	YY	B. PLACE OF SERVICE	C. EMG	D. PROCEDURES, SERVICES, OR SUPPLIES (Explain Unusual Circumstances) CPT/HCPCS	MODIFIER	E. DIAGNOSIS POINTER	F. $ CHARGES	G. DAYS OR UNITS	H. EPSDT Family Plan	I. ID. QUAL.	J. RENDERING PROVIDER ID. #
ZZKaye Walker													N	G2	12345678901
10	01	05	10	01	05	12		E1399		12	165 00	1	N	NPI	0123456789

NDC Code:

24. A. DATE(S) OF SERVICE From MM	DD	YY	To MM	DD	YY	B. PLACE OF SERVICE	C. EMG	D. PROCEDURES, SERVICES, OR SUPPLIES (Explain Unusual Circumstances) CPT/HCPCS	MODIFIER	E. DIAGNOSIS POINTER	F. $ CHARGES	G. DAYS OR UNITS	H. EPSDT Family Plan	I. ID. QUAL.	J. RENDERING PROVIDER ID. #
N459148001665 UN1													N	G2	12345678901
10	01	05	10	01	05	11		J0400		1	250 00	40	N	NPI	0123456789

Vendor Product Number Health Industry Business Communications Council (HIBCC):

24. A. DATE(S) OF SERVICE From MM	DD	YY	To MM	DD	YY	B. PLACE OF SERVICE	C. EMG	D. PROCEDURES, SERVICES, OR SUPPLIES (Explain Unusual Circumstances) CPT/HCPCS	MODIFIER	E. DIAGNOSIS POINTER	F. $ CHARGES	G. DAYS OR UNITS	H. EPSDT Family Plan	I. ID. QUAL.	J. RENDERING PROVIDER ID. #
N449500267230 UN1 50.00													N	G2	12345678901
10	01	05	10	01	05	11		J7603		1	50 00	2.5	N	NPI	0123456789

Product Number Health Care Uniform Code Council – Global Trade Item Number (GTIN):

24. A. DATE(S) OF SERVICE From MM	DD	YY	To MM	DD	YY	B. PLACE OF SERVICE	C. EMG	D. PROCEDURES, SERVICES, OR SUPPLIES (Explain Unusual Circumstances) CPT/HCPCS	MODIFIER	E. DIAGNOSIS POINTER	F. $ CHARGES	G. DAYS OR UNITS	H. EPSDT Family Plan	I. ID. QUAL.	J. RENDERING PROVIDER ID. #
OXZ00301134678906												2	N	G2	12345678901
10	01	05	10	01	05	12		A6410		13	500 00	2	N	NPI	0123456789

Tooth Number:

24. A. DATE(S) OF SERVICE From MM	DD	YY	To MM	DD	YY	B. PLACE OF SERVICE	C. EMG	D. PROCEDURES, SERVICES, OR SUPPLIES (Explain Unusual Circumstances) CPT/HCPCS	MODIFIER	E. DIAGNOSIS POINTER	F. $ CHARGES	G. DAYS OR UNITS	H. EPSDT Family Plan	I. ID. QUAL.	J. RENDERING PROVIDER ID. #
JP1													N	1B	12345678901
10	01	05	10	01	05	11		D7240		1	500 00	1	N	NPI	0123456789

Multiple Tooth Numbers:

24. A. DATE(S) OF SERVICE From MM	DD	YY	To MM	DD	YY	B. PLACE OF SERVICE	C. EMG	D. PROCEDURES, SERVICES, OR SUPPLIES (Explain Unusual Circumstances) CPT/HCPCS	MODIFIER	E. DIAGNOSIS POINTER	F. $ CHARGES	G. DAYS OR UNITS	H. EPSDT Family Plan	I. ID. QUAL.	J. RENDERING PROVIDER ID. #
JP1 16 17 32													N	G2	12345678901
10	01	05	10	01	05	11		D7240		1	500 00	4	N	NPI	0123456789

Area of Oral Cavity:

24. A. DATE(S) OF SERVICE From MM	DD	YY	To MM	DD	YY	B. PLACE OF SERVICE	C. EMG	D. PROCEDURES, SERVICES, OR SUPPLIES (Explain Unusual Circumstances) CPT/HCPCS	MODIFIER	E. DIAGNOSIS POINTER	F. $ CHARGES	G. DAYS OR UNITS	H. EPSDT Family Plan	I. ID. QUAL.	J. RENDERING PROVIDER ID. #
JO10													N	G2	12345678901
10	01	05	10	01	05	11		41820		1	500 00	1	N	NPI	0123456789

Multiple Areas of Oral Cavity:

24. A. DATE(S) OF SERVICE From MM	DD	YY	To MM	DD	YY	B. PLACE OF SERVICE	C. EMG	D. PROCEDURES, SERVICES, OR SUPPLIES (Explain Unusual Circumstances) CPT/HCPCS	MODIFIER	E. DIAGNOSIS POINTER	F. $ CHARGES	G. DAYS OR UNITS	H. EPSDT Family Plan	I. ID. QUAL.	J. RENDERING PROVIDER ID. #
JO10 20													N	G2	12345678901
10	01	05	10	01	05	11		D7310		1	500 00	2	N	NPI	0123456789

Item 25

Enter the federal tax ID number (employer identification number or social security number) of the billing provider identified in item 33. This is the tax ID number intended to be used for 1099 reporting purposes. Enter an X in the appropriate box to indicate which number is being reported. Only one box may be marked.

Do not enter hyphens with numbers. Enter numbers left justified in this field.

For Medicare claims, providers are not required to complete this item for crossover purposes since the Medicare contractor will retrieve the tax identification information from their internal provider file for inclusion on the COB outbound claim. However, tax ID information is used in the determination of accurate NPI reimbursement. Thus, reimbursement of claims submitted without this information will/may be delayed.

Item 26

Enter the patient's account number assigned by the service provider's or supplier's accounting system.

Do not enter hyphens with numbers. Enter numbers left justified in this field. For Medicare claims this item is optional to help the provider identify the patient. As a service, any account numbers entered here will be returned to the provider.

Item 27

Enter an X in the correct box to indicate whether the provider accepts assignment under the terms of the payers program

For Medicare claims, if Medigap is indicated in item 9 and Medigap payment authorization is given in item 13, the provider of service or supplier should also be a Medicare participating provider of service or supplier and accept assignment of Medicare benefits for all covered charges for all patients.

5010A1 Alert: Report "Accept Assignment?" for all payers.

The following providers of service/suppliers and claims can be paid only on an assignment basis:

- Clinical diagnostic laboratory services
- Physician services to individuals dually entitled to Medicare and Medicaid
- Participating physician or supplier services
- Services of physician assistants, nurse practitioners, clinical nurse specialists, nurse midwives, certified registered nurse anesthetists, clinical psychologists, and clinical social workers
- Ambulatory surgery center services for covered ASC procedures
- Home dialysis supplies and equipment paid under Method II

- Ambulance services
- Drugs and biologicals
- Simplified Billing Roster for influenza virus vaccine and pneumococcal vaccine

Item 28

Enter total charges for the services (i.e., total of all charges in item 24f). Enter number right justified in the dollar area of the field. Do not use commas when reporting dollar amounts. Negative dollar amounts are not allowed and dollar signs should not be entered. When the amount is a whole number, enter 00 in the cents area.

Item 29

Enter the total amount the patient and/or other payers paid on the covered services only. Enter number right justified in the dollar area of the field. Do not use commas when reporting dollar amounts. Negative dollar amounts are not allowed and dollar signs should not be entered. When the amount is a whole number, enter 00 in the cents area.

Item 30

Enter the total amount due. Enter number right justified in the dollar area of the field. Do not use commas when reporting dollar amounts. Negative dollar amounts are not allowed and dollar signs should not be entered. When the amount is a whole number, enter 00 in the cents area.

837p Alert: Balance due does not exist in the electronic 837 Professional 4010A1 or 5010A1. The NUCC recommends not reporting this field.

5010A1 Alert: The "Balance Due" field does not exist in either the 4010A1 or 5010A1 formats. The NUCC recommends that this field be left blank.

For Medicare claims, leave blank as this field is not required by Medicare.

Item 31

Enter the legal signature of the practitioner or supplier, signature of the practitioner or supplier representative, "SIGNATURE ON FILE", or "SOF." Enter either the six- or eight-digit date format or alphanumeric date the form was signed.

837p Alert: Signature of physician or supplier including degrees or credential does not exist in the electronic 837 Professional 4010A1 and 5010A1.

For Medicare claims please note that in the case of a service that is provided incident to the service of a physician or nonphysician practitioner, when the ordering physician or nonphysician practitioner is directly supervising the service as in 42 CFR 410.32, the signature of the ordering physician or nonphysician practitioner shall be entered in item 31. When the ordering physician or nonphysician practitioner is not supervising the service, enter the signature of the physician or nonphysician practitioner providing the direct supervision in item 31.

Furthermore, although this is a required item, the claim can be processed if any of the following is true: A physician, supplier, or authorized person's signature is missing, but the signature is on file; an authorization is attached to the claim, or the signature item has "SIGNATURE ON FILE" and/or a computer generated signature.

Item 32

Enter the name, address, city, state, and ZIP code of the location where the services were rendered. Providers of service (namely physicians) must identify the supplier's name, address, ZIP code, and NPI number when billing for purchased diagnostic tests. When more than one supplier is used, a separate CMS-1500 claim form should be used to bill for each supplier.

If the "Service Facility Location" is a component or subpart of the billing provider and their own NPI is being reported on the claim, the subpart is then reported as the Billing Provider and "Service Facility Location" would not be used. When an NPI in the "Service Facility Location" is reported, the entity must be an external organization to the billing provider.

Enter the name and address information in the following format:

1st Line—Name

2nd Line—Address

3rd Line—City, State, and ZIP Code

Do not use commas, periods, or other punctuation in the address (e.g., 123 N Main Street 101 instead of 123 N. Main Street, #101). Enter a space between town name and state code; do not include a comma. When entering a nine-digit ZIP code, include the hyphen.

If a foreign address is provided, contact payer for specific reporting instructions.

5010A1 Alert: Enter the 9-digit ZIP code. Include the hyphen.

For Medicare claims, the following applies:

Only one name, address, and ZIP code may be entered in this field. If additional entries are needed, separate CMS-1500 claim forms must be submitted.

Providers of service (namely physicians) must identify the supplier's name, address, and ZIP code when billing for purchased diagnostic tests. If more than one supplier is used, a separate CMS-1500 form should be used to bill for each supplier.

For foreign claims, only the enrollee can file for Part B benefits rendered outside of the United States. These claims will not include a valid ZIP code. The contractor processing the foreign claim will follow instructions provided in chapter 1 of Pub.100-04 Claims Processing Manual for proper disposition of the claim.

DMEPOS claims, the name and address of the location where the order was accepted must be entered (DME MAC only). When more than one supplier is used, separate CMS-1500 forms must be used to bill for each supplier. This field should be completed whether the supplier's personnel performs the work at the physician's office or another location. This is a required field.

If a modifier is billed that indicates the service was rendered in a health professional shortage area (HPSA) or physician scarcity area (PSA), the physical location where the service was rendered must be entered, if other than home.

If the supplier is a certified mammography screening center, enter the six-digit FDA approved certification number in this item.

Complete this item for all laboratory work performed outside a physician's office. If an independent lab is billing, enter the place where the test was performed.

Item 32a
Enter the NPI of the service facility.

5010A1 Alert: Enter the Service Facility Location NPI ONLY when the NPI is different from the billing provider's NPI.

For Medicare claims, if required by Medicare claims processing policy, enter the NPI of the service facility.

Item 32b
Enter the two-digit qualifier identifying the non-NPI number followed by the ID number. Do not enter a space, hyphen, or other separator between the qualifier and number.

The NUCC defines the following qualifiers, since they are the same as those used in the electronic 837 Professional 4010A1 and 5010A1.

4010A1	
0B	State License Number
1A	Blue Cross Provider Number
1B	Blue Shield Provider Number
1C	Medicare Provider Number
1D	Medicaid Provider Number
1G	Provider UPIN Number
1H	CHAMPUS Identification Number
G2	Provider Commercial Number
LU	Location Number
N5	Provider Plan Network Identification Number
TJ	Federal Taxpayer's Identification Number
X4	Clinical Laboratory Improvement Amendment Number
X5	State Industrial Accident Provider Number
ZZ	Provider Taxonomy

5010A1	
0B	State License Number
G2	Provider Commercial Number
LU	Location Number

The aforementioned list contains provider identifiers and provider taxonomy codes. The provider identifiers are assigned to providers by a specific payer or a third party in order to uniquely identify the provider. Taxonomy codes are designated by providers to identify his or her provider type, classification, and/or area of specialization. Both provider identifiers and taxonomy codes may be used in this field.

For Medicare claims, leave blank as this field is not required by Medicare.

Item 33
Enter the provider or supplier's billing name, address, ZIP code, and telephone number. The phone number is to be entered in in the area to the right of the field title.

Enter the name and address information in the following format:

1st Line—Name

2nd Line—Address

3rd Line—City State and Zip Code

This field identifies the provider who is requesting payment for services rendered and should always be completed.

Do not use commas, periods, or other punctuation in the address (e.g., 123 N Main Street 101 instead of 123 N. Main Street, #101). Enter a space between town name and state code; do not include a comma. When entering a nine-digit ZIP code, include the hyphen. Check with the payer for reporting instructions if reporting a foreign address.

5010A1 Alert: 5010A1 requires the "Billing Provider Address" to be a street address or physical location. The NUCC recommends that the same requirements be reported here.

Item 33a
Enter the NPI of the billing provider.

Item 33b
Enter the two-digit qualifier identifying the non-NPI number followed by the ID number. The non-NPI number of the billing provider refers to the unique identifier of the provider or the provider designated taxonomy code. Do not enter a space, hyphen, or other separator between the qualifier and number.

The NUCC defines the following qualifiers, since they are the same as those used in the electronic 837 Professional 4010A1 and 5010A1.

4010A1	
0B	State License Number
1A	Blue Cross Provider Number
1B	Blue Shield Provider Number
1C	Medicare Provider Number
1D	Medicaid Provider Number
1G	Provider UPIN Number
1H	CHAMPUS Identification Number
IJ	Facility ID Number
B3	Preferred Provider Organization Number
BQ	Health Maintenance Organization Code Number
FH	Clinic Number
G2	Provider Commercial Number
G5	Provider Site Number
U3	Unique Supplier Identification Number (USIN)
X5	State Industrial Accident Provider Number
ZZ	Provider Taxonomy

5010A1	
0B	State License Number
G2	Provider Commercial Number
ZZ	Provider Taxonomy (The qualifier in the 5010A1 for Provider Taxonomy is PXC, but ZZ will remain the qualifier for the 1500 claim form. Note: This identifier is not included in this data element in 5010A1.)

The aforementioned list contains provider identifiers and provider taxonomy codes. The provider identifiers are assigned to providers by a specific payer or a third party in order to uniquely identify the provider. Taxonomy codes are designated by providers to identify his or her provider type, classification, and/or general area of specialization. Both of these codes may be used in this field.

For Medicare claims, leave blank as this field is not required by Medicare.

0212 1500 Claim Form

On March 27, 2012, the National Uniform Claim Committee released a copy of the revised 1500 Health Insurance Claim (HIC) form, version 02/12. This new version was created in order to allow for the Version 5010 837p changes as well as the implementation of ICD-10 and will eventually replace the current version 08/05, commonly referred to as the CMS 1500. NUCC began working on the revision to the 1500 claim form in 2009 with the goal of aligning the paper format to some of the changes in the electronic health care claim.

On June 17, 2013, the National Uniform Claims Committee (NUCC) announced that the Office of Management and Budget (OMB) had approved Version 02/12 1500 Health Insurance Claim Form under OMB number 0938-1197. The OMB approval is required for any form used in government programs including government health care payers. The NUCC had been working on the revisions to determine how the changes could be made to minimize the impact on re-programming within the health care industry since 2009. The process included two different public comment periods in October 2009 and June 2011; the final draft was approved by the NUCC in February 2012 and was subsequently submitted to CMS for its approval process with OMB. CMS also conducted a 60-day public comment period as part of its approval process, with the OMB conducting its own additional 30-day comment period in October 2012. On June 11, 2013, the OMB granted approval of the form. This new form successfully addresses reporting needs identified for reporting of ICD-10 codes as well as meets requirements in the Accredited Standards Committee X12 (ASC X12) Health care claim (Professional (837P) Version 5010 Technical Report Type 3.

During the course of working on the document, the health care industry identified two main areas of focus that lead to the revised form. First, it was a priority to include an indicator in Item 21 that would permit identification of which diagnosis code set (ICD-9 or ICD-10) was being reported. This was a key need especially during the ICD-10 implementation period. Secondly, expansion of Item 21 from four diagnosis codes to 12 was done to ensure additional codes could be reported, as needed. In addition to these revisions, other changes were adopted in order to increase the accuracy of the data being reported; for example, identification of the provider role in Item number 17 and the specific dates reported in Item number 14.

Note that the revised form contains a symbol at the top left hand corner that is referred to as a Quick Response (QR) code. By taking a picture of the symbol with a smartphone that has the appropriate app downloaded to it, the user can be taken directly to the NUCC website. Additionally, scanners can be programmed to read the QR symbol and identify that that the 1500 claim form is the 02/12 version.

Some of the additional changes made include the elimination of certain fields such as Item numbers 8, 9b, 9c, 11b, and 30 because the data in those fields is not reported in the 837P electronic version. The NUCC has indicated its intention to mirror reporting requirements from the paper 1500 claim form with the 837P electronic version whenever possible.

Other changes include:

- Changing Item number 10d from Reserved for Local Use to Claim Codes. This was done to limit the use of the field for reporting of various claims codes (e.g., condition codes). The NUCC will be accepting requests for any additional codes that the health care industry would like to have reported in this field as well as the need to report any other data in this field. Requests can be submitted by e-mailing info@nucc.org.
- Item 11b was changed to Other Claim ID. This was done in response to input from the health care industry that this field could serve a broader need by using this existing field with the ability to report an indicator that would describe the type of number being reported. The format permits greater flexibility to add additional qualifiers and number types in the future, as necessary.
- The addition of a qualifier to Item number 14. This was done to specifically allow for the identification of which date is being reported in the field.
- Changing Item number 15 from "Same or Similar Illness" to "Other Date." NUCC received input from the health care industry that a date for "same or similar illness" was not necessary but instead, would benefit from the ability to report other dates that may be associated with the claim. Thus, a qualifier was added to indicate which date is being reported. The format permits greater flexibility to add additional qualifiers and number types in the future, as necessary.
- The addition of a qualifier to Item number 17. This was done to permit the identity of the provider's role in this field.
- Changing Item number 19 from "Reserved for Local Use" to "Additional Claim Information." The field was renamed in order to the limit the use of it as an open text field. As specific needs for reporting data in this field are identified, requests can be made by e-mailing info@nucc.org.
- Indicator space added in Item number 21. This was done to identify which codes (ICD-9 or ICD-10) are being reported on the claim; this is necessary for the transition period during the ICD-10 implementation.
- Line labels in Item 21 changed from numbers to letters. Line labels are the diagnosis pointers that are reported in Item 24E. Each service line can "point" up to four diagnosis codes; changing to letters was required because an entry of "12" in Item 24E could be interpreted to mean "1" and "2" or simply "12." Further, there was not enough space in Item 24E to permit the reporting of two-digit pointers and still include up to four pointers.
- Removal of "Medicaid" from the title of Item number 22. Medicaid was removed to ensure the field was no longer specific to Medicaid submissions and can now be used for submissions with any payer.
- Reserved for NUCC Use fields. These fields are not open fields for the use of reporting any data and should not be used. In the event a need is determined for these fields, a request can be submitted to NUCC at info@nucc.org.
- No "Pay-to" Address included in the revised form. After lengthy discussions, the NUCC concluded that payers use the address they have on file for a provider when sending payment. If the "pay-to" address is different from the address the payer has on file, the payer would want to contact the provider to verify the address prior to sending payment to an address on the form. Thus, NUCC determined that it is not necessary to have a "pay-to address" on the form.

The NUCC has indicated that in order for the form to be read by a scanner, the form must be in red ink which allows scanners to drop the form template during imaging of the paper; this creates a "cleaner" image that allows for easier and quicker processing with data capture automation such as ICR/OCR software.

Lastly, the NUCC developed the 1500 Claim Form Reference Instruction Manual to provide a standardized manner in which the 1500 form should be completed; however, NUCC recognizes that, at times, a payer may give providers different instructions on how to complete certain fields within the form. Consequently, the title page of the instruction manual states the following regarding this:

> "The NUCC has developed this general instructions document for completing the 1500 Claim Form. This document is intended to be a guide for completing the 1500 Claim Form and not definitive instructions for this purpose. Any user of this document should refer to the most current federal, state, or other payer instructions for specific requirements applicable to using the 1500 Claim Form."

Transition Timeline

Currently, the NUCC is conducting a review of the initial proposed timeline, shown below, and will announce a finalized transition timeline after seeking input from its members, including CMS. However, until then, health care entities should begin working on any programming and implementation needs that may be required for the new form. Further, providers should begin checking with their payers, vendors, and/or clearinghouses to determine appropriate steps needed to ensure readiness for this new form.

June 1, 2013	June 1 – October 1, 2013	October 1, 2013
Health plans, clearinghouses, and other IS vendors ready to handle and accept the new (02/12) 1500 claim form.	Providers can use either the (08/05) or (02/12) claim form; billing vendors can accept and process either version.	Discontinue use of (08/05) 1500 claim form; only use the (02/12) version; rebilling of any claims will be reported on the new (02/12) version from this point forward despite original claim being on the (08/05) version.

NOTE: The aforementioned timeline will be revised after input from NUCC members and CMS.

In addition to the revised form, a 0212 Change Log has been released that details the changes between the two versions as well as a V1.1 0613 0212 NUCC 1500 0212 Instruction Manual. Copies of both can be viewed at:
http://nucc.org/images/stories/PDF/1500_claim_form_change_log_2012_02.pdf

and

http://nucc.org/images/stories/PDF/1500_claim_form_instruction_manual_2012_02.pdf

Copies of the 02/12 1500 claim form can be obtained from your current forms vendor, by contacting TFP Data Systems at 1-800-482-9367 ext. 58029, by e-mailing 1500form@tfpdata.com, or from the Government Printing Office (GPO) website http://bookstore.gpo.gov/catalog/government-forms-phone-directories or calling 1-866-512-1800.

Print files and specifications are available from TFP as of June, 20, 2013.

A copy of the new Version 02/12 1500 form follows.

HEALTH INSURANCE CLAIM FORM

APPROVED BY NATIONAL UNIFORM CLAIM COMMITTEE (NUCC) 02/12

PICA PICA

CARRIER

1. MEDICARE (Medicare#) MEDICAID (Medicaid#) TRICARE (ID#/DoD#) CHAMPVA (Member ID#) GROUP HEALTH PLAN (ID#) FECA BLK LUNG (ID#) OTHER (ID#)

1a. INSURED'S I.D. NUMBER (For Program in Item 1)

2. PATIENT'S NAME (Last Name, First Name, Middle Initial)

3. PATIENT'S BIRTH DATE MM DD YY SEX M F

4. INSURED'S NAME (Last Name, First Name, Middle Initial)

5. PATIENT'S ADDRESS (No., Street)

6. PATIENT RELATIONSHIP TO INSURED Self Spouse Child Other

7. INSURED'S ADDRESS (No., Street)

CITY STATE

8. RESERVED FOR NUCC USE

CITY STATE

ZIP CODE TELEPHONE (Include Area Code) ( )

ZIP CODE TELEPHONE (Include Area Code) ( )

9. OTHER INSURED'S NAME (Last Name, First Name, Middle Initial)

10. IS PATIENT'S CONDITION RELATED TO:

11. INSURED'S POLICY GROUP OR FECA NUMBER

a. OTHER INSURED'S POLICY OR GROUP NUMBER

a. EMPLOYMENT? (Current or Previous) YES NO

a. INSURED'S DATE OF BIRTH MM DD YY SEX M F

b. RESERVED FOR NUCC USE

b. AUTO ACCIDENT? PLACE (State) YES NO

b. OTHER CLAIM ID (Designated by NUCC)

c. RESERVED FOR NUCC USE

c. OTHER ACCIDENT? YES NO

c. INSURANCE PLAN NAME OR PROGRAM NAME

d. INSURANCE PLAN NAME OR PROGRAM NAME

10d. CLAIM CODES (Designated by NUCC)

d. IS THERE ANOTHER HEALTH BENEFIT PLAN? YES NO *If yes*, complete items 9, 9a, and 9d.

READ BACK OF FORM BEFORE COMPLETING & SIGNING THIS FORM.

12. PATIENT'S OR AUTHORIZED PERSON'S SIGNATURE I authorize the release of any medical or other information necessary to process this claim. I also request payment of government benefits either to myself or to the party who accepts assignment below.

SIGNED DATE

13. INSURED'S OR AUTHORIZED PERSON'S SIGNATURE I authorize payment of medical benefits to the undersigned physician or supplier for services described below.

SIGNED

PATIENT AND INSURED INFORMATION

14. DATE OF CURRENT ILLNESS, INJURY, or PREGNANCY (LMP) MM DD YY QUAL.

15. OTHER DATE QUAL. MM DD YY

16. DATES PATIENT UNABLE TO WORK IN CURRENT OCCUPATION FROM MM DD YY TO MM DD YY

17. NAME OF REFERRING PROVIDER OR OTHER SOURCE 17a. 17b. NPI

18. HOSPITALIZATION DATES RELATED TO CURRENT SERVICES FROM MM DD YY TO MM DD YY

19. ADDITIONAL CLAIM INFORMATION (Designated by NUCC)

20. OUTSIDE LAB? YES NO $ CHARGES

21. DIAGNOSIS OR NATURE OF ILLNESS OR INJURY Relate A-L to service line below (24E) ICD Ind.

A. B. C. D.
E. F. G. H.
I. J. K. L.

22. RESUBMISSION CODE ORIGINAL REF. NO.

23. PRIOR AUTHORIZATION NUMBER

	24. A. DATE(S) OF SERVICE From MM DD YY To MM DD YY	B. PLACE OF SERVICE	C. EMG	D. PROCEDURES, SERVICES, OR SUPPLIES (Explain Unusual Circumstances) CPT/HCPCS MODIFIER	E. DIAGNOSIS POINTER	F. $ CHARGES	G. DAYS OR UNITS	H. EPSDT Family Plan	I. ID. QUAL.	J. RENDERING PROVIDER ID. #
1									NPI	
2									NPI	
3									NPI	
4									NPI	
5									NPI	
6									NPI	

PHYSICIAN OR SUPPLIER INFORMATION

25. FEDERAL TAX I.D. NUMBER SSN EIN

26. PATIENT'S ACCOUNT NO.

27. ACCEPT ASSIGNMENT? (For govt. claims, see back) YES NO

28. TOTAL CHARGE $

29. AMOUNT PAID $

30. Rsvd for NUCC Use

31. SIGNATURE OF PHYSICIAN OR SUPPLIER INCLUDING DEGREES OR CREDENTIALS (I certify that the statements on the reverse apply to this bill and are made a part thereof.)

SIGNED DATE

32. SERVICE FACILITY LOCATION INFORMATION

a. NPI b.

33. BILLING PROVIDER INFO & PH # ( )

a. NPI b.

NUCC Instruction Manual available at: www.nucc.org *PLEASE PRINT OR TYPE* APPROVED OMB-0938-1197 FORM 1500 (02-12)

SAMPLE

Claims Processing

Place of Service Codes (POS) and Definitions

The Health Insurance Portability and Accountability Act of 1996 (HIPAA) became effective October 16, 2003, for all covered entities. Medicare is a covered entity under HIPAA.

The final rule, "Health Insurance Reform: Standards for Electronic Transactions," published in the *Federal Register*, August 17, 2000, adopts the standards to be used under HIPAA and names the implementation guides to be used for these standards. The ASC X12 837 professional is the standard to be used for transmitting health care claims electronically, and its implementation guide requires the use of POS codes from the National POS code set, currently maintained by CMS.

As a covered entity, Medicare must use the POS codes from the National POS code set for processing its electronically submitted claims. Medicare must also recognize as valid POS codes from the POS code set when these codes appear on such a claim.

It should be noted that the Office of the Inspector General (OIG) has consistently reported that physicians and other suppliers frequently fail to report correctly the POS in which they furnish services. This can result in inappropriate payment. Additionally, as a result of these findings, payers are more apt to closely scrutinize place of service reporting for accuracy. A complete list of the official POS codes can be found in appendix B.

Medicare requires that the provider indicate the POS where the patient received face-to-face services with two exceptions: In the event that the provider is performing an interpretation of a test off-site, the POS identified is for the location where the service is provided. For example, if the provider is interpreting a CT scan in the office and the CT scan is performed in the hospital on an inpatient, the place of service the provider indicates is 21 or inpatient hospital. Likewise, if in the scenario above, the patient was a hospital outpatient, place of service 22 would be identified. Appropriate place of service reporting and the payment ramifications for global services are discussed in more detail in the Clarifications Regarding Global Services section later in this chapter.

There are special considerations which apply to some POS codes.

Special Considerations for Homeless Shelter (Code 04)

Note that for the purposes of receiving durable medical equipment (DME), a homeless shelter is considered the beneficiary's home. Because DME is payable in the beneficiary's home, the crosswalk for Homeless Shelter (code 04) to Office (code 11) that was mandated effective January 1, 2003, may need to be adjusted or local policy developed so that HCPCS codes for DME are covered when other conditions are met and the beneficiary is in a homeless shelter. If desired, local contractors are permitted to work with their medical directors to determine a new crosswalk such as from Homeless Shelter (code 04) to Home (code 12) or Custodial Care Facility (code 33) for DME provided in a homeless shelter setting. If a local contractor is currently paying claims correctly, however, it is not necessary to change the current crosswalk.

Special Considerations for Indian Health Service (Codes 05, 06) and Tribal 638 Settings (Codes 07, 08)

Medicare does not currently use the POS codes designated for these settings. Follow the instructions you have received regarding how to process claims for services rendered in IHS and Tribal 638 settings. If you receive claims with these codes, you must initially accept them in terms of HIPAA compliance. However, follow your "return as unprocessable" procedures after this initial compliance check. Follow your "return as unprocessable" procedures when you receive paper claims with these codes. (Note that while these codes became part of the National POS code set effective January 1, 2003, Medicare contractors received instructions regarding how to process claims with these codes effective October 1, 2003, so that Medicare could be HIPAA compliant by October 16, 2003).

Special Considerations for Prison/Correctional Facility Settings (Code 09)

The addition of code 09 to the POS code set and Medicare claims processing reflects Medicare's compliance with HIPAA laws and regulations. Local contractors must continue to comply with CMS current policy that does not allow payment for Medicare services in a penal institution in most cases. The addition of a POS code for a prison/correctional facility setting does not supersede this policy. (See Pub. 100-04, *Medicare Claims Processing Manual*, chapter 1, section 10.4.)

Special Considerations for Mobile Unit Settings (Code 15)

When services are furnished in a mobile unit, they are often provided to serve an entity for which another POS code exists. For example, a mobile unit may be sent to a physician's office or a skilled nursing facility. If the mobile unit is serving an entity for which another POS code already exists, providers should use the POS code for that entity. However, if the mobile unit is not serving an entity that could be described by an existing POS code, the providers are to use the Mobile Unit POS code 15. Apply the nonfacility rate to payments for services designated as being furnished in POS code 15; apply the appropriate facility or nonfacility rate for the POS code designated when a code other than the mobile unit code is indicated.

Special Consideration for Walk-in Retail Health Clinics (Code 17)

Medicare has specific billing rules for immunizations claims (see Pub 104, chapter 18). Some providers may elect to use POS 17 to track the setting where immunizations are performed. However, Medicare does not recognize this code. Nevertheless, Medicare contractors will accept and adjudicate claims containing POS code 17, even if the presence of this code on a claim is contrary to these billing instructions.

Special Consideration for Services Rendered to Registered Inpatients (Code 21)

When a provider furnishes services to a registered inpatient, payment is made under the Physician Fee Schedule at the facility rate. Therefore, the provider furnishing services to a patient who is a registered inpatient should, at a minimum, report the inpatient hospital POS code 21 irrespective of the setting where the patient actually receives the face-to-face encounter. However, if the provider is aware of the exact setting at which the patient is a registered inpatient, the appropriate inpatient POS code may be reported instead of POS 21. For example, POS 31 for a patient in an SNF receiving inpatient skilled nursing care, POS 51 for a patient registered in a Psychiatric Inpatient Facility, and POS 61 for patients registered in a Comprehensive Inpatient Rehabilitation Facility may be reported, if and, when known.

Special Consideration for Services Rendered in Outpatient Hospital Departments (Code 22)

When a provider renders services in the outpatient department of a facility, payment is made under the "at the facility" rate. Providers who furnish services to a hospital outpatient (including in a provider-based department of that hospital) or under arrangement to a hospital should, at a minimum, report the outpatient hospital POS code 22 irrespective of the setting where the patient actually receives the face-to-face encounter. If the provider is aware of the exact setting at which the patient is a registered hospital outpatient, the appropriate outpatient facility POS code may be reported instead of POS 22. For example, the provider may use POS code 23 for services furnished to a patient registered in the emergency room, POS 24 for patients registered in an ambulatory surgical center, and POS 56 for patients registered in a psychiatric residential treatment center.

Providers who perform services in a separately maintained physician office space in the hospital or on the hospital campus not considered a provider-based hospital department, will indicate place of service code 11 (office) on the claim.

Special Consideration for Services Rendered in an Ambulatory Surgical Center (Code 24)

When the service is rendered in a Medicare-participating ambulatory surgical center (ASC), the provider should indicate POS code 24 on the claim. However, if the physician has an office at the same physical location of the ASC and all other requirements for operating as a physician office at the same physical location of the ASC are met—including the distinct entity criteria as defined in the ASC State Operations Manual—place of service code 11 (office) may be reported.

Special Considerations for Hospice (Code 34)

When the patient is in an "inpatient" respite or general "inpatient" care stay, or has elected coverage under the Hospice benefit and is receiving inpatient hospital care in a hospital, SNF, or hospice inpatient facility the place of service code 34 (hospice) is reported.

When services are provided in an outpatient setting that is not operated by the hospice, for example, the provider's office (POS 11), or the patient's home (POS 12), the place of service indicating that site is used.

CMS has also recently published clarification of how the place of service can affect payment.

Clarification Regarding Global Services

Some diagnostic tests are provided to patients under arrangements with a hospital and the test and interpretation of that test are not separately billable; for example, the physician may not bill separately for the interpretation. In this situation, the hospital is the only provider who can bill for the diagnostic test. There is no POS code for the interpretation because a physician claim is not generated.

When the global diagnostic service code is billed, the biller reports the address and ZIP code where the test was performed in item 32 on the CMS 1500 claim form.

Other procedures have both a professional component (PC) and technical component (TC). When a procedure that has both the PC and TC component is performed, it is possible that each entity will bill for the component they provided. For example, if the procedure is performed in the hospital and the physician interprets the results, the hospital would bill the TC portion and the provider would bill the PC portion of the service.

In the event that the service has both a PC and TC component, the entity performing the test (the technical portion) would bill the appropriate CPT code with the TC modifier appended; enter the POS where the test was performed and indicate the address in item 32 of the CMS-1500 claim form. The provider interpreting the procedure (the PC portion) would report the CPT code with modifier 26 (professional component), the POS where the procedure was performed, and the billing address and NPI in item 32 and 32a, respectively. The place of service indicated should be the place where the test was performed. For example, a chest x-ray is performed (the patient is considered to be an outpatient) and is interpreted by the provider in the provider's office. The hospital would bill for the TC component by entering code 71010-TC and POS 22. The physician would enter code 71010-26 and POS 22 even though the interpretation was performed in the office.

Paper Claims

Adjudicate paper claims with codes from the National POS code set as you would for electronic claims.

Contractor Instructions for Place of Service Codes

If the physician bills for lab services performed in his/her office, the code for "Office" is shown. If the physician bills for a lab test furnished by another physician who maintains a lab in his/her office, the code for "Other" is shown. If the physician bills for a lab service furnished by an independent lab, the code for "Independent Laboratory" is used. Items 21 and 22 on the CMS-1500 must be completed for all laboratory work performed outside a physician's office. If an independent lab bills, the place where the sample was taken is shown. An independent laboratory taking a sample in its laboratory shows "IL" as place of service. If an independent laboratory bills for a test on a sample drawn on a hospital inpatient, it uses the code for "Hospital Inpatient."

For hospital visits by physicians, presume, in the absence of evidence to the contrary, that visits billed for were made. However, review a sample of physician's records when there are questionable patterns of utilization. Confirm these visits where the medical facts do not support the frequency of the physician's visits or in cases of beneficiary complaints.

If questioning whether the visit had been made, ascertain whether the physician's own entry is in the patient's record at the provider's office. Accept an entry where the nurses' notes indicate that the physician saw the patient on a given day. A statement by the beneficiary is also acceptable documentation if it was made close to the alleged date of the visit. Entries in the physician's records represent possible secondary evidence. However, these are of less value since they are self-serving statements. Exercise judgment regarding their authenticity. The policy requiring daily physician visits is not conclusive if, in the individual case, the facts did not support a finding that daily visits were made. If the place of service is not specified, then edit and review claims for missing place of service information.

If a claim lacks a valid POS code in 24b or contains an invalid POS in item 24b, return the claim as unprocessable to the provider or supplier using RA remark code M77. Effective for claims received on or after April 1, 2004, only one POS code may be submitted on the CMS-1500 form.

If the place of service is not indicated and the carrier cannot infer the place of service from the procedure code billed (e.g., a procedure code for which the definition is not site specific or that can be performed in more than one setting), then return assigned services as unprocessable and develop for the place of service on nonassigned claims.

If the place of service is inconsistent with the procedure code billed, then edit for consistency or compatibility between the place of service and site-specific procedure codes.

If the place of service is valid but inconsistent or incompatible with the procedure billed (e.g., the place of service is inpatient hospital and the procedure code billed is office visit), then return assigned services as unprocessable and develop nonassigned services since the carrier typically will not know whether the procedure code or the place of service is incorrect in such instances.

If the place of service is invalid, edit for the validity of the place of service coding.

If the place of service code is not valid (e.g., the number designation has not been assigned or defined by CMS), return assigned services as unprocessable and develop for a valid place of service on nonassigned line items.

Type of Service (TOS)

For submitting a claim to the Common Working File (CWF), use the following table to assign the proper TOS. The only exceptions are:

- Surgical services billed for dates of service through December 31, 2007 containing the ASC facility service modifier SG must be reported as TOS F. The indicator F does not appear on the TOS table because its use is dependent upon claims submitted with POS 24 (ASC Facility) from an ASC (specialty 49). This is effective for service dates of January 1, 2008 and later.
- Surgical services billed with an assistant-at-surgery modifier (80–82, AS) must be reported with TOS 8. The 8 indicator does not appear on the TOS table because its use is dependent upon the use of the appropriate modifier. (See Pub 100-4, *Medicare Claims Processing Manual*, chapter 12, "Physician/Practitioner Billing," for instructions on when assistant-at-surgery is allowable.)
- Psychiatric treatment services that are subject to the outpatient mental health treatment limitation should be reported with TOS T.
- TOS H appears in the list of descriptors. However, it does not appear in the table. In CWF, "H" is used only as an indicator for hospice. You should not submit TOS H to CWF at this time.
- For outpatient services, when a transfusion medicine code appears on a claim that also contains a blood product, the service is paid under reasonable charge at 80 percent, coinsurance and deductible apply. When transfusion medicine codes are paid under the clinical laboratory fee schedule pay at 100 percent, coinsurance and deductible do not apply.

Note: For injection codes with more than one possible TOS designation, use the following guidelines when assigning the TOS:

When the choice is L or 1:

- Use TOS L when the drug is used related to ESRD
- Use TOS 1 when the drug is not related to ESRD and is administered in the office

When the choice is G or 1:

- Use TOS G when the drug is an immunosuppressive drug
- Use TOS 1 when the drug is used for other than immunosuppression

When the choice is P or 1:

- Use TOS P if the drug is administered through durable medical equipment (DME)
- Use TOS 1 if the drug is administered in the office

You may consider the place of service or diagnosis when determining the appropriate TOS. The descriptors for each of the TOS codes are:

Type of Service Indicators

0 Whole Blood

1 Medical Care

2 Surgery

3 Consultation

4 Diagnostic Radiology

5 Diagnostic Laboratory

6 Therapeutic Radiology

7 Anesthesia

8 Assistant at Surgery

9 Other Medical Items or Services

A Used DME

B High Risk Screening Mammography

C Low Risk Screening Mammography

D Ambulance

E Enteral/Parenteral Nutrients/Supplies

F Ambulatory Surgical Center (Facility Usage for Surgical Services)

G Immunosuppressive Drugs

H Hospice

J Diabetic Shoes

K Hearing Items and Services

L ESRD Supplies

M Monthly Capitation Payment for Dialysis

N Kidney Donor

P Lump Sum Purchase of DME, Prosthetics, Orthotics

Q Vision Items or Services

R Rental of DME

S Surgical Dressings or Other Medical Supplies

T Outpatient Mental Health Treatment Limitation

U Occupational Therapy

V Pneumococcal/Flu Vaccine

W Physical Therapy

For more information on CMS-1500 claim forms as well as information on where to purchase forms, please go to http://www.cms.gov/Medicare/Billing/ElectronicBillingEDITrans/index.html?redirect=/ElectronicBillingEDITrans/16_1500.asp. You can also find basic form completion instructions and print specifications for the CMS-1500 form in chapter 26 of the *Medicare Claims Processing Manual* (Pub.100-04).

Clean Claims

Claims submitted with all of the information necessary for processing are referred to as "clean" and are usually paid in a timely manner. Paying careful attention to what should appear on your claim form helps produce these clean claims. Now we'll discuss some of the common reasons that claims are denied. Being aware of common mistakes helps you avoid them. It's extremely important to read the communications you receive from insurers. Their information will often put you on the right track to correct your errors through resubmission.

Common Errors

- The patient's ID number is incorrect
- The patient's name and address does not match the insurer's records
- The physician's tax ID number, provider number, or social security number is missing

- There is little or no information regarding primary or secondary coverage
- The physician's or authorized person's signature is missing
- Dates of service are incorrect or do not relate to the claims information from other providers (hospital, nursing homes, etc.)
- Dates are not six or eight digits as required
- The fee column is blank or not itemized and totaled
- The patient information is incomplete
- The CPT, HCPCS Level II, and ICD-9-CM codes are invalid, or the diagnostic codes are not linked to the correct services, procedures, or supplies
- The claim is illegible

Signature Requirements

All documentation in the patient's medical chart *must* be signed and dated by the provider. Many electronic medical records require the provider's unique electronic signature to close and lock the record. Dictated and handwritten documentation must also be signed and dated by the practitioner. In addition, dictated documentation should be read and reviewed to ensure accuracy and to validate revisions before being initialed. Some payers, including Medicare, will not accept unsigned notes, whether electronic, dictated, or handwritten.

Remember, commonly accepted documentation standards always include a physician signature or "identifier." However, Medicare and commercial payers require a handwritten or electronic signature for all services provided or ordered. Stamp signatures are not permitted, although facsimile of original written or electronic signatures are accepted when certifying terminal illnesses for hospice care. *Note:* A possibility of misuse or abuse for providers opting to use electronic systems may exist when used. Appropriate administrative procedures should be in place to protect against modifications and should correlate to recognized existing standards and laws. Keep in mind that the individual whose name is listed as the alternate signature, as well as the provider, shares the responsibility for authenticity of all information being attested to. Finally, all state licensure and practice regulations continue to apply and where state law is more restrictive than Medicare, the state law standard is applied.

On May 31, 2009, CMS modified CERT medical review criteria to state that during the course of a complex medical review (a manual review of claims and supporting documentation), a claim must be **denied** if the signature on the medical record is absent or illegible. Despite this, the Office of the Inspector General found that many CMS contractors were not applying this policy consistently and recommended that CMS provide guidance to the CERT contractor that claims should be counted as an error if a reviewer could not identify the author of a medical record entry. Previously, a CERT reviewer could apply clinical review judgment in considering medical record entries with missing or illegible signatures.

CMS considers the signature requirement met when:

- Initials are shown over a typed or printed name
- Initials NOT over a typed or printed name but *accompanied* by:
  - a signature log, or
  - an attestation statement
- Unsigned handwritten note with other entries on same page, in same handwriting are signed

Timely Filing

Timely Filing Requirements for Medicare Fee-For-Service Claims

On March 23, 2010, the President signed into law the Patient Protection and Affordable Care Act (PPACA), which amended the time period for filing Medicare fee-for-service (FFS) claims as one of many provisions aimed at curbing fraud, waste, and abuse in the Medicare program.

The time period for filing Medicare FFS claims is specified in Sections 1814(a), 1835(a)(1), and 1842(b)(3) of the Social Security Act and in the Code of Federal Regulations (CFR), 42 CFR section 424.44. Section 6404 of the PPACA amended the timely filing requirements to reduce the maximum time period for submission of all Medicare FFS claims to one calendar year after the date of service.

Under this law, claims for dates of service provided on or after January 1, 2010, must have been filed within one calendar year after the date of service. In addition, section 6404 mandates that claims for services furnished before January 1, 2010, must have been filed no later than December 31, 2010. The following rules apply to claims with dates of service prior to January 1, 2010. Claims with dates of service before October 1, 2009, must follow the pre-PPACA timely filing rules. Claims with dates of service October 1, 2009, through December 31, 2009, must have been submitted by December 31, 2010.

In addition, section 6404 of the PPACA permits the Secretary to make certain exceptions to the one-year filing deadline. Presently, one exception exists at 42 CFR section 424.44(b)(1), for "error or misrepresentation" of an employee, Medicare contractor, or agent of the Department that was performing Medicare functions and acting within the scope of its authority. In the event that CMS should add other exceptions, or modifications to this current exception, specific instructions and information will be provided in a future update.

In some states, timely filing limits have been established which would override any limits stated in payer contractual agreements. Check with your state insurance commissioner's office for filing limits that may be applicable to your local area.

Note: When another state or federal law requires filing before these timeframes, the state or federal deadline is to be followed in lieu of the aforementioned time limits.

In order to ensure compliance with timely filing requirements, the following items should be checked prior to submitting a claim:

- Use the appropriate form
- Verify the payer claims mailing address and/or Plan ID (PayerID)
- Report the member's name as it appears on the insurance identification card
- Indicate the correct member or dependent identification number, based on who the patient is, as applicable
- Ensure the dates of service are during an authorized coverage period
- Validate the number of units and type of service submitted is within the parameters of authorization
- Verify the CPT and ICD-9-CM codes reported are correct and support the services rendered
- Report the correct EIN
- Identify the degree level of the service provider

There may be times when a claim is submitted properly yet fails to reach the insurance carrier or is somehow misrouted. In order to avoid an outright denial, you may be required to submit documentation as evidence that you did, in fact, send the claim in within the payer timely filing limit guidelines. Therefore, it is important to note that each payer may have a different definition of what constitutes "proof" of timely filing. This information may be available in the provider manual or handbook or it may be located on the payer's website. It is always a good idea to ask the provider relations representative for this information, in writing, and maintain it in your office policy and procedure manual.

As a general rule, some insurance companies will request a computer generated ledger that includes the following information that cannot be altered or revised in any way:

- Member name
- Insurance ID number
- Billed amount
- Date of service
- Address where the claim was sent for paper claims
- 997 report for electronic claims that indicates a successful transmission to the proper Plan ID (PayerID)

Oftentimes, submitting paper claims by certified mail requesting a signature from the recipient or tracking the claims is another means of demonstrating confirmation that the claims were submitted timely and received by the insurance company.

Again, this is an area where each payer may have distinctly different rules and regulations and as such it is best to verify with the specific insurance company what their particular requirements are in this regard.

Preauthorization

A preauthorization should supply and organize the information regarding a procedure's insurance coverage. Determining, in advance, the benefits and allowable provides you with reimbursement figures in advance. Under most circumstances you'll be able to discuss the deductible, copayment, and balance over and above the allowable with the patient prior to providing costly surgical services. Asking a few pointed questions of the patient and insurer will provide you with additional information regarding allowable, for example:

- How much is the deductible and has it been met for the current year?
- What is the allowable for the quoted procedure?
- What percent of the allowable will be paid?

Be prepared to answer questions regarding any proposed procedures and the diagnosis for each. In other words, have your CPT, HCPCS Level II, and ICD-9-CM codes ready.

Involve your patient when an insurer refuses to provide the information. Most patients don't like surprises in the form of a large unpaid balance after the insurance company has determined its benefits. Submitting your claim is the next (though not final) step toward receiving payment. Verify the insurance company's name and address before mailing the claim and you may save the time and aggravation of having it returned.

CMS -1500 (08-05) Form

1500

HEALTH INSURANCE CLAIM FORM

APPROVED BY NATIONAL UNIFORM CLAIM COMMITTEE 08/05

PICA PICA

CARRIER

1. MEDICARE (Medicare #) MEDICAID (Medicaid #) TRICARE CHAMPUS (Sponsor's SSN) CHAMPVA (Member ID#) GROUP HEALTH PLAN (SSN or ID) FECA BLK LUNG (SSN) OTHER (ID)

1a. INSURED'S I.D. NUMBER (For Program in Item 1)

2. PATIENT'S NAME (Last Name, First Name, Middle Initial)

3. PATIENT'S BIRTH DATE MM DD YY SEX M F

4. INSURED'S NAME (Last Name, First Name, Middle Initial)

5. PATIENT'S ADDRESS (No., Street)

6. PATIENT RELATIONSHIP TO INSURED Self Spouse Child Other

7. INSURED'S ADDRESS (No., Street)

CITY STATE

8. PATIENT STATUS Single Married Other

CITY STATE

ZIP CODE TELEPHONE (Include Area Code) ( )

Employed Full-Time Student Part-Time Student

ZIP CODE TELEPHONE (Include Area Code) ( )

9. OTHER INSURED'S NAME (Last Name, First Name, Middle Initial)

10. IS PATIENT'S CONDITION RELATED TO:

11. INSURED'S POLICY GROUP OR FECA NUMBER

a. OTHER INSURED'S POLICY OR GROUP NUMBER

a. EMPLOYMENT? (Current or Previous) YES NO

a. INSURED'S DATE OF BIRTH MM DD YY SEX M F

b. OTHER INSURED'S DATE OF BIRTH MM DD YY SEX M F

b. AUTO ACCIDENT? PLACE (State) YES NO

b. EMPLOYER'S NAME OR SCHOOL NAME

c. EMPLOYER'S NAME OR SCHOOL NAME

c. OTHER ACCIDENT? YES NO

c. INSURANCE PLAN NAME OR PROGRAM NAME

d. INSURANCE PLAN NAME OR PROGRAM NAME

10d. RESERVED FOR LOCAL USE

d. IS THERE ANOTHER HEALTH BENEFIT PLAN? YES NO *If yes*, return to and complete item 9 a-d.

READ BACK OF FORM BEFORE COMPLETING & SIGNING THIS FORM.

12. PATIENT'S OR AUTHORIZED PERSON'S SIGNATURE I authorize the release of any medical or other information necessary to process this claim. I also request payment of government benefits either to myself or to the party who accepts assignment below.

SIGNED ______ DATE ______

13. INSURED'S OR AUTHORIZED PERSON'S SIGNATURE I authorize payment of medical benefits to the undersigned physician or supplier for services described below.

SIGNED ______

PATIENT AND INSURED INFORMATION

14. DATE OF CURRENT: MM DD YY ILLNESS (First symptom) OR INJURY (Accident) OR PREGNANCY(LMP)

15. IF PATIENT HAS HAD SAME OR SIMILAR ILLNESS. GIVE FIRST DATE MM DD YY

16. DATES PATIENT UNABLE TO WORK IN CURRENT OCCUPATION MM DD YY FROM TO

17. NAME OF REFERRING PROVIDER OR OTHER SOURCE

17a.

17b. NPI

18. HOSPITALIZATION DATES RELATED TO CURRENT SERVICES MM DD YY FROM TO

19. RESERVED FOR LOCAL USE

20. OUTSIDE LAB? YES NO $ CHARGES

21. DIAGNOSIS OR NATURE OF ILLNESS OR INJURY (Relate Items 1, 2, 3 or 4 to Item 24E by Line)

1. ___ . ___ 3. ___ . ___

2. ___ . ___ 4. ___ . ___

22. MEDICAID RESUBMISSION CODE ORIGINAL REF. NO.

23. PRIOR AUTHORIZATION NUMBER

24. A. DATE(S) OF SERVICE From MM DD YY To MM DD YY	B. PLACE OF SERVICE	C. EMG	D. PROCEDURES, SERVICES, OR SUPPLIES (Explain Unusual Circumstances) CPT/HCPCS MODIFIER	E. DIAGNOSIS POINTER	F. $ CHARGES	G. DAYS OR UNITS	H. EPSDT Family Plan	I. ID. QUAL.	J. RENDERING PROVIDER ID. #
1								NPI	
2								NPI	
3								NPI	
4								NPI	
5								NPI	
6								NPI	

25. FEDERAL TAX I.D. NUMBER SSN EIN

26. PATIENT'S ACCOUNT NO.

27. ACCEPT ASSIGNMENT? (For govt. claims, see back) YES NO

28. TOTAL CHARGE $

29. AMOUNT PAID $

30. BALANCE DUE $

31. SIGNATURE OF PHYSICIAN OR SUPPLIER INCLUDING DEGREES OR CREDENTIALS (I certify that the statements on the reverse apply to this bill and are made a part thereof.)

SIGNED DATE

32. SERVICE FACILITY LOCATION INFORMATION

a. b.

33. BILLING PROVIDER INFO & PH # ( )

a. b.

PHYSICIAN OR SUPPLIER INFORMATION

NUCC Instruction Manual available at: www.nucc.org **PLEASE PRINT OR TYPE** APPROVED OMB-0938-0999 FORM CMS-1500 (08-05)

Monitoring Claims

A Day in the Life of a Claim

Once the payer has received a claim, the process of adjudication follows a well-established path. Hopefully, the claim will proceed unimpeded toward reimbursement, but along the way the claim may be stopped and returned to your office for lack of information. Let's look at this adjudication process so you know what to expect and how to speed up your payment.

The Claim Arrives

Upon receipt, paper claims are either manually entered or scanned into the payer's adjudication system. Electronic claims are screened to determine that all necessary data elements are present. If the payer uses an optical recognition scanner (OCR), any attachments, such as operative reports, cover letters, pathology reports, etc., are separated from the claim and scanned in. You may save a few headaches by stamping your practice name, provider number, address, and phone number on all forms and attachments. The same information should be recorded for electronic claims. This helps the payer avoid losing the documentation necessary to pay the claim.

The Claims Adjudicator

After the data has been entered into the payer's computer system, and if the claim is "clean" (no problems) it's paid. But first, claims must pass through a series of edits to verify the patient's coverage and eligibility as well as check for medical necessity and noncovered services. If the claim requires additional information, also known as development, the insurer contacts either you or your patient. Let your patients know you're available to help them with questions. This contact for development is usually by mail, but it can also be by phone. Many problem claims are denied immediately or placed at the bottom of the pile due to lack of information. The best way to receive prompt and correct payment is to submit a clean claim. This is definitely a case where time well spent is money earned.

Occasionally, your office will submit a claim that contains all pertinent information needed for payment but requires examination by the payer's medical review department. This will delay your payment. However, if your office has a program or process for monitoring claims, you'll not only be watching your claims for timely payment, you'll also know where your claim is in the processing system when payment is delayed. Carefully tracking the progress of your claims will alert you to those unpaid claims that have been lost and need to be resubmitted.

Why Monitor?

Monitoring insurance submissions can significantly improve cash flow and profit position because, as you track specific claims, you assure timely and appropriate payment. Leaving your claims to chance can cause problems that can easily be solved if brought to the processor's attention at first submission. Since some insurance companies have been found to commit errors on as many as 25 percent of all claims, monitoring should be an ongoing process. The payer may have neither the information nor the incentive to catch mistakes made in payment. When a patient receives an incorrect payment, the error may go unnoticed. An alert insurance clerk carefully monitoring reimbursement is the best safeguard against insurance company errors.

Once you've sent a claim, either on paper or electronically, you need a mechanism for following it through to reimbursement. Commonly, this takes four weeks to six weeks, but it may vary geographically or by payer. Most software packages should include a reporting system for tracking claims. You need to define "prompt payment" for the computer system. In other words, you have to tell the computer what you feel is a reasonable time delay before the computer alerts you that no payment has been received. Optimally, your computerized system allows you to set this parameter for individual payers.

Furthermore, careful and consistent review of electronic claims submission reports will show you, at a glance, whether all of your claims were successfully transmitted. Claims with errors are easily determined and a policy should be instated that requires immediate correction of claims errors. Some claims will transmit to the carrier despite containing an error whereas other claims simply reject from the onset. Once the error has been remedied, resubmit the claim right away. Oftentimes, offices and clinics who have adopted such a policy will receive a denial or notification of the error from the payer days or weeks relating to the original denial after they had already corrected and resubmitted the claim versus waiting for that notification from the insurance company, saving the provider and the practice time and money.

For Medicare, verifying within one business day that a claim is on file is another good habit to develop. If one or two claims in a transmitted batch are on file, then all claims within that particular batch are on file. Again, this is another mechanism that can be employed when there may be uncertainty as to the success of the transmission.

Many commercial payers offer free online provider access to check eligibility, claims status, and obtain referrals or preauthorizations among other things. This is a great resource and tool to utilize when monitoring claims status. The provider will likely be required to register with the payer site and receive a username and password in order to use the service.

One downfall of most computer systems is found in payment posting. Do you relate portions of a payment to each individual service or to the original service date? The former is generally referred to as "open item billing" and is considered a more accurate tracking method. Unfortunately, many offices don't use this capability, ultimately reducing the accuracy of claims tracking. If you lack the ability to track your claims via the computer, you will want to use a manual tracking system.

Tracking Systems

The Suspension File System

For nonautomated offices filing paper claims, it's wise to create a suspension file. Simply set up a series of files for a month at a time. Usually it's better not to mix claims that are current (less than 30 days) with claims more than 30 days. Depending on your practice, you may find it necessary to have a current file, a 30-day file, and a 60+-day file.

A practical method for creating your suspension file is to use three separate hanging files, each with four separate folders marked Week 1, Week 2, etc.—one folder for each week of the month. Mark the hanging files Month 1, Month 2, and Month 3. Place the current month's claims in the hanging file marked Month 1. Place the claims over one month old in the file for Month 2 and claims 60+ days old in Month 3. As each week goes by, roll the outstanding claims to the next file. Keep the claims in each file in alphabetic order to eliminate the time and energy spent looking for them when the payment is received.

Claims review should be given a high priority and be a regularly scheduled part of your work week. Insurance claims that are current, or have been filed in the current month, generally require no additional work until the Explanation of Benefits (EOB) and payment are received. Claims more than 30 days old should be reviewed for possible inquiries to the payer.

Make it a rule in your office that most inquiries are written. Notably, this rule applies to Medicare and Medicaid carriers, many of whom require their own forms. Some inquiries are most efficiently made by phone. For example, if a claim has been denied for a simple reason, without notification, a quick phone call is time well spent. If resubmission is the solution, always attach a note with the date, contact person's name, and a

INSURANCE CLAIM REGISTER

Filing Date	Chart Number	Patient's Name	Name & Address Where Claim Submitted	Amount Billed	Amount Paid	Difference	Status or Comment
7/30	1221	Matthew Kramer	First Insurance 1st Avenue, Newark, NJ 12345	$525.00			9/26 busy 9/27 busy 9/28 " "
8/30	1032	Mark Lane	Fine Insurance 2nd Avenue New Haven, CT 12346	$50.00	$40.00	$10.00	Pd. at 80% Pt. owes balance
8/30	1350	Luke Myers	Better Insurance 3rd Avenue New York City, NY 02111	$1,200.00	$700.00	$500.00	Requested review 9/23
8/30	1118	John Jacobs	Gold Insurance 4th Avenue Newton, WI 12456	$50.00			9/23 claim being processed today
8/30	1179	Mary Byer	Transaccident Insurance 5th Avenue New Hill, NC 24567	$50.00			9/23 no record of claim–resubmit
8/30	1098	Christi Wilson	County Farm Insurance 6th Avenue New Era, IA 45678	$125.00	$50.00	$75.00	$75.00 deductible; bill patient
8/30	1352	Rose Larsen	Last Insurance 7th Avenue New Hope, MS 56789	$1,500.00	$0.00		Sent to medical review 9/10

description of the conversation. This provides you with the documentation needed if you have to repeat this process.

Your office computer software program may provide you with a comment field or area for "collection" notes. If you don't have this luxury, keep hard copy files of your claims inquiries.

The Log System

An alternative to the suspension file is to record your claims information on a log sheet. When a claim is submitted, record the filing date, patient's name and chart number, account number, name and address of the payer, and the amount billed. The claim itself can be filed temporarily in either the patient's chart or an unpaid insurance file.

After all of the day's or week's claims have been recorded, leave a blank space to tag the claims submitted during that time frame. You may want to highlight those dates in a specific color for review in about three to four weeks.

As payments come in, pull the original claim form and compare it to the EOB. Record the amount paid along with any difference on your log sheet. Any notations such as "claim sent to review" or "claim denied for additional information" should be recorded in the status column.

Understanding Explanation Of Benefits (EOB)

The EOB is the key to knowing what you were paid and why, but understanding what this document really means is sometimes not as easy as it sounds. An EOB has its own language: "applied to deductible," "above usual and customary," "patient co-pay," "allowable," and so on. Often hidden in this language is the explanation of what the patient is responsible for paying. Too many offices write off thousands of dollars of earned income each year because the EOBs are misunderstood or not carefully read.

Each payer EOB follows its own format. Some can be very confusing and may even lead the patient to believe he/she is not responsible for a balance. Knowing how to read an EOB can help you collect full reimbursement, including any balances owed by the patient.

Sometimes payers change your CPT codes and pay you based on a CPT code different from the one you submitted. Watch for these types of changes carefully, as many payment mistakes occur from simple data entry errors by the insurer. Read and learn from your EOB because you may be the one making a common coding error that is easily corrected.

A wise tactic is to "volunteer" to review EOBs sent to your patients. This accomplishes two things: first, it provides assurance that your office receives the payment, and secondly, you demonstrate to your patients that your practice takes an interest in their financial well-being.

Monitoring EOBs and comparing payments allows you to track your claims and tells you which claims have been sent for medical review. There's also the benefit of understanding why insurance companies pay the way they do.

Medicare Summary Notice

The Explanation of Medicare Benefits (EOMB) shares the same problem as the EOB: they are both confusing to the provider and the beneficiary. To resolve the problem, at least for Medicare beneficiaries, CMS has developed the Medicare Summary Notice (MSN). The MSN lists all claims filed during each month for each beneficiary. One type covers inpatient and outpatient facility services, another type includes all Part B physician and other services, and a third type covers durable medical equipment (DME). Additionally, each document periodically carries messages pertinent to the beneficiary, such as the hotline for reporting fraud and abuse.

Common Payment Errors

There will be times when your diligent monitoring shows claim problems that are difficult to resolve. The following chart may help you determine what caused an incorrect payment.

Common Payment Errors

Result	Why?
A service is reduced.	The adjudicator may have down coded the claim for lack of documentation.
Reimbursement is made at a significantly reduced rate.	Possibly a data entry error. Compare the CPT code submitted to the actual code paid.
Low or no reimbursement.	Precertification was not obtained. Insufficient documentation to establish medical necessity.

Common Payment Errors (Continued)	
Result	**Why?**
Multiple units are paid as one unit.	The insurer "missed" the number in the units column. Determine if there is third-party payer instruction or policies regarding the number of units that may be billed for the service either at a single encounter or during the patient's lifetime. Appeal the payment amount if appropriate.
The reimbursement for a procedure or service suddenly drops.	This could mean a recalculation of allowables or an error. Contact the payer.
Payment is not received.	Claim is lost or "caught in the system." Begin an inquiry.
Multiple procedures were not paid.	The insurance company either ignored the additional procedures or bundled them in with the primary procedure. Verify CCI edits and, if appropriate, contact the payer.

Insurance Payment Log

CPT Code	Payment	Payment	Payment	Payment	Payment
	$1,832	$1,600			
	$1,950				
47600	$1,250				
	$2,150				
	$2,000	$1,900			
	$2,460	$2,158			
47605	$2,833				
	$2,112				
	$2,150	$2,066			
	$2,380				
47610	$2,740				
	$2,950				

Gathering Information

Most physicians' offices have contractual arrangements with government or private third-party payers. Many of these payers provide your office with a "fee schedule" or other type of payment information. Medicare payment is based on the Medicare Fee Schedule, also known as Resource Based Relative Value Scale or RBRVS. The locality-specific fees are available from CMS on their website or from other commercial sources such as Optum.

Another good source of information is available in those states that have developed a Relative Value Study (RVS) or fee schedule for their state workers' compensation payers. When using an RVS, these states usually pay at a set rate based on the relative value of a procedure multiplied by a dollar conversion factor. Workers' compensation rates based on a fee schedule usually provide the dollar value, sometimes called the maximum allowable rate (MAR) for the service.

As a rule, commercial insurers don't readily provide fee information, but it can be obtained. When a payment is received, record the amount in a payment log. For frequently billed payers, devote a column to each payer. List all procedures performed and be conscientious in keeping this information up-to-date. This helps you develop a UCR (usual, customary, and reasonable) reimbursement amount by payer for each procedure and service performed by your practice.

Information from a variety of sources helps you develop a fee schedule that is "in-step" with accepted relative values. It also helps you identify reimbursement errors. If you know your fee for a service is fair, low reimbursement indicates an error may have occurred in processing the claim.

When it's apparent an error has been made, don't hesitate to challenge the payment. Medicare and private payers will correct proven mistakes, when brought to their attention. Errors such as billing the wrong procedure code, omitting a procedure code usually billed with that service, or omitting a standard supply are acceptable reasons for resubmission. Payers usually require this resubmission in a timely manner.

Payment Rationales

Contrary to popular belief, most payers do follow logical mechanisms for reimbursing claims. Many insurers base payments on UCR amounts adjusted for specific geographic areas. Payers acquire this information from several sources and then adjust accordingly to fit their needs in written policies. This UCR information is gathered within specific geographic boundaries though it is not broken down by specialty. Other payers gather their own data for the regions they service and base their payment on a percentage of the UCR charge they've established for your area.

Workers' compensation payers often use a straightforward relative value study chosen by that state. Payments are determined by multiplying a conversion factor, usually established by the state's industrial commission, against the relative value for the service.

HMO and PPO fee schedules are usually developed internally by each organization and are often published, on request, for their participants. These fee schedules are generally updated on a yearly basis.

Downcoding

Downcoding or recoding by an insurance company is another possible cause of reduced payments. Downcoding occurs when a payer either reviews a claim and determines that the code selected is not correct and a lesser valued code is substituted. It may also occur when the payer uses statistical frequencies to evaluate coding patterns and determines that the provider is oversubmitting higher valued codes. This occurs most frequently with evaluation and management (E/M) services. If the payer determines E/M levels are higher than the norm, the payer may downcode the services to the next lower level E/M service.

Recoding often occurs when claims are submitted with deleted or invalid CPT codes. In this case, the payer may assign a current code. The opposite may occur in billing workers' compensation. Many workers' compensation payers are RVS-based or based on the CPT code set from a previous year, and if the CPT code submittted doesn't match the RVS code or code set currently being used, the code may be reassigned or denied. Knowing which coding systems and code sets your payers use can avoid these problems.

Inquiries, Reviews, and Appeals

Inquiries, reviews, and appeals are the final essential component to monitoring your payments whether you choose the suspension file or log system, or create your own method of tracking claims.

When your claims and EOB monitoring turns up an error (provider or payer), correct the claim and resubmit it for appropriate reimbursement. If this does not resolve the issue, immediately appeal.

Claims Correction

When a claims error is discovered that could result, or already has resulted, in inaccurate reimbursement, send a corrected claim. Clearly mark this claim as "CORRECTED BILLING—NOT A DUPLICATE CLAIM." Include a note describing the error, plus any additional documentation necessary to support your position. Do not be tempted to keep overpayments; bring it to the attention of the insurance company with a refund as soon as possible. Medicare does not look favorably on practices holding claim overpayments and will prosecute.

Medicare law contains provisions dealing with liability for and recovery of overpayments that can be found in the *Medicare Financial Management Manual*, Pub. 100-06, chapter 3, section 200.

Appealing Incorrect Payments

Before appealing a claim, whether with Medicare or a private insurer, notify the insurer in writing that an error has occurred. Many payers have established time allowances for claims appeals and often print this on their EOBs. Do not let appeals slide. Actively monitor your claims and stay current with any appeals in progress.

One of the basic rules for appealing a claim is to always include a copy of the original claim, EOB or EOMB (or MSN), and any additional documentation necessary to provide evidence for the appeal. Cover letters are also effective for appeals and will "set the stage" with the claims reviewer. If you feel the payer has not responded to your complaint, do not give up—there are alternatives. Contact your state's insurance commissioner and send a clear, well-documented account of your dissatisfaction. Your argument carries greater weight if you have several examples of the problem from the same insurance company.

Appealing a Part B Medicare Claim

Medicare claims appeals have five levels supported by numerous regulations. The journey starts when either the physician or beneficiary disagrees with the carrier's determination as explained on the EOMB (or MSN). If the claim was assigned, only the physician can initiate the review. If the claim was unassigned, the beneficiary usually initiates the review or can stipulate in writing that the physician is authorized to act on his/her behalf.

The appeals process consists of five levels:

- Redetermination
- Reconsideration
- Administrative Law Judge (ALJ) Hearing
- Review by the Medicare Appeals Council
- Federal District Court Review

Level 1, Redetermination, is the only level that a contractor performs. It should be noted that each level of appeal must be completed for each claim before proceeding on to the next level.

The time limit for filing the request is 120 days for level 1, 180 days for level 2, and 60 days from previous determinations for the remaining three levels. However, extensions may be granted in certain situations and when "good cause" can be shown. An example of "good cause" includes natural disasters and other unavoidable circumstances.

The First Level of Appeal—Redetermination

If you are dissatisfied with the outcome of your initial appeal determination, you may request, in writing, to have the contractor review its determination by a different person than the employee who made the original determination. This step is considered the first level of appeal for both Part A and Part B claims. Essentially, this is a "second look" at the claim and supporting documentation. Previously, telephone requests for reviews or reconsiderations could be made over the telephone; however, regulations no longer permit this right though contractors may choose to conduct a telephone reopening for clerical errors or omissions.

In the past, *revised* initial determinations were afforded appeal rights to a hearing officer for Part B claims where the amount in controversy was greater than $100. For amounts less than $100, appeal rights to the review level for Part B claims were afforded. However, for all Part B *revised* initial determinations issued on or after January 1, 2006, the first level of appeal is a redetermination.

As mentioned, all appeals for redetermination must be made in writing. There are two ways of doing this:

- Completed CMS-20027 form
- Written request not on Form 20027 that contains all of the following:
  —. Beneficiary Name
  —. Medicare health insurance claim number (HIC)
  —. The specific service(s) and/or item(s) for which the redetermination is being requested
  —. Date(s) of service
  —. Name and signature of the party or representative of the party

Note: For a claim containing a minor error or omission, request a correction of the claim through the "reopening" process rather than submitting an appeal reconsideration. The specific steps in the processes can be found at: http://www.cms.gov/Regulations-and-Guidance/Guidance/Manuals/downloads/clm104c34.pdf with additional information in the *Medicare Claims Processing Manual* (Pub. 100-04), chapter 1 General Billing Requirements, § 80.3.2—Handling Incomplete or Invalid Claims and § 70.2.3.1—Incomplete or Invalid Submissions.

DEPARTMENT OF HEALTH AND HUMAN SERVICES
CENTERS FOR MEDICARE & MEDICAID SERVICES

MEDICARE REDETERMINATION REQUEST FORM — 1ST LEVEL OF APPEAL

1. Beneficiary's name:____________________

2. Medicare number: ____________________

3. Item or service you wish to appeal: ____________________

4. Date the service or item was received: ____________________

5. Date of the initial determination notice (please include a copy of the notice with this request):
(If you received your initial determination notice more than 120 days ago, include your reason for the late filing.)

____

____

____

5a. Name of the Medicare contractor that made the determination (not required):

____

5b. Does this appeal involve an overpayment? ☐ Yes ☐ No
(for providers and suppliers only)

6. I do not agree with the determination decision on my claim because:

____

____

____

7. Additional information Medicare should consider:

____

____

____

8. ☐ I have evidence to submit. Please attach the evidence to this form or attach a statement explaining what you intend to submit and when you intend to submit it. You may also submit additional evidence at a later time, but all evidence must be received prior to the issuance of the redetermination.

☐ I do not have evidence to submit.

9. Person appealing: ☐ Beneficiary ☐ Provider/Supplier ☐ Representative

10. Name, address, and telephone number of person appealing: ____________________

____

11. Signature of person appealing: ____________________

12. Date signed:____________________

PRIVACY ACT STATEMENT: The legal authority for the collection of information on this form is authorized by section 1869 (a)(3) of the Social Security Act. The information provided will be used to further document your appeal. Submission of the information requested on this form is voluntary, but failure to provide all or any part of the requested information may affect the determination of your appeal. Information you furnish on this form may be disclosed by the Centers for Medicare and Medicaid Services to another person or government agency only with respect to the Medicare Program and to comply with Federal laws requiring or permitting the disclosure of information or the exchange of information between the Department of Health and Human Services and other agencies. Additional information about these disclosures can be found in the system of records notice for system no. 09-70-0566, as amended, available at 71 Fed. Reg. 54489 (2006) or at http://www.cms.gov/PrivacyActSystemofRecords/downloads/0566.pdf

Form CMS-20027 (12/10)

Monitoring Claims

The Second Level of Appeal—Reconsideration

A request for reconsideration must be submitted in writing on either the CMS-20033 form or, if not on the 20033 form, it should contain all of the same information identified above for the Redetermination process as well as the name of the contractor who made the redetermination along with the Medicare Redetermination Notice (MRN). Requests for reconsideration must be filed with the QIC specified in the redetermination notice and who has the jurisdiction.

Reconsiderations are processed within 60 days upon receipt of the required information by entities called qualified independent contractors or QICs. QIC reconsiderations consist of a panel that includes physicians and other health professionals. Services or items rendered or ordered by a physician under reconsideration will have at least one physician on the panel.

A list of the QICs and the jurisdictions that they serve is shown below:

Part A East Jurisdiction:	Maximus, Inc.
Part A West Jurisdiction:	Maximus, Inc.
Part B North Jurisdiction:	C2C Solutions, Inc.
Part B South Jurisdiction:	Q2 Administrators, LLC
DME Jurisdiction:	RiverTrust Solutions, Inc.

DEPARTMENT OF HEALTH AND HUMAN SERVICES
CENTERS FOR MEDICARE & MEDICAID SERVICES

MEDICARE RECONSIDERATION REQUEST FORM — 2ND LEVEL OF APPEAL

1. Beneficiary's name: ______________________

2. Medicare number: ______________________

3. Item or service you wish to appeal: ______________________

4. Date the service or item was received: ______________________

5. Date of the redetermination notice (please include a copy of the notice with this request):
(If you received your redetermination notice more than 180 days ago, include your reason for the late filing.)

____

____

____

5a. Name of the Medicare contractor that made the redetermination (not required if copy of notice attached):

____

5b. Does this appeal involve an overpayment? ☐ Yes ☐ No
(for providers and suppliers only)

6. I do not agree with the redetermination decision on my claim because:

____

____

____

7. Additional information Medicare should consider:

____

____

____

8. ☐ I have evidence to submit. Please attach the evidence to this form or attach a statement explaining what you intend to submit and when you intend to submit it. You may also submit additional evidence at a later time, but all evidence must be received prior to the issuance of the reconsideration.

☐ I do not have evidence to submit.

9. Person appealing: ☐ Beneficiary ☐ Provider/Supplier ☐ Representative

10. Name, address, and telephone number of person appealing: ______________________

____

11. Signature of person appealing: ______________________

12. Date signed: ______________________

PRIVACY ACT STATEMENT: The legal authority for the collection of information on this form is authorized by section 1869 (a)(3) of the Social Security Act. The information provided will be used to further document your appeal. Submission of the information requested on this form is voluntary, but failure to provide all or any part of the requested information may affect the determination of your appeal. Information you furnish on this form may be disclosed by the Centers for Medicare and Medicaid Services to another person or government agency only with respect to the Medicare Program and to comply with Federal laws requiring or permitting the disclosure of information or the exchange of information between the Department of Health and Human Services and other agencies. Additional information about these disclosures can be found in the system of records notice for system no. 09-70-0566, as amended, available at 71 Fed. Reg. 54489 (2006) or at http://www.cms.gov/PrivacyActSystemofRecords/downloads/0566.pdf

Form CMS-20033 (12/10)

The Third Level of Appeal—Administrative Law Judge (ALJ)
There are three circumstances whereby a party can request an Administrative Law Judge hearing:

- If the request for an ALJ hearing was submitted within 60 days after receipt of the notice of the QIC's reconsideration and the amount in question requirement is met
- When the QIC's decision making time period has expired and you submit a written request to escalate the appeal to an ALJ to the QIC but no action is taken within five days of the QIC receiving said request
- A dismissal of a request for reconsideration by the QIC can be reviewed by the ALJ if the amount in question meets the requirement

The amount in controversy requirement for all ALJ hearings made on or after January 1, 2013 is $140.

Note: The amount in controversy required to request an ALJ hearing is increased annually by the percentage increase in the medical care component of the consumer price index for all urban consumers.

CHART 1 – The Medicare Fee-for-Service Appeals Process

APPEAL LEVEL	TIME LIMIT FOR FILING REQUEST	MONETARY THRESHOLD TO BE MET
1. Redetermination	120 days from date of receipt of the notice initial determination	None
2. Reconsideration	180 days from date of receipt of the redetermination	None
3. Administrative Law Judge (ALJ) Hearing	60 days from the date of receipt of the reconsideration	At least $100 remains in controversy.* For requests filed on or after January 2010, at least $130 remains in controversy.
4. Departmental Appeals Board (DAB) Review/Appeals Council	60 days from the date of receipt of the ALJ hearing decision	None
5. Federal Court Review	60 days from date of receipt of the Appeals Council decision or declination of review by DAB	At least $1,000 remains in controversy.* For requests filed on or after January 2010, at least $1,260 remains in controversy.

In order to request an ALJ hearing, you must submit the request in writing, on either the CMS-20034A/B form or the request should contain all of the following information:

- Name, address and Medicare health insurance claim number of the beneficiary whose claims is being appealed
- Name and address of the appellant, when not the beneficiary
- Name and address of designated representative, if any
- Document control number assigned to the appeal by the QIC, if any
- Date(s) of service
- Reasons appellant disagrees with the decision by the QIC during reconsideration or other determination being appealed.
- Statement of additional evidence to be submitted and when it will be submitted, if any

ALJ hearing requests should be filed with the entity specified in the reconsideration notice from the QIC.

DEPARTMENTOF HEALTH AND HUMAN SERVICES
OFFICE OF MEDICARE HEARINGS AND APPEALS

REQUEST FOR MEDICARE HEARING BY AN ADMINISTRATIVE LAW JUDGE

❑ Part A
❑ Part B

Effective July 1, 2005. For use by party to a reconsideration determination issued by a Qualified Independent Contractor (QIC)
(Amount in controversy must be $100 or more.)

Send copies of this completed form to:
Original — *Office of Medicare Hearings and Appeals Field Office specified in the QIC Reconsideration Notice*
Copy — *Appellant* ***Copy*** — *All other parties*
Failure to send a copy of this completed request to the other parties to the appeal will delay the start date of your appeal.
Did you send all required copies? ❑ Yes ❑ No

Appellant *(The party appealing the reconsideration determination)*

Beneficiary *(Leave blank if same as the appellant.)*	Provider or Supplier *(Leave blank if same as the appellant.)*
AddressAddress	
CityStateZip Code	CityStateZip Code
Area Code/Telephone NumberE-mail Address	Area Code/Telephone NumberE-mail Address
Health Insurance (Medicare) Claim Number	Document control number assigned by the QIC
QIC that made the reconsideration determination	Dates of Service FromTo

I DISAGREE WITH THE DETERMINATION MADE ON MY APPEAL BECAUSE:

____

____

You have a right to be represented at the hearing. If you are not represented but would like to be, your Office of Medicare Hearings and Appeals Field Office will give you a list of legal referral and service organizations. *(If you are represented and have not already done so, complete form CMS-1696.)*

Check **Only One** Statement:
- ❑ I **wish** to have a hearing.
- ❑ I **do not wish** to have a hearing and I request that a decision be made on the basis of the evidence in my case. *(Complete form HHS-723, "Waiver of Right to an ALJ Hearing.")*

Check **Only One** Statement:
- ❑ I **have** additional evidence to submit.
- ❑ I **have no** additional evidence to submit.

If you have additional evidence to submit, please attach the evidence or attach a statement explaining what you intend to submit and when you intend to submit it. If you are a provider, supplier, or beneficiary represented by a provider or supplier, the evidence must be accompanied by a good cause statement explaining why the evidence is being submitted for the first time at the ALJlevel.

The appellant should complete No. 1 and the representative, if any, should complete No.2. If a representative is not present to sign, print his or her name in No.2. Where applicable, check to indicate if appellant will accompany the representative at the hearing. ❑ Yes ❑ No

1. (Appellant's Signature)Date	**2.** (Representative's Signature/Name)Date
Address	Address ❑ Attorney ❑ Non-Attorney
CityStateZip Code	CityStateZip Code
Area Code/Telephone NumberE-mail Address	Area Code/Telephone NumberE-mail Address

Answer the following questions that apply:
A)Does request involve multiple claims? (If yes, a list of all the claims must be attached.) ❑ Yes ❑ No
B)Does request involve multiple beneficiaries? (If yes, a list of beneficiaries, their HICNs and the dates of service.) ❑ Yes ❑ No
C)Did the beneficiary assign his or her appeal rights to you as the provider/supplier? ❑ Yes ❑ No
(If yes, you must complete and attach form CMS-20031. Failure to do so will prevent approval of the assignment.)

Must be completed by the provider/supplier if representing the beneficiary:

I waive my rights to charge and collect a fee for representing ______________________ before the Office of Medicare Hearings and Appeals. (Beneficiary name)

Signature of provider/supplier representing beneficiaryDate

CMS-20034 A/B U3 (08/05) EF 08/2005 ATTACH ACOPYOF THE RECONSIDERATION DETERMINATION (IF AVAILABLE) TO THIS COPY.

DEPARTMENTOF HEALTH AND HUMAN SERVICES
OFFICE OF MEDICARE HEARINGS AND APPEALS

REQUEST FOR MEDICARE HEARING BY AN ADMINISTRATIVE LAW JUDGE

❑ Part A
❑ Part B

Effective July 1, 2005. For use by party to a reconsideration/fair hearing determination issued by a Fiscal Intermediary (FI), Carrier, or Quality Improvement Organization (QIO)
(Amount in controversy must be $100 or more.)

Send copies of this completed form to:
Original *— The FI, Carrier, or QIO that issued the Reconsideration/Fair Hearing Notice*
Copy *— Appellant*

Appellant *(The party appealing the reconsideration determination)*

Beneficiary *(Leave blank if same as the appellant.)*	Provider or Supplier *(Leave blank if same as the appellant.)*
AddressAddress	
CityStateZip Code	CityStateZip Code
Area Code/Telephone NumberE-mail AddressArea Code/Telephone NumberE-mail Address	
Health Insurance (Medicare) Claim Number	Document control number assigned by the FI, Carrier, or QIO
FI, Carrier, or QIO that made the reconsideration/fair hearing determination	Dates of Service From / To

I DISAGREE WITH THE DETERMINATION MADE ON MY APPEAL BECAUSE:

You have a right to be represented at the hearing. If you are not represented but would like to be, your Office of Medicare Hearings and Appeals Field Office will give you a list of legal referral and service organizations. *(If you are represented and have not already done so, complete form CMS-1696.)*

Check **Only One** Statement:	❑ I **wish** to have a hearing. ❑ I **do not wish** to have a hearing and I request that a decision be made on the basis of the evidence in my case. *(Complete form HHS-723, "Waiver of Right to an ALJ Hearing.")*	Check **Only One** Statement:	❑ I **have** additional evidence to submit. ❑ I **have no** additional evidence to submit.

The appellant should complete No. 1 and the representative, if any, should complete No.2. If a representative is not present to sign, print his or her name in No.2. Where applicable, check to indicate if appellant will accompany the representative at the hearing. ❑ Yes ❑ No

1. (Appellant's Signature)Date	**2.** (Representative's Signature/Name)Date
Address	Address ❑ Attorney ❑ Non-Attorney
CityStateZip Code	CityStateZip Code
Area Code/Telephone NumberE-mail Address	Area Code/Telephone NumberE-mail Address

Answer the following questions that apply:

A)Does request involve multiple claims? ❑ Yes ❑ No
(If yes, a list of all the claims must be attached.)

B)Does request involve multiple beneficiaries? ❑ Yes ❑ No
(If yes, a list of beneficiaries, their HICNs and the dates of the applicable reconsideration determinations must be attached.)

C)Did the beneficiary assign his or her appeal rights to you as the provider/supplier? ❑ Yes ❑ No
(If yes, you must complete and attach form CMS-20031. Failure to do so will prevent approval of the assignment.)

D)If there was no assignment, are you a physician being held liable pursuant to 1842(I)(1)(A) of the Social Security Act? ❑ Yes ❑ No

CMS-5011A/B U2 (08/05) EF 08/2005ATTACH ACOPYOF THE RECONSIDERATION/FAIR HEARING DETERMINATION (IF AVAILABLE) TO THIS COPY.

The Fourth Level of Appeal—Review by the Medicare Appeals Council

This is the level available to appellants after the ALJ hearing decision or dismissal order has been issued. The Appeals Council may receive the decision and can adopt, modify, or reverse the ALJ's decision, or remand the case back to an ALJ for further proceedings. In the event of a dismissal from the ALJ, the Council may deny review or remand the case back to an ALJ for further proceedings.

In most cases, the Council renders a decision within 90 days after receiving a request for review. However, the time period may extend beyond the 90-day period or extended at the discretion of the Council for a number of reasons that include, but are not limited to, the case escalating from the ALJ level.

DEPARTMENT OF HEALTH AND HUMAN SERVICES (DHHS) / DEPARTMENTAL APPEALS BOARD Form DAB-101 (08/09)

REQUEST FOR REVIEW OF ADMINISTRATIVE LAW JUDGE (ALJ) MEDICARE DECISION / DISMISSAL

1. APPELLANT (the party requesting review)	2. ALJ APPEAL NUMBER (on the decision or dismissal)
3. BENEFICIARY*	4. HEALTH INSURANCE CLAIM NUMBER (HICN)*

*If the request involves multiple claims or multiple beneficiaries, attach a list of beneficiaries, HICNs, and any other information to identify all claims being appealed.

5. PROVIDER, PRACTITIONER, OR SUPPLIER	6. SPECIFIC ITEM(S) OR SERVICE(S)

7. Medicare claim type: ☐ Part A ☐ Part B ☐ Part C - Medicare Advantage
☐ Part D - Medicare Prescription Drug Plan ☐ Entitlement/enrollment for Part A or Part B

8. Does this request involve authorization for an item or service that has not yet been furnished?
☐ Yes If Yes, skip to Block 9.
☐ No If No, Specific Dates of Service:

9. If the request involves authorization for a prescription drug under Medicare Part D, would application of the standard appellate timeframe seriously jeopardize the beneficiary's life, health, or ability to regain maximum function (as documented by a physician) such that expedited review is appropriate? ☐ Yes ☐ No

I request that the Medicare Appeals Council review the ALJ's ☐ decision or ☐ dismissal order [check one] dated ______________________ . I disagree with the ALJ's action because (specify the parts of the ALJ's decision or dismissal you disagree with and why you think the ALJ was wrong):

____

____

____

____

(Attach additional sheets if you need more space)

PLEASE ATTACH A COPY OF THE ALJ DECISION OR DISMISSAL ORDER YOU ARE APPEALING.

DATE			DATE		
APPELLANT'S SIGNATURE (the party requesting review)			REPRESENTATIVE'S SIGNATURE (include signed appointment of representative if not already submitted.)		
PRINT NAME			PRINT NAME		
ADDRESS			ADDRESS		
CITY, STATE, ZIP CODE			CITY, STATE, ZIP CODE		
TELEPHONE NUMBER	FAX NUMBER	E-MAIL	TELEPHONE NUMBER	FAX NUMBER	E-MAIL

(SEE FURTHER INSTRUCTIONS ON PAGE 2)

Form DAB-101 (08/09)

If you have additional evidence, submit it with this request for review. If you need more time, you must request an extension of time in writing now, explaining why you are unable to submit the evidence or legal argument now.

If you are a provider, supplier, or a beneficiary represented by a provider or supplier, and your case was reconsidered by a Qualified Independent Contractor (QIC), the Medicare Appeals Council will not consider new evidence related to issues the QIC has already considered unless you show that you have a good reason for submitting it for the first time to the Medicare Appeals Council.

IMPORTANT: Include the HICN and ALJ Appeal Number on any letter or other material you submit.

This request must be received within 60 calendar days after you receive the ALJ's decision or dismissal, unless we extend the time limit for good cause. We assume you received the decision or dismissal 5 calendar days after it was issued, unless you show you received it later. If this request will not be received within 65 calendar days from the date on the decision or dismissal order, please explain why on a separate sheet.

You must file your request for review in writing with the Medicare Appeals Council at:

Department of Health and Human Services
Departmental Appeals Board
Medicare Appeals Council, MS 6127
Cohen Building Room G-644
330 Independence Ave., S.W.
Washington, D.C. 20201

You may send the request for review by U.S. Mail, a common carrier such as FedEx, or by fax to (202) 565-0227. If you send a fax, please do not also mail a copy. ***You must send a copy of your appeal to the other parties and indicate that all parties, to include all beneficiaries, have been copied on the request for review. For claims involving multiple beneficiaries, you may submit a copy of the cover letters issued or a spreadsheet of the beneficiaries and addresses who received a copy of the request for review.***

If you have any questions about your request for review or wish to request expedited review of a claim involving authorization of your prescription drug under Medicare Part D, you may call the Medicare Appeals Council's staff in the Medicare Operations Division of the Departmental Appeals Board at (202) 565-0100. You may also visit our web site at www.hhs.gov/dab for additional information on how to file your request for review.

PRIVACY ACT STATEMENT

The collection of information on this form is authorized by the Social Security Act (section 205(a) of title II, section 702 of title VII, section 1155 of Title XI, and sections 1852(g)(5), 1869(b)(1), 1871, 1872, and 1876(c)(5)(B) of title XVIII, as appropriate). The information provided will be used to further document your claim. Information requested on this form is voluntary, but failure to provide all or any part of the requested information may affect the determination of your claim. Information you furnish on this form may be disclosed by the Department of Health and Human Services or the Social Security Administration to another person or governmental agency only with respect to programs under the Social Security Act and to comply with Federal laws requiring the disclosure of information or the exchange of information between the Department of Health and Human Services, the Social Security Administration, or other agencies.

The Fifth Level of Appeal—U.S. District Court Review
There are limited circumstances whereby an appeal or escalation to the U.S. District Court level of review would be permitted and those circumstances are outlined in 42 CFR 405.1136.

After the Departmental Appeals Board issues a decision, the appellant must file a complaint with the U.S. District Court. A contractor is not permitted to accept requests for court review. The disputed amount for requests made on or after January 1, 2013 is $1,400.

The address to file with the U.S. District Court is:

Department of Health and Human Services
General Counsel
200 Independence Avenue, S.W.
Washington, D.C., 20201

Appealing a Part A Medicare Claim
The process for appealing a Part A Medicare claim is similar to that of appealing a Part B claim. Requests for redetermination begin with the filing of the Form CMS-20027, Medicare Redetermination Request Form. If the filing party is dissatisfied following the redetermination and the amount in controversy is $140 for claims filed on or after January 1, 2013, the party is entitled to a hearing before a federal ALJ. If the dissatisfaction continues after the ALJ's decision, the appellant may request the Department of Appeals Board (DAB) review the decision. The DAB may, on its own motion, review an ALJ decision. After DAB review or its denial of review, an appellant who is dissatisfied may file a civil action in the U.S. District Court for a review of the final administrative decision if the amount in controversy is $1,400 for requests made on or after January 1, 2013.

Fostering a Spirit of Cooperation
Combative behavior toward a claims reviewer never works in your favor. Concentrate instead on developing a respectful working relationship with one person in each frequently billed insurance company. If you've worked with a particularly good reviewer, send your review requests to that individual's attention.

Measuring Your Success

One way of viewing the financial health of a practice is with an accounts receivable report. The age (30, 60, 90 days, etc.) of each unpaid balance should be calculated every month. Offices that develop good monitoring systems and collection plans find their outstanding accounts are more current. Receivables can also be influenced by the physician's specialty, type of practice, and participation agreements with insurance companies.

Periodically review your billing, monitoring, and collection policies. Don't hesitate to adjust them if necessary. Set goals for your accounts receivable and track them carefully. This will help you develop greater efficiency in your claims monitoring habits.

Collecting the remainder (co-insurance, deductible, and unpaid amounts) after the insurer has paid is also important. If you don't already have a good plan for collecting these balances, you should: (1) predetermine insurance coverage while patients are in your office and have them pay the anticipated remainder at the time of the service, and (2) regularly bill and follow up on all unpaid balances.

Summary

The claims monitoring process should include a system to:

- Label all attachments to claims with identifying information
- Actively monitor claims payments by comparing the EOB to the original claim
- Gather reimbursement data to help evaluate your fee schedule
- Resubmit claims if necessary to correct errors
- Avoid payer downcoding or coding changes by using current CPT, HCPCS Level II, and ICD-9-CM codes
- Follow the correct steps when appealing claims
- Frequently evaluate your office's billing and monitoring patterns

The Payers

Today's health insurance industry is comprised of many companies each with its own policies, plans, rules, and regulations. The benefits available to groups or individuals vary and the definitions for medical exclusions and pre-existing conditions are almost certain to differ among comparable policies. This variability makes it difficult for billing staff to predict an insurance company's response to a particular claim submission.

There are ways around the problem. First, gather as much information as possible. The policyholder may be the best place to start because he/she may be aware of how their insurance plan works. But you might have to ask the following questions:

- Are you aware of any policy exclusions?
- Is there an annual or lifetime maximum defined in your policy?
- Was there a waiting period for the policy to take effect?
- Are there any coverage limitations based on a specific illness, such as mental disorders?
- Does your plan include a health saving account (HSA)?
- Is your plan a consumer-directed health plan (CDHP)?

These variables as well as the policy deductible and copayment can create an endless number of challenges in preparing a claim for submission.

Patients with dual coverage (more than one policy) present special billing challenges. Generally, the primary payer will pay the full benefit (allowable less copayments and/or deductible) on an individual's plan. The secondary and supplemental payers will pay an additional amount up to the allowable or contracted rate or the difference between the actual (billed) charge and the amount paid by the primary payer. The total of the combined payments from the primary and subsequent payers should not exceed the total billed charges. When an overpayment occurs, contact payers as soon as possible.

When setting standards for dealing with payers, a good rule of thumb is to contact them directly for certain basic facts regarding claims submission. Record the information on 3x5 cards indexed alphabetically for quick reference. Always attempt to get the answers from a supervisor or a provider relations person to help ensure the accuracy of the claim processing information.

Many times, the information you are seeking to summarize in the creation of an insurance matrix or "quick reference" cards can be located in the provider's contract and/or handbook from the payer. It is strongly advised to ensure the information in the provider contract or manual is the most up to date. Maintaining copies of addendums or policy changes in the proper location of the contract manual is helpful in making sure that all revisions or changes to the contract terms are readily available. Key components of a matrix or the "quick reference" cards should include: information on requirements such as timely filing, copays, referrals, preauthorization, laboratory and other ancillary services.

Payer Comparisons

The following sections discuss a variety of payers and payer types. This is a general discussion only. Specific information on payers and plans should be obtained directly from the payer. Specific information can be obtained by contacting the payer by phone or accessing the payer's website.

Blue Cross/Blue Shield Plans

Blue Cross is a nonprofit health organization providing hospital benefits. In most states, this plan has merged with its counterpart, Blue Shield, which offers physician services benefits to provide total health care coverage for its subscribers. Although all of the plans in the United States, the District of Columbia, and Puerto Rico are separate entities, they are coordinated through the national Blue Cross/Blue Shield Plan Association headquartered in Chicago.

Like Medicare, Blue Cross/Blue Shield plans have provider I.D. numbers and participating and nonparticipating provider arrangements. Most plans pay participating providers directly, and the providers agree not to bill the patient for the difference between the allowable and the fee.

Blue Cross/Blue Shield payments are subject to deductibles and copayments that vary according to the patient's plan. A tip: Your office should request a recent provider manual for your state's Blue Cross/Blue Shield plans. It is a good idea to obtain a current provider manual from all participating major health plans. This will be invaluable to understanding how and why you are paid.

Some of the coverage options available through Blue Cross Blue Shield companies include:

- Flexible Spending Accounts (FSAs)
- Health Maintenance Organizations (HMOs)
- Health Savings Accounts (HSAs)
- Health Reimbursement Arrangements (HRAs)
- Indemnity and Traditional Coverage
- Point of Service (POS)
- Preferred Provider Organizations (PPOs)

TRICARE

TRICARE (formerly CHAMPUS) is a regionally managed health care program serving active duty National Guard and Reserve members as well as retired members of the uniformed services, their families, and survivors. TRICARE brings together the health care resources of the Army, Navy, and Air Force and supplements them with networks of civilian health care professionals to provide better access and high quality service while maintaining the capability to support military operations.

TRICARE offers a number of health plan options to choose from:

- TRICARE for Life
- TRICARE Prime Remote Overseas
- TRICARE Prime
- TRICARE Prime Overseas
- TRICARE Prime Remote
- TRICARE Reserve Select
- TRICARE Retired Reserve
- TRICARE Standard and Extra
- TRICARE Standard Overseas
- TRICARE Young Adult
- US Family Health Plan

TRICARE for Life, TRICARE Prime and TRICARE Standard and Extra are the main programs for military members and their dependents stationed in the United States and a summary of each is provided below:

TRICARE for Life: This program acts as the Medicare supplement option of the TRICARE family of health insurance plans provided the TRICARE beneficiary has both Medicare Part A and B. Medicare beneficiaries with TFL do not have to file their own claims. The patient's Medicare provider will file the claim for payment and Medicare will electronically forward the claim to the TFL claims processor who forwards payment directly to the provider for TRICARE covered services. TRICARE serves as the supplemental payer to Medicare and benefits include covering the Medicare deductible and coinsurance.

TRICARE Prime: This program is the managed care option of the TRICARE family of health insurance plans and offers full comprehensive coverage at the most affordable rates. Some of the key features of this program include:

- Required enrollment via online beneficiary website or hard copy forms
- Reduced out of pocket expenses for the patient
- Expanded vision and preventive services
- Priority access to military treatment facilities
- Primary care provider assigned
- Referrals required from PCP for access to specialists
- No claims for patient to file
- Standards for time and distance access for care established

TRICARE Standard and Extra: This program is a fee-for-service option of the TRICARE family of health plans and is available to all nonactive duty beneficiaries throughout the United States. Enrollment is not required. Coverage is automatic as long as your information is current in the Defense Enrollment Eligibility Reporting System (DEERS).

The patient may visit any TRICARE-authorized provider, network or non-network. Care at military treatment facilities is on a space-available basis only. No referral is required though some services may require prior authorization.

The type of provider determines your options and how much you'll pay out-of-pocket. For example, if a non-network provider is seen, you're using the Standard option whereas when you visit an in-network provider, this is considered the Extra option. Utilizing the Extra option means less out of pocket expense for the patient and ensures the provider will file claims on your behalf.

Costs may also vary depending on your military status (active duty family members vs. retirees, their families and others). After meeting an annual deductible, the patient is still responsible to pay a coinsurance (or percentage).

Benefits and requirements vary based on the plan. Providers should consult the TRICARE website http://www.tricare.mil/mybenefit/home/overview/Plans for detailed information on these plans.

Health Maintenance Organizations (HMOs)

HMOs are the most common form of managed care. Generally, they incorporate a number of cost containment techniques to manage care, such as utilization management, development of provider networks, and financial incentives for both providers and members. HMOs must follow the requirements of P.L. 1301 of the Public Health Service Act and 43 CFR 417.100-417.109.

There are a number of models under which HMOs can be organized. HMOs can be staff model plans, Independent Practice Association (IPA), Point-of-Service (POS), and Consumer Direcrted Health Plans (CDHP).

Staff Model Plans

Staff model plans, also called group models, are HMOs that own the facilities and employ personnel to provide care to their enrollees. A staff model may provide all the services required by their members or they may provide only the more frequently utilized services and contract with other providers for less frequently utilized services such as cardiovascular surgery, burn care, and organ and tissue transplant services.

Independent Practice Association (IPA)

An Independent Practice Association (IPA) consists of physicians who have not combined their assets and liabilities and are not practicing in a truly integrated fashion. They maintain their separate practices and participate in the IPA as a means to contract with HMOs or other health plans. Providers may also see patients who are not enrolled in HMO plans. Where IPAs primarily contract with the HMO to provide services to the HMO's members, the HMO model typically is called the IPA model HMO.

IPAs are developed in two ways. Providers may market themselves as an IPA group and perform their own administrative functions, or payers may develop an IPA from a panel of contracted providers. Whether developed by the providers or a payer, provider members of the IPA should appoint a committee to meet with payer representatives to negotiate contracts, review financial performance of the plan, and settle payer-provider or provider-enrollee disputes. In addition, the committee should be responsible for sanctioning IPA providers and adding/deleting providers from the panel.

Point-of-Service Plan (POS)

A point-of-service health plan allows the covered person to choose to receive a service from a participating or nonparticipating provider, with different benefit levels associated with the use of participating providers. If a POS is purchased, a nonparticipating provider may cost the subscriber the deductibles and 30 percent of the remaining costs up to a set limit. When the costs exceed the limit, the HMO assumes the remaining expenses.

Point-of-service can be provided in several ways (and in various combinations):

- An HMO may allow members to obtain limited services from nonparticipating providers
- An HMO may provide nonparticipating benefits through a supplemental major medical policy
- A PPO may be used to provide both participating and nonparticipating levels of coverage and access

Consumer-directed Health Plans

Consumer-directed health plans (CDHP) give the patient more choices in selecting their providers and are intended to make patients aware of how their health care dollars are being spent, as well as the cost of the services they receive. Health savings accounts (HSAs) and flexible spending accounts (FSAs) are the most common models of these plans. The health savings account is used to reimburse services at the full contracted rate or billed charges.

Usually, services received within network are obtained at a lower cost, allowing the consumer to retain more dollars in their spending accounts. Once the HSA is exhausted, members may still have a deductible. Usually, there is no copay, but there may be a coinsurance and/or deductible remaining after the claim is adjudicated. Many payers advise members to pay nothing in advance, since the actual amount owed by the patient (if any) may be impacted by the status of the HSA, FSA, deductible status, etc.

Preferred Provider Organizations (PPOs)

A Preferred Provider Organization (PPO) typically contracts on behalf of employer groups or other plans with hospital and physician providers at reduced rates. The hospitals and physicians participating in the preferred provider network generally are called either preferred or participating providers. Usually, there is an incentive to the patient to use a preferred provider. A patient who visits a physician who is not a preferred provider likely will have to pay a higher copayment or deductible. Providers offer discounts to PPOs in anticipation of achieving additional patient volumes or to minimize the chances that their patient volume will go to another provider.

Exclusive Provider Organizations (EPOs)

An Exclusive Provider Organization (EPO) is a variation of a PPO. EPOs contract with providers on a discounted basis, but enrollees must receive care within the network. EPOs, like PPOs, provide no penalties to providers if the patient opts to obtain care outside the network. Instead, the enrollee assumes responsibility for out-of-network costs.

Third-Party Administrators (TPAs) and Administrative Services Organizations (ASOs)

TPAs and ASOs are neither health plans nor insurers, rather they are organizations that provide claims-paying functions for the clients which they service. Many self-insured groups, such as employers and union trusts, use TPAs or ASOs to manage and pay their claims. In lieu of paying premiums to health insurers who would charge group premiums, these self-insured groups assume the risk of the provision of such services on their own, usually with some stop loss insurance. The self-insured group may contract directly with providers and it may use the services of a PPO. Although historically such TPAs and ASOs merely paid claims, their functions have expanded. Many have some function in the management of care. In addition, many self-insured groups were pioneers in PPO development, and thus a TPA or ASO may be paying claims based on discounted rates negotiated by a PPO on behalf of a self-insured group.

Single or Specialty Service Plans

There also are single or specialty service plans, such as health plans that provide services only in the mental health area or plans for vision and dental services. Plans for mental health were developed to slow the rising costs of care. Employer groups can contract with these specialty health plans for services that focus on mental health. Vision and dental plans often have been add-on or supplemental coverage to health plans. They vary greatly in the benefits and services that they offer, and represent another example of single specialty service plans.

Medicaid

Federal and state governments jointly administer Medicaid, a program that may go by another name in your state (e.g., Welfare, Title XIX, or Medi-Cal). Medicaid payers do share some characteristics. For example, payers are subject to the same federal guidelines, although there may be individual guidelines for claims submission. Each payer publishes a handbook that outlines and updates the Medicaid rules for that state.

The program issues each recipient an eligibility card that indicates coverage dates. Examine this card carefully to confirm coverage on the date of service. Coverage can change monthly so verify coverage frequently. This card also contains the ID number, which must be included on your claim. A photocopy of the Medicaid card should be placed in the patient's file.

Medicaid, Blue Cross/Blue Shield, and Medicare assign each physician and supplier a local provider number that must be printed in the appropriate box on the claim form. An obvious difficulty arises when a physician provides care to a patient residing in a different state. When this happens, make it a priority to apply immediately for a provider number in that state before submitting the claim. If your office is in a border town or close to a state line, apply for a provider number in both states.

Medicare

The Medicare program, created in 1966, was originally intended to provide health insurance benefits (both hospital and nonhospital) to people older than age 65. The program was expanded in July 1973 to include persons of any age who are entitled to monthly disability benefits for 24 consecutive months under Social Security or the Railroad Retirement program. Additionally, end-stage renal disease (ESRD) patients requiring hemodialysis or kidney transplant are eligible. The Centers for Medicare and Medicaid Services (CMS) was established in 1977 to administer this growing program and is headquartered in Baltimore with 10 regional offices.

As with Medicaid, each Medicare patient is issued an identification card listing a Medicare number and letter combination. The letter suffix identifies the patient's status, e.g., A (wage earner), B (wife of wage earner), D (widow). A complete listing is available from your local Social Security office.

The Medicare program is divided into four components. Part A covers hospital facility services (operating suites, hospital rooms, and supplies), skilled nursing facilities, home health services, and hospice care. Part B covers medical or nonhospital services such as office visits, outpatient surgery and supplies, etc. Part B is voluntary, with premiums deducted from the beneficiary's social security check, allowing the beneficiary to refuse this portion of the Medicare program and maintain only Part A coverage. Part C has been renamed "Medicare Advantage." Medicare Advantage plans are health plan options that are part of the Medicare program. Beneficiaries who join one of these plans generally get all of their Medicare-covered health care through that plan. Coverage may include prescription drug coverage. In order to enroll in a Medicare Advantage plan, you must have Medicare Parts A and B.

Part D refers to the outpatient prescription drug benefit that was implemented in 2006, enacted under the Medicare Prescription Drug, Improvement, and Modernization Act (MMA) of 2003.

Both Part A and Part B have deductibles, but are handled in different ways. The Part A deductible is based on benefit periods and may have to be satisfied for each hospitalization. The deductible for Part B is met yearly and renews each January 1. Under most circumstances, Medicare benefits are paid at 80 percent of the allowable and the patient is responsible for the remaining 20 percent if the claim is assigned. When a claim is unassigned, the patient is responsible for the entire amount remaining after Medicare makes its payment up to the limiting charge. When assignment is accepted, the supplier or physician cannot seek additional payment—beyond the Medicare allowable—from the beneficiary or co-insurer. Participating physicians can only submit assigned claims and always check "yes" in box 27 on the CMS-1500 form.

The Medicare Advantage Plan modifies the method the federal government uses to establish capitation rates for Medicare beneficiaries enrolled in managed care plans. Under this program, eligible individuals may elect to receive Medicare benefits through enrollment in one of many private health plans choices beyond the original Medicare programs or plans not available through MCOs. A Medicare Advantage plan is required to provide their Medicare enrollees with those services that are covered under Medicare and available to other fee-for-service Medicare beneficiaries residing in the geographic area covered by the plan.

Currently, Medicare offers five Advantage plans:

- Medicare HMO Plans
- Preferred Provider Organization (PPO) Plans
- Special Needs Plans (SNP)
- Private Fee-for-Service (PFFS) Plans
- Medical Savings Account (MSA) Plans

A Medicare Advantage Plan is required to issue a notice when it denies an enrollee's request for medical service, or whenever there is a request for payment for services already received. Information regarding two standardized appeal notices—Notice of Denial of Medical Services and the Notice of Denial of Request for Payment—were published in the *Federal Register* on June 8, 2000 and March 22, 2001.

Indemnity Plans

Even though MCOs dominate the health insurance market, many indemnity plans continue to exist. Usually, the indemnity carrier will pay the provider directly where the patient has assigned his/her benefits to the provider. Many of the indemnity carriers have attempted to include PPO like characteristics to reduce their costs.

Physician Hospital Organizations (PHOs)

A physician hospital organization (PHO) is created by a hospital and a physician organization, or physicians and physician groups, to assist in managed care contracting on behalf of the parties. The best PHOs include a physician organization that has its own structure, providing a means for reviewing pertinent issues both internal and external, such as contracts, payer disputes, or physician monitoring.

Management Services Organizations (MSOs)

A Management (or Medical) Services Organization (MSO) provides services to physicians and physician groups. It also may provide services to a hospital or hospitals. An MSO may acquire physicians' tangible assets and certain intangible assets, as with the PHO. An MSO, like a PHO, is generally not a provider or supplier of hospital or medical services for Medicare purposes. Goods and services provided by the MSO should be provided to the physicians and not patients, unless the MSO can practice medicine.

MSOs unable to employ physicians contract with them. MSOs might provide office space, equipment, furnishings, management information systems, nonprofessional and certain professional personnel, and services to physicians on a turnkey basis.

MSOs generally are good vehicles for physician recruitment because physicians can contract with the MSO to run their practices. The costs of opening and operating a practice can be offered by the MSO to the physicians on a flat fee, percentage, or hybrid basis.

State Children's Health Insurance Program (SCHIP)

Children who are not covered under a group health plan or other health insurance coverage are often eligible to participate in SCHIP if they meet the income and state-specific standards. Eligibility requirements vary from state-to-state, but in most states uninsured children 18 years of age and younger, whose families earn less than a state specific maximum, qualify for coverage.

For children in families with income at or below 150 percent of poverty, cost-sharing charges cannot exceed the limits for the medically needy under Medicaid. For children in families with income above 150 percent of the poverty line, cost sharing is on a sliding scale related to income, but the total annual cost-sharing for all children in the family cannot exceed 5 percent of the family's annual income.

Covered services vary from state-to-state, but at a minimum SCHIP covers:

- Physician visits
- Prescription medicines
- Hospitalizations
- Immunizations recommended by the Advisory Committee on Immunization Practices (ACIP) in accordance with the ACIP schedule

Workers' Compensation

All states require workers' compensation benefits to provide medical and disability coverage for employees who are injured, contract an illness or disease, or become disabled as a result of their employment. In most states, employers voluntarily provide these benefits, but the criteria for mandatory coverage vary. Some states require employers to carry workers' compensation coverage only if they hire a certain number of people.

The requirements for filing a claim also vary from state to state. In some states the claim is sent directly to a court or the workers' compensation office, while others want it sent to the employer or directly to the insurance carrier.

There does seem to be a common denominator for claims payment. The amount paid is based on an allowable for that service, and the physician doesn't bill the patient for an unpaid balance. When your practice accepts a workers' compensation case, you've essentially agreed to accept the allowable as payment in full.

Most programs do require an initial accident or medical report, a periodic progress report, and a final report if the patient is temporarily disabled and unable to return to work.

Supplemental Insurance

Supplemental Insurance for Medicare

Many private insurance companies sell Medicare supplement (Medigap) insurance policies for the specific purpose of filling the "gaps" in Medicare coverage. Other supplemental coverage may also be available through an employer or union health plan. The American Association of Retired Persons (AARP) is another source of supplemental coverage. AARP member coverage may be for both hospital and nonhospital charges. AARP does not require an insurance form, only a copy of the benefits summary. The national headquarters for AARP is in Philadelphia, PA. Inquiries are handled at this location for the insurance program itself.

AARP Health Care Options
PO Box 1017
Montgomeryville, PA 18936
800.523.5800

Send claims to the following address:
United Healthcare Claim Division
PO Box 740819
Atlanta, GA 30374-0819
800.523.5880

Though a benefit for the patient, supplemental insurance is added paperwork for your practice. Since the September 1, 1990 law requiring physicians to file all primary Medicare claims, many practices have felt the need to analyze their stance on filing supplemental insurance claims.

Medicare patients may subscribe to an additional policy with an automatic coordination of benefits. The provider must list the secondary coverage in the appropriate space on the CMS-1500 and Medicare does the rest of the work.

Medigap

"Gaps" in the original Medicare plan are costs that are not covered under Medicare, like deductibles and coinsurance. Medigap policies may pay for some or all of the Medicare coinsurance and copayment amounts, and some or all deductibles. Some standardized Medigap plans also pay for services not covered by Medicare, such as coverage for foreign travel or hospital stays after Medicare coverage is exhausted.

In most states, there are 10 standard Medigap plans available; some states offer alternative sets of standardized plans under a federal waiver.

Only the supplemental insurance coverage that has been privately purchased directly by the beneficiary meets the definition of a Medigap policy. The Omnibus Budget Reconciliation Act (OBRA) of 1990 requires all Medigap insurance policies to conform to minimum standards including loss ratio requirements, standardized benefit packages, and consumer protection requirements. Companies selling these policies cannot place conditions on the policy (such as an exclusion of benefits based on a pre-existing condition) or discriminate in the price of the policy because of health status, claims experience, receipt of health care, or medical condition.

To facilitate this process, OBRA created a mechanism to pay participating physicians directly for supplemental benefits. This process allows your Medicare carrier to send an Explanation of Medicare Benefits (EOMB) directly to the Medigap carrier. The Centers for Medicare and Medicaid Services (CMS) requires Medigap carriers to accept the EOMB (or MSN) as a replacement for the CMS-1500 form, eliminating the need for an additional claim. The Medigap carrier issues the payment for coinsurance, deductible, or other charges directly to participating physicians.

New laws have brought some changes to the Medigap policies, including offering two new plans, M and N, as well as extending basic benefits. For policies effective on or after June 1, 2010, Hospice Part A coinsurance will be covered. Plans E, H, I, and J are no longer available for purchase. However, if a patient already has one of these policies or purchased one prior to June 1, 2010, they may keep the plan.

In addition, plans D and G will have different benefits after June 1, 2010; again, plans purchased before that date will retain the same benefits. Lastly, plans K, L, and N will have lower premiums though they will require the beneficiary to pay a portion of the Part B coinsurance and copayments, while other Medigap policies pay these amounts in full. All other plans will still be in effect (A, B, C, and F). However, not all Medigap policies may be available in every state.

Coordination of Benefits Agreement Overview

CMS developed a model national contract, called the Coordination of Benefits Agreement (COBA), which standardizes the way that eligibility and Medicare claims payment information within a claims crossover context is exchanged. COBAs permit other insurers and benefit programs (also known as trading partners) to send eligibility information to CMS and receive Medicare paid claims data for processing supplemental insurance benefits for Medicare beneficiaries from CMS' national crossover contractor or Coordination of Benefits Contractor (COBC). The COBC transmits eligibility information that COBA trading partners send to the COBC for purposes of initiating the crossing over of claims for their members to CMS' Common Working File (CWF), the central system through which all Medicare claims are sent for payment authorization. The CWF houses COBA trading partner's eligibility information for crossover purposes only in those instances where the information successfully matches with the in-file CMS entitlement information. COBA trading partners are apprised of situations where their eligibility information matches CMS eligibility data as well as when their submitted information does not result in a match. The COBC, under direction from CMS, also supports the COBA Medigap claim-based crossover process.

The COBA program establishes a uniform national contract between CMS and other health insurers and benefit programs. The COBA program is a standard processing methodology used by the national Medicare community. The COBA allows greater efficiency and simplification via consolidation of the claims crossover process.

The COBA allows other insurers and benefit programs to send eligibility information to CMS and receive Medicare paid claims data, along with other coordination of benefits data, from one source, the COBC. While not widely encouraged, CMS also supports a COBA Medigap claim-based crossover process, which is driven by a Medicare participating provider's entry of a 5-byte COBA ID on incoming 837 Professional claims or hard copy CMS-1500 claims. Under this process, the COBC will **only** transfer Part B Medicare Administrative Contractor (MAC) and Durable Medical Equipment Medicare Administrative Contractor (DME MAC) 837 Professional claims to a Medigap insurer with whom it has executed a crossover agreement (or COBA) when: 1) the physician or supplier is participating with the Medicare program: 2) the beneficiary assigns his/her benefits (rights to payment) to the physician or supplier; and 3) the incoming claim contains a valid Medigap claim-based COBA ID within the range of 55000 to 59999.

Conveying the Correct Information

When completing an electronic media claim or the CMS-1500 form, provide your Medicare carrier with the appropriate information. Refer to the *2014 Insurance Directory* section describing the CMS-1500 form for further instructions on paper claims. Refer to instructions in the ASC X12 837 implementation guide for submission of supplemental insurance information on electronic claims.

Your local carrier may have special instructions regarding addresses, so watch for this information in carrier newsletters. If a patient has more than one Medigap policy, Medicare will send this payment information to only one of the carriers.

For participating physicians, the assignment of benefits on the claim form must authorize the payment to be made directly to your practice. In addition to the Medicare assignment of benefits, you must have a Medigap assignment of benefits.

Medigap carriers may require the assignment of benefits for this supplemental insurance to be carrier specific. You could add a statement to your current Medicare assignment of benefits stating:

I authorize payment of all medical benefits to apply to all occasions for primary and supplemental (Medigap) coverage to be paid to (physician's name). This assignment will remain in effect until revoked by me in writing.

A photocopy of this assignment is considered as valid as the original.

Once the claim has been processed, Medicare has 30 days to forward the EOMB or Medicare Summary Notice (MSN) to the Medigap carrier.

Participating physicians receive notification on the EOMB or an MSN stating that a copy has been sent to the Medigap carrier. Medicare will not forward an EOMB or an MSN to a Medigap carrier if the charges are denied as noncovered.

If you don't accept assignment on Medicare claims, either you or your patients need to submit claims directly to the supplemental insurance carrier to receive benefits. To assist your patients, present them with an itemized statement (at the time of service) and instructions, such as the following:

As of September 4, 20XX, Dr. ____________ is required by law to submit your claim to Medicare. You will still receive an explanation of Medicare benefits (EOMB) from Medicare identifying any coinsurance and deductible in most cases. An exception to this is laboratory services, which have been billed separately to Medicare. When you receive your EOMB or Medicare Summary Notice (MSN), attach it to this itemized statement and forward both to your supplemental carrier. If we can assist you in billing your supplemental carrier, please notify our billing and insurance department.

These instructions may be preprinted on a separate sheet or on the back of your itemized statement. Stamp or print the following phrase on your statement: "Medicare has been billed for these charges." This prevents your patient from sending a duplicate bill to Medicare.

Supplemental Ins

See the section "Payer Comparisons" for information about Medicare and Medicare Advantage programs.

Nonparticipating physicians treating Medicare patients who have secondary coverage through Medicaid must accept assignment on these claims. In most states, the Medicare carrier automatically transmits the forms to Medicaid for payment.

Insurance Commissioners

The following is a list of state insurance commissioners. They function as a source of appeal against commercial insurers just as the Medicare appeals process is set up to ensure fair treatment from Medicare payers (see chapter 2). To appeal to an insurance commissioner, carefully document the problems you are experiencing, particularly repeated problems with an individual payer. Forward this information to the appropriate office as listed on the following pages.

Alabama Dept of Insurance
201 Monroe St, Ste 502
Montgomery, AL 36104
Mailing address:
PO Box 303351
Montgomery, AL 36130-3351
334.269.3550
www.aldoi.gov/

Alaska Division of Insurance
Juneau Office
9th Fl State Office Bldg
333 Willoughby Ave
Juneau, AK 99801
Mailing address:
PO Box 110805
Juneau, AK 99811-0805
907.465.2515
Fax: 907.465.3422
TDD: 907.465.5437

Anchorage Office
Robert B. Atwood Bldg
550 W 7th Ave, Ste 1560
Anchorage, AK 99501-3567
907.269.7900
Fax: 907.269.7910
TDD: 907.465.5437
www.commerce.state.ak.us/insurance/

American Samoa Government
Insurance Commissioner
Pago Pago, AS 96799 USA
011.684.633.4116
Fax: 011.684.633.2269
www.americansamoa.gov

Arizona Dept of Insurance
2910 N 44th St, Ste 210
Phoenix, AZ 85018-7269
602.364.2499 or 800.325.2548
www.id.state.az.us

Arkansas Insurance Dept
1200 W Third St
Little Rock, AR 72201
501.371.2600 or 800.282.9134
Fax: 501.371.2618
www.insurance.arkansas.gov

California Dept of Insurance
Consumer Services Division
300 S Spring St South Tower
Los Angeles, CA 90013
Outside California: 213.897.8921
Within California only:
800.927.4357
TDD: 800.482.4833
www.insurance.ca.gov

Colorado Division of Insurance
1560 Broadway, Ste 110
Denver, CO 80202
303.894.7855 or 800.886.7675
Fax: 303.894.7885
www.dora.state.co.us/insurance/

Connecticut Insurance Dept
153 Market St
Hartford, CT 06103
Mailing address:
PO Box 816
Hartford, CT 06142-0816
860.297.3800
800.203.3447
Fax: 860.566.7410
www.ct.gov/cid/site/default.asp

Delaware Insurance Dept
841 Silver Lake Blvd
Dover, DE 19904
302.674.7300 or 800.282.8611
www.state.de.us/inscom/

District of Columbia
Dept of Insurance, Securities and Banking
810 First St NE, Ste 701
Washington, DC 20002
202.727.8000
Fax: 202.535.1196
www.disb.dc.gov

Florida Office of Insurance Regulation
200 E Gaines St
Tallahassee, FL 32399
877.693.5236 or 850.413.3089
www.fldfs.com

Georgia Insurance and Safety Fire Commission
Two Martin Luther King, Jr Dr
West Tower, Ste 704
Atlanta, GA 30334
404.656.2070 or 800.656.2298
Fax: 404.657.8542
www.gainsurance.org

Government of Guam
Dept of Revenue and Taxation
Insurance and Banking
1240 Army Dr
Barrigada, GU 96913
PO Box 23607
GMF, Guam 96921
671.635.1835
Fax: 671.633.2643
www.guamtax.com

Hawaii Dept of Commerce and Consumer Affairs
Division of Insurance
King Kalakaua Bldg
335 Merchant St, Rm 213
Honolulu, HI 96813
Mailing address:
PO Box 3614
Honolulu, HI 96811
808.586.2790
Fax: 808.586.2806
www.state.hi.us/dcca/ins/

Idaho Dept of Insurance
Boise Main Office
700 W State St, 3rd Fl
PO Box 83720
Boise, ID 83720-0043
208.334.4250
Fax: 208.334.4398

Coeur d'Alene Regional Office
2005 Ironwood Parkway, Ste 143
Coeur d'Alene, ID 83814
Consumer Affairs: 800.488.5725 or 208.666.6850
Fax: 208.666.6767

Pocatello Regional Office
353 N 4th Ave, Ste 200
Pocatello, ID 83201
Consumer Affairs: 208.236.6411
Fax: 208.236.6351
www.doi.idaho.gov

Illinois Div of Insurance
Springfield Office
320 W Washington St
Springfield, IL 62767-0001
217.782.4515
Fax: 217.782.5020
TDD: 866.323.5321

Chicago Office
James R. Thompson Center
122 S. Michigan Ave., 19th Floor
Chicago, IL 60603
312.814.2420
Fax: 312.814.5416
www.insurance.illinois.gov

Indiana Dept of Insurance
311 W Washington St, Ste 300
Indianapolis, IN 46204
317.232.2385 or 800.622.4461
www.in.gov/idoi

Iowa Insurance Division
330 Maple St
Des Moines, IA 50319-0065
515.281.5705 or 877.955.1212
Fax: 515.281.3059
www.iid.state.ia.us/

Kansas Insurance Dept
Topeka Office
420 SW 9th St
Topeka, KS 66612
785.296.3071 or 800.432.2484
Fax: 785.296.7805
TTY:TDD: 877.235.3151
www.ksinsurance.org/

Kentucky Office of Insurance
215 W Main St
Frankfort, KY 40601
Mailing Address:
PO Box 517
Frankfort, KY 40602
502.564.3630 or 800.595.6053
TTY: 800.648.6056
http://insurance.ky.gov/Home.aspx

Louisiana Dept of Insurance
1702 N Third St
Baton Rouge, LA 70802
Mailing address:
PO Box 94214
Baton Rouge, LA 70804
225.342.5900 or 800.259.5300
www.ldi.la.gov/

Maine Bureau of Insurance
76 Northern Ave
Gardiner, ME 04345
Mailing address:
34 State House Station
Augusta, ME 04333-0034
207.624.8475
Within ME only: 800.300.5000
Fax: 207.624.8599
TTY: 888.577.6690
www.maine.gov/pfr/insurance

Maryland Insurance Administration
200 St Paul Place, Ste 2700
Baltimore, MD 21202-2272
410.468.2000 or 800.492.6116
TTY: 800.735.2258
www.mdinsurance.state.md.us/

Massachusetts Division of Insurance
1000 Washington St, Ste 810
Boston, MA 02118-6200
617.521.7794
or 877.563.4467
TTD/TDD: 617.521.7490
www.mass.gov/doi

Michigan Office of Financial and Insurance Services
611 W Ottawa St, 3rd Fl
Lansing, MI 48933
Mailing address:
PO Box 30220
Lansing, MI 48909-7720
517.373.0220 or 877.999.6442
Fax: 517.335.4978
http://www.michigan.gov/difs/

Minnesota Dept of Commerce
85 7th Place E, Ste 500
St. Paul, MN 55101
651.296.4026
Fax: 651.297.1959
TTY: 651.296.2860
www.commerce.state.mn.us/

Mississippi Insurance Dept
1001 Woolfolk State Office Bldg
501 N West St
Jackson, MS 39201
Mailing address:
PO Box 79
Jackson, MS 39205-0079
601.359.3569
Within MS only: 800.562.2957
www.mid.state.ms.us/

Missouri Dept of Insurance
301 W High St, Rm 530
Jefferson City, MO 65101
Mailing Address:
PO Box 690
Jefferson City, MO 65102-0690
573.751.4126 or 800.726.7390
TTY: 573.526.4536
www.insurance.mo.gov

Montana State Auditor
Insurance Division
840 Helena Ave
Helena, MT 59601
406.444.2040 or 800.332.6148
Fax: 406.444.3497
TDD: 406.444.3246
www.sao.mt.gov

Nebraska Dept of Insurance
Terminal Bldg
941 O St, Ste 400
Lincoln, NE 68508-3639
Mailing address:
PO Box 82089
Lincoln, NE 68501-2089
402.471.2201 or 877.564.7323
TDD: 800.833.7352
www.doi.ne.gov

Nevada Division of Insurance
Carson City Office
1818 E College Pkwy, Ste 103
Carson City, NV 89706
775.687.0700
Fax: 775.687.0787

Las Vegas Office
2501 E Sahara Ave, Ste 302
Las Vegas, NV 89104
702.486.4009
Fax: 702.486.4007
www.doi.state.nv.us/

New Hampshire Insurance Dept
21 S Fruit St, Ste 14
Concord, NH 03301
603.271.2261 or 800.852.3416
Fax: 603.271.1406
www.state.nh.us/insurance/

New Jersey Dept of Banking and Insurance
20 W State St
PO Box 325
Trenton, NJ 08625-0325
609.292.7272 or 800.446.7467
www.state.nj.us/dobi/index.html

New Mexico Insurance Division
PERA Bldg, 4th Fl
1120 Paseo de Peralta
Santa Fe, NM 87501
PO Box 1269
505.827.4601
888.427.5772
Fax: 505.827.4734
www.nmprc.state.nm.us/id.htm

New York State Insurance Dept
Albany Office
One Commerce Plaza
Albany, NY 12257
518.474.6600

Buffalo Office
Walter Mahoney Office Bldg
65 Court St, Rm 7
Buffalo, NY 14202
716.847.7618

Long Island Office
163 Mineola Blvd
Mineola, NY 11501
516.248.5886

New York City Office
25 Beaver St
New York, NY 10004
212.480.6400
www.dfs.ny.gov

North Carolina Dept of Insurance
Dobbs Bldg
430 N Salisbury St
Raleigh, NC 27603-5926
Mailing address:
1201 Mail Service Center
Raleigh, NC 27699-1201
In NC Only: 800.546.5664
Outside NC: 919.807.6750

Eastern Regional Office
1410 McCarthy Blvd
New Bern, NC 28562
252.514.4813

Western Regional Office
537 College St
Asheville, NC 28801
828.251.6483
www.ncdoi.com/

North Dakota Insurance Dept.
State Capitol, 5th Fl
600 E Boulevard Ave
Bismarck, ND 58505-0320
701.328.2440 or 800.247.0560
Fax: 701.328.4880
TTY: 800.366.6888
www.nd.gov/ndins/

Ohio Dept of Insurance
50 W Town St, Ste 300
Columbus, OH 43215
614.644.2658
TDD: 614.644.3745
www.insurance.ohio.gov/

Oklahoma Insurance Dept
Oklahoma City Office
Five Corporate Plaza
3625 NW 56th, Ste 100
Oklahoma City, OK 73112
405.521.2828 or 800.522.0071
Fax: 405.521.6635

Tulsa Office
7645 E 63rd St, Ste 102
Tulsa, OK 74133
918.295.3700 or 800.994.7916
Fax: 918.994.7916
www.ok.gov/oid

Oregon Dept of Consumer and Business Services
Oregon Insurance Division
350 Winter St NE
Salem, OR 97309-0405
503.378.4100
Fax: 503.378.6444
http://egov.oregon.gov/DCBS

Pennsylvania Insurance Dept
1326 Strawberry Sq
Harrisburg, PA 17120
717.787.2317 or 877.881.6388
Fax: 717.787.8585
TTY/TDD: 717.783.3898

Puerto Rico Dept of Insurance
B5 Calle Tabonuco St, Ste 216
PMB 356
Guaynabo, PR 00968-3029
787.304.8686
Fax: 787.273.6082
www.ocs.gobierno.pr

Rhode Island Division of Insurance
1511 Pontiac Ave
Cranston, RI 02920
401.462.9500
Fax: 401.462.9532
www.dbr.state.ri.us/

South Carolina Dept of Insurance
Capital Center
1201 Main St, Ste 1000
Columbia, SC 29201
Mailing address:
PO Box 100105
Columbia, SC 29202-3105
803.737.6160
Fax: 803.737.6205
www.doi.sc.gov

South Dakota Div of Insurance
445 E Capitol Ave
Pierre, SD 57501
605.773.3563
Fax: 605.773.5369
http://dlr.sd.gov/insurance/default.aspx

Tennessee Dept of Commerce and Insurance
Davy Crocket Tower
500 James Robertson Pkwy
Nashville, TN 37243-0565
615.741.2241
www.state.tn.us/commerce/

Texas Dept of Insurance
333 Guadalupe
Austin, TX 78701
Mailing address:
PO Box 149104
Austin, TX 78714-9104
512.463.6169 or 800.252.3439
www.tdi.state.tx.us/

Utah Insurance Department
State Office Bldg, Ste 3110
Salt Lake City, UT 84114-6901
801.538.3800 or 800.439.3805
Fax: 801.538.3829
TDD: 801.538.3826
www.insurance.utah.gov

Vermont Insurance Div
89 Main St, Drawer 20
Montpelier, VT 05620-3101
802.828.3301
www.bishca.state.vt.us/insurance/insurance-division

Virgin Islands Dept of Finance
No. 5049 Kongens Gade
Charlotte Amalie
St. Thomas, VI 00802
340.774.7166
Fax: 340.774.9458
http://ltg.gov.vi/division-of-banking-and-insurance.html

Virginia Bureau of Insurance
Tyler Bldg, 9th FL
1300 E Main St
Richmond, VA 23219
Mailing address:
PO Box 1157
Richmond, VA 23218
804.371.9741
Within VA only: 800.552.7945
TDD: 804.371.9206
www.state.va.us/scc/division/boi/index.htm

Washington Insurance Commission
Insurance Bldg
5000 Capitol Blvd, SE
Tumwater, WA 98501
Mailing address:
PO Box 40255
Olympia, WA 98504-0255
360.725.7080 or 800.562.6900
Fax: 360.586.2018
TDD: 360.586.0241
www.insurance.wa.gov/

West Virginia Insurance Commission
1124 Smith St, Rm 309
Charleston, WV 25301
Mailing address:
PO Box 50540
Charleston, WV 25305-0540
304.558.3386 or 888.879.9842
www.wvinsurance.gov

Wisconsin Office of the Commissioner of Insurance
125 S Webster St
Madison, WI 53703-3474
608.266.3585 or 800.236.8517
Fax: 608.266.9935
TDD: 711 ask for 608.266.3586
www.oci.wi.gov/

Wyoming Insurance Dept
106 E 6th Ave
Cheyenne, WY 82002
307.777.7401
Within WY only: 800.438.5768
Fax: 307.777.2446
http://insurance.state.wy.us/

Workers' Compensation

Workers' compensation laws are designed to ensure that employees who are injured or disabled on the job are provided with fixed monetary awards, eliminating the need for litigation. These laws also provide benefits for dependents of those workers who are killed because of work-related accidents or illnesses. Some laws also protect employers and fellow workers by limiting the amount an injured employee can recover from an employer and by eliminating the liability of coworkers in most accidents. State workers' compensation statutes establish this framework for most employment. Federal statutes are limited to federal employees or those workers employed in some significant aspect of interstate commerce.

In most cases, an individual must have a burden of proof to be entitled to workers' compensation benefits. Burden of proof involves providing the information to support the claim. Discovery is a formal way of obtaining information about the other side's case. Only limited discovery is available in workers' compensation cases. Documents that can be used in discovery include medical and hospital records, physician reports, and vocational counselor reports if provided to the other side at before the hearing. Once the hearing begins, each side can introduce relevant evidence to prove its case.

Alabama

Department of Industrial Relations
Workers' Compensation Division
649 Monroe St
Montgomery, AL 36131
334.242.2868
800.528.5166
http://dir.alabama.gov/wc/

Alaska

Division of Workers' Compensation
Anchorage Office
3301 Eagle St, Ste 304
Anchorage, AK 99503
PO Box 107019
Anchorage, AK 99510-7019
907.269.4980
http://labor.state.ak.us/wc/home.htm

Fairbanks Office
675 Seventh Ave, Station K
Fairbanks, AK 99701-4531
907.451.2889
Fisherman's Fund
PO Box 111149
Juneau, AK 99811-1149
907.465.2766

Juneau Office
1111 W 8th St, Rm 305
Juneau, AK 99801
PO Box 115512
Juneau, AK 99811-5512
907.465.2790

State Employees Claims
Harbor Adjustment Services
1900 W Benson Blvd, Ste 101
Anchorage, AK 99517
907.277.1377

American Samoa

Workers' Compensation
Office of Governor
Pago Pago, AS 96799
684.633.4116
http://americansamoa.gov

Arizona

Industrial Commission of Arizona
Phoenix Office
800 W Washington St
Phoenix, AZ 85007
Mailing address:
PO Box 19070
Phoenix, AZ 85005
602.542.4661
www.ica.state.az.us

Tucson Office
2675 E Broadway Blvd
Tucson, AZ 85716
520.628.5181

Arkansas

Workers' Compensation Commission
324 Spring St
PO Box 950
Little Rock, AR 72203-0950
501.682.3930
800.622.4472
www.awcc.state.ar.us/

California

Division of Workers' Compensation
Anaheim Office
1065 N PacifiCenter Dr Ste 170
Anaheim, CA 92806
714.414.1800
www.dir.ca.gov

Bakersfield Office
1800 30th St, Ste 100
Bakersfield, CA 93301-1929
661.395.2723

Eureka Office
100 "H" Street, Ste 202
Eureka, CA 95501-0481
707.445.6518

Fresno Office
2550 Mariposa Mall, Ste 4078
Fresno, CA 93721-2219
559.445.5051

Goleta Office
6755 Hollister Ave, Ste 100
Goleta, CA 93117-5551
805.968.0258

Long Beach Office
300 Oceangate St, Ste 200
Long Beach, CA 90802-4304
562.590.5001

Los Angeles Office
320 W Fourth St, 9th Fl
Los Angeles, CA 90013-2329
213.576.7335

Marina del Rey Office
4720 Lincoln Blvd, 2-3 Fls
Marina del Rey, CA 90292
310.482.3820

Oakland Office (Headquarters)
1515 Clay St, 6th Fl
Oakland, CA 94612-1402
510.622.2866

Oxnard Office
1901 N Rice Ave, Ste 200
Oxnard, CA 93030
805.485.2533

Pomona Office
732 Corporate Center Dr
Pomona, CA 91768
909.623.4301

Redding Office
2115 Civic Center Dr, Ste 15
Redding, CA 96001-2796
530.225.2845

Riverside Office
3737 Main St, Ste 300
Riverside, CA 92501-3337
951.782.4269

Sacramento Office
160 Promenade Cir, Ste 300
Sacramento, CA 95834
916.928.3101

Salinas Office
1880 N Main St, Ste 100 & 200
Salinas, CA 93906-2037
831.443.3060

San Bernardino Office
464 W Fourth St, Ste 239
San Bernardino, CA 92401-1411
909.383.4341

San Diego Office
7575 Metropolitan Dr, Ste 202
San Diego, CA 92108-4424
619.767.2083

San Francisco Office
455 Golden Gate Ave, 2nd Fl
San Francisco, CA 94102
415.703.5011

San Jose Office
100 Paseo de San Antonio, Rm 241
San Jose, CA 95113-1402
408.277.1246

San Luis Obispo Office
4740 Allene Way, Ste 100
San Luis Obispo, CA 93401
805.596.4153

Santa Ana Office
605 W Santa Ana Blvd, Bldg 28
Ste 451
Santa Ana, CA 92701
714.558.4121

Santa Rosa Office
50 "D" Street, Ste 420
Santa Rosa, CA 95404-4771
707.576.2391

Stockton Office
31 E Channel St, Rm 344
Stockton, CA 95202
209.948.7759

Van Nuys Office
6150 Van Nuys Blvd, Ste 105
Van Nuys, CA 91401-3370
818.901.5367

Colorado
Division of Workers' Compensation
633 17th St, Ste 400
Denver, CO 80202
Mailing address:
PO Box 18291
Denver, CO 80218-0291
303.318.8131
888.390.7936
www.coworkforce.com/dwc/

Connecticut
Workers' Compensation Commission
First District Office – Hartford
999 Asylum Ave
Hartford, CT 06105
860.566.4154
wcc.state.ct.us/

Second District Office – Norwich
55 Main St
Norwich, CT 06360
860.823.3900

Third District Office – New Haven
700 State St
New Haven, CT 06511-6500
203.789.7512

Fourth District Office – Bridgeport
350 Fairfield Ave
Bridgeport, CT 06604
203.382.5600

Fifth District Office – Waterbury
55 W Main St
Waterbury, CT 06702
203.596.4207

Sixth District Office – New Britain
233 Main St
New Britain, CT 06051
860.827.7180

Seventh District Office – Stamford
111 High Ridge Rd
Stamford, CT 06905
203.325.3881

Eighth District Office – Middletown
90 Court St
Middletown, CT 06457
860.344.7453

Office of the Chairman
Capitol Place
21 Oak Street, 4th Fl
Hartford, CT 06106
860.493.1500

Delaware
Office of Workers' Compensation
Milford Office
The Windsor, Ste 100
24 NW Front St
Milford, DE 19963
302.422.1392
www.delawareworks.com/

Wilmington Office
4425 N Market Street, 3rd Fl
Wilmington, DE 19802
PO Box 9954
Wilmington, DE 19809-9954
302.761.8200

District of Columbia
Office of Workers' Compensation
4058 Minnesota Ave, NE
Washington, DC 20019
202.724.7000
www.does.dc.gov/does

Florida
Division of Workers' Compensation
200 E Gaines St
Tallahassee, FL 32399-4220
800.342.1741
www.fldfs.com/WC/index.htm

Georgia
State Board of Workers' Compensation
270 Peachtree Street NW
Atlanta, GA 30303-1299
404.656.3818
800.533.0682
http://sbwc.georgia.gov

Guam
Department of Labor
Workers' Compensation Commission
PO Box 9970
Tamuning, GU 96931-9970
671.475.7046
www.dol.guam.gov

Hawaii
Department of Labor and Industrial Relations
Disability Compensation Division
830 Punchbowl St, Rm 404
Honolulu, HI 96813
PO Box 3769
Honolulu, HI 96812-3769
808.586.9174
http://hawaii.gov/labor/dcd/aboutwc.shtml

Idaho
Industrial Commission
700 S Clearwater Ln
Boise, ID 83712
PO Box 83720
Boise, ID 83720-0041
208.334.6000
800.950.2110
www.iic.idaho.gov

Illinois
Workers' Compensation Commission
Chicago Office
100 W Randolph St, Ste 8-200
Chicago, IL 60601
312.814.6611
866.352.3033
www.iwcc.il.gov/

Collinsville Office
1014 Eastport Plaza Dr
Collinsville, IL 62234
618.346.3450
866.352.3033

Peoria Office
401 Main St, Ste 640
Peoria, IL 61602
309.671.3019
866.352.3033

Rockford
200 S Wyman
Rockford, IL 61101
815.987.7292
866.352.3033

Springfield Office
4500 S Sixth St Frontage Rd
Springfield, IL 62703
217.785.7087

Indiana
Workers' Compensation Board
402 W Washington St, Rm W-196
Indianapolis, IN 46204
317.232.3808
http://www.in.gov/wcb/

Iowa
Division of Workers' Compensation
1000 E Grand Ave
Des Moines, IA 50319-0209
515.281.5387
800.562.4692
www.iowaworkforce.org/wc/

Kansas
Div of Workers' Compensation
401 SW Topeka Blvd, Ste 2
Topeka, KS 66603-3105
785.296.4000
800.332.0353
www.dol.ks.gov

Kentucky
Department of Workers' Claims
657 Chamberlin Ave
Frankfort, KY 40601
502.564.5550 ext. 4423
800.554.8601
www.labor.ky.gov/workersclaims/

Louisiana
Office of Workers' Compensation Admin
1001 N 23rd St
Baton Rouge, LA 70802
PO Box 94040
Baton Rouge, LA 70804-9040
225.342.7970
800.201.2499
www.laworks.net/WorkersComp/OWC_MainMenu.asp

District 1 East (Monroe)
1401 Hudson Ln Ste 301
Monroe, LA 71201
318.362.3078
800.209.7321

District 1 West (Shreveport)
9234 Linwood
Shreveport, LA 71106
318.676.5331
800.209.7173

District 2 (Alexandria)
3724 Government St, Ste 114
Alexandria, LA 71302
318.487.5966
800.209.7329

District 3 (Lake Charles)
4250 Fifth Ave., Ste 3
Lake Charles, LA 70607
337.475.4882
888.768.8745

District 4 (Lafayette)
556 Jefferson St, First Fl
Lafayette, LA 70501-6947
337.262.1057
800.209.7174

District 5 (Baton Rouge)
224 Florida St., Ste 100
Baton Rouge, LA 70801
225.219.4378
800.209.7175

District 6 (Covington)
19374 N Third St
Covington, LA 70433-8813
985.871.1258
888.575.6149

District 7 (Harahan)
880 W Commerce Rd, Ste 401
Harahan, LA 70123-3330
504.736.8606
866.253.5830

District 8 (New Orleans)
1450 Poydras St, Ste 838
Mailbox 24
New Orleans, LA 70112-2001
504.568.6952
800.209.7232

District 9 (Houma)
8026 Main St, Ste 404
Houma, LA 70360-3407
985.857.3775
800.262.1497

Maine
Workers' Compensation Board
27 State House Station
Augusta, ME 04333-0027
207.287.3751
www.maine.gov/wcb/

Augusta Regional Office
24 Stone St
Augusta, ME 04330
207.287.2308
800.400.6854

Bangor Regional Office
106 Hogan Rd
Bangor, ME 04401
207.941.4550
800.400.6856

Caribou Regional Office
One Vaughn Pl
43 Hatch Dr
Caribou, ME 04736
207.498.6428
800.400.6855

Lewiston Regional Office
36 Mollison Wy
Lewiston, ME 04240
207.753.7700
800.400.6857

Portland Regional Office
62 Elm St
Portland, ME 04101
207.822.0840
800.400.6858

Maryland
Workers' Compensation Commission
10 E Baltimore St
Baltimore, MD 21202-1641
410.864.5100
800.492.0479
www.wcc.state.md.us/

Massachusetts
Workers' Compensation Advisory Council
1 Congress St, Ste 100
Boston, MA 02114
617.727.4900
www.mass.gov

Michigan
Workers' Compensation Agency
General Office Bldg
7150 Harris Dr, 1st Fl, B-Wing
Dimondale, MI 48821
PO Box 30016
Lansing, MI 48909
888.396.5041
www.michigan.gov/wca

Minnesota
Workers' Compensation Division
443 Lafayette Rd N
St Paul, MN 55155-4319
651.284.5032
800.342.5354
www.doli.state.mn.us/workcomp.asp

Mississippi
Workers' Compensation Commission
1428 Lakeland Dr
Jackson, MS 39216
PO Box 5300
Jackson, MS 39296-5300
601.987.4200
www.mwcc.state.ms.us/

Missouri
Division of Workers' Compensation
3315 West Truman Blvd, Rm 131
PO Box 58
Jefferson City, MO 65102-0058
573.751.4231
800.775.2667
www.labor.mo.gov/DWC/about.asp

Montana
Workers' Compensation Claims Assistance Bureau
1805 Prospect Ave
Helena, MT 59601
PO Box 8011
Helena, MT 59624-8011
406.444.6451
http://erd.dli.mt.gov/

Navajo Nation
Workers' Compensation Program
PO Box 2489
Window Rock, AZ 86515
928.871.6389
www.isd.wcp.navajo-nsn.gov

Nebraska
Workers' Compensation Court
1010 Lincoln Mall, Ste 100
Lincoln, NE 68508
PO Box 98908
Lincoln, NE 68509-8908
402.471.6468
800.599.5155
www.wcc.ne.gov/

Nevada
Workers' Compensation Section
Northern District Office
400 W King St, Ste 400
Carson City, NV 89703
775.684.7270
http://dirweb.state.nv.us/WCS/wcs.htm

Southern District Office
1301 No Green Valley Pky, Ste 200
Henderson, NV 89074
702.486.9080

New Hampshire
Workers' Compensation Division
95 Pleasant St
Concord, NH 03301
603.271.3176
www.labor.state.nh.us/workers_compensation.asp

New Jersey
Division of Workers' Compensation
1 John Fitch Plz
PO Box 381
Trenton, NJ 08625-0381
609.292.2515
http://lwd.dol.state.nj.us/labor/wc/wc_index.html

Atlantic City
1333 Atlantic Ave, 4th Fl
Atlantic City, NJ 08401-7084
609.441.3160

Bridgeton
40 E Broad St, Ste 203
Bridgeton, NJ 08302-2880
856.453.3930

Camden
2 Riverside Dr, 3rd Fl
Camden, NJ 08103
856.614.2850

Elizabeth
295 N Broad St, 2nd Fl
Elizabeth, NJ 07208
908.820.3062

Freehold
2 Paragon Way
Freehold, NJ 07728
732.462.9321

Hackensack
60 State St
Hackensack, NJ 07601-5427
201.996.8930

Jersey City
438 Summit Ave, 3rd Fl
Jersey City, NJ 07306-0603
201.217.7205

Lebanon
Hunterdon Hills Plz
1390 Route 22 W
Lebanon, NJ 08833
908.236.8026

Mt. Arlington
100 Valley Rd, Bldg 3, Ste 100
Mt. Arlington, NJ 07856
973.770.4480

Mt. Holly
555 High St, Fairground Plz
Mt. Holly, NJ 08060
609.518.1790

Newark
124 Halsey St, 2nd Fl
Newark, NJ 07101-0226
973.648.2663

New Brunswick
550 Jersey Ave
New Brunswick, NJ 08901-2549
732.937.6333

Paterson
100 Hamilton Plz, 8th Fl
Clark St
Paterson, NJ 07505
973.977.4526

Toms River
954 Rt 166
Toms River, NJ 08753
732.349.9592

Trenton
Station Plaza 4, PO Box 958
Trenton, NJ 08625-0958
609.292.2508

New Mexico
Workers' Compensation Administration
Main Office
2410 Centre Ave SE
PO Box 27198
Albuquerque, NM 87125-7198
505.841.6000
800.255.7965
www.workerscomp.state.nm.us/

Farmington Office
2700 Farmington Ave Bldg E, Ste 2
Farmington, NM 87402
505.599.9746
800.568.7310

Las Cruces Office
1120 Commerce Dr, Ste B-1
Las Cruces, NM 88011
575.524.6246
800.870.6826

Las Vegas Office
32 N M 65
Las Vegas, NM 87701
505.454.9251
800.281.7889

Lovington Office
100 West Central, Ste A
Lovington, NM 88260
575.396.3437
800.934.2450

Roswell Office
Penn Plaza Bldg
400 N Pennsylvania Ave, Ste 425
Roswell, NM 88201
575.623.3781
866.311.8587

Santa Fe Office
810 West San Mateo, Ste A2
Sante Fe, NM 87505
505.476.7381

New York
Workers' Compensation Board
Albany District Office
100 Broadway-Menands
Albany, NY 12241
866.750.5157
www.wcb.ny.gov

Binghamton District Office
44 Hawley St
Binghamton, NY 13901
866.802.3604

Brooklyn District Office
111 Livingston St, 22nd Fl
Brooklyn, NY 11201
PO Box 5205
Binghamton, NY 13902-5205
800.877.1373

Buffalo District Office
Cyclorama Building
295 Main St, Ste 400
Buffalo, NY 14203
866.211.0645

Long Island District Office
220 Rabro Dr, Ste 100
Hauppauge, NY 11788-4230
866.681.5354

Manhattan District Office
215 W 125th St
New York, NY 10027
PO Box 5205
Binghamton, NY 13902-5205
800.877.1373

Peekskill District Office
41 N Division St
Peekskill, NY 10566
PO Box 5205
Binghamton, NY 13902-5205
866.746.0552

Queens District Office
168-46 91st Ave, 3rd Fl
Jamaica, NY 11432
PO Box 5205
Binghamton, NY 13902-5205
800.877.1373

Rochester District Office
130 Main St W
Rochester, NY 14614
PO Box 5205
Binghamton, NY 13902-5205
866.211.0644

Syracuse District Office
935 James St
Syracuse, NY 13203
866.802.3730

North Carolina
Industrial Commission
430 N Salisbury St
Raleigh, NC 27603
4340 Mail Service Center
Raleigh, NC 27699-4340
919.807.2501
800.688.8349
www.ic.nc.gov/

North Dakota
Workforce Safety and Insurance
1600 E Century Ave, Ste 1
Bismarck, ND 58503-0644
PO Box 5585
Bismarck, ND 58506-5585
701.328.3800
800.777.5033
www.workforcesafety.com/

Northern Mariana Islands
Commonwealth of the Northern Mariana Islands
Caller Box 10,007
Saipan, MP 96950 USA
670.664.2200
www.gov.mp/

Ohio
Bureau of Workers' Compensation
30 W Spring St
Columbus, OH 43215-2256
614.644.6292
800.644.6292
www.ohiobwc.com/Default.aspx

Oklahoma
Workers' Compensation Court
Oklahoma City Office
1915 N Stiles Ave
Oklahoma City, OK 73105-5212
405.522.8600
800.522.8210
www.owcc.state.ok.us

Tulsa Office
440 S Houston, Ste 300
Tulsa, OK 74127
918.581.2400

Oregon
Workers' Compensation Division
350 Winter St NE, Rm 27
Salem, OR 97309
PO Box 14480
Salem, OR 97309-0405
503.947.7810
800.452.0288
http://wcd.oregon.gov/

Pennsylvania
Bureau of Workers' Compensation
1171 S Cameron St, Rm 103
Harrisburg, PA 17104
717.783.4151
800.482.2383
www.dli.state.pa.us/landi/cwp/view.asp?a=138&q=220671

Puerto Rico
Workers' Compensation Commission
Industrial Commissioner Office
GPO Box 364466
San Juan, PR 00936-4466
787.781.0545
www.cipr.gobierno.pr/

Rhode Island
Division of Workers' Compensation
1511 Pontiac Ave, Bldg 71-1, 1st Fl
Cranston, RI 02920
PO Box 20190
Cranston, RI 02920-0942
401.462.8100
www.dlt.ri.gov/wc

South Carolina
Workers' Compensation Commission
1333 Main St, Ste 500
Columbia, SC 29202-1715
PO Box 1715
Columbia, SC 29202-1715
803.737.5700
www.wcc.sc.gov/

South Dakota
Division of Labor and Management
Kneip Building
700 Governors Dr
Pierre, SD 57501-2291
605.773.3681
http://dol.sd.gov/workerscomp/default.aspx

Tennessee
Workers' Compensation Division
220 French Landing Dr
Nashville, TN 37243-1002
615.741.6642 or 800.332.2667
www.tn.gov/labor-wfd/wcomp.html

Texas
Division of Workers' Compensation
Central Office
7551 Metro Center Dr, Ste 100
Austin, TX 78744-1645
512.804.4000
www.tdi.state.tx.us/wc/indexwc.html

Abilene Office
1290 S Willis, Ste 102
Abilene, TX 79605-4064
325.695.4992

Amarillo Office
7112 IH-40 W, Bldg D
Amarillo, TX 79106-2503
806.351.1222

Austin Office
4616 W Howard Ln, Ste 130
Austin, TX 78728
512.933.1899

Beaumont Office
Concord Square Office Park
6430 Concord Rd
Beaumont, TX 77708-4315
409.899.5589

Bryan/College Station
4001 E 29th St, Ste 185
Bryan, TX 77802-4211
979.268.6766

Corpus Christi Office
5155 Flynn Pkwy, Ste 218
Corpus Cristi, TX 78411
361.883.2551

Dallas Office
1515 W Mockingbird, Ste 100
Dallas, TX 75235-5078
214.350.9299

Denton Office
Dallas Dr Tech Center
625 Dallas Dr, Ste 475
Denton, TX 76205-5299
940.380.1400

El Paso Office
El Paso State Office Bldg
401 Franklin Ave, Ste 330
El Paso, TX 79901
915.351.5260

Fort Worth
Walton Bldg
6900 Anderson Blvd, Ste 200
Fort Worth, TX 76120-3030
817.446.4488

Houston East Office
Elias Ramirez Bldg
5425 Polk St, Ste 130
Houston, TX 77023-1454
713.924.2200

Houston West Office
350 N Sam Houston Pkwy E Ste 110
Houston, TX 77060
281.260.3035

Laredo Office
5420 Springfield Ave
Laredo, TX 78041
956.718.2040

Lubbock Office
22 Briercroft Office Park, Ste A
Lubbock, TX 79412-3089
806.744.4569

Lufkin Office
310 Harmony Hill Dr, Ste 100
Lufkin, TX 75901
936.639.6425

Midland/Odessa Office
Executive Office Park
4500 W Illinois Ave, Ste 315
Midland, TX 79703-5486
432.699.1281

Missouri City Office
2440 Texas Pkwy, Ste 240
Missouri City, TX 77489
281.403.7050

San Angelo Office
State of Texas Services Center
622 S Oakes, Ste M
San Angelo, TX 76903-7035
325.657.0404

San Antonio Office
9514 Console Dr, Ste 200
San Antonio, TX 78229-2043
210.593.0070

Tyler Office
3800 Paluxy Dr, Ste 570
Tyler, TX 75703-1665
903.534.6250

Victoria Office
American General Bldg
3001 N Cameron St
Victoria, TX 77901-3942
361.576.9612

Waco Office
Raleigh Bldg
801 Austin Ave, Ste 840
Waco, TX 76701-1937
254.755.7011

Weslaco Office
1108 Pike Blvd
Weslaco, TX 78596
956.447.4416

Wichita Falls
Chelsea Plaza
909 8th St, Ste 112
Wichita Falls, TX 76301
940.767.2691

Utah
Industrial Accidents Division
160 East 300 South, 3rd Fl
Salt Lake City, UT 84111
PO Box 146610
Salt Lake City, UT 84114-6610
801.530.6800
800.530.5090
www.laborcommission.utah.gov/IndustrialAccidents/index.html

Vermont
Workers' Compensation & Safety Division
5 Green Mountain Drive
PO Box 488
Montpelier, VT 05601-0488
802.828.2286
http://labor.vermont.gov/

Virgin Islands
Division of Workers' Compensation
2353 Kronprindsens Gade
St Thomas, VI 00802
340.776.3700
www.vidol.gov

Virginia
Workers' Compensation Commission
Central Office
1000 DMV Dr
Richmond, VA 23220
877.664.2566
www.vwc.state.va.us/

Fairfax Regional Office
3020 Hamaker Ct, Ste 100
Fairfax, VA 22031-2220
703.269.2276

Harrisonburg Regional Office
41 Court Sq, Ste B
Harrisonburg, VA 22801
540.433.7701

Lebanon Regional Office
Center One
1114 E Main St, Ste 4
Lebanon, VA 24266
PO Box 98
Lebanon, VA 24266
276.415.3022

Manassas Regional Office
7900 Sudley Rd, Ste 619
Manassas, VA 20109
703.334.2602

Roanoke Regional Office
3959 Electric Rd SW
Roanoke, VA 24018
PO Box 21634
Roanoke, VA 24018
540.283.5006

Virginia Beach Regional Office
281 Independence Blvd
Pembroke One, Ste 600
Virginia Beach, VA 23462
757.648.7111

Washington
Department of Labor and Industries
7273 Linserson Way SW
Tumwater, WA 98501-5414
PO Box 44000
Olympia, WA 98504-4000
360.902.5800
800.547.8367
www.lni.wa.gov/

West Virginia
Offices of the Insurance Commissioner
1124 Smith St
Charleston, WV 25301
PO Box 50540
Charleston, WV 25305-0540
304.558.5838
866.452.7425
www.wvinsurance.gov

Wisconsin
Workers' Compensation Division
Main Office
201 E Washington Ave, Rm C100
Madison, WI 53703
PO Box 7901
Madison, WI 53707-7901
608.266.1340
www.dwd.state.wi.us/wc/default.htm

Milwaukee Office
State Office Bldg
819 N 6th St, Rm 330
Milwaukee, WI 53203
414.227.4381

Appleton Office
54 Parkway Pl, Ste 900
Appleton, WI 54914
920.832.5450

Wyoming
Department of Employment
Workers' Safety and Compensation Division
Cheyenne Business Center
PO Box 20070
Cheyenne, WY 82003
307.777.7441
http://wyomingworkforce.org

Using the Directory

FORMATTING

The format for the *2014 Insurance Directory* has been updated to make it more user-friendly. The directory is formatted in a three-column-per-page style for easy reference. All listings are alphabetized by company name and printed in large, bold type. The mailing addresses, phone numbers, and internet addresses direct users to the claim information resources provided by the payer or insurer.

The addresses are printed in capital letters with no punctuation. This follows guidelines set by the U.S. Postal Service to facilitate more efficient electronic scanning. See appendix A for acceptable abbreviations. We have also included the postal service recommendations for addressing envelopes.

When available, the PayerID has been included for each insurance carrier listed.

Appendix C contains a Glossary with commonly used terms in the health insurance and payer environments. Terms contained in *2014 Insurance Directory* can be found in the glossary as well as number of other widely referenced acronyms, abbreviations, and terms.

1199 NATIONAL BENEFIT FUND

Payer ID 13162	ADA PO BOX 1144 NEW YORK, NY 10108	(646) 473-7160 WWW.1199NBF.ORG
Payer ID 13162	UB04 PO BOX 933 NEW YORK, NY 10108	(646) 473-7160 WWW.1199NBF.ORG
Payer ID 13162	CMS 1500 PO BOX 1007 NEW YORK, NY 10108-1007	(646) 473-7160 HTTP://1199SEIUBENEFITS.ORG/PROVIDERS/ CLAIMS/

21ST CENTURY HEALTH AND BENEFITS

Payer ID 59069 | 220 LAKE DR E #300
CHERRY HILL, NJ 08002-1165 | (856) 321-9460
www.21stcenturybenefit.com/

21ST CENTURY INSURANCE AND FINANCIAL SERVICES

Payer ID 51028 | PO BOX 52041
PHOENIX, AZ 85072 | (888) 244-6163
WWW.21ST.COM

360 ALLIANCE PPO GILSBAR

Payer ID 07205 | PO BOX 998
COVINGTON, LA 70434 | (888) 215-9841
WWW.GILSBAR360ALLIANCE.COM/CONTACT-
US

3P ADMINISTRATORS

Payer ID 20413 | 1113 RIDERS CLUB RD
ONALASKA, WI 54650 | (888) 540-0094
www.3pa.com/

8TH DISTRICT ELECTRICAL BENEFIT FUND

Payer ID 74234 | PO BOX 30101
SALT LAKE CITY, UT 84130 | (800) 628-6562
WWW.8THDIST.ORG

A & I BENEFIT PLAN ADMINISTRATORS

Payer ID 93044 | 1220 SW MORRISON STE 300
PORTLAND, OR 97205-2222 | (503) 224-0048
(800) 547-4457
WWW.AIBPA.COM/

A-PLUS BENEFITS

| PO BOX 849
PLEASANT GROVE, UT 84062 | (208) 639-5220
(800) 748-5102
WWW.APLUSBENEFITS.COM

AAG BENEFIT PLAN ADMINISTRATORS

Payer ID 75240 | 4500 MERCANTILE PLAZA DR
FORT WORTH, TX 76137 | (682) 647-3400
WWW.AAGBENEFITS.COM

AAOMS NATIONAL INSURANCE COMPANY

| 6113 N RIVER RD STE 650
ROSEMONT, IL 60018 | (800) 522-6670
WWW.AAOMSNATIONAL.COM

AARP MEDICARE

Payer ID 36273 | PO BOX 740819
ATLANTA, GA 30374-0819 | (800) 523-5880
HTTP://
AARPPROVIDERONLINETOOL.UHC.COM

ABBA INDEMNITY COMPANY

| 1421 TELEPHONE RD
HOUSTON, TX 77023 | (800) 228-3927

ABC MASSACHUSETTS W.C. SELF INSURANCE GROUP

| 1 WALL ST
BURLINGTON, MA 01803 | (781) 273-0123
WWW.ABCMA.ORG/ABC_INSURANCE.ASPX

ABRAZO ADVANTAGE HEALTH PLAN

Payer ID 03443	PO BOX 81200 PHOENIX, AZ 85069	(602) 824-3861 (888) 864-1114 WWW.ABRAZOADVANTAGE.COM/ PROVIDERS.ASPX

ABRI HEALTHPLAN

Payer ID ABRI1	PO BOX 22815 LONG BEACH, CA 90801	(414) 847-1776 (888) 999-2404 WWW.MOLINAHEALTHCARE.COM/COMMON/ PAGES/SELECT.ASPX?FINDP=TRUE

ACCESS BEHAVIORAL CARE

Payer ID COACC	PO BOX 17470 DENVER, CO 80217-0470	(800) 984-9133 WWW.COACCESS.COM/OUR-PROVIDERS

ACCIDENT FUND INSURANCE COMPANY OF AMERICA

	PO BOX 40790 LANSING, MI 48901-7990	(866) 206-5851 WWW.ACCIDENTFUND.COM

ACCIDENT INSURANCE COMPANY

	1 HARBISON WAY STE 115 COLUMBIA, SC 29112 PO BOX 2908 KENNESAW, GA 30156	(800) 638-1120 WWW.ACCIDENTINSURANCE.COM

ACCLAIM BENEFITS

Payer ID 64071	2302 INTERNATIONAL LANE MADISON, WI 53704	(800) 777-4925 WWW.ACCLAIMBENEFITS.COM

ACCLAIM INC

Payer ID 64071	808 VARSITY DR TUPELO, MS 38801-4613	(800) 317-2324 HTTP://ACCLAIMTPA.COM/DEFAULT.ASP

ACCLAM REPRICING

Payer ID 21356	808 VARSITY DR TUPELO, MS 38801-4613	(800) 317-2324 HTTP://ACCLAIMTPA.COM/DEFAULT.ASP

ACCLARIS, INC.

	1511 N W SHORE BLVD STE 350 TAMPA, FL 33607	(813) 873-2020 WWW.ACCLARIS.COM

ACCORD HUMAN RESOURCES, INC

	450 7TH AVE STE 207 NEW YORK, NY 10123	(212) 239-0422 WWW.ACCORDHR.COM

ACCORD INSURANCE COMPANY

	1 FLORIDA PARK DRIVE SOUTH 300 PALM COAST, FL 32137	(386) 447-8950 WWW.ACCORDINS.NET

ACCOUNTABLE HEALTH PLAN OF OHIO

Payer ID 31138	94947 CLEVELAND, OH 44101	(216) 902-7529 (866) 744-5152 WWW.AHPOHIO.COM

ACE AMERICAN INSURANCE COM.

	2 LIBERTY PLACE PHILADELPHIA, PA 19192 PO BOX 41484 PHILADELPHIA, PA 19192	(215) 640-1000 WWW.ACE-INS.COM

ACH

Payer ID 20029

PO BOX 922043
HOUSTON, TX 77292-2043

(877) 224-3627
HTTPS://SECURE.ACHONLINE.COM/PROVIDERS/DEFAULT.ASP

ACS BENEFIT SERVICES

Payer ID 72467

PO BOX 2000
WINSTON SALEM, NC 27102-2000

(336) 759-2013
(800) 849-5370
WWW.ACSBENEFITSERVICESINC.COM

ACTIVA BENEFITS SERVICES, LLC

Payer ID 38254

2905 LUCERNE DR SE STE 110
GRAND RAPIDS, MI 49546-7116

(877) 827-1414
WWW.ACTIVABENEFITS.COM

ACUITY

Payer ID ACU99

PO BOX 58
SHEBOYGAN, WI 53082

(920) 458-9131
(800) 242-7666
WWW.ACUITY.COM

ADMINISTRATION SYSTEMS RESEARCH CORP

Payer ID 38265

PO BOX 6392
GRAND RAPIDS, MI 49516-6392

(616) 957-1751
(800) 968-2449
WWW.ASRHEALTHBENEFITS.COM

ADMINISTRATIVE CONCEPTS, INC

Payer ID 22384

994 OLD EAGLE SCHOOL RD STE 1005
WAYNE, PA 19087-1802

(610) 293-9229
(888) 293-9229
WWW.VISIT-ACI.COM

ADMINISTRATIVE SERVICES, INC.

Payer ID 59141

7990 SW 117TH AVE 200
MIAMI, FL 33183-3845

(305) 595-4040
(800) 959-3953
WWW.ABPA.COM

ADMIRAL INSURANCE CO

1000 HOWARD BLVD STE 300
MOUNT LAUREL, NJ 08054

(856) 429-9200
WWW.ADMIRALINS.COM

ADVANCED MEDICAL MANAGEMENT

Payer ID AMM01

5000 AIRPORT PLAZA DR STE 150
LONG BEACH, CA 90815-1260

(562) 766-2000
WWW.AMM.CC

ADVANSTAFF, INC

Payer ID 74234

8925 RUSSEL RD STE 100
LAS VEGAS, NV 89148

(702) 598-0000
WWW.ADVANSTAFF.COM/

ADVANTAGE BY BRIDGEWAY HEALTH SOLUTIONS

Payer ID 68056

PO BOX 3040
FARMINGTON, MO 63640-3814

(866) 516-7224
WWW.BRIDGEWAYHS.COM

ADVANTAGE BY BUCKEYE COMMUNITY HEALTH PLAN

Payer ID 68056

PO BOX 3060
FARMINGTON, MO 63640

(866) 296-8731
HTTP://ADVANTAGE.BCHPOHIO.COM/

ADVANTAGE BY MANAGED HEALTH SERVICES

Payer ID 68056

PO BOX 3001
FARMINGTON, MO 63640-3801

(800) 222-9831
WWW.MHSWI.COM

ADVANTAGE CARE IPA

Payer ID ACIPA

1540 BRIDGEGATE DR #400
DIAMOND BAR, CA 91765

(626) 388-2300
WWW.CHMSO.ORG/MSO/SUBIPAS.HTM

A

ADVANTAGE HEALTH SOLUTIONS, INC

Payer ID 35209

PO BOX 310
SCRANTON, PA 18512

(800) 523-7533
WWW.ADVANTAGEPLAN.COM

ADVANTAGE PREFERRED PLUS

Payer ID 77070

PO BOX 310
SCRANTON, PA 18512

(317) 573-6644
(800) 523-7533
WWW.ADVANTAGEPLAN.COM

ADVANTEK BENEFIT ADMINISTRATORS

Payer ID 83077

PO BOX 45007
FRESNO, CA 93718

(866) 556-7655
WWW.ADVANTEKBENEFIT.COM/PROVIDERS-OVERVIEW.PHP

ADVANTICA BENEFITS

Payer ID 59374

19321 US HIGHWAY 19 N BLDG C STE 320
CLEARWATER, FL 33764

(727) 538-7719
(866) 354-2020
WWW.ADVANTICABENEFITS.COM/PROVIDERS/PROVIDERS.ASPX

ADVENTIST HEALTH SYSTEM

Payer ID 95340

PO BOX 619031
ROSEVILLE, CA 95661

(916) 781-2000
(800) 441-2524
WWW.ADVENTISTHEALTH.ORG/FOR-PHYSICIANS

ADVICA- NEW YORK HOSPITAL COMMUNITY HEALTH PLAN

Payer ID 13373

PO BOX 6008
HAUPPAUGE, NY 11788

(800) 558-7970
WWW.GETNHP.COM/

ADVOCARE

Payer ID 31147

25001 EMERY RD STE 300
CLEVELAND, OH 44128

(800) 659-4025
WWW.ADVOCARE-INC.COM

ADVOCATE HEALTH CENTERS

Payer ID 36320

PO BOX 0838
MOUNT PROSPECT, IL 60056-0838

(630) 572-9393
WWW.ADVOCATEHEALTH.COM

ADVOCATE PHYSICIANS PARTNERS

Payer ID 65093

PO BOX 0357
MT PROSPECT, IL 60056

(630) 572-9393
WWW.ADVOCATEHEALTH.COM/HOME_PROFESSIONAL.CFM

AECC TOTAL VISION HEALTH PLAN OF TEXAS

112 ZEBULON CT
ROCKY MOUNT, NC 27804
PO BOX 7548
ROCKY MOUNT, NC 27804

(800) 465-6972
WWW.OPTIMCARE.COM/

AEGIS ADMINISTRATIVE SERVICES

6970 W DIVERSEY AVE
CHICAGO, IL 60707-1725

(888) 881-2307
WWW.AEGISADMIN.COM

AETNA AFFORDABLE HEALTH CHOICES (SM)-SRC

Payer ID 57604

PO BOX 14079
LEXINGTON, KY 40512

(888) 772-9682
WWW.AETNA.COM/SRC/

AETNA BETTER HEALTH MEDICAID IL

Payer ID 26337

PO BOX 66545
PHOENIX, AZ 85082

(866) 212-2851
WWW.AETNABETTERHEALTH.COM/ILLINOIS/PROVIDERS/

AETNA BETTER HEALTH-PA

Payer ID 23228

PO BOX 62198
PHOENIX, AZ 85082-2198

(866) 638-1232
WWW.AETNABETTERHEALTH.COM/PENNSYLVANIA/PENNPROVIDERS.ASPX?MENU=3

AETNA TX MEDICAID & CHIP

Payer ID 38692

PO BOX 60938
PHOENIX, AZ 85082

(800) 306-8612
WWW.AETNAMEDICAID.COM/FAQ3_EN.ASP?OPTION=PROVIDER

AETNA U.S. HEALTHCARE

Payer ID 60054

151 FARMINGTON AVE
HARTFORD, CT 06156-0002
PO BOX 981106
EL PASO, TX 79998-1106

(888) 632-3862
www.aetna.com/healthcare-professionals/index.html

AFFILIATED DOCTORS OF ORANGE COUNTY

Payer ID ADOCS

12966 EUCLID STE 340
GARDEN GROVE, CA 92840

(714) 539-3100
(800) 747-2362
WWW.ADOC.US/INDEX.PHP/PROVIDER-INFORMATION.HTML

AFFINITY HEALTH PLANS

Payer ID 13334

PO BOX 981726
EL PASO, TX 79998-1726

(866) 247-5678
WWW.AFFINITYPLAN.ORG

AFFINITY HEALTH PLANS (MEDICARE)

Payer ID 13333

PO BOX 4018
SCRANTON, PA 18505-6018

(866) 247-5678
WWW.AFFINITYPLAN.ORG

AFFINITY MEDICAL GROUP

Payer ID 46594

PO BOX 21390
EL SOBRANTE, CA 94820

(800) 615-0261
WWW.AFFINITYMD.COM/PROVIDERS/SUBMITTING-A-CLAIM/

AFFORDABLE BENEFIT ADMINISTRATORS, INC

Payer ID 95426

PO BOX 10787
BURBANK, CA 91510-0787

(818) 842-0147
(800) 350-0148
WWW.BENEFITSABA.COM

AFLAC

1932 WYNNTON RD
COLUMBUS, GA 31999-7251

(800) 992-3522
WWW.AFLAC.COM

AFTRA HEALTH FUND

Payer ID 13346

PO BOX 188004
CHATANOOGA, TN 37422

(800) 562-4690
WWW.AFTRAHR.COM

AGATE RESOURCES

Payer ID 20048

1800 MILLRACE DR
EUGENE, OR 97403

(541) 762-9088
WWW.AGATEHEALTHCARE.COM

AGIA, INC

Payer ID 95241

PO BOX 9060
PHOENIX, AZ 85068

(800) 782-7267
WWW.AGIA.COM

AGRI SERVICES AGENCY

PO BOX 4844
SYRACUSE, NY 13221-4910

(315) 433-0100
(800) 654-8838
WWW.DAIRYLEA.COM

A

AHI-HEALTHLINK

	PO BOX 42096 OKLAHOMA, OK 73123-3096	(405) 848-1975 (800) 825-3540 WWW.MAA-TPA.COM/PROVIDERS

AHPO

Payer ID 31138	PO BOX 94947 CLEVELAND, OH 44101	(866) 744-5152 WWW.AHPOHIO.COM

AIM MUTUAL INSURANCE COMPANY

	PO BOX 4070 BURLINGTON, MA 01803	(866) 270-3354 WWW.AIMMUTUAL.COM/SERVICE-DEPARTMENTS/CLAIM/REPORT-A-CLAIM/

AKM MEDICAL GROUP

Payer ID IP080	PO BOX 261760 ENCINO, CA 91426	(818) 461-5055 (888) 445-0062 WWW.CAPCMS.COM/DEFAULT.ASPX

ALABAMA TRUCKING ASSOCIATION WORKERS COMPENSATION FUND

Payer ID WB186	PO BOX 241605 MONTGOMERY, AL 36124	(334) 834-7911 (800) 277-7500 www.atacompfund.org/index.htm

ALAMEDA ALLIANCE FOR HEALTH

Payer ID 95327	PO BOX 2460 ALAMEDA, CA 94501-0460	(510) 747-4510 WWW.ALAMEDAALLIANCE.ORG/PROVIDERS/

ALASKA CHILDRENS SERVICES, INC

Payer ID 91136	4600 ABBOTT RD ANCHORAGE, AK 99507-4314	(907) 346-2101 WWW.AKCHILD.ORG

ALASKA ELECTRICAL HEALTH AND WELFARE FUND

Payer ID 92600	2600 DENALI ST STE 200 ANCHORAGE, AK 99503-2782	(800) 478-1246 WWW.AETF.COM/HW_MEDICAL_FILING.ASP

ALASKA LABORERS CONSTRUCTION INDUSTRY TRUST

Payer ID 91136	PO BOX 34567 SEATTLE, WA 98124-1567	(800) 331-6158 HTTP://LOCAL341.COM/BENEFITINFORMATION/TABID/61/DEFAULT.ASPX

ALASKA NATIONAL INSURANCE COMPANY

Payer ID 19010	7001 JEWEL LAKE RD ANCHORAGE, AK 99502-2825	(907) 266-9227 (877) 248-2642 WWW.ALASKANATIONAL.COM
Payer ID 19010	601 CALIFORNIA STE 1000 SAN FRANCISCO, CA 94108 PO BOX 193970 SAN FRANCISCO, CA 94119-3970	(415) 248-5030 (866) 355-2642 WWW.ALASKANATIONAL.COM
Payer ID 19010	776 E RIVERSIDE DR STE 200 BOISE, ID 83616	(208) 955-8336 WWW.ALASKANATIONAL.COM
Payer ID 19010	1111 THIRD AVE STE 2600 SEATTLE, WA 98101	(206) 292-6360 (800) 292-0588 WWW.ALASKANATIONAL.COM

ALASKA PIPE TRADERS LOCAL 375

Payer ID 91136	PO BOX 34687 SEATTLE, WA 98124-1687	(907) 479-6221 WWW.UALOCAL375.ORG

ALASKA UNITED FOOD &COMMERCIAL WORKERS HEALTH &WELFARE TRUST

Payer ID 91136

PO BOX 34945
SEATTLE, WA 98124-1945

(800) 325-6532
WWW.WPAS-INC.COM/AKUFCW/

ALFA INSURANCE CORP

PO BOX 11000
MONTGOMERY, AL 36191-0001

(800) 964-2532
WWW.ALFAINS.COM

ALICARE

Payer ID 13550

333 WEST CHESTER
WHITE PLANES, NY 10604

(914) 367-5365
WWW.ALICARE.COM

ALL SAVERS INSURANCE (UNITEDHEALTHONE)

Payer ID 81400

PO BOX 19032
GREEN BAY, WI 54307-9032

(800) 232-5432
WWW.MYALLSAVERS.COM/ASIONLINE/DEFAULT.ASPX

ALL SAVERS INSURANCE CO.

Payer ID 37602

PO BOX 19032
GREEN BAY, WI 54307-9032

(877) 775-3338
WWW.MYALLSAVERS.COM

ALLEGIANCE BENEFIT PLAN MANAGEMENT, INC.

Payer ID 81040

PO BOX 4346
MISSOULA, MT 59806

(800) 877-1122
WWW.ALLEGIANCEFLEXADVANTAGE.COM/PARTICIPANT/P_CLAIMFORMS.ASP

ALLIANT HEALTH PLANS OF GEORGIA

Payer ID 58234

PO BOX 3708
CORPUS CHRISTI, TX 78463-3708

(800) 811-4793
WWW.ALLIANTPLANS.COM/PROVIDERS.PHP

ALLIED ADMINISTRATORS, INC

Payer ID 94177

PO BOX 2500
SAN FRANCISCO, CA 94126-2500

(415) 989-7443
(888) 877-8363
WWW.ALLIEDADMINISTRATORS.COM

ALLIED BENEFIT SYSTEMS, INC

Payer ID 37308

PO BOX 909786-60690
CHICAGO, IL 60690

(800) 288-2078
WWW.ALLIEDBENEFIT.COM/PROVIDERS.ASPX

ALLIED HEALTH SYSTEMS CHIROPRACTIC

Payer ID SX156

867 E 9400 S
SANDY, UT 84094

(800) 339-5958
WWW.ALLIEDHEALTHSYSTEMS.COM

ALLIED NATIONAL

PO BOX 29186
SHAWNEE MISSION, KS 66201

(800) 825-7531
WWW.ALLIEDNATIONAL.COM/PROVIDER.HTM

ALLSTATE INSURANCE CO.

Payer ID WR378

PO BOX 12055
ROANOKE, VA 24018

(800) 255-7828
WWW.ALLSTATE.COM

ALOHA CARE OF HAWAII

Payer ID ALOHA

1357 KAPIOLANI BLVD STE 1250
HONOLULU, HI 96814-4538

(808) 973-1650
(866) 973-6395
WWW.ALOHACARE.ORG/PROVIDERS/DEFAULT.ASPX

ALPHA DATA SYSTEMS

Payer ID TH085

2001 THOMASVILLE ROAD
TALLAHASSEE, FL 32308

(850) 385-7000
HTTP://ALPHADATASYS.COM

A

ALPS SERVICES

Payer ID 10050	10653 CHESTER RD CINCINNATI, OH 45215-1205	(800) 835-2577 WWW.ALPSSERVICES.COM

ALTA BATES MEDICAL GROUP

Payer ID A0701	PO BOX 649010 SAN FRANCISCO, CA 94164	(866) 681-0737 WWW.ALTABATESMD.COM

ALTAMED SENIOR CARE

Payer ID E3510	2040 CAMFIELD AVENUE LOS ANGELES, CA 90040	(877) 462-2582 WWW.ALTAMED.ORG

ALTIUS

Payer ID 25133	UT CLAIMS PO BOX 7147 LONDON, KY 40742	(800) 377-4161 HTTP://ALTIUS.COVENTRYHEALTHCARE.COM/SERVICES-AND-SUPPORT/PROVIDERS/INDEX.HTM
Payer ID 25133	NV CLAIMS PO BOX 7801 LONDON, KY 40742	(800) 377-4161 HTTP://ALTIUS.COVENTRYHEALTHCARE.COM/SERVICES-AND-SUPPORT/PROVIDERS/INDEX.HTM

ALWAYSCARE BENEFITS

	PO BOX 14389 BATON ROUGE, LA 70898	(888) 729-5433 WWW.ALWAYSCAREBENEFITS.COM/PROVIDERSRVC.ASP

AMA & ASSOCIATES

	PO BOX 659570 SAN ANTONIO, TX 78265-9570	(210) 829-7407 (800) 456-7480 WWW.AMAOFSA.COM/

AMA INSURANCE AGENCY, INC

Payer ID AMAIA	PO BOX 804238 CHICAGO, IL 60680-4104	(888) 627-5883 WWW.AMAINSURE.COM

AMALGAMATED LIFE INSURANCE CO.

Payer ID 13550	PO BOX 5431 WHITE PLAINS, NY 10602	(914) 367-5365 (866) 995-9011 WWW.AMALGAMATEDLIFE.COM/PROVIDERS/MAIN_CONTENT.PHP

AMALGAMATED LIFE- PA/ ALICARE

Payer ID 13343	333 WESTCHESTER AVE WHITE PLAINS, NY 10604	(914) 367-5000 WWW.AMALGAMATEDLIFE.COM

AMALGAMATED TRANSIT UNION DIVISION 1001 HEALTH & WELFARE FUND

Payer ID COMPU	PO BOX 188004 CHATTANOOGA, TN 37422	(303) 745-7004 WWW.ATU1001.ORG

AMCO

Payer ID 62176	2700 SOUTH INTERSTATE 35 AUSTIN, TX 78704	(800) 282-2000 WWW.GETAMCO.COM

AMCOMP

Payer ID WB184	3626 E TREMONT AVE STE 203 THROGGS NECK, NY 10465	(718) 892-0228 WWW.AMCOMPPRO.COM

AMERAPLAN

Payer ID 38219	3001 W BIG BEAVER STE 320 TROY, MI 48084-3003	(248) 643-9400 WWW.AMERAPLAN.COM/PROVIDER.HTML

AMERIBEN SOLUTIONS

Payer ID 75137 | PO BOX 7186
BOISE, ID 83707-1186 | (800) 786-7930
WWW.AMERIBEN.COM

AMERICA 1ST CHOICE PLANS OF NORTH CAROLIINA

Payer ID 26078 | PO BOX 210459
COLUMBIA, SC 29221-0459 | (803) 748-4533
(866) 321-3947
HTTP://NC.AMERICAS1STCHOICE.COM/NODE/62

AMERICA FIRST INSURANCE

1600 N COLLINS BLVD
RICHARDSON, TX 75080-3519 | (972) 231-7175
(800) 443-2533
WWW.AMERICAFIRST-INS.COM

AMERICA'S CHOICE NMA

Payer ID 20029 | PO BOX 922043
HOUSTON, TX 77292 | (877) 224-3627
HTTPS://SECURE.ACHONLINE.COM/PROVIDERS/LOOKUPCLAIMS.ASP

AMERICA'S PPO

Payer ID 41178 | PO BOX 398220
MINNEAPOLIS, MN 55439 | (800) 948-9451
WWW.AMERICASPPO.COM/HOW_TO_SUBMIT_CLAIMS.ASPX

AMERICAID COMMUNITY CARE DALLAS/FORT WORTH

Payer ID 27514 | PO BOX 61010
VIRGINIA BCH, VA 23466 | (800) 454-3730
HTTPS://PROVIDERS.AMERIGROUP.COM/PAGES/CONTACT.ASPX#PROVIDER%20SERVICES

AMERICAID COMMUNITY CARE HOUSTON

Payer ID 27515 | PO BOX 61010
VIRGINIA BEACH, VA 23466 | (800) 454-3730
HTTPS://PROVIDERS.AMERIGROUP.COM/PAGES/CONTACT.ASPX#PROVIDER%20SERVICES

AMERICAID COMMUNITY CARE MARYLAND

Payer ID 27517 | PO BOX 61010
VIRGINIA BEACH, VA 23466 | (800) 454-3730
HTTPS://PROVIDERS.AMERIGROUP.COM/PAGES/CONTACT.ASPX#PROVIDER%20SERVICES

AMERICAID COMMUNITY CARE NEW JERSEY

Payer ID 27516 | PO BOX 61010
VIRGINIA BEACH, VA 23466 | (800) 454-3730
HTTPS://PROVIDERS.AMERIGROUP.COM/PAGES/CONTACT.ASPX#PROVIDER%20SERVICES

AMERICAN ADMINISTRATORS

Payer ID 42112 | PO BOX 65887
WEST DES MOINES, IA 56265 | (800) 456-4584

AMERICAN ADMINISTRATORS OF FLORIDA

Payer ID 65064 | PO BOX 2278
HALLANDALE, FL 33008-2278 | (262) 241-7460
(800) 508-4893
WWW.THERAPYADMIN.COM

AMERICAN BEHAVIORAL (MBH & FEP/ITS)

Payer ID 63103 | FEP/ITS PO BOX 981698
EL PASO, TX 79998 | (877) 660-6646
WWW.AMERICANBEHAVIORAL.COM/CONTENT.ASP?ID=257578

Payer ID 63103 | MBH PO BOX 981699
EL PASO, TX 79998 | (877) 660-6646
WWW.AMERICANBEHAVIORAL.COM/CONTENT.ASP?ID=257578

AMERICAN BENEFIT PLAN ADMINISTRATORS

Payer ID 59140 | PO BOX 43569, LAS VEGAS, NV 89116 | (800) 959-3953, WWW.CIGNASHAREDADMINISTRATION.COM

AMERICAN BENEFITS MANAGEMENT

Payer ID 34187 | 8310 PORT JACKSON AVE NW, NORTH CANTON, OH 44720-7340 | (330) 966-5500, (800) 456-4002, WWW.AMERICANBENEFITS.ORG/GROUP%20SERVICES%20MAIN.HTML

AMERICAN BENEFITS PLAN ADMINISTRATORS INC

Payer ID 95170 | PO BOX 3604, SEATTLE, WA 98124 | (800) 966-5387, WWW.ABPA.COM/HOME/PROVIDER.ASPX

AMERICAN CHIROPRACTIC NETWORK

Payer ID ACN01 | PO BOX 212, MINNEAPOLIS, MN 55440 | (800) 873-4575, WWW.OPTUMHEALTH.COM

AMERICAN CLAIMS MANAGEMENT

Payer ID WA065 | PO BOX 85251, SAN DIEGO, CA 92186 | (065) 866-6715, WWW.ACMCLAIMS.COM

AMERICAN CONTRACTORS INSURANCE GROUP

Payer ID WC232 | 12222 MERIT DR STE 1660, DALLAS, TX 75251 | (972) 687-0602, WWW.ACIG.COM

AMERICAN FAMILY (ADMINISTERED BY AMERICAN REPUBLIC)

Payer ID 56071 | PO BOX 14511, DES MOINES, IA 50306-3511 | (888) 755-3064, HTTP://AMFAM.AMERICANREPUBLIC.COM/PROVIDERS/DEFAULT.ASPX

AMERICAN FAMILY INSURANCE

Payer ID TH095 | PO BOX 7430, MADISON, WI 53783-0001 | (800) 333-6886, WWW.AMFAM.COM/CLAIMS/CLAIMS-BASICS.ASP

AMERICAN FIDELITY ASSURANCE CO

PO BOX 268898, OKLAHOMA CITY, OK 73125-8898 | (800) 437-1011, WWW.AFADVANTAGE.COM/CUSTOMER-SUPPORT/CLAIM-FLEX-FORMS.ASPX

AMERICAN GENERAL

Payer ID 62030 | PO BOX 1500, NASHVILLE, TN 37230-1500 | (800) 888-2452, WWW.AMERICANGENERAL.COM/LIFE/LIFE.NSF/CONTENTS/CLAIMS_HOME

AMERICAN GENERAL LIFE & ACCIDENT INSURANCE CO

Payer ID 87726 | PO BOX 4443, HOUSTON, TX 77210-4443 | (800) 521-2773, WWW.AIGAG.COM

AMERICAN HEALTH UNDERWRITERS

830 TAYLOR ST, FORT WORTH, TX 76102 | (800) 772-2355, WWW.AHUINC.COM

AMERICAN HEALTHCARE ALLIANCE

Payer ID 01066 | PO BOX 8530, KANSAS CITY, MO 64114-8530 | (800) 870-6252, WWW.AHAPPO.COM

AMERICAN HERITAGE

Payer ID 77083 | PO BOX 43067, JACKSONVILLE, FL 32203-3067 | (800) 348-4489, WWW.ALLSTATEATWORK.COM/

AMERICAN IMAGING MANAGEMENT, INC

Payer ID 36369
PO BOX 1328
NORTHBROOK, IL 60015-1167
(847) 564-8500
WWW.AMERICANIMAGING.NET

AMERICAN INCOME LIFE INSURANCE CO

PO BOX 2608
WACO, TX 76797-2608
(254) 761-6400
(800) 433-3405
WWW.AMERICAN-INCOME-LIFE.COM/SUPPORT/AMERICAN-INCOME-LIFE-INSURANCE-COMPANY-CLAIM-SERVICES.ASPX

AMERICAN INSURANCE COMPANY OF TX

Payer ID 81949
PO BOX 25326
OVERLAND PARK, KS 66225
(800) 237-4463

AMERICAN INTERNATIONAL GROUP, INC

Payer ID 87726
PO BOX 2066
JACKSONVILLE, FL 32203
(866) 960-0772
WWW.AIGCORPORATE.COM/INDEX.HTML

AMERICAN INTERSTATE INSURANCE COMPANY

Payer ID WB100
2301 HIGHWAY 190 WEST
DERIDDER, LA 70634
(337) 463-9052
(800) 256-9052

AMERICAN MEDICAL & LIFE

Payer ID 23212
PO BOX 34912
PHILADELPHIA, PA 19101
(888) 264-1512
WWW.USAMLI.COM/MEMBER-SERVICES.HTML

AMERICAN MEDICAL SECURITY

Payer ID 81400
PO BOX 19032
GREEN BAY, WI 54307-9032
(800) 232-5432
WWW.EAMS.COM

AMERICAN NATIONAL INSURANCE CO

Payer ID 74048
PO BOX 696800
SAN ANTONIO, TX 78269
(800) 899-6520
WWW.ANICO.COM

AMERICAN POSTAL WORKERS UNION HEALTH PLAN

Payer ID 62308
PO BOX 188004
CHATTANOOGA, TN 37422
(800) 222-2798
WWW.APWUHP.COM/PROVIDERS.PHP

AMERICAN PROGRESSIVE LIFE & HEALTH INSURANCE CO

Payer ID 48055
PO BOX 130
PENSACOLA, FL 32591
(800) 332-3377
WWW.AMERPROG.COM

AMERICAN PUBLIC LIFE INSURANCE CO

PO BOX 925
JACKSON, MS 39205-0925
(800) 256-8606
WWW.AMPUBLIC.COM/PROVIDERSERVICE/

AMERICAN REPUBLIC INSURANCE CO

Payer ID 42011
PO BOX 21670
EAGAN, MN 55121
(515) 247-2435
(800) 247-2190
WWW.AMERICANREPUBLIC.COM/PROVIDERS/DEFAULT.ASPX

AMERICAN RISK SERVICES

Payer ID WB103
11135 KENWOOD RD
CINCINNATI, OH 45242
(877) 313-7301
WWW.AMERICANRISKSERVICES.COM

AMERICAN SENTINEL INSURANCE CO

Payer ID 17965
PO BOX 61140
HARRISBURG, PA 17106-1140
(717) 540-0600
(800) 692-7338
WWW.AMERICANSENTINEL.CC

AMERICAN SPECIALTY HEALTH INCORPORATED

Payer ID ASH01

PO BOX 509001
SAN DIEGO, CA 92510

(800) 972-4226
WWW.ASHCOMPANIES.COM/PROVIDERS/CLAIMS/CLAIMS.ASPX

AMERICAN TRUST ADMINISTRATORS, INC

255 NW BLUE PKWY STE 100
LEE'S SUMMIT, MO 64063

(800) 843-4121
WWW.ATAAMERICA.COM/PROVIDERS.HTM

AMERICAN UNDERWRITERS LIFE INSURANCE CO

PO BOX 9510
WICHITA, KS 67277-9510

(316) 794-2200
WWW.IAI-ONLINE.COM

AMERICAN WHOLE HEALTH NETWORKS, INC

Payer ID 58213

PO BOX 3192
MILWAUKEE, WI 53201

(800) 274-7526
HTTP://HEALTHWAYS.WHOLEHEALTHMD.COM/

AMERICAN WORKER HEALTH PLAN

Payer ID 37322

33 WEST HIGGINS RD STE 910
SOUTH BARRINGTON, IL 60010-9320

(866) 215-9300
WWW.THEAMERICANWORKER.COM

AMERICAS 1ST CHOICE HEALTH PLANS OF SOUTH CAROLINA

Payer ID 20553

PO BOX 210769
COLUMBIA, SC 29221

(866) 321-3947
HTTP://SC.AMERICAS1STCHOICE.COM/NODE/152

AMERICAS 1ST CHOICE INSURANCE CO OF NORTH CAROLINA

Payer ID 26078

PO BOX 210459
COLUMBIA, SC 29221-0459

(866) 321-3947
HTTP://NC.AMERICAS1STCHOICE.COM/NODE/153

AMERICHOICE OF CT, FL, MD, RI, TX, WI

Payer ID 87726

PO BOX 31362
SALT LAKE CITY, UT 84131

(877) 842-3210
WWW.UHCCOMMUNITYPLAN.COM/HEALTH-PROFESSIONALS/TX/PROVIDER-INFORMATION

AMERICHOICE OF FLORIDA

Payer ID 87726

PO BOX 31362
SALT LAKE CITY, UT 84131

(877) 842-3210
WWW.UHCCOMMUNITYPLAN.COM/HEALTH-PROFESSIONALS/FL/PROVIDER-INFORMATION

AMERICHOICE OF ILLINOIS

Payer ID 87726

PO BOX 30555
SALT LAKE CITY, UT 84130

(877) 842-3210
WWW.UHCCOMMUNITYPLAN.COM/HEALTH-PROFESSIONALS/IL/PROVIDER-INFORMATION

AMERICHOICE OF IOWA

Payer ID 95375

PO BOX 30555
SALT LAKE CITY, UT 84130

(877) 842-3210
WWW.UHCCOMMUNITYPLAN.COM/HEALTH-PROFESSIONALS/IA/PROVIDER-INFORMATION

AMERICHOICE OF MARYLAND

Payer ID 87726

PO BOX 31365
SALT LAKE CITY, UT 84131

(877) 841-3210
WWW.UHCCOMMUNITYPLAN.COM/HEALTH-PROFESSIONALS/MD/PROVIDER-INFORMATION

AMERICHOICE OF MISSISSIPPI

Payer ID 95378

PO BOX 5032
KINGSTON, NY 12402-5032

(800) 557-9933
WWW.UHCCOMMUNITYPLAN.COM/HEALTH-PROFESSIONALS/MS/PROVIDER-INFORMATION

AMERICHOICE OF NEBRASKA

Payer ID 87726

PO BOX 31365
SALT LAKE CITY, UT 84131

(866) 331-2243
WWW.UHCCOMMUNITYPLAN.COM/HEALTH-PROFESSIONALS/NE/PROVIDER-INFORMATION

AMERICHOICE OF NEW JERSEY PERSONAL CARE PLUS

Payer ID 86001

PO BOX 5250
KINGSTON, NY 12402-5250

(888) 362-3368
WWW.UHCCOMMUNITYPLAN.COM/HEALTH-PROFESSIONALS/NJ/PROVIDER-INFORMATION

AMERICHOICE OF NEW YORK PERSONAL CARE PLUS

Payer ID 86002

PO BOX 5240
KINGSTON, NY 12402-5240

(877) 842-3210
WWW.UHCCOMMUNITYPLAN.COM/HEALTH-PROFESSIONALS/NY/PROVIDER-INFORMATION

AMERICHOICE OF NJ MEDICAID & FAMILY CARE

Payer ID 86047

PO BOX 5250
KINGSTON, NY 12402-5250

(888) 362-3368
WWW.UHCCOMMUNITYPLAN.COM/HEALTH-PROFESSIONALS/NJ/PROVIDER-INFORMATION

AMERICHOICE OF NY MEDICAID & CHILD HEALTH PLUS

Payer ID 86048

PO BOX 5240
KINGSTON, NY 12402-5240

(877) 842-3210
WWW.UHCCOMMUNITYPLAN.COM/HEALTH-PROFESSIONALS/NY/PROVIDER-INFORMATION

AMERICHOICE OF PA CHILDREN'S HEALTH INSURANCE PROGRAM

Payer ID 86049

PO BOX 8207
KINGSTON, NY 12402-8207

(800) 600-9007
WWW.AMERICHOICE.COM

AMERICHOICE OF PA MEDICAID

Payer ID 86049

PO BOX 8207
KINGSTON, NY 12402-5250

(800) 345-3627
WWW.AMERICHOICE.COM

AMERICHOICE OF PENNSYLVANIA PERSONAL CARE PLUS

Payer ID 86003

PO BOX 8207
KINGSTON, NY 12402-8207

(800) 600-9007
WWW.AMERICHOICE.COM

AMERICHOICE OF RHODE ISLAND

Payer ID 87726

PO BOX 31361
SALT LAKE CITY, UT 84131

(877) 842-3210
WWW.UHCCOMMUNITYPLAN.COM/HEALTH-PROFESSIONALS/RI/PROVIDER-INFORMATION

AMERICHOICE OF TENNESSEE

Payer ID 95378

PO BOX 5220
KINGSTON, NY 12402-5220

(800) 690-1606
WWW.UHCCOMMUNITYPLAN.COM/HEALTH-PROFESSIONALS/TN/PROVIDER-INFORMATION

AMERIGROUP CORP.

PO BOX 61010
VIRGINIA BEACH, VA 23466

(757) 490-6900
(800) 454-3730
WWW.AMERIGROUP.COM

AMERIGROUP FLORIDA

Payer ID 28809

PO BOX 61010
VIRGINIA BEACH, VA 23466

(757) 490-6900
(800) 454-3730
WWW.AMERIGROUP.COM

AMERIGROUP GEORGIA

Payer ID 27514

PO BOX 61010
VIRGINIA BEACH, VA 23466-1010

(800) 454-3730
WWW.AMERIGROUP.COM

A

AMERIGROUP MARYLAND

Payer ID 28807

PO BOX 61010
VIRGINIA BEACH, VA 23466

(410) 859-5800
(800) 454-3730
WWW.AMERIGROUP.COM

AMERIGROUP NEW JERSEY

Payer ID 28806

PO BOX 61010
VIRGINIA BEACH, VA 23466

(732) 452-6000
(800) 454-3730
WWW.AMERIGROUP.COM

AMERIGROUP TENNESSEE

Payer ID 27514

PO BOX 61010
VIRGINIA BEACH, VA 23466

(800) 454-3730
WWW.AMERIGROUP.COM

AMERIGROUP/AMERICAID FT WORTH, NEW MEXICO

Payer ID 28804

PO BOX 61010
VIRGINIA BEACH, VA 23466

(800) 454-3730
WWW.AMERIGROUP.COM

AMERIGROUP/AMERICAID HOUSTON

Payer ID 28805

PO BOX 61010
VIRGINIA BEACH, VA 23466

(800) 454-3730
WWW.AMERIGROUP.COM

AMERIHEALTH

Payer ID 54704

PO BOX 41574
PHILADELPHIA, PA 19101-1574

(800) 841-5328
WWW.AMERIHEALTH.COM/

AMERIHEALTH ADMINISTRATORS

Payer ID 54763

720 BLAIR MILL RD
HORSHAM, PA 19044-2269

(800) 841-5328
WWW.AHATPA.COM/PROVIDERS

AMERIHEALTH DC

Payer ID 77002

PO BOX 7342
LONDON, KY 40742

(202) 408-2237
WWW.AMERIHEALTHDC.COM/

AMERIHEALTH HMO NEW JERSEY AND DELAWARE

Payer ID 23037

PO BOX 41574
PHILADELPHIA, PA 19101-1574

(800) 275-2583
WWW.AMERIHEALTH.COM/PROVIDERS/INDEX.HTML

AMERIHEALTH MERCY HEALTH PLAN

Payer ID 22248

PO BOX 7118
LONDON, KY 40742

(800) 521-6007
WWW.AMERIHEALTHMERCYHP.COM/PROVIDER/INDEX.ASPX

AMERIHEALTH NEW JERSEY

Payer ID SX075

PO BOX 41574
PHILADELPHIA, PA 19101-1574

(800) 275-2583
WWW.AMERIHEALTH.COM/PROVIDERS/INDEX.HTML

AMERIHEALTH NORTHEAST

Payer ID 77001

PO BOX 7118
LONDON, KY 40742

(888) 208-7370
WWW.AMERIHEALTHNORTHEAST.COM/

AMERIKIDS DALLAS/FT. WORTH

Payer ID 26375

PO BOX 61010
VIRGINIA BEACH, VA 23466

(800) 454-3730
WWW.AMERIGROUP.COM

AMERIPRISE AUTO AND HOME INSURANCE

Payer ID WA054

PO BOX 19018
GREEN BAY, WI 54307

(800) 872-5246
WWW.AMERIPRISE.COM

AMERISURE COMPANIES

Payer ID WC422	26777 HALSTED RD FARMINGTON HILLS, MI 48331-3586 PO BOX 2060 FARMINGTON HILLS, MI 48333-2060	(248) 615-9000 (800) 257-1900 WWW.AMERISURE.COM

AMICA MUTUAL INSURANCE

Payer ID WA056	100 AMICA WAY LINCOLN, RI 02865-1167	(401) 334-6000 (800) 242-6422 WWW.AMICA.COM

AMIDA CARE

Payer ID 24818	PO BOX 6022 HAUPPAUGE, NY 11788	(800) 556-0674 WWW.AMIDACARENY.ORG/PROVIDERS-SERVICES.HTM

AMTRUST FINANCIAL SERVICES

	59 MAIDEN LN 6TH FL NEW YORK, NY 10038	(212) 220-7120 WWW.AMTRUSTGROUP.COM

AMTRUST INSURANCE COMPANY OF KANSAS INC

Payer ID 12491	PO BOX 105074 ATLANTA, GA 30348-5074	(888) 239-3909 WWW.AMTRUSTGROUP.COM/

AMVI

Payer ID IP080	1920 E 17TH ST STE 200 SANTA ANA, CA 92705-8606	(800) 708-3230 WWW.PROSPECTAMVI.COM/PROVIDERS/INDEX.HTML

AMWAY CORPORATION

Payer ID 38254	7575 FULTON ST E ADA, MI 49355	(616) 336-8808 WWW.IBOAI.COM

ANCHOR BENEFIT CONSULTING

Payer ID 53085	PO BOX 945260 MAITLAND, FL 32794-5260	(800) 845-7629 WWW.ANCHORBENEFIT.COM

ANCHOR CLAIMS MANAGEMENT

Payer ID CQ554	PO BOX 819045 DALLAS, TX 75381	(800) 275-3193 WWW.ANCHOR-CLAIMS.COM

APEX BENEFIT SERVICES

Payer ID 34196	PO BOX 3620 AKRON, OH 44309	(800) 996-8401 WWW.APEX-BENEFITS.COM/LOGIN/PROVIDER/

APPLECARE MEDICAL MGMT

Payer ID APP01	PO BOX 6014 ARTESIA, CA 90702	(714) 443-4500 (800) 864-8160 WWW.APPLECAREMEDICAL.COM/PHYSICIAN_LOGIN.HTM

APPLIED RISK SERVICES

Payer ID WB164	3 GARBER HILL ROAD BLAUVELT, NY 10913	(845) 365-2444 WWW.APPLIEDRISK CONTROL.COM

APS HEALTHCARE INC

Payer ID 54160	7125 COLUMBIA GAEWAY DR STE 250 COLUMBIA, MD 21046	(877) 490-6854 WWW.APSHEALTHCARE.COM/PROVIDERS.ASPX

A

ARAZ

Payer ID 16120

PO BOX 398220
MINNEAPOLIS, MN 55439

(952) 896-1200
(800) 444-3005
WWW.ARAZ.COM

ARBOR HEALTH PLAN

Payer ID 52312

PO BOX 7336
LONDON, KY 40742

(866) 423-2337
WWW.ARBORHEALTHPLAN.COM/PROVIDER/RESOURCES/INDEX.ASPX

ARCADIAN MANAGEMENT SERVICES, INC

Payer ID 77045

PO BOX 4198
COVINA, CA 91723-4198

(800) 573-8597
WWW.ARCADIANHEALTH.COM/PROVIDER.HTML

ARGUS SERVICES CORP

9101 LBJ FWY STE 600
DALLAS, TX 75243

(214) 459-2000
(800) 720-6787
WWW.ARGUSSERVICES.NET

ARIZONA FOUNDATION FOR MEDICAL CARE

Payer ID AZFMC

PO BOX 2909
PHOENIX, AZ 85062-2909

(800) 624-4277
WWW.AZFMC.COM/INDEX/PROVIDER

ARIZONA MEDICAID

Payer ID AZMCD

PO BOX 1700
PHOENIX, AZ 85002-1700

(800) 523-0231
WWW.AZAHCCCS.GOV/COMMERCIAL/DEFAULT.ASPX

ARIZONA MEDICAID HMO (AZ PHYSICIANS IPA)

Payer ID 03432

PO BOX 5290
KINGSTON, NY 12402-5290

(800) 445-1638
WWW.UHCCOMMUNITYPLAN.COM/HEALTH-PROFESSIONALS/AZ/PROVIDER-INFORMATION

ARIZONA MEDICAID HMO (HEALTH CHOICE AZ)

Payer ID 62179

410 N 44TH ST STE 500
PHOENIX, AZ 85008-6572

(800) 322-8670
WWW.HEALTHCHOICEAZ.COM/GENERALPROVIDERS/

ARIZONA MEDICAID HMO (PHOENIX HEALTH PLAN)

Payer ID 3440

PO BOX 81000
PHOENIX, AZ 85069

(602) 824-3743
(800) 747-7997
WWW.PHOENIXHEALTHPLAN.COM/PROVIDERS.ASPX

ARIZONA PHYSICIANS IPA INC

Payer ID 03432

PO BOX 5290
KINGSTON, NY 12402

(800) 445-1638
WWW.MYAPIPA.COM

ARIZONA PIPE TRADES

Payer ID 74234

PO BOX 21240
DENVER, CO 80221

(877) 429-7473
WWW.AZPIPE.ORG

ARKANSAS BEST CORP

Payer ID 75278

PO BOX 10048
FORT SMITH, AR 72917-0048

(479) 785-6178
(800) 451-6907
WWW.CHOICEBENEFITS.COM/PROVIDERENTRY.ASP?CONTENT=PAGE1

A

ARKANSAS MANAGED CARE ORGANIZATION

Payer ID 62176	PO BOX 8219 LITTLE ROCK, AR 72221-8219	(501) 225-8470 (800) 278-8470 WWW.AMCOPPO.COM/ _PROVIDERS_ONLY.ASP

ARKANSAS MUNICIPAL LEAGUE

Payer ID 71603	PO BOX 38 NORTH LITTLE ROCK, AR 72115	(501) 374-3484 WWW.ARML.ORG

ARROW MUTUAL LIABILITY INSURANCE CO

	23 COMMONWEALTH AVE CHESTNUT HILL, MA 02467-1099	(617) 244-5730 (800) 457-9753 WWW.ARROWMUTUAL.COM

ASOCIACION DE MAESTROS

Payer ID 94027	PO BOX 191088 SAN JUAN, PR 00919-1088	(787) 767-2020 WWW.AMPRNET.ORG/

ASR CORPORATION

Payer ID 38265	PO BOX 6392 GRAND RAPIDS, MI 49516-6392	(800) 968-2449 WWW.ASRHEALTHBENEFITS.COM/

ASRM CORP

Payer ID ASRM1	505 S LENOLA RD STE 231 MOORESTOWN, NJ 08057-1542	(800) 359-7475 WWW.CLAIM.MD/PAYER.HTML?P=ASRM1

ASSOCIATED BENEFITS CORP

Payer ID FAABC	1415 28TH ST STE 100 WEST DES MOINES, IA 50266	(800) 747-4370 WWW.ASSOCIATEDBENEFITS.COM

ASSOCIATED THIRD PARTY ADMINISTRATION

Payer ID ATPA1	1640 S LOOP RD ALAMEDA, CA 94502-7089	(510) 451-8564 WWW.ATPA.COM/

ASSOCIATES FOR HEALTH CARE

Payer ID 36326	18650 W CORPORATE DR STE 310 BROOKFIELD, WI 53008-0981	(262) 879-0100

ASSOCIATION & SOCIETY INSURANCE CORP

	PO BOX 2510 ROCKVILLE, MD 20847-2510	(301) 816-0045 (800) 638-2610 WWW.ASICORPORATION.COM/PROVIDERS/ INDEX.HTML

ASSOCIATION CASUALTY INSURANCE GROUP

Payer ID WP987	3420 EXECUTIVE CENTER DR STE 200 AUSTIN, TX 78731	(800) 252-9641 WWW.COLINSGRP.COM

ASSURANCE RESOURCES

Payer ID WE044	3430 S SAM HOUSTON PKWY STE 400 HOUSTON, TX 77047 PO BOX 84525 PEARLAND, TX 77584	(888) 266-6401 WWW.ASSURANCERESOURCES.ORG

ASSURANT EMPLOYEE BENEFITS

Payer ID 70408	PO BOX 2940 CLINTON, IA 52733	(800) 443-2995 WWW.ASSURANTEMPLOYEEBENEFITS.COM/

ASSURANT HEALTH

PO BOX 3050
MILWAUKEE, WI 53201-0624

(800) 800-1212
WWW.ASSURANTHEALTH.COM/CORP/AH/PROVIDERS/CLAIMSSUBMISSION.HTM

ASSURANT HEALTH SELF FUND

Payer ID 37313

PO BOX 1239
FT MILL, SC 29716-1239

(866) 387-0489
WWW.GROUPSELFFUNDED.COM/

ASSURE CARE

Payer ID 88035

340 QUADRANGLE DR
BOLINGBROOK, IL 60440-3448

(603) 759-1311
(800) 759-7422
WWW.ASSURECARE.COM/PROVIDERS/PROVIDERSERVICES.HTM

ASSURECARE

Payer ID 88035

13700 WATERTOWER CIR STE D
PLYMOUTH, MN 55441

(800) 328-0927
WWW.ASSURECARE.COM

ASSURED BENEFITS ADMINISTRATORS

Payer ID 74240

4855 N MESA STE 130
EL PASO, TX 79912-5901

(915) 532-2100
(800) 247-7114
WWW.ABADMIN.COM/SERVICES.HTM

ASURIS NORTHWEST/MEDADVANTAGE

Payer ID SX179

PO BOX 30271
SALT LAKE CITY, UT 84130-0271

(888) 344-5587
WWW.ASURIS.COM/PROVIDER

ATHENS HEALTH PLAN

Payer ID 95691

PO BOX 382767
BIRMINGHAM, AL 35238-2767

(706) 549-0549
(800) 293-6260
WWW.AAHPS.COM/PROVIDERS.HTML

ATLANTICARE ADMINISTRATORS, INC

Payer ID 22304

PO BOX 786361
PHILADELPHIA, PA 19178-6361

(888) 569-1000

ATLAS ADMINISTRATORS

Payer ID ATLAD

PO BOX 801234
DALLAS, TX 75380-1234

(800) 256-2657
WWW.ATLASADMIN.COM/

ATRIO HEALTH PLANS

PO BOX 5490
SALEM, OR 97304

(866) 672-8620
HTTP://WWW.ATRIOHP.COM/FOR-PROVIDERS.ASPX

AULTCARE

Payer ID MNAUL

PO BOX 6910
CANTON, OH 44706-0910

(330) 363-6360
(800) 344-8858
WWW.AULTCARE.COM/APPLICATION/UCL/R/PROVIDERS/LANDING/AULTCARE/UCPORTAL.ASPX

AULTCOMP MCO

Payer ID 10016

PO BOX 4817
MASSILLON, OH 44648-4817

(330) 830-4919
(888) 738-5800
WWW.AULTCOMP.COM/APPLICATION/UCL/R/PROVIDERS/LANDING/AULTCOMP/UCPORTAL.ASPX

AULTRA ADMINISTRATIVE GROUP

Payer ID 37242

PO BOX 35276
CANTON, OH 44735

(800) 325-8424
WWW.AULTRAGROUP.COM/APPLICATION/UCL/R/PROVIDERS/LANDING/AULTRAGROUP/UCPORTAL.ASPX

AUSTIN MUTUAL INSURANCE CO

Payer ID WZ744

15490 101ST AVE NORTH
MAPLE GROVE, MN 55369-9725
PO BOX 1420
MAPLE GROVE, MN 55311

(800) 328-4628
WWW.AUSTINMUTUAL.COM

AUTO CLUB INSURANCE ASSOCIATION

Payer ID WA053

1 AUTO CLUB DR
DEARBORN, MI 48126
PO BOX 920
SUISUN CITY, CA 94586

(313) 336-1234
(888) 222-0086
WWW.AAA.COM

AUTO-OWNERS

Payer ID 10190

PO BOX 100044
DULUTH, GA 30096

(770) 931-7766
WWW.AUTO-OWNERS.COM

AUTOMATED BENEFITS SERVICES, INC

Payer ID 38259

PO BOX 37506
OAK PARK, MI 48237-7705

(800) 521-1321
WWW.ABS-TPA.COM/ABS/PROVIDERS.HTM

AUTOMATED GROUP ADMINISTRATION INC

Payer ID 37280

7605 WESTFIELD DR
FORT WAYNE, IN 46825

(260) 489-6447
WWW.AGA-TPA.COM/PROVIDERS/

AUTOMOTIVE MACHINISTS LOCAL 289 HEALTH & WELFARE TRUST - GRP#F32

Payer ID 91136

9135 15TH PL
SEATTLE, WA 98108

(206) 441-7574
WWW.IAMLL289.COM

AV-MED HEALTH PLAN

Payer ID 59274

PO BOX 569000
MIAMI, FL 33256-9000

(800) 346-0231
HTTP://WWW.AVMED.ORG/PROVIDERS/INDEX.ASPX

AVALON IPA

Payer ID IP080

PO BOX 261040
ENCINO, CA 91426

(818) 461-5055
(888) 445-0062
WWW.CAPCMS.COM/DEFAULT.ASPX

AVERA HEALTH PLANS

Payer ID 46045

3816 S ELM WOOD AVE
SIOUX FALLS, SD 57105

(888) 605-1331
WWW.AVERA.ORG

AVERDE HEALTH

Payer ID 26355

PO BOX 5223
JANESVILLE, WI 53547-5223

(877) 283-7331
WWW.AVERDEHEALTH.COM/PHYSICIANS/LOGIN

AVESIS THIRD PARTY ADMINISTRATORS

Payer ID 87098

PO BOX 7777
PHOENIX, AZ 85012

(800) 952-6674
WWW.AVESIS.COM/DOCTORS.HTML

AVIZENT

Payer ID WX601

5000 BRADENTON AVE
DUBLIN, OH 43017-3520
PO BOX 182364
COLUMBUS, OH 43218-2364

(888) 296-4283
WWW.AVIZENTRISK.COM

AVMED

Payer ID 59274

PO BOX 569000
MIAMI, FL 33256

(305) 671-5437
(800) 882-8633
WWW.AVMED.ORG/PROVIDERS/INDEX.ASPX

BABB, INC

850 RIDGE AVE
PITTSBURGH, PA 15212-6095

(800) 245-6102
WWW.BABBINS.COM

BAKERSFIELD FAMILY MEDICAL CENTER

Payer ID BKRFM

PO BOX 10749
BAKERSFIELD, CA 93389-0749

(661) 846-4726
(800) 763-7732
WWW.BFMC.COM

BANKERS FIDELITY LIFE INSURANCE

PO BOX 105652
ATLANTA, GA 30348-5185

(404) 266-5500
(800) 241-1439
WWW.BFLIC.COM

BANKERS INSURANCE GROUP

PO BOX 33061
ST PETERSBURG, FL 33733-8061

(727) 803-4084
(800) 765-9700
WWW.BANKERSINSURANCE.COM/CLAIMS-SUPPORT.HTML

BANKERS LIFE & CASUALTY CO

PO BOX 1935
CARMEL, IN 46082-1935

(800) 773-4760
WWW.BANKERSLIFE.COM/SERVICECLAIMS.ASPX

BANNER HEALTH CO

Payer ID SX145

PO BOX 16423
MESA, AZ 85211-6423

(480) 684-7070
(800) 827-2464
WWW.BANNERHEALTHPLANS.COM

BANNER MEDISUN

Payer ID 77078

PO BOX 16423
MESA, AZ 85211-6423

(800) 446-8331
WWW.BANNERHEALTH.COM/_MEDISUN/PROVIDERS/_PROVIDERS.HTM

BAPTIST HEALTH SERVICES GROUP

Payer ID SX002

350 N HUMPHREYS BLVD 4TH FL
MEMPHIS, TN 38120

(800) 522-2474
WWW.BHSGONLINE.COM

BASCOM PALMER EYE CARE NETWORK

Payer ID NCH06

7101 FAIRWAY DR
PALM BEACH GARDENS, FL 33418

(305) 243-9999
WWW.BASCOMPALMER.ORG

BCI ADMINISTRATORS, INC

Payer ID 49153

PO BOX 250878
W BLOOMFIELD, MI 48325-0878

(248) 626-8896
WWW.MYBCI.COM

BEACON HEALTH STRATEGIES

Payer ID 43324

500 UNICORN PARK DR 401
WOBURN, MA 01801-3353

(781) 994-7500
WWW.BEACONHEALTHSTRATEGIES.COM

BEACON INSURANCE COMPANY OF AMERICA

Payer ID WZ806

1 PARK CIR
WESTFIELD CENTER, OH 44251-9700
PO BOX 5001
WESTFIELD CENTER, OH 44521

(866) 937-2663
WWW.WESTFIELDINSURANCE.COM

BEECH STREET CORP.

Payer ID 95377

PO BOX 853925
RICHARDSON, TX 75085-3925

(800) 877-1444
WWW.BEECHSTREET.COM

BEHAVIORAL HEALTH SYSTEMS

Payer ID 63100

TWO METROPLEX DR STE 500
BIRMINGHAM, AL 35209
PO BOX 830724
BIRMINGHAM, AL 35283-0724

(205) 879-1150
(800) 245-1150
WWW.BEHAVIORALHEALTHSYSTEMS.COM/PROVIDERS/ECLAIMS.ASP

BEHAVIORAL HEALTHCARE OPTIONS

PO BOX 36040
LAS VEGAS, NV 89133

(877) 393-6094
WWW.BEHAVIORALHEALTHCAREOPTIONS.COM/BODY.CFM?ID=29

BEHAVIORAL HEALTHCARE, INC

Payer ID BHI00

PO BOX 17448
DENVER, CO 80217

(720) 490-4413
WWW.BHICARES.ORG/PROVIDERS.HTM

BELLA VISTA MEDICAL GROUP IPA

Payer ID MPM10

PO BOX 572066
TARZANA, CA 91357

(818) 702-0100
WWW.MEDPOINTMANAGEMENT.COM/MPM/PROVIDERAB1455

BENCHMARK INSURANCE

Payer ID WP049

775 PRAIRIE CENTER DR STE 420
EDEN PRARIE, MN 55344

(952) 974-2200
WWW.BENCHMARKINSCO.COM

BENECARD SERVICES INC.

5040 RITTER RD
MECHANICSBURG, PA 17055

(800) 734-9528
WWW.BENECARD.COM

BENEFIT & RISK MANAGEMENT SERVICES

Payer ID 99320

PO BOX 2140
FOLSOM, CA 95763

(916) 858-2950
(888) 326-2555
WWW.BRMSONLINE.COM/ABOUT/SUPPORT.ASPX

BENEFIT ADMINISTRATIVE SYSTEMS

Payer ID 36149

PO BOX 2920
MILWAKEE, WI 53201

(708) 799-7400
(800) 523-0582
WWW.BENADMSYS.COM

BENEFIT ASSISTANCE CORPORATION

PO BOX 950
HURRICANE, WV 25526-0950

(304) 562-1913
(800) 448-1131
WWW.BACWV.COM

BENEFIT COORDINATORS CORP

Payer ID 25145

100 RYAN CT STE 200
PITTSBURGH, PA 15205-1310

(800) 685-6100
WWW.BENXCEL.COM/CONTACT.PHP#1

BENEFIT MANAGEMENT GROUP

Payer ID 20018

1520 KENSINGTON RD STE 200
OAKBROOK, IL 60523

(630) 472-0626
WWW.BMGIWEB.COM/

BENEFIT MANAGEMENT SERVICES

Payer ID 56139

PO BOX 1178
MATTHEWS, NC 28106-1178

(800) 228-1803
WWW.INTEGRAHEALTH.COM

BENEFIT MANAGEMENT SYSTEMS, INC OF MISSISSIPPI

Payer ID 37212

PO BOX 2058
MADISON, MS 39130

(601) 856-9029
WWW.BENEFITMGT.COM

BENEFIT MANAGEMENT SYSTEMS, INC. OF LOUSIANA

Payer ID 00999

PO BOX 98044
BATON ROUGE, LA 70898-9044

(225) 295-3307
(800) 603-2299
WWW.BMSHEALTH.COM/

BENEFIT MANAGEMENT, INC OF KANSAS

Payer ID 48611

PO BOX 1090
GREAT BEND, KS 67530

(800) 290-1368
WWW.BMIKANSAS.COM/PROVIDER.ASPX

BENEFIT PLAN ADMINISTRATION OF WI, INC

11270 W PARK PL STE 950
MILWAUKEE, WI 53224-3642

(414) 577-3700
(800) 425-1272
WWW.BPALJA.COM

BENEFIT PLAN ADMINISTRATORS CO

Payer ID 39081

PO BOX 1128
EAU CLAIRE, WI 54702

(715) 832-5535
(800) 236-7789
WWW.BPACO.COM

BENEFIT PLAN ADMINISTRATORS NORTH DAKOTA

Payer ID 37286

518 NP AVENUE N STE 400
FARGO, ND 58102

(701) 237-4787

BENEFIT PLAN ADMINISTRATORS, INC

Payer ID 37286

PO BOX 11746
ROANOKE, VA 24022-1746

(800) 277-8973
WWW.BPATPA.COM

BENEFIT PLAN SERVICES, INC

PO BOX 2793
HIGH POINT, NC 27261-2793

(336) 889-2003
WWW.BPSTPA.COM

BENEFIT PLANNERS, INC

Payer ID 74223

PO BOX 690450
SAN ANTONIO, TX 78269-0450

(800) 769-1452
WWW.BENPLAN.COM

BENEFIT SUPPORT, INC

PO BOX 2977
GAINESVILLE, GA 30503

(800) 777-4782
HTTP://BENEFITSUPPORT.BIZ/

BENEFIT SYSTEMS & SERVICES, INC

Payer ID 36342

225 SMITH RD
ST. CHARLES, IL 60174

(800) 423-1841
WWW.BENEFIT-SYS.COM

BENESIGHT

Payer ID 87265

PO BOX 8077
WAUSAU, WI 54402-8077

(800) 826-9781
WWW.BENESIGHT.COM

BENESYS, INC

Payer ID 38238

700 TOWER DR STE 300
TROY, MI 48098-2863

(248) 813-9800
WWW.BENESYSINC.COM

BENICOMP, INC

8310 CLINTON PARK DR
FT WAYNE, IN 46825-3171

(260) 482-7400
(800) 837-7400
WWW.BENICOMP.COM

BERKLEY RISK SERVICES

2000 S COLORADO BLVD ANNEX BLDG STE 410
DENVER, CO 80222-4356

(303) 504-6133
(800) 449-7707
WWW.BERKLEYRISK.COM

B

BERKSHIRE HATHAWAY HOMESTATE COMPANIES

PO BOX 31361
OMAHA, NE 68131

(402) 393-7255
(800) 488-2930
WWW.BHHC.COM/REPORT_A_CLAIM

BERKSHIRE HEALTH PARTNERS

Payer ID 23243

50 COMMERCE DR
READING, PA 19610

(610) 372-8044
(866) 257-0445
WWW.BHP.ORG/PROVIDERS/

BEST LIFE AND HEALTH INSURANCE CO

Payer ID 95604

PO BOX 890
MERRIDIAN, ID 83680

(949) 253-4080
(800) 433-0088
WWW.BESTLIFE.COM/CONTACT-US.HTM

BETTER HEALTH PLAN OF FLORIDA

Payer ID 20488

PO BOX 211665
EAGAN, MN 55121

(800) 514-4561
WWW.BETTERHEALTHFLORIDA.COM/
PROVIDER.HTML

BHP

Payer ID 44219

50 COMMERCE DR
READING, PA 19610

(610) 372-8044
WWW.BHP.ORG/PROVIDERS/

BITUMINOUS INSURANCE CO

Payer ID WZ570

320 18TH ST
ROCK ISLAND, IL 61201-8744

(800) 475-4477
WWW.BITUMINOUSINSURANCE.COM

BLOCK VISION

PO BOX 14035
MILWAUKEE, WI 53214

(866) 265-0517
WWW.BLOCKVISION.COM

BLOCK VISION INC

Payer ID BV001

939 ELKRIDGE LANDING RD
LINTHICUM, MD 21090

(410) 752-0121
(800) 243-1401
WWW.BLOCKVISION.COM

BLOCK VISION OF TEXAS

Payer ID BVTX1

6737 W WASHINGTON ST STE 2202
MILWAKEE, WI 53214-5644

(800) 883-5747
WWW.BLOCKVISION.COM

BLUE ADVANTAGE OF ARKANSAS

Payer ID ARBLS

PO BOX 1460
LITTLE ROCK, AR 72203

(888) 872-2531
WWW.BLUEADVANTAGEARKANSAS.COM/
PROVIDERS/CLAIMS_GUIDE.ASPX

BLUE BELL HEALTH BENEFITS

Payer ID 37308

PO BOX 909786-60690
CHICAGO, IL 60690

(979) 830-7388
WWW.ALLIEDBENEFIT.COM/PROVIDERS.ASPX

BLUE BENEFIT ADMINISTRATORS

Payer ID 03036

PO BOX 55917
BOSTON, MA 02205-5917

(877) 707-2583
WWW.BLUEBENEFITMA.COM

BLUE CARE NETWORK OF MICHIGAN

PO BOX 68767
GRAND RAPIDS, MI 49516-8767

(800) 662-6667
WWW.MICBN.COM

BLUE CHOICE MEDICAID

Payer ID 00403

PO BOX 100124
COLUMBIA, SC 29202-3124

(866) 577-9710
WWW.BLUECHOICESMEDICAID.COM

B

BLUE CHOICE OF SOUTH CAROLINA

Payer ID 00922

PO BOX 6170
COLUMBIA, SC 29260

(800) 868-2528
WWW.BLUECHOICESC.COM/PROVIDERS.ASPX

BLUE CROSS BLUE SHIELD- BLUE CHIP OF RHODE ISLAND

Payer ID RICHP

500 EXCHANGE STREET
PROVIDENCE, RI 02903

(800) 267-0439
WWW.BCBSRI.COM

BLUE CROSS BLUE SHIELD-ALABAMA

Payer ID ALBLS

PO BOX 2294
BIRMINGHAM, AL 35201

(205) 733-7016
(800) 292-8868
WWW.BCBSAL.ORG/PROVIDERS/INDEX.CFM

BLUE CROSS BLUE SHIELD-ALASKA

Payer ID AKBLS

PO BOX 240609
ANCHORAGE, AK 99524-0609

(907) 258-5065
(800) 722-4714
WWW.PREMERA.COM

BLUE CROSS BLUE SHIELD-ARIZONA

Payer ID AZBLS

PO BOX 2924
PHOENIX, AZ 85062-2924

(602) 864-4400
(800) 232-2345
WWW.AZBLUE.COM

BLUE CROSS BLUE SHIELD-ARKANSAS

Payer ID ARBLS

PO BOX 2181
LITTLE ROCK, AR 72203

(501) 378-2307
(800) 827-4814
WWW.ARKANSASBLUECROSS.COM/PROVIDERS/
PROVIDERMANUAL_DISCLAIMER.ASPX

BLUE CROSS BLUE SHIELD-COLORADO

Payer ID COBLS

PO BOX 5747
DENVER, CO 80217-5747

(877) 833-5742
WWW.ANTHEM.COM/WPS/PORTAL/
AHPPROVIDER?CONTENT_PATH=PROVIDER/CO/
F1/S0/T0/PW_AD071001.HTM&ROOTLEVEL=0&
STATE=CO&LABEL=PROVIDER%20HOME

BLUE CROSS BLUE SHIELD-CONNECTICUT

Payer ID CTBLS

PO BOX 533
NORTH HAVEN, CT 06473-0533

(800) 895-9915
WWW.ANTHEM.COM/WPS/PORTAL/
AHPPROVIDER?CONTENT_PATH=PROVIDER/CT/
F1/S0/T0/PW_AD076835.HTM&ROOTLEVEL=0&
STATE=CT&LABEL=PROVIDER%20HOME

BLUE CROSS BLUE SHIELD-DELAWARE

Payer ID DEBLS

PO BOX 8831
WILMINGTON, DE 19899-8831

(302) 421-3330
(800) 346-6262
WWW.BCBSDE.COM/PROVIDERS/

BLUE CROSS BLUE SHIELD-DISTRICT OF COLUMBIA

PO BOX 14116
LEXINGTON, KY 40512-4116

(202) 488-4900
(800) 854-5256
WWW.PROVIDER.CAREFIRST.COM/WPS/PORTAL/
PROVIDER/PROVIDERHOME

BLUE CROSS BLUE SHIELD-FLORIDA

Payer ID FLBLS

PO BOX 1798
JACKSONVILLE, FL 32231-0014

(904) 791-6111
(800) 727-2227
WWW.BCBSFL.COM

BLUE CROSS BLUE SHIELD-GEORGIA

Payer ID GABLS

PO BOX 9907
COLUMBUS, GA 31908

(404) 842-8000
(800) 441-2273
WWW.BCBSGA.COM

BLUE CROSS BLUE SHIELD-HAWAII

Payer ID HIBLS

PO BOX 44500
HONOLULU, HI 96804-4500

(800) 790-4672
WWW.HMSA.COM/PORTAL/PROVIDER/ZAV_WP001.HTM#NAV_CLAIMSCLAIMS

BLUE CROSS BLUE SHIELD-ILLINOIS

Payer ID ILBLS

PO BOX 805107
CHICAGO, IL 60680-4112

(312) 653-6000
(800) 972-8088
WWW.BCBSIL.COM/PROVIDER/CLAIMS/CLAIM_SUBMISSION.HTML

BLUE CROSS BLUE SHIELD-INDIANA

Payer ID INBLS

PO BOX 105187
ATLANTA, GA 30348

(800) 345-4344
WWW.ANTHEM.COM

BLUE CROSS BLUE SHIELD-IOWA

Payer ID IABLS

PO BOX 9291
DES MOINES, IA 50306

(800) 362-2218
WWW.WELLMARK.COM/PROVIDER/CLAIMSANDPAYMENTS/CLAIMSANDPAYMENTSHOME.ASPX

BLUE CROSS BLUE SHIELD-KANSAS

Payer ID KSBLS

1133 SW TOPEKA BLVD
TOPEKA, KS 66629

(800) 432-3990
WWW.BCBSKS.COM/CUSTOMERSERVICE/PROVIDERS/INDEX.HTM

BLUE CROSS BLUE SHIELD-KANSAS CITY MO

Payer ID KCBLS

PO BOX 419169
KANSAS CITY, MO 64141

(816) 395-2222
(800) 456-3759
WWW.BLUEKC.COM

BLUE CROSS BLUE SHIELD-KENTUCKY

Payer ID KYBLS

PO BOX 105187
ATLANTA, GA 30348

(800) 205-5870
WWW.ANTHEM.COM

BLUE CROSS BLUE SHIELD-LOUISIANA

Payer ID LABLS

PO BOX 98024
BATON ROUGE, LA 70898-9024

(225) 291-5370
(800) 599-2583
WWW.BCBSLA.COM/PROVIDERS/PAGES/CONTACTUS.ASPX

BLUE CROSS BLUE SHIELD-MARYLAND

Payer ID MDBLS

PO BOX 14115
LEXINGTON, KY 40512-4115

(410) 581-3581
(800) 842-5975
WWW.CAREFIRST.COM

BLUE CROSS BLUE SHIELD-MASSACHUSETTS

Payer ID MABLS

PO BOX 986020
BOSTON, MA 02298

(617) 246-5000
(800) 771-4097
WWW.BLUECROSSMA.COM/PORTAL/DT?PROVIDER=PROVIDERHOME

BLUE CROSS BLUE SHIELD-MICHIGAN

Payer ID MIBLS

PO BOX 2500
DETROIT, MI 48226

(313) 225-9000
WWW.BCBSM.COM/INDEX.SHTML

BLUE CROSS BLUE SHIELD-MINNESOTA

Payer ID MNBLS

PO BOX 64338
ST PAUL, MN 55164-0338

(651) 662-5200
(800) 262-0820
WWW.BLUECROSSMN.COM

BLUE CROSS BLUE SHIELD-MISSISSIPPI

Payer ID MSBLS

PO BOX 1043
JACKSON, MS 39215-1043

(601) 932-1122
WWW.BCBSMS.COM/INDEX.PHP?Q=IM-A-PROVIDER.HTML

BLUE CROSS BLUE SHIELD-MISSOURI

Payer ID MOBLS

PO BOX 105187
ATLANTA, GA 30348

(888) 571-9054
WWW.ANTHEM.COM

BLUE CROSS BLUE SHIELD-MONTANA

Payer ID MTBLS

PO BOX 7982
HELENA, MT 59604

(406) 444-8200
(800) 447-7828
WWW.BCBSMT.COM

BLUE CROSS BLUE SHIELD-NEBRASKA

Payer ID NEBLS

PO BOX 3248
OMAHA, NE 68180-3248

(402) 390-1890
(800) 642-8516
WWW.NEBRASKABLUE.COM/PROVIDERS/

BLUE CROSS BLUE SHIELD-NEVADA

Payer ID NVBLS

PO BOX 60007
LOS ANGELES, CA 90060-0007

(866) 754-3077
WWW.ANTHEM.COM

BLUE CROSS BLUE SHIELD-NEW HAMPSHIRE

Payer ID NHBLS

PO BOX 533
NORTH HAVEN, CT 06473

(800) 332-6558
WWW.ANTHEM.COM/HEALTH-INSURANCE/HOME/OVERVIEW

BLUE CROSS BLUE SHIELD-NEW JERSEY

Payer ID 22099

PO BOX 820
NEWARK, NJ 07101-0820

(800) 624-1110
WWW.HORIZON-BCBSNJ.COM/PROVIDERS.HTML?WT.SVL=HOMETAB

BLUE CROSS BLUE SHIELD-NEW MEXICO

Payer ID NMBLS

PO BOX 11968
ALBUQUERQUE, NM 87192

(505) 291-3500
(888) 349-3706
WWW.BCBSNM.COM

BLUE CROSS BLUE SHIELD-NEW YORK

Payer ID NYBLS

PO BOX 1407 CHURCH ST STATION
NEW YORK, NY 10008-1407

(800) 552-6630
WWW.EMPIREBLUE.COM

BLUE CROSS BLUE SHIELD-NORTH CAROLINA

Payer ID NCBLS

PO BOX 35
DURHAM, NC 27702

(800) 214-4844
WWW.BCBSNC.COM/CONTENT/PROVIDERS/INDEX.HTM

BLUE CROSS BLUE SHIELD-NORTH DAKOTA

Payer ID NDBLS

4510 13TH AVE SOUTH
FARGO, ND 58121

(701) 282-1090
(800) 368-2312
WWW.THORCONNECT.ORG/PROVIDER-SERVICES/

BLUE CROSS BLUE SHIELD-NORTHEASTERN NY

Payer ID N5BLS

PO BOX 80
BUFFALO, NY 14240-0080

(716) 884-3461
(800) 544-2583
HTTPS://SECUREWS.BSNENY.COM/WEB/CONTENT/BSNENY_BROCHURE/HOME/ABOUT-US/CONTACT-US.HTML

BLUE CROSS BLUE SHIELD-OHIO

Payer ID OHBLS

PO BOX 105187
ATLANTA, GA 30348

(800) 345-4344
WWW.ANTHEM.COM

BLUE CROSS BLUE SHIELD-OKLAHOMA

Payer ID OKBLS	PO BOX 3283 TULSA, OK 74102-3283	(918) 560-3500 (800) 942-5837 WWW.BCBSOK.COM/PROVIDER/

BLUE CROSS BLUE SHIELD-OREGON

Payer ID ORBLS	PO BOX 30805 SALT LAKE CITY, UT 84130-0805	(503) 225-5336 (800) 452-7278 WWW.OR.REGENCE.COM/PROVIDER/

BLUE CROSS BLUE SHIELD-PENNSYLVANIA

Payer ID PABLS	PO BOX 890179 CAMP HILL, PA 17089-0179	(888) 829-8599 WWW.BCNEPA.COM/PROVIDERS/
Payer ID PABLS	PO BOX 41474 PHILADELPHIA, PA 19101	(800) 275-2583 WWW.IBX.COM/PROVIDERS/
Payer ID PABLS	PO BOX 890062 CAMP HILL, PA 17089-0062	(800) 248-4180 WWW.HIGHMARKBLUESHIELD.COM

BLUE CROSS BLUE SHIELD-PUERTO RICO

Payer ID PRBLS	PO BOX 363628 SAN JUAN, PR 00936-3628	(787) 774-6060 (800) 676-2583 WWW.SSSPR.COM/SSSPORTAL/PROVIDER/

BLUE CROSS BLUE SHIELD-RHODE ISLAND

Payer ID RIBLS	500 EXCHANGE ST PROVIDENCE, RI 02903	(800) 230-9050 WWW.BCBSRI.COM/PROVIDERS

BLUE CROSS BLUE SHIELD-ROCHESTER NY

Payer ID N7BLS	PO BOX 22999 ROCHESTER, NY 14692-2999	(585) 454-4951 (800) 462-0116 WWW.EXCELLUSBCBS.COM/WPS/PORTAL/XL/PRV/

BLUE CROSS BLUE SHIELD-SOUTH CAROLINA

Payer ID SCBLS	PO BOX 100300 COLUMBIA, SC 29202	(803) 736-1576 (800) 334-2583 WWW.SOUTHCAROLINABLUES.COM/PROVIDERS.ASPX

BLUE CROSS BLUE SHIELD-SOUTH DAKOTA

Payer ID SDBLS	PO BOX 5023 SIOUX FALLS, SD 57117-5023	(800) 831-4818 WWW.WELLMARK.COM/PROVIDER/CLAIMSANDPAYMENTS/CLAIMSANDPAYMENTSHOME.ASPX

BLUE CROSS BLUE SHIELD-TENNESSEE

Payer ID TNBLS	1 CAMERON HILL CIR STE 0002 CHATTANOOGA, TN 37402-0002	(800) 924-7141 WWW.BCBST.COM/PROVIDERS/

BLUE CROSS BLUE SHIELD-TEXAS

Payer ID TXBLS	PO BOX 660044 DALLAS, TX 75266-0044	(972) 766-6900 (800) 451-0287 WWW.BCBSTX.COM/PROVIDER/

BLUE CROSS BLUE SHIELD-UTAH

Payer ID UTBLS	PO BOX 30270 SALT LAKE CITY, UT 84130-0270	(801) 333-2100 (877) 417-6222 WWW.UT.REGENCE.COM/PHYSICIAN/

BLUE CROSS BLUE SHIELD-UTICA NY

Payer ID N4BLS	PO BOX 4809 SYRACUSE, NY 13221-4809	(315) 671-6400 (800) 920-8889 WWW.EXCELLUSBCBS.COM/WPS/PORTAL/XL/PRV/

BLUE CROSS BLUE SHIELD-VERMONT

Payer ID VTBLS	PO BOX 186 MONTPELIER, VT 05601-0186	(800) 395-3389 WWW.BCBSVT.COM/PROVIDER/CLAIMS/CLAIMSUBMISSION.HTML

BLUE CROSS BLUE SHIELD-VIRGINIA

Payer ID VABLS	PO BOX 14113 LEXINGTON, KY 40512-4113	(202) 479-6560 (800) 842-5975 WWW.CAREFIRST.COM
Payer ID VABLS	PO BOX 27401 RICHMOND,, VA 23279	(800) 533-1120 WWW.ANTHEM.COM

BLUE CROSS BLUE SHIELD-WASHINGTON

	PO BOX 30271 SALT LAKE CITY, UT 84130-0271	(206) 464-3600 (800) 458-3523 WWW.WA.REGENCE.COM/PROVIDER/
	PO BOX 91059 SEATTLE, WA 98111-9159	(877) 342-5258 WWW.PREMERA.COM/STELLENT/GROUPS/PUBLIC/DOCUMENTS/ASSOCIATEDFILES/PROVIDERSHOME.ASP

BLUE CROSS BLUE SHIELD-WEST VIRGINIA

Payer ID WVBLS	PO BOX 7026 WHEELING, WV 26003	(304) 234-7012 (800) 543-7822 WWW.HIGHMARKBCBSWV.COM

BLUE CROSS BLUE SHIELD-WESTERN NEW YORK

Payer ID N1BLS	PO BOX 80 BUFFALO, NY 14240-0080	(716) 884-2800 (800) 544-2583 WWW.BCBSWNY.COM/WPS/PORTAL/WNY/PROVIDERSHOME

BLUE CROSS BLUE SHIELD-WISCONSIN

Payer ID WIBLS	PO BOX 105187 ATLANTA, GA 30348	(888) 571-9055 WWW.ANTHEM.COM/HOME-PROVIDERS.HTML

BLUE CROSS BLUE SHIELD-WYOMING

Payer ID WYBLS	PO BOX 2266 CHEYENNE, WY 82003-2266	(888) 442-2376 WWW.BCBSWY.COM/PROVIDERS/

BLUE CROSS CANADA

	10009 108TH ST NW EDMONTON, AB T5J 3C5	(780) 498-8000 (800) 661-6995 WWW.AB.BLUECROSS.CA/CLAIMING.HTML
	PO BOX 1046 STN MAIN WINNIPEG, MB R3C-2X7	(204) 775-0151 (800) 873-2583 WWW.MB.BLUECROSS.CA
	PO BOX 4433 STATION A TORONTO, ON M5W 3Y7	(866) 732-2583 WWW.USEBLUE.COM

B

BLUE CROSS OF CALIFORNIA

Payer ID 47198	PO BOX 60007 LOS ANGELES, CA 90060-0007	(800) 677-6669 WWW.ANTHEM.COM/CA/HOME-PROVIDERS.HTML

BLUE CROSS OF IDAHO

Payer ID IDBLC	PO BOX 7408 BOISE, ID 83707	(208) 345-4550 (800) 274-4018 WWW.BCIDAHO.COM/PROVIDERS/SIGNON.ASP

BLUE CROSS OF NORTHEASTERN PENNSLYVANIA

Payer ID 23241	PO BOX 890179 CAMP HILL, PA 17089-0179	(800) 822-8752 WWW.BCNEPA.COM/PROVIDERS/

BLUE CROSS-CENTRAL PENNSYLVANIA

	PO BOX 779519 HARRISBURG, PA 17177-9519	(866) 688-2242 WWW.CAPBLUECROSS.COM/PROVIDERS/

BLUE CROSS-PENNSYLVANIA (INDEPENDENCE)

	PO BOX 41474 PHILADELPHIA, PA 19101	(800) 275-2583 WWW.IBX.COM/PROVIDERS/

BLUE SHIELD OF CALIFORNIA

Payer ID BS001	PO BOX 272510 CHICO, CA 95927-2510	(800) 824-8839 WWW.BLUESHIELDCA.COM/PROVIDER/HOME.SP
Payer ID BS001	PO BOX 1505 REDBLUFF, CA 96080-1505	(800) 622-0632 WWW.BLUESHIELDCA.COM/PROVIDER/HOME.SP
Payer ID BS001	PO BOX 272570 CHICO, CA 95927-2570	(800) 241-4896 WWW.BLUESHIELDCA.COM/PROVIDER/HOME.SP
Payer ID BS001	PO BOX 272540 CHICO, CA 95927-2540	(800) 541-6652 WWW.BLUESHIELDCA.COM/PROVIDER/HOME.SP

BLUE SHIELD OF CENTRAL NEW YORK

	333 BUTTERNUT DRIVE SYRACUSE, NY 13214-1803 P.O. BOX 22999 ROCHESTER, NY 14692	(800) 920-8889 (800) 548-6017 HTTPS://WWW.EXCELLUSBCBS.COM/WPS/PORTAL/XL/PRV/

BLUE SHIELD OF IDAHO

Payer ID IDBLS	PO BOX 31603 SALT LAKE CITY, UT 84131-0603	(800) 475-1149 WWW.ID.REGENCE.COM/PHYSICIAN/CLAIMS-AND-BILLING/SUBMITTING-CLAIMS/

BLUE SHIELD OF MAINE

Payer ID MEBLS	PO BOX 533 NORTH HAVEN, CT 06473	(800) 832-6011 WWW.ANTHEM.COM

BLUEGRASS FAMILY HEALTH

Payer ID 61124	PO BOX 22738 LEXINGTON, KY 40522-2738	(859) 269-4475 (800) 787-2680 WWW.BGFH.COM

BMC HEALTHNET

Payer ID 13337	PO BOX 55282 BOSTON, MA 02205-5282	(888) 566-0008 WWW.BMCHP.ORG

BMI HEALTH PLANS

PO BOX 2187
BARTLESVILLE, OK 74005

(918) 335-0387
(800) 824-5034
WWW.BMI-HEALTHPLANS.COM

BOILERMAKERS NATIONAL HEALTH & WELFARE FUND

Payer ID 36609

PO BOX 182223
CHATTANOOGA, TN 37422

(800) 244-6224
WWW.BNF-KC.COM/PROVIDERS.ASPX

BOLLINGER, INC

Payer ID BOLL1

PO BOX 5000
SHORT HILLS, NJ 07078-0727

(973) 467-0444
(800) 526-1379
WWW.BOLLINGERINSURANCE.COM/CONTACTUS/CLAIMS.ASPX

BOON GROUP

Payer ID BOONG

PO BOX 14079
LEXINGTON, KY 40512-4079

(800) 368-2666
WWW.BOONGROUP.COM

BOON-CHAPMAN BENEFIT ADMINISTRATORS

Payer ID 74238

PO BOX 9201
AUSTIN, TX 78766-9201

(800) 252-9653
WWW.BOONCHAPMAN.COM/PROVIDERPAGE.ASPX

BOSTON MEDICAL CENTER HEALTHNET

Payer ID 13337

PO BOX 55282
BOSTON, MA 02205-5282

(888) 566-0008
HTTP://PORTALS.BMCHP.ORG/PAGES/PROVIDERS/PROVIDER_HOME.ASPX

BOULDER ADMINISTRATION SERVICES

Payer ID 20381

PO BOX 1046
BOULDER, MT 59632

(406) 225-3699
(877) 406-3699
WWW.BOULDERADMIN.COM/

BPS INC

Payer ID 48964

PO BOX 2793
HIGH POINT, NC 27261-2793

(336) 889-2003
WWW.MYBENEFITS.BZ

BRAVO HEALTH

Payer ID 52192

PO BOX 981706
EL PASO, TX 79998-1706

(800) 291-0396
WWW.BRAVOHEALTH.COM/PROVIDERS

BRIDGESTONE/FIRESTONE

Payer ID 88033

PO BOX 5224
JANESVILLE, WI 53547

(330) 379-4500

BRIDGEWAY ARIZONA

Payer ID 68054

PO BOX 3040
FARMINGTON, MO 63640

(866) 475-3129
WWW.BRIDGEWAYHS.COM/FOR-PROVIDERS/

BROADSPIRE AUTO

Payer ID TP021

1001 SUMMIT BLVD
ATLANTA, GA 30319

(866) 830-2383
WWW.CHOOSEBROADSPIRE.COM

BROKERAGE CONCEPTS

Payer ID 51037

PO BOX 60608
KING OF PRUSSIA, PA 19406-0608

(610) 337-2600
WWW.BCITPA.COM/MAIN.CFM

BROWARD HEALTH

Payer ID 37314

303 SE 17TH STREET
FORT LAUDERDALE, FL 33316

(954) 847-4315
WWW.BROWARDHEALTH.ORG

B

BROWN & BROWN

Payer ID 59069 | PO BOX 7048
ORANGE, CA 92863 | (714) 939-0800
(800) 821-0540
WWW.BBINSURANCE.COM

BROWN & TOLAND MEDICAL GROUP

Payer ID 94316 | PO BOX 640469
SAN FRANCISCO, CA 94164-0469 | (415) 972-6002
(800) 225-5637
WWW.BROWNANDTOLAND.COM/

BROWN AND TOLAND SUTTERSELECT

Payer ID BTSS1 | PO BOX 640469
SAN FRANCISCO, CA 94164-0469 | (415) 972-6002
(800) 225-5637
WWW.BROWNANDTOLAND.COM/

BUCKEYE COMMUNITY HEALTH

Payer ID 32004 | PO BOX 6200
FARMINGTON, MO 63640 | (866) 296-8731
WWW.BCHPOHIO.COM/FOR-PROVIDERS/

BUILDERS INSURANCE GROUP

Payer ID WE078 | PO BOX 723099
ATLANTA, GA 31139-0099 | (678) 309-4000
(800) 883-9305
WWW.BLDRS.COM

BUNCH & ASSOCIATES

Payer ID WC812 | 3500 REYNOLDS RD
LAKELAND, FL 33803 | (863) 669-0861
WWW.BUNCHCARE.COM

BUNKER HILL INSURANCE

Payer ID WE043 | 695 ATLANTIC AVE
BOSTON, MA 02111 | (617) 956-1775
(866) 322-2442
WWW.BUNERHILLINS.COM

BUTLER BENEFITS

Payer ID 42150 | PO BOX 3310
DAVENPORT, IA 52808-3310 | (563) 327-2200
(866) 927-2200
WWW.BUTLERINS.COM/PROVIDERS/

C AND O EMPLOYEES' HOSPITAL ASSOCIATION

Payer ID 23708	511 MAIN ST 2ND FL CLIFTON FORGE, VA 24422-1166	(540) 862-5728 (800) 679-9135 WWW.COEHA.COM

CA KAISER PERMANENTE

Payer ID KS003	PO BOX 12923 OAKLAND, CA 94604-2923	(800) 390-3510 WWW.KAISERPERMANENTE.ORG/

CAC

Payer ID 62413	PO BOX 8402 LONDON, KY 40742	(800) 410-7778 WWW.MHBP.COM

CADENT ADMINISTRATORS

Payer ID 33192	100 1ST AVE S ST PETERSBURG, FL 33701	(727) 824-0800

CAL-OPTIMA DIRECT

Payer ID CALOP	PO BOX 11037 ORANGE, CA 92856	(714) 246-8600 (888) 587-8088 WWW.CALOPTIMA.ORG/HOME/ PROVIDERS.ASPX

CALIFORNIA CARE

Payer ID IP059	PO BOX 1395 EUREKA, CA 95502	(707) 443-4563 (866) 443-4563 WWW.HDNFMC.COM

CALIFORNIA EYE CARE - NEW CENTURY HEALTH

Payer ID NCH05	1141 W. REDONDO BEACH, SUITE 101 GARDENA, CA 90247	(310) 767-7814 WWW.CENTURYEYECARE.COM

CALIFORNIA MEDICAID HMO (CALOPTIMA)

Payer ID CALOP	PO BOX 11037 ORANGE, CA 92856	(714) 246-8600 WWW.CALOPTIMA.ORG/HOME/ PROVIDERS.ASPX

CALIFORNIA MEDICAID HMO (HEALTHNET)

Payer ID 95567	PO BOX 14702 LEXINGTON, KY 40512	(800) 675-6110 WWW.HEALTHNET.COM

CALIFORNIA MEDICAID HMO (INLAND EMPIRE)

	PO BOX 10129 SAN BERNADINO, CA 92423	(909) 890-2054 (866) 223-4347 HTTPS://WW3.IEHP.ORG/EN/PROVIDERS/

CALIFORNIA MEDICAID HMO (KEARN HEALTH SYSTEMS)

	PO BOX 25003 BAKERSFIELD, CA 93311	(661) 664-5000 WWW.KEARNHEALTHSYSTEMS.COM

CALIFORNIA MEDICAID HMO (LA CARE)

Payer ID LACAR	PO BOX 811580 LOS ANGELES, CA 90081	(866) 522-2736 WWW.LACARE.ORG/PROVIDERS

CALIFORNIA STATE COMPENSATION INSURANCE FUND

Payer ID WR839	PO BOX 8192 PLEASANTON, CA 94588	(888) 782-8338 WWW.STATEFUNDCA.COM

CAMERON AND ASSOCIATES

Payer ID CAMAA	55 YORK ST STE 400 TORONTO, ON CANADA, M5J1R7	(866) 779-7953 WWW.CAMERONASSOCIATES.COM

CANNON COCHRAN MANAGEMENT SERVICES, INC.

Payer ID 71057

PO BOX 19600
IRVINE, CA 92623

(949) 743-1230
(800) 277-6512
WWW.STRATACARE.COM

CAP MANAGEMENT SYSTEMS

Payer ID IP080

15821 VENTURA BLVD STE 600
ENCINO, CA 91436
PO BOX 261040
ENCINO, CA 91426

(818) 461-5000
WWW.CAPCMS.COM/DEFAULT.ASPX

CAPE HEALTH PLAN

Payer ID 38245

PO BOX 22812
LONG BEACH, CA 90801

(888) 562-5442
WWW.MOLINAHEALTHCARE.COM/

CAPITAL BLUE CROSS

Payer ID 23045

PO BOX 779503
HARRISBURG, PA 17177-9503

(717) 541-7000
(800) 962-2242
WWW.CAPBLUECROSS.COM

CAPITAL DISTRICT PHP

Payer ID SX065

PO BOX 66602
ALBANY, NY 12206-6602

(800) 926-7526
WWW.CDPHP.COM/

CAPITAL HEALTH PLAN

Payer ID 95112

PO BOX 15349
TALLAHASEE, FL 32317

(850) 383-3311
WWW.CAPITALHEALTH.COM/

CAPITOL ADMINISTRATORS

Payer ID 68011

PO BOX 2318
RANCHO CORDOVA, CA 95741-2318

(800) 331-5301
WWW.CAPITOLADM.COM

CAPITOL INDEMNITY CORP

Payer ID WB239

1600 ASPEN COMMONS
MIDDLETON, WI 53562
PO BOX 5900
MADISON, WI 53705-0900

(608) 829-4200
(800) 475-4450
WWW.CAPITOLINDEMNITY.COM

CAPROCK HEALTH PLANS INC.

4401 82ND ST
LUBBOCK, TX 79424
PO BOX 21548
EAGAN, MN 55121-0548

(800) 747-9446
WWW.CAPROCKHP.COM/PROVIDER.PHP

CAPSTONE HEALTH PLAN, INC

Payer ID 86044

914 N SAN FRANCISCO ST STE A
FLAGSTAFF, AZ 86001-3236

(928) 779-2113
(800) 336-3874
WWW.NAZCAP.COM

CARE 1ST HEALTH PLAN OF ARIZONA

Payer ID 57116

2355 E CAMELBACK RD STE 300
PHOENIX, AZ 85016-3417

(866) 560-4042
WWW.CARE1ST.COM/AZ

CARE 1ST HEALTH PLAN OF CA

Payer ID 57115

601 POTRERO GRANDE DR MAIL STOP: CL001
MONTEREY PARK, CA 91755

(800) 605-2556
WWW.CARE1ST.COM

CARE ACCESS HEALTH PLAN

PO BOX 4276
HALLANDALE, FL 33008

(305) 614-5010
(877) 411-2247
HTTP://MYCAREACCESS.COM/

CARE FIRST BLUE CROSS BLUE SHIELD

PO BOX 14116
LEXINGTON, KY 40512-4116

(202) 479-6560
(800) 842-5975
WWW.PROVIDER.CAREFIRST.COM

CARE IMPROVEMENT PLUS

Payer ID 77082

PO BOX 488
LINTHICUM, MD 21090-0488

(866) 679-3119
WWW.CAREIMPROVEMENTPLUS.COM

CARE PARTNERS

Payer ID 43172

68 SWEETEN CREEK RD
ASHEVILLE, NC 28803-2318

(828) 277-4800
WWW.CAREPARTNERS.ORG

CARE PLUS CARDIOLOGY- NEW CENTURY HEALTH

Payer ID NCH04

675 PLACENTIA AVE STE 300
BREA, CA 92821

(888) 999-7713
WWW.NEWCENTURYHEALTH.COM/

CARE PLUS HEALTH PLANS

Payer ID 65031

PO BOX 31286
TAMPA, FL 33631-3286

(866) 313-7587
WWW.CAREPLUSHEALTHPLANS.COM

CARE TO CARE RADIOLOGY BENEFIT MANAGEMENT

Payer ID 41222

755 SECOND AVE 2ND FL
NEW YORK, NY 10017

(212) 747-1000
WWW.CARETOCARE.COM

CARE WISCONSIN HEALTH PLAN

Payer ID 27004

PO BOX 849
BUCKEYSTOWN, MD 21717

(877) 496-3858
WWW.CAREWISCONSINHEALTHPLAN.ORG

CARECENTRIX

Payer ID 11345

111 FOUNDERS PLAZA STE 801
EAST HARTFORD, CT 06108

(860) 528-4038
WWW.CARECENTRIXPORTAL.COM

CARECORE NATIONAL

Payer ID 14182

PO BOX 798
LAKE KATRINE, NY 12449

(800) 420-3471
WWW.CARECORENATIONAL.COM

CARECORE NATIONAL OXFORD

Payer ID 14180

PO BOX 680
LAKE KATRINE, NY 12449

(800) 420-3471
WWW.CARECORENATIONAL.COM

CARECORE NATIONAL WELLCARE

Payer ID 14188

PO BOX 758
LAKE KATRINE, NY 12449

(800) 420-3471
WWW.CARECORENATIONAL.COM

CARECORE NATIONAL, LLC - AETNA CLAIMS

Payer ID 14179

PO BOX 660
LAKE KATRINE, NY 12449

(800) 420-3471
WWW.CARECORENATIONAL.COM

CARECORE NATIONAL, LLC - HEALTH NET NEW JERSEY

Payer ID 14185

PO BOX 759
LAKE KATRINE, NY 12449

(800) 420-3471
WWW.CARECORENATIONAL.COM

CARECORE-HEALTHNET

Payer ID 14184

PO BOX 14702
LEXINGTON, KY 40512

(800) 441-5741
WWW.HEALTHNET.COM

CAREFIRST ADMINISTRATORS

Payer ID 75191

PO BOX 3900
MERRIFIELD, VA 22116-3900

(866) 945-9839
WWW.CFABLUE.COM

CAREFIRST BCBS - DC, NATIONAL CAPITAL AREA

Payer ID SB580

PO BOX 14116
LEXINGTON, KY 40512

(202) 479-6560
(800) 842-5975
WWW.PROVIDER.CAREFIRST.COM

CARELINK HEALTH PLAN

Payer ID 25139

PO BOX 7373
LONDON, KY 40742-7103

(800) 348-2922
HTTP://
CHCWESTVIRGINIA.COVENTRYHEALTHCARE.COM/

CARELINK MEDICAID

Payer ID 25140

PO BOX 7373
LONDON, KY 40742

(888) 348-2966
HTTP://CHCMEDICAID-
WESTVIRGINIA.COVENTRYHEALTHCARE.COM/

CAREMORE

Payer ID CM001

12900 PARK PLAZA DR STE 150 MS-6110
CERRITOS, CA 90703

(888) 291-1358
WWW.CAREMORE.COM

CARENET OF VIRGINIA

Payer ID 25142

PO BOX 7702
LONDON, KY 40742

(800) 449-1944
HTTP://CHCMEDICAID-
VIRGINIA.COVENTRYHEALTHCARE.COM/

CAREOREGON, INC.

Payer ID 93975

PO BOX 40328
PORTLAND, OR 97240

(503) 416-8080
(800) 224-4840
WWW.CAREOREGON.ORG

CAREPLUS HEALTH PLANS

Payer ID 65031

11430 NW 20TH ST STE 300
DORAL, FL 33172

(855) 605-6171
WWW.CARE-PLUS-HEALTH-PLANS.COM

CAREPOINT HEALTH PLAN

Payer ID 77023

PO BOX 3236
SCRANTON, PA 18505

(888) 657-1207
HTTP://CAREPOINTHEALTHPLANS.ORG/
PROVIDERS/

CARESOURCE

Payer ID 31114

PO BOX 8730
DAYTON, OH 45401-8730

(800) 488-0134
WWW.CARESOURCE.COM

CARESOURCE OF INDIANA

Payer ID 37311

PO BOX 8730
DAYTON, OH 45401

(800) 488-0134
WWW.CARESOURCE.COM

CAREWORKS

Payer ID 10010

PO BOX 94748
CLEVELAND, OH 44101

(888) 627-7586
WWW.CAREWORKSMCO.COM/

CAREWORKS OF OHIO (OH BWC)

Payer ID CAREW

PO BOX 8101
DUBLIN, OH 43016

(800) 837-3200
WWW.CCI.WORKSCOMP.COM

CARILION CLINIC MEDICARE HEALTH PLAN

Payer ID 77015

PO BOX 3237
SCRANTON, PA 18505

(800) 779-2285
WWW.CARILIONMEDICARE.COM

CAROLINA CARE PLAN

Payer ID 29076

PO BOX 6018
CLEVELAND, OH 44101

(800) 232-2821
WWW.CAROLINACAREPLAN.COM

CAROLINA CRESCENT

Payer ID 68055 | PO BOX 5386
RICHMOND, VA 23220-5386 | (866) 748-8661
WWW.CAROLINACHP.COM

CAROLINA CRESCENT HEALTH PLAN

Payer ID SX191 | PO BOX 5386
RICHMOND, VA 23220-5386 | (866) 748-8661
WWW.CAROLINACHP.COM

CAROLINA SUMMIT HEALTHCARE, INC

Payer ID 56195 | PO BOX 14669
CINCINNATI, OH 45250-0669 | (877) 507-7360
WWW.SECURE.HEALTHX.COM/PROVIDER.ASP

CARPENTER'S OF GREATER ST. LOUIS H&W FUND

Payer ID 25125 | 1419 HAMPTON AVE
ST LOUIS, MO 63139-3115 | (877) 232-3863
WWW.CARPDC.ORG

CARPENTERS BENEFITS FUNDS

1811 SPRING GARDEN ST
PHILADELPHIA, PA 19130-3916 | (215) 568-0430
HTTPS://WWW.PHILACARPENTERFUNDS.ORG/DEFAULT.ASPX

CARPENTERS' AND MILLWRIGHTS' HEALTH BENEFIT TRUST FUND

Payer ID COMPU | PO BOX 182223
CHATANOOGA, TN 37422-7223 | (800) 244-6224
HTTPS://CARPENTERS-MILLWRIGHTSBENEFITS.COM/

CARPET, LINOLEUM AND RESILIENT TILE LAYERS HEALTH AND WELFARE FUND

Payer ID COMPU | PO BOX 188004
CHATTANOOGA, TN 37422 | (303) 745-1941

CASCADE HEALTH SOLUTIONS

2650 SUZANNE WAY, SUITE 200
EUGENE, OR 97408 | (541) 228-3000
HTTP://WWW.CASCADEHEALTH.ORG/

CATHOLIC HEALTHCARE WEST

Payer ID SX183 | 185 BERRY ST STE 300
SAN FRANCISCO, CA 94107 | (415) 438-5500
WWW.CHWHEALTH.ORG

CATHOLIC MUTUAL

Payer ID WP870 | 10843 OLD MILL RD
OMAHA, NE 68154-2600 | (800) 228-6108
WWW.CATHOLICMUTUAL.ORG

CBA BLUE

Payer ID 03036 | PO BOX 2365
SOUTH BURLINGTON, VT 05407-2365 | (888) 222-9206
WWW.CBABLUEVT.COM

CBA, INC. (COOPERATIVE BENEFITS ADMINISTRATORS)

Payer ID 52132 | PO BOX 6249
LINCOLN, NE 68506 | (402) 483-9200

CBCA ADMINISTRATORS, INC

Payer ID 55438 | PO BOX 9888
SAVANNAH, GA 31412 | (912) 691-1551
(800) 631-3441
WWW.CBCA.COM

Payer ID 55438 | PO BOX 1272
MINNEAPOLIS, MN 55440-1272 | (952) 829-3500
(888) 446-5710
WWW.CBCA.COM

CBHA CAROLINA BEHAVIORAL HEALTH ALLIANCE

Payer ID 56215

PO BOX 571137
WINSTON-SALEM, NC 27157-1137

(800) 475-7900
WWW.CBHALLC.COM/

CBHNP HEALTH CHOICES

Payer ID 65391

PO BOX 6600
HARRISBURG, PA 17112

(888) 700-7370
WWW.CBHNP.ORG/HCPROVIDERS.ASPX

CBIZ BENEFITS & INSURANCE SERVICES

Payer ID 31158

6050 OAK TREE BLVD SOUTH STE 500
CLEVELAND, OH 44131

(216) 447-9000
(800) 895-0002
WWW.CBIZ.COM/BENEFITS

CBSA

Payer ID 41124

PO BOX 27267
MINNEAPOLIS, MN 55427-0267

(877) 637-4824
WWW.MERITAIN.COM

CCMC - COMPREHENSIVE CARE MANAGEMENT CORP.

Payer ID CCMC1

1250 WATERS PLACE STE 602
BRONX, NY 10461-2704

(800) 761-5602
WWW.CCMNY.ORG

CCMSI

2 E MAIN ST STE 208
DANVILLE, IL 61832

(217) 446-1089
(800) 252-5059
WWW.CCMSI.COM

CCMSI-MIDLAND LLC

Payer ID WR322

2 E MAIN ST
DANVILLE, IL 61832
PO BOX 1430
DANVILLE, IL 61834-1430

(217) 446-1089
(800) 252-5059
WWW.CCMSI.COM

CDO TECHNOLOGIES

Payer ID 87065

5200 SPRINGFIELD ST STE 320
DAYTON, OH 45431-1255

(937) 258-0022
WWW.CDOTECH.COM

CDS GROUP HEALTH

Payer ID 88022

PO BOX 50190
SPARKS, NV 89435-0190

(775) 352-6900
(800) 455-4236
WWW.CDSGROUPHEALTH.COM

CEDARS-SINAI MEDICAL NETWORK SERVICES CLAIMS

Payer ID 95166

PO BOX 6250
NEWPORT BEACH, CA 92658

(800) 700-6424
WWW.CEDARS-SINAI.EDU

CELTIC INSURANCE CO

Payer ID CELTC

PO BOX 26440
LITTLE ROCK, AR 72221

(312) 332-5401
(800) 477-7870
WWW.CELTIC-NET.COM

CELTICARE

Payer ID 68060

PO BOX 3000
FARMINGTON, MO 63640-3824

(866) 895-1786
WWW.CELTICAREHEALTHPLAN.COM

CEMENT MASONS & PLASTERERS HEALTH & WELFARE TRUST

Payer ID 91136

PO BOX 34203
SEATTLE, WA 98124-1203

(800) 735-7053
WWW.WPAS-INC.COM

CENCAL HEALTH

4050 CALLE REAL
SANTA BARBARA, CA 93110

(805) 562-1676
HTTP://WWW.CENCALHEALTH.ORG/
FOR_PROVIDERS/INDEX.HTML

CENPATICO BEHAVIORAL HEALTH AZ

Payer ID 68048	PO BOX 6500 FARMINGTON, MO 63640	(866) 495-6738 WWW.CENPATICOAZ.COM

CENPATICO FLORIDA

Payer ID 68058	PO BOX 6900 FARMINGTON, MO 63640-3818	(877) 730-2117 WWW.CENPATICO.COM

CENPATICO GEORGIA

Payer ID 68050	PO BOX 6700 FARMINGTON, MO 63640	(866) 324-3632 WWW.CENPATICO.COM

CENPATICO INDIANA

Payer ID 68052	PO BOX 6800 FARMINGTON, MO 63640	(800) 224-1991 WWW.CENPATICO.COM

CENPATICO KANSAS

Payer ID 68047	PO BOX 6400 FARMINGTON, MO 63640-3807	(866) 896-7293 WWW.CENPATICO.COM

CENPATICO MASSACHUSETTS

Payer ID 68061	PO BOX 7200 FARMINGTON, MO 63640-3818	(866) 324-3632 WWW.CENPATICO.COM

CENPATICO OHIO

Payer ID 68051	PO BOX 6150 FARMINGTON, MO 63640	(800) 224-1991 WWW.CENPATICO.COM

CENPATICO WISCONSIN

Payer ID 68046	PO BOX 6123 FARMINGTON, MO 63640-6123	(877) 730-2117 WWW.CENPATICO.COM

CENTENE ADVANTAGE PLANS

Payer ID 68056	7700 FORSYTH BLVD ST LOUIS, MO 63105-1810	(314) 725-4477 WWW.CENTENE.COM

CENTER LIGHT HEALTH CARE

	1250 WATERS PLACE TOWER 1 STE 602 BRONX, NY 10461	(877) 226-8500 WWW.CENTERLIGHTHEALTHCARE.ORG/FOR-PROVIDERS

CENTER POINT HUMAN SERVICES

	4045 UNIVERSITY PKWY WINSTON-SALEM, NC 27106	(336) 714-9100 WWW.CPHS.ORG

CENTERCARE

Payer ID 13357	1225 FAIRWAY ST BOWLING GREEN, KY 42103-2477	(800) 972-7038 WWW.CENTERCARE.COM/

CENTINELA IPA

Payer ID IP080	PO BOX 4069 COVINA, CA 91723	(909) 971-6717

CENTRAL BENEFITS MUTUAL

Payer ID 31118	PO BOX 1224 LITTLE ROCK, AR 72203-1224	(800) 972-3025 WWW.HEALTHSCOPEBENEFITS.COM

CENTRAL CALIFORNIA ALLIANCE

Payer ID CALL	PO BOX 660015 SCOTTS VALLEY, CA 95066-4924	(831) 430-5503 (800) 700-3874 WWW.CCAH-ALLIANCE.ORG/

C

C

CENTRAL DATA SERVICES, INC

5 HOT METAL ST STE 200
PITTSBURGH, PA 15203-2329

(412) 432-1125
WWW.CDSADMINISTRATORS.COM

CENTRAL PENNSYLVANIA TEAMSTERS HEALTH & WELFARE FUND

PO BOX 15224
READING, PA 19612-5224

(610) 320-5500
(800) 331-0420
WWW.CENTRALPATEAMSTERS.COM

CENTRAL RESERVE LIFE

Payer ID 34097

PO BOX 21680
EAGAN, MN 55121

(800) 321-3997
WWW.GASBINSURANCE.COM

CENTRAL STATES FUNDS

PO BOX 5111
DES PLAINES, IL 60017-5111

(800) 323-5000
WWW.CENTRALSTATESFUNDS.ORG

CENTRAL STATES SOUTHEAST AND SOUTHWEST AREAS HEALTH AND WELFARE AND PENSIONS FUNDS

Payer ID 36215

PO BOX 5113
DES PLAINES, IL 60017-5113

(800) 323-2190
WWW.CENTRALSTATESFUNDS.ORG

CENTRAL VALLEY MEDICAL GROUP

Payer ID E3510

1101 SYLVAN AVE STE C-103
MODESTO, CA 95350

(209) 573-7401
(800) 956-8000
WWW.CENTRALVALLEYMEDICALGROUP.COM

CENTURY HEALTH SOLUTIONS

Payer ID 48120

PO BOX 1676
TOPEKA, KS 66601-1676

(785) 233-1816
(800) 227-0089
WWW.CENTURY-HEALTH.COM

CHA- COMMONWEALTH HEALTH ALLIANCE

Payer ID 23171

PO BOX 6602
ASHLAND, VA 23116

(804) 402-3833
WWW.THEDOCSALLIANCE.COM/

CHAMPVA-HAC

Payer ID 84146

PO BOX 469064
DENVER, CO 80246-9064

(800) 733-8387
WWW.VA.GOV

CHATWINS HEALTHCARE ADMINISTRATORS

Payer ID CHAT1

11 STANWIX ST
PITTSBURGH, PA 15222

(412) 281-7555

CHAUTAUQUA COUNTY HEALTH PLAN

Payer ID 16600

7 N ERIE ST HRC BLDG 4TH FL
MAYVILLE, NY 14757-1095

(716) 753-4314
WWW.CO.CHAUTAUQUA.NY.US

CHCS SERVICES, INC

411 NORTH BAYLEN
PENSACOLA, FL 32501-3901

(800) 370-7684
WWW.CHCSSERVICES.COM

CHESAPEAKE LIFE INSURANCE CO.

Payer ID 59223

PO BOX 981606
EL PASO, TX 79998

(800) 733-8880
WWW.CHESAPEAKEINS.COM

CHESTERFIELD RESOURCES, INC

Payer ID 34154

3520 FOREST LAKE DR
UNIONTOWN, OH 44685-8105
PO BOX 1884
AKRON, OH 44309-1884

(330) 896-4311
(800) 321-0935

Payer ID 34154	PO BOX 610 GREEN, OH 44232	(330) 896-4311 (800) 321-0935

CHESTERFIELD SERVICES

Payer ID WB193	4544 W 103RD ST STE 101 OAK LAWN, IL 60453	(708) 529-7800 WWW.CHESTERFIELD-INS.COM

CHILD HEALTH AND DISABILITY PREVENTION TREATMENT

Payer ID AMM03	PO BOX 3689 LONG BEACH, CA 90853	(800) 206-6591 HTTPS://OCHCA.AMM.CC/ BILLINGINSTRUCTIONS.ASPX?P=CTU

CHILDREN FIRST MEDICAL GROUP

Payer ID 94321	6425 CHRISTIE AVE #110 EMERYVILLE, CA 94608	(510) 428-3154 WWW.CHILDREN-FIRST-MEDICAL- GROUP.COM

CHILDREN'S COMMUNITY HEALTH PLAN

Payer ID 39113	PO BOX 56099 MADISON, WI 53705	(800) 482-8010 WWW.CHILDRENSCHP.COM

CHILDREN'S PHYSICIANS MEDICAL GROUP

Payer ID CPMG1	3860 CALLE FORTUNADA #210 SAN DIEGO, CA 92123	(858) 309-6270 WWW.CPMGSANDIEGO.COM/

CHILDRENS HOSPITAL OF ORANGE COUNTY HEALTH ALLIANCE

Payer ID 33065	PO BOX 62108 PHOENIX, AZ 85082-2108	(800) 387-1103 WWW.CHOCHEALTHALLIANCE.COM

CHINESE COMMUNITY HEALTH PLAN

Payer ID 94302	445 GRANT AVE STE 700 SAN FRANCISCO, CA 94108-3250	(415) 955-8800 (888) 775-7888 WWW.CCHPHMO.COM

CHIROCARE

Payer ID ACN01	12400 W HWY 71 STE 350-428 AUSTIN, TX 78738-6517	(866) 209-0070 WWW.CHIROCAREPLAN.COM/

CHIROPRACTIC ASSOCIATION OF SOUTH DAKOTA

Payer ID CASD1	2301 RESEARCH PARK WAY STE 221 BROOKINGS, SD 57006	(800) 658-2214 WWW.CASD.US

CHIROPRACTIC CARE OF MINNESOTA, INC

Payer ID LNDMK	1000 COUNTY RD EAST STE 230 SHOREVIEW, MN 55126	(888) 638-7719 WWW.CHIROCARE.COM

CHIROPRACTIC CARE OF WISCONSIN, INC.

Payer ID ACN01	2825 N MAYFAIR RD STE 106 WAUWATOSA, WI 53222-4404	(414) 476-4733 WWW.CHIROCAREWI.COM

CHIROPRACTIC LIFECARE OF AMERICA

	1031 PARKSIDE COMMONS STE 202 GREENSBORO, GA 30642	(800) 775-7900 HTTP://CLAHEALTHCARE.COM

CHOC

Payer ID 33065	PO BOX 62108 PHOENIX, AZ 85082-2108	(714) 565-5100 (800) 387-1103 WWW.CHOCHEALTHALLIANCE.COM

C

CHOICE CARE NETWORK

PO BOX 19013
GREEN BAY, WI 54307

(800) 626-2741
WWW.CHOICECARENETWORK.COM

CHOICE ONE

Payer ID 76049

PO BOX 15485
AUSTIN, TX 78761

(409) 766-4064
(866) 735-3281
WWW.UTMBHCS.ORG

CHOICE PLUS

1001 AVENIDA DEL CIRCO
VENICE, FL 34285

(941) 234-4985
WWW.CHOICEPLUSLLC.COM/EN-US/HOME.ASPX

CHOICENET

Payer ID CHCNT

PO BOX 3559
ENGLEWOOD, CO 80155-3559

(800) 426-7453
WWW.CNICHS.COM

CHP DIRECT SUPERMED

Payer ID 90441

PO BOX 6018
CLEVELAND, OH 44101

(800) 362-1279
WWW.SUPERMEDNETWORK.COM

CHP/DMBA

Payer ID UH133

PO BOX 70097
SALT LAKE CITY, UT 84170

(801) 352-7270
WWW.ALLIEDHEALTHSYSTEMS.COM

CHP/EMIA

PO BOX 70097
SALT LAKE CITY, UT 84170

(801) 352-7270
WWW.ALLIEDHEALTHSYSTEMS.COM

CHP/MEDICAID

Payer ID UH135

PO BOX 70097
SALT LAKE CITY, UT 84170

(801) 352-7270
WWW.ALLIEDHEALTHSYSTEMS.COM

CHP/UUHP

Payer ID UH137

PO BOX 70097
SALT LAKE CITY, UT 84170

(801) 352-7270
WWW.ALLIEDHEALTHSYSTEMS.COM

CHP/WISE

PO BOX 70097
SALT LAKE CITY, UT 84170

(801) 352-7270
WWW.ALLIEDHEALTHSYSTEMS.COM

CHRISTIAN BROTHERS SERVICES

Payer ID 61271

1205 WINDHAM PKWY
ROMEOVILLE, IL 60446-1672

(800) 807-0100
WWW.CBSERVICES.ORG/

CHRISTUS SPOHN HEALTH NETWORK

Payer ID SPOHN

PO BOX 3947
CORPUS CHRISTI, TX 78463-3947

(361) 881-3000
WWW.CHRISTUSSPOHN.ORG

CIGNA

Payer ID 62308

PO BOX 182223
CHATTANOOGA, TN 37422-7223

(800) 882-4462
WWW.CIGNAFORHCP.CIGNA.COM

CIGNA BEHAVIORAL HEALTH

Payer ID MCCBV

PO BOX 188022
CHATTANOOGA, TN 37422

(800) 274-7603
WWW.CIGNABEHAVIORAL.COM

CIGNA HEALTHCARE FOR SENIORS - ARIZONA MEDICARE

Payer ID 86033

PO BOX 38639
PHOENIX, AZ 85069-8639

(800) 627-7534
WWW.CIGNAMEDICARE.COM

CIGNA INTERNATIONAL EXPATRIATE BENEFITS

590 NAAMANS RD
CLAYMONT, DE 19703-2308

(302) 797-3100
(800) 339-6922
WWW.CIGNAENVOY.COM

CINCINNATI CASUALTY COMPANY

Payer ID 28665

PO BOX 145496
CINCINNATI, OH 45250-5496

(888) 242-8811
WWW.CINFIN.COM

CINCINNATI INSURANCE CO

Payer ID 10677

6200 S GILLMORE RD
FAIRFIELD, OH 45014-5141
PO BOX 145496
CINCINNATI, OH 45250-5496

(513) 870-2000
WWW.CINFIN.COM

CINNCINNATI FINANCIAL CORPORATION

Payer ID 46871

PO BOX 182223
CHATTANOOGA, TN 37422-7223

(800) 244-6224
WWW.CINFIN.COM

CITIZENS INSURANCE CO

Payer ID 31534

808 N HIGHLANDER WAY
HOWELL, MI 48843-1020
PO BOX 15146
WORCESTER, MA 01615

(800) 388-1300
WWW.HANOVER.COM/THG/CITIZENS/
INDEX.HTM

CITRUS HEALTH CARE

Payer ID 10207

PO BOX 20547
TAMPA, FL 33622

(877) 624-8787
WWW.CITRUSHC.COM

CITY OF AMARILLO

Payer ID COA01

PO BOX 15130
AMARILLO, TX 79105-5130

(806) 378-4235
WWW.CI.AMARILLO.TX.US

CITY OF AUSTIN

Payer ID 74234

PO BOX 30555
SALT LAKE CITY, UT 84130-0555

(800) 430-7316
WWW.CI.AUSTIN.TX.US/BENEFITS/ENROLLMENT/
EMPLOYEE_INFO.HTM

CITY OF ODESSA

Payer ID 75600

PO BOX 4398
ODESSA, TX 79760

(432) 335-3276
WWW.ODESSA-TX.GOV

CL FRATES

Payer ID CLFR2

PO BOX 26967
OKLAHOMA CITY, OK 73126-0967

(405) 290-5696
(800) 850-7166
WWW.CLFRATES.COM/

CLAIMPATH, LTD.

605 FULTON AVE STE 2002
ROCKFORD, IL 61103-4179

(815) 964-6334

CLAIMS ADMINISTRATIVE SERVICES

Payer ID WR889

501 SHELLEY DRIVE
TYLER, TX 75701

(903) 509-8484
(800) 765-2412
WWW.CAS-SERVICES.COM

CLAIMS MANAGEMENT SERVICES

Payer ID 39141

PO BOX 10
CANTON, MA 02021

(781) 793-7800
WWW.CMSCLAIMS.COM

C

CLAIMSWARE, INC. DBA MANAGEMED

Payer ID 57080

PO BOX 6125
GREENVILLE, SC 29606-6125

(800) 992-8088
WWW.CWIBENEFITS.COM

CLARIAN HEALTH PLANS

Payer ID 95444

PO BOX 447
LINTHICUM, MD 21090-0447

(317) 963-9920
(866) 218-1524
WWW.CLARIANHEALTHPLANS.ORG

CM ADMINISTRATORS

Payer ID 56211

2543 RAVENHILL DR STE E
FAYETTEVILLE, NC 28303

(910) 484-3303

CMS CAP MANAGEMENT SYSTEMS

PO BOX 261040
ENCINO, CA 91426

(818) 461-5000
WWW.CAPCMS.COM

CNA INSURANCE

Payer ID WB168

333 S WABASH AVE
CHICAGO, IL 60604

(312) 822-2000
(888) 600-4776
WWW.CNA.COM

CNA MAILHANDERS

Payer ID 62413

PO BOX 8402
LONDON, KY 40742-8402

(800) 410-7778
WWW.DIRECTPROVIDER.COM

CNIC HEALTH SOLUTIONS

PO BOX 3559
ENGLEWOOD, CO 80155

(877) 321-4412
WWW.CNICHS.COM

COALITION AMERICA, INC

TWO CONCOURSE PARKWAY STE 300
ATLANTA, GA 30328-5347

(404) 459-7201
(888) 266-3053
WWW.COALITIONAMERICA.COM

COASTAL ADMINISTRATIVE SERVICES

Payer ID 77052

PO BOX 3070
BELLINGHAM, WA 98227

(360) 746-8386
(800) 870-1831
WWW.COASTALADMIN.COM

COASTAL COMMUNITIES PHYSICIAN NETWORK

661
SAN LUIS OBISPO, CA 93406

(800) 604-8752
WWW.CCPNHPN.COM/FOR-OUR-PROVIDERS

COFINITY

Payer ID 38335

PO BOX 2720
FARMINGTON HILLS, MI 48333

(800) 831-1166
WWW.COFINITY.NET

COLONIAL HEALTHCARE

Payer ID 37123

PO BOX 827
LANHAM, MD 20703

(301) 306-3020
(800) 344-9885
WWW.ASSURECARE.COM

COLONIAL MEDICAL

Payer ID 22284

4400 N SCOTTSDALE RD STE 9-393
SCOTTSDALE, AZ 85251

(441) 296-3200
WWW.CGIGROUP.BM

COLORADO ACCESS HMO

Payer ID COACC

PO BOX 17470
DENVER, CO 80217-0470

(303) 751-2657
(877) 441-6032
WWW.COACCESS.COM

COLORADO KAISER PERMANENTE

Payer ID COKSR
PO BOX 373150
DENVER, CO 80237
(800) 382-4661
WWW.KAISERPERMANENTE.ORG/

COLORADO LABORERS HEALTH AND WELFARE FUND

Payer ID COMPU
PO BOX 188004
CHATTANOOGA, TN 37422
(303) 597-0113

COLUMBIA UNITED PROVIDERS

Payer ID 91162
19120 SE 34TH ST STE 201
VANCOUVER, WA 98683-1430
(360) 891-1520
(800) 315-7862
WWW.CUPHEALTH.COM

COMBINED BENEFITS ADMINISTRATORS

4704 W JENNIFER AVE STE 104
FRESNO, CA 93722-6419
(559) 275-3984
(800) 709-4734
WWW.CBAADMIN.COM

COMBINED INSURANCE

PO BOX 6700
SCRANTON, PA 18505-0700
(773) 275-8000
(800) 225-4500
WWW.COMBINEDINSURANCE.COM

COMMERCE BENEFITS GROUP

Payer ID 34181
PO BOX 900
ELYRIA, OH 44036
(800) 223-9941
WWW.COMMERCEBENEFITSGROUP.COM

COMMONWEALTH CARE ALLIANCE

Payer ID 14315
148 STATE ST 10TH FL
BOSTON, MA 02109
(800) 306-0732
WWW.COMMONWEALTHCARE.ORG/

COMMUNITY CARE ASSOCIATES

Payer ID 17902
PO BOX 44230
DETROIT, MI 48244
(313) 961-3100
WWW.CCAREI.COM

COMMUNITY CARE BEHAVIORAL HEALTH ORG.

Payer ID 23282
PO BOX 2972
PITTSBURGH, PA 15230
(888) 251-2224
WWW.CCBH.COM

COMMUNITY CARE MANAGED HEALTH CARE PLANS OF OKLAHOMA

Payer ID 73143
PO BOX 3249
TULSA, OK 74101-3249
(405) 843-1887
WWW.CCOK.COM

COMMUNITY CARE ORGANIZATION

Payer ID 39126
PO BOX 341997
MILWAUKEE, WI 53234
(414) 902-2375
(866) 937-2783
WWW.COMMUNITYCAREINC.ORG

COMMUNITY CARE PLUS

Payer ID 00330
601 MONROE AVE
PITTSBURGH, PA 15202
(412) 367-3110

COMMUNITY CHOICE OF MICHIGAN

Payer ID 38325
PO BOX 1307
DAYTON, OH 45401-1307
(800) 390-7102
WWW.CARESOURCE.COM

COMMUNITY CONNECT MEDICAID

Payer ID 95192
PO BOX 3157
EAU CLAIRE, WI 54702-3157
(877) 350-6074
WWW.COMMUNITYCONNECTHEALTHPLAN.COM

COMMUNITY FAMILY CARE SYNERMED

Payer ID SYMED	PO BOX 2002 MONTEREY PART, CA 97154	(213) 406-2853 WWW.ISYNERMED.COM

COMMUNITY FIRST HEALTH PLAN, INC.

Payer ID COMMF	12238 SILICON DRIVE STE 100 SAN ANTONIO, TX 78249	(210) 227-2347 WWW.CFHP.COM

COMMUNITY HEALTH ALLIANCE

Payer ID 35193 HEADQUARTERS	PO BOX 94365 LUBBOCK, TX 79493	(888) 689-2242 WWW.CHANETWORK.COM

COMMUNITY HEALTH CENTER NETWORK

	101 CALLAN AVE STE 300 SAN LEANDRO, CA 94577	(510) 297-0210 WWW.CHCNETWORK.ORG/MANAGED-CARE-SERVICES/INFORMATION-FOR-PROVIDERS

COMMUNITY HEALTH CHOICE

Payer ID 48145	PO BOX 301412 HOUSTON, TX 77230-1404	(713) 295-2295 (888) 760-2600 WWW.CHCHEALTH.ORG

COMMUNITY HEALTH ELECTRONIC CLAIMS

Payer ID 75261	PO BOX 99906 GRAPEVINE, TX 76099	(877) 593-2872 WWW.WEBTPA.COM

COMMUNITY HEALTH NETWORK OF CONNECTICUT

Payer ID 62149	11 FAIRFIELD BLVD WALLINGFORD, CT 06492-1828	(800) 440-5071 WWW.CHNCT.ORG

COMMUNITY HEALTH PLAN OF WASHINGTON

Payer ID SB613	PO BOX 269002 PLANO, TX 75026-9002	(800) 440-1561 HTPPS://JIVA.CHPW.ORG

COMMUNITY HEALTH SOLUTIONS (LOUISIANA)

Payer ID CLA11	PO BOX 23199 ST. PETERSBURG, FL 33742-3199	(855) 247-5248 HTTP://LOUISIANA.CHSAMERICA.COM/

COMMUNITY MEDICAL GROUP OF THE WEST VALLEY

Payer ID CMGWV	PO BOX 371390 RESEDA, CA 91337	(818) 707-9603

COMMUNITY PARTNERS HEALTH PLANS INC

	1605 S STATE ST STE 104 CHAMPAIGN, IL 61820-7249	(217) 355-0055 HTTP://CPHP.COM

COMPBENEFITS CORPORATION

Payer ID 37297	PO BOX 14284 LEXINGTON, KY 40512	(800) 342-5209 WWW.COMPBENEFITS.COM

COMPENSATION PROGRAMS OF OHIO, INC

Payer ID 34177	33 FITCH BLVD AUSTINTOWN, OH 44515-2202	(330) 652-9821

COMPIQ

Payer ID WE042	35 TESLA WAY STE 100 IRVINE, CA 92618	(949) 923-4000 (800) 293-3131 WWW.COMPIQ.COM

COMPLEMENTARY HEALTHCARE PLANS

Payer ID 93101
PO BOX 278
BEAVERTON, OR 97075-0278
(503) 203-8333
(800) 449-9479
HTTP://CHPGROUP.COM

COMPLIMENTARY HEALTHCARE PLANS

6600 SW 105TH AVE STE 114
BEAVERTON, OR 97008
(503) 203-8333

COMPMANAGEMENT HEALTH SYSTEMS, INC.

Payer ID 10005
PO BOX 1040
DUBLIN, OH 43017
(888) 247-7799
WWW.CHSMCO.COM/

COMPREHENSIVE BEHAVIORAL CARE

Payer ID 59314
3405 W DR MLK JR BLVD STE 101
TAMPA, FL 33607-6207
(813) 288-4808
WWW.COMPCARE.COM/

COMPREHENSIVE BENEFITS ADMINISTRATOR, INC.

Payer ID 03036
PO BOX 2365
SOUTH BURLINGTON, VT 05407-2365
(800) 525-8788
WWW.EBPABENEFITS.COM

COMPREHENSIVE CARE SOLUTIONS (CCS)

333 WEST END AVE STE 9C
NEW YORK, NY 10023
(602) 206-4018
WWW.COMPREHENSIVECARESOLUTIONS.COM

COMPSERVICES

Payer ID WB194
1717 ARCH ST 45TH FL
PHILADELPHIA, PA 19103
(215) 587-1901
(800) 393-7196
WWW.COMPSERVICESINC.COM

COMPSYCH

Payer ID 37363
PO BOX 8379
CHICAGO, IL 60680-8379
(312) 595-4000
WWW.COMPSYCH.COM

COMPUSYS INC

Payer ID 74234
2156 W 2200 S
SALT LAKE CITY, UT 84119-1326
(801) 973-1001
WWW.COMPUSYSCORP.COM/

COMPUSYS INC NEW MEXICO

Payer ID 74234
PO BOX 26068
SALT LAKE CITY, UT 84126
(800) 926-5581
WWW.COMPUSYSERISA.COM/

COMPUSYS INCORPORATED OF COLORADO

Payer ID COMPU
2821 S PARKER RD STE 1005
AURORA, CO 80014-2703
(800) 659-0841
WWW.COMPUSYSERISA.COM/

CONFEDERATION ADMIN/LIFE INSURANCES

Payer ID 80705
393 UNIVERSITY AVE STE 1100
TORONTO, ON M5G 2N9 CANADA
(416) 323-7600
HTTP://CONFEDERATIONLIFE.COM/

CONIFER INSURANCE AGENCY

Payer ID CQ142
26300 NORTHWESTERN HWY STE 410
SOUTHFIELD, MI 48076
(866) 412-2424
WWW.CONIFERINSURANCE.COM

CONNECTICARE INC

Payer ID 06105
PO BOX 4000
FARMINGTON, CT 06034-4000
(860) 674-5850
(800) 251-7722
WWW.CONNECTICARE.COM

CONNECTICARE-MEDICARE

PO BOX 4000
FARMINGTON, CT 06034-4000

(860) 674-5850
(800) 828-3407
WWW.CONNECTICARE.COM/PROVIDER

CONNECTICUT CARPENTERS HEALTH FUND

Payer ID 37307

10 BROADWAY
HAMDEN, CT 06518

(203) 281-5511
WWW.CTCARPENTERSFUNDS.ORG

CONNECTICUT GENERAL LIFE INSURANCE

PO BOX 30365
TAMPA, FL 33630-3365

(877) 484-5967
WWW.CIGNA.COM

CONNECTICUT MEDICAID HMO (AETNA)

PO BOX 61445
PHOENIX, AZ 85082

(866) 716-3356
WWW.AETNABETTERHEALTH.COM

CONNECTICUT MEDICAID HMO (COMMUNITY HEALTH NETWORK)

11 FAIRFIELD BLVD STE 1
WALLINGFORD, CT 06492-1828

(800) 440-5071
WWW.CHNCT.ORG

CONSECO

PO BOX 2024
CARMEL, IN 46082

(317) 817-6200
(800) 244-1423
WWW.CONSECO.COM

CONSOCIATE GROUP

Payer ID 37135

PO BOX 1068
DECATUR, IL 62525-1068

(217) 423-7788
(800) 798-2422
WWW.CONSOCIATEDANSIG.COM

CONSOLIDATED ASSOCIATES RAILROAD

Payer ID 75284

2080 N HWY 360 STE 375
GRAND PRAIRIE, TX 75050-1423

(972) 602-9322
(888) 463-4137
WWW.ACCESSPPO.COM

CONSOLIDATED ASSOCIATION OF RAILROAD EMPLOYEES

PO BOX 6130
TEMPLE, TX 76503-6130

(254) 773-1330
(800) 334-1330
WWW.CAREHEALTHPLAN.COM

CONSOLIDATED GROUP RESOURCES INC

43097 WOODWARD AVE STE 103
BLOOMFIELD HILLS, MI 48302

(248) 352-6220
(800) 273-3299
WWW.CGRBENEFITS.COM/INDEX.HTML

CONSOLIDATED HEALTH PLANS

Payer ID 87843

2077 ROOSEVELT AVE
SPRINGFIELD, MA 01104-1657

(413) 733-4540
(800) 633-7867
WWW.CONSOLIDATEDHEALTHPLAN.COM

CONTAINCARE

Payer ID 36439

19065 HICKORY CREEK DR STE 240
MOKENA, IL 60448-8596

(800) 331-6062
WWW.DIATRI.NET

CONTINENTAL GENERAL INSURANCE CO

Payer ID 71404

PO BOX 21680
EAGAN, MN 55121-0680

(800) 545-8905
WWW.WORLDINSCOCGI.COM

CONTRA COSTA HEALTH PLAN

PO BOX 2157
SAN LEANDRO, CA 94577

(925) 313-6000
WWW.CCHEALTH.ORG

CONTRACT CLAIMS SERVICES

Payer ID WX244	PO BOX 541388 DALLAS, TX 75354	(800) 743-2231 WWW.CCSAPPS.COM

CONTRACTORS, LABORERS, TEAMSTERS & ENGINEERS

Payer ID 47046	10334 ELLISON CIR OMAHA, NE 68134-1024	(402) 491-3751

COOK & CO, INC

	PO BOX 1068 MARSHFIELD, MA 02050-1068	(781) 837-7300 (800) 281-9696 WWW.COOKANDCOMPANY.COM

COOK CHILDREN'S HEALTH PLAN

Payer ID CCHP1	PO BOX 961295 FORT WORTH, TX 76161-1295	(800) 964-2247 WWW.COOKCHP.ORG/

COOK GROUP HEALTH PLAN TRUST

Payer ID 35149	PO BOX 1608 BLOOMINGTON, IN 47402	(812) 339-2235 (800) 457-4500 WWW.COOKGROUP.COM

COOPERATIVE BENEFIT ADMINISTRATORS, INC

Payer ID 52132	PO BOX 6249 LINCOLN, NE 68506-0249	(402) 483-9200

COOPERATIVE MANAGED CARE SERVICES

Payer ID 35199	PO BOX 502090 INDIANAPOLIS, IN 46250	(317) 578-4300 (866) 873-4515 WWW.CMCS-INDY.COM

COORDINATED BENEFIT PLAN

Payer ID 14829	PO BOX 26222 TAMPA, FL 33623-6222	(727) 799-9188 (800) 753-1000 WWW.CBPINSURE.COM/PROCESS.CFM ?PAGEID=14

COORDINATED MEDICAL SPECIALISTS (CMS)

Payer ID 58204	223 E HALLANDALE BEACH BLVD STE A HALLANDALE BEACH, FL 33009-5542	(954) 458-3668 WWW.CLAIM.MD/PAYER.HTML?P=58204

CORE ADMINISTRATIVE SERVICES

Payer ID 58231	PO BOX 90 MACON, GA 31202-0090	(888) 741-2673 WWW.COREMRG.COM

CORESOURCE

Payer ID 35182	PO BOX 2920 CLINTON, IA 52733-2920	(800) 888-7202 WWW.CORESOURCE.COM

CORESOURCE LITTLE ROCK

Payer ID 75136	PO BOX 8215 LITTLE ROCK, AR 72211	(888) 604-9397 WWW.CORESOURCE.COM

CORESOURCE-OHIO

	5200 UPPER METRO PL STE 300 DUBLIN, OH 43017	(614) 336-9604 (800) 282-3920 WWW.CORESOURCE.COM/PROVIDER.ASPX

CORIZON INC

	PO BOX 981639 EL PASO, TX 79998	(800) 729-0069 WWW.CORIZONHEALTH.COM

C

CORNERSTONE BENEFIT ADMINISTRATORS

Payer ID 35202

PO BOX 1007
ELKHART, IN 46516

(574) 296-9990
WWW.CBATPA.COM

CORPHEALTH INC

2101 W. JOHN CARPENTER FREEWAY
IRVING, TX 75063-3228

(817) 870-9103
WWW.LIFESYNCH.COM

CORPORATE BENEFITS SERVICE, INC

Payer ID 56116

PO BOX 981800
EL PASO, TX 79998

(704) 373-0447
(800) 277-9476
WWW.CORBENSER.COM

CORPORATE SYSTEMS ADMINISTRATION, INC

Payer ID 37246

PO BOX 4985
JOHNSON CITY, TN 37602-4985

(423) 282-3420
(800) 829-7566
WWW.CSABENEFITS.COM

CORRECTIONAL HEALTH PARTNERS

Payer ID PHPMC

PO BOX 1738
DENVER, CO 80201

(866) 932-7185
WWW.CORRECTIONALHEALTHPARTNERS.COM

CORRECTIONAL MEDICAL SERVICES

Payer ID 43160

PO BOX 981639
EL PASO, TX 79998

(800) 395-3500
(800) 325-4809
WWW.CMSSTL.COM

CORSOLUTIONS

Payer ID 48146

1850 PARKWAY PLACE
MARIETTA, GA 30067-7826

(800) 343-6311
WWW.CORSOLUTIONS.COM

CORVEL CORPORATION

Payer ID 31147

3001 NE BROADWAY ST
MINNEAPOLIS, MN 55413-1707

(612) 436-2400
(888) 726-7835
WWW.CORVEL.COM

COTTAGE HEALTH SYSTEM

PO BOX 689
SANTA BARBARA, CA 93102-0689

(805) 682-7111
WWW.COTTAGEHEALTHSYSTEM.ORG

COTTINGHAM AND BUTLER

800 MAIN ST
DUBUQUE, IA 52001-6822
PO BOX 28
DUBUQUE, IA 52004

(563) 583-7301
(800) 793-5235
WWW.CB-SISCO.COM

COTTON STATES INSURANCE COMPANIES

244 PERIMETER CTR PKWY NE
ATLANTA, GA 30346-2302
PO BOX 105303
ATLANTA, GA 30348-5303

(770) 391-8600
(800) 457-1658
WWW.COTTONSTATESINSURANCE.COM

COUNTRY FINANCIAL INSURANCE COMPANY

Payer ID WZ905

1701 N TOWANDA AVE
BLOOMINGTON, IL 61701-2057

(866) 268-6879
WWW.COUNTRYFINANCIAL.COM

COUNTRY INSURANCE AND FINANCIAL SERVICES

Payer ID 23655

1705 N TOWANDA AVE
BLOOMINGTON, IL 61701-2040
PO BOX 2100
BLOOMINGTON, IL 61702-2100

(888) 211-2555
WWW.COUNTRYFINANCIAL.COM

Payer ID 23655	TWO PINE TREE DR ARDEN HILLS, MN 55112-3715 PO BOX 64035 ST PAUL, MN 55164-0035	(651) 631-7000 (888) 211-2555 WWW.COUNTRYFINANCIAL.COM
Payer ID 23655	2150 COUNTRY DR SALEM, OR 97302-9459	(888) 211-2555 WWW.COUNTRYFINANCIAL.COM

COUNTRY LIFE INSURANCE COMPANY

Payer ID 62553	PO BOX 2000 BLOOMINGTON, IL 61702	(866) 268-6879 WWW.COUNTRYFINANCIAL.COM

COUNTY CARE

	9370 MCKNIGHT RD PITTSBURGH, PA 15237	(312) 864-8200 (855) 444-1661 HTTP://COUNTYCARE.COM/PROVIDERS.ASPX

COVENANT ADMINISTRATORS

Payer ID 58102	PO BOX 105738 ATLANTA, GA 30348-5738	(678) 258-8200 (800) 680-8728 WWW.COVENANTADMINISTRATORS.NET

COVENANT MANAGEMENT SYSTEMS EMPLOYEE BENEFIT PLAN

Payer ID CMSEB	PO BOX 26159 AUSTIN, TX 78755	(512) 420-2785 HTTP://THEARIANETWORK.COM/

COVENTRY HEALTH CARE OF DELAWARE

Payer ID 25130	PO BOX 7713 LONDON, KY 40742-7713	(800) 833-7423 HTTP:// CHCDELAWARE.COVENTRYHEALTHCARE.COM/

COVENTRY HEALTH CARE OF GEORGIA

Payer ID 25127	PO BOX 7711 LONDON, KY 40742-7711	(800) 470-2004 HTTP:// CHCGEORGIA.COVENTRYHEALTHCARE.COM/

COVENTRY HEALTH CARE OF ILLINOIS

Payer ID 25133	PO BOX 7141 LONDON, KY 40742	(800) 562-5792 WWW.CHCIL.COM/

COVENTRY HEALTH CARE OF IOWA

Payer ID 25132	4320 114TH ST URBANDALE, IA 50322	(800) 470-6352 HTTP://CHCIOWA.COVENTRYHEALTHCARE.COM/

COVENTRY HEALTH CARE OF KANSAS - KANSAS CITY

Payer ID 25133	PO BOX 7109 LONDON, KY 40742-7124	(800) 664-9251 HTTP:// CHCKANSAS.COVENTRYHEALTHCARE.COM/

COVENTRY HEALTH CARE OF LOUISIANA

Payer ID 25135	3838 N CAUSEWAY BLVD 3350 METAIRIE, LA 70002-8500	(800) 341-6613 HTTP:// CHCLOUISIANA.COVENTRYHEALTHCARE.COM/

COVENTRY HEALTH CARE OF NEBRASKA

Payer ID 25136	PO BOX 7705 LONDON, KY 40742-7705	(800) 471-0240 HTTP:// CHCNEBRASKA.COVENTRYHEALTHCARE.COM/

COVENTRY HEALTH CARE OF NORTH CAROLINA

Payer ID 25129	PO BOX 7102 LONDON, KY 40742	(800) 935-7284 HTTP:// CHCNORTHCAROLINA.COVENTRYHEALTHCARE.COM

C

COVERCOLORADO

Payer ID CHCNT	PO BOX 3559 ENGLEWOOD, CO 80155-3559	(303) 749-1111 (888) 770-1120 WWW.COVERCOLORADO.ORG

COVERDELL & COMPANY INC

	8770 W. BRYN MAWR STE 1000 CHICAGO, IL 60631-3506	(800) 308-0374 (866) 440-0528 HTTP://WWW.FINDBESTBENEFITS.COM/

COX HEALTH PLAN

Payer ID 00019	PO BOX 5750 SPRINGFIELD, MO 65801-5750	(800) 205-7665 WWW.COXHEALTHPLANS.COM

CRA MANAGED CARE

Payer ID 10014	PO BOX 94748 CLEAVELAND, OH 44101-4748	(888) 627-7586 WWW.CAREWORKSMCO.COM/

CRAWFORD AND COMPANY

Payer ID WB195	2387 ROSEGATE ROSEVILLE, MN 55113	(877) 346-0300 WWW.CRAWFORDANDCOMPANY.COM

CREATIVE PLAN ADMINISTRATORS

Payer ID 37320	PO BOX 734 BUCKEYSTOWN, MD 21717	(860) 656-7956 WWW.CPATPA.COM

CREATIVE RISK SOLUTIONS

Payer ID TP038	PO BOX 9207 DES MOINES, IA 50306	(515) 223-6990 (877) 544-7843 WWW.CREATIVERISKSOLUTIONS.COM

CRESCENT HEALTH SOLUTIONS (NORTH CAROLINA)

	1200 RIDGEFILED BLVD STE 215 ASHEVILLE, NC 28806	(828) 670-9145 WWW.CRESCENTHS.COM

CRESCENT PPO SOLUTIONS

	1200 RIDGEFIELD BLVD STE 215 ASHEVILLE, NC 28806	(828) 670-9145 (800) 707-7726 HTTP://CRESCENTHS.COM/

CRUM & FORSTER INSURANCE

Payer ID 31348	305 MADISON AVE MORRISTOWN, NJ 07962 PO BOX 1973 MORRISTOWN, NJ 07962-1960	(973) 490-6600 (888) 890-1500 WWW.CFINS.COM

CT GENERAL LIFE INSURANCE

Payer ID 59225	900 COTTAGE GROVE RD BLOOMFIELD, CT 06002-2920	(860) 226-6000 WWW.CIGNA.COM

CULINARY HEALTH & WELFARE FUND

Payer ID 59140	1901 LAS VEGAS BLVD S STE 107 LAS VEGAS, NV 89104-1309	WWW.CULINARYHEALTHFUND.ORG
Payer ID 59140	PO BOX 94469 SEATTLE, WA 98124	(702) 733-9938 WWW.CULINARYHEALTHFUND.ORG

CUMIS INSURANCE SOCIETY

Payer ID WC132	PO BOX 1221 MADISON, WI 53701-1221	(800) 356-2644 WWW.CUNAMUTUAL.COM

CUNNINGHAM LINDSEY

Payer ID WB196	405 STATE HWY 121 BYPASS BLD A STE 200 LEWISVILLE, TX 75067 PO BOX 703689 DALLAS, TX 75370-3689	(214) 488-6530 WWW.CUNNINGHAMLINDSEY.COM

CUSTOM BENEFIT ADMINISTRATORS

Payer ID 39170	PO BOX 1385 LA CROSSE, WI 54602-1385	(608) 784-2442 (800) 944-2188 WWW.CUSTOMBENEFIT.NET

CUSTOMCARE

Payer ID 68241	#210, 200 QUARRY PARK BLVD SE CALGARY, AB T2C 5E3	(866) 820-2188 WWW.CUSTOMCARE.CA/

CUSTOME DESIGN BENEFITS, INC.

Payer ID 82056	5589 CHEVIOT RD CINCINNATI, OH 45247-7548	(513) 598-2929 (800) 598-2929 WWW.CUSTOMDESIGNBENEFITS.COM/

CWI BENEFITS

	PO BOX 6125 GREENVILLE, SC 29606-6125	(864) 234-8200 (800) 992-8088 WWW.CWIBENEFITS.COM

CYPRESS BENEFIT ADMINISTRATORS

	PO BOX 7020 APPLETON, WI 54912	(877) 236-0844 WWW.CYPRESSBENEFIT.COM

CYPRESS CARE INC

	PO BOX 2829 SUWANEE, GA 30024	(800) 419-7191 HTTP://CYPRESSCARE.COM

C

D

D H EVANS & ASSOCIATES

Payer ID 25172

PO BOX 6480
HARRISBURG, PA 17112-0480

(717) 671-8551
(800) 636-7632
WWW.DHEVANSASSOC.COM

DAKOTACARE

Payer ID DAK01

PO BOX 7406
SIOUX FALLS, SD 57717-7406

(605) 334-4000
(800) 325-5598
HTTPS://ACCESS.DAKOTACARE.COM/

DALLAS NATIONAL INSURANCE

Payer ID WB197

5501 LBJ FREEWAY STE 1200
DALLAS, TX 75240

(800) 533-0457
WWW.DALLASNATIONALINS.COM

DART CONTAINER CORPORATION

Payer ID 06172

600 DART RD STE 3000
MASON, MI 48854

(800) 248-5960
WWW.DART.BIZ

DAVIS VISION

PO BOX 1525
LATHAM, NY 12110

(800) 933-9371
WWW.DAVISVISION.COM/PROVIDERS/

DEACONESS HEALTH PLANS

350 W COLUMBIA ST STE 400
EVANSVILLE, IL 47710

(812) 450-7265
(812) 450-7265
WWW.DEACONESS.COM/DEACONESS-HEALTH-PLANS/FOR-PROVIDERS.ASPX

DEAN HEALTH PLAN

Payer ID DEAN1

PO BOX 56099
MADISON, WI 53705-9399

(608) 828-1301
(800) 279-1301
WWW.DEANCARE.COM/PROVIDERS/

DECARE DENTAL NETWORK

PO BOX 1348
MINNEAPOLIS, MN 55440-1348

(800) 587-6857
WWW.DECARE.COM

DECISION SCIENCE BENEFIT FUND

5901 HARFORD RD STE C
BALTIMORE, MD 21214-1846

(410) 254-9595
(800) 367-7848
WWW.DSIBENEFITFUND.ORG/INDEX.HTML

DEEP EAST TEXAS SELF INSURANCE FUND

Payer ID WE040

PO BOX 960
JASPER, TX 75951

(800) 944-0859
WWW.DETSIF.COM

DELAWARE HEALTH PLAN CONSORTIUM

Payer ID 63081

100 W 10TH ST STE 415
WILMINGTON, DE 19801

(302) 654-5471
WWW.DELAWAREHIV.ORG

DELAWARE MEDICAID HMO (DELAWARE PHYSICIANS CARE)

Payer ID 27009

PO BOX 61145
PHOENIX, AZ 85082-1145

(800) 287-9860
WWW.DELAWAREPHYSICIANSCARE.COM/PROVIDERS.ASPX

DELAWARE PHYSICIANS CARE, INC

Payer ID 27009

PO BOX 61145
PHOENIX, AZ 85082-1145

(800) 287-9860
WWW.DELAWAREPHYSICIANSCARE.COM/PROVIDERS.ASPX

DELMARVA HEALTH PLAN

	301 BAY ST STE 401 EASTON, MD 21601	(410) 822-7223 (800) 334-3427

DELTA HEALTH SYSTEMS

Payer ID DHS01	PO BOX 80 STOCKTON, CA 95201	(800) 422-6099 WWW.DELTAHEALTHSYSTEMS.COM/PAGES/ LOGIN.ASPX

DENCAP DENTAL PLANS

	45 E MILWAUKEE ST DETROIT, MI 48202	(800) 875-2400 WWW.DENCAP.COM

DENTAL BENEFIT PROVIDERS

	PO BOX 30566 SALT LAKE CITY, UT 84130-0566	(800) 822-5353 WWW.DBP.COM

DENTAL SELECT

	5373 S GREEN ST 4TH FL SALT LAKE CITY, UT 84123	(800) 999-9789 WWW.DENTALSELECT.COM/CLIENT-SOLUTIONS/ PROVIDERS/

DENVER HEALTH AND HOSPITAL AUTHORITY

Payer ID 84133	777 BANNOCK ST DENVER, CO 80204	(303) 436-6000 WWW.DENVERHEALTH.ORG

DENVER HEALTH MEDICAL PLAN, INC

Payer ID 84135	777 BANNOCK ST MAIL CODE 6000 DENVER, CO 80204	(303) 602-2046 WWW.DENVERHEALTHMEDICALPLAN.COM/

DEPT OF LABOR BLACK LUNG PROGRAM

Payer ID 77044	PO BOX 8302 LONDON, KY 40742-8302	(800) 638-7072 HTTP://OWCP.DOL.ACS-INC.COM

DERMATOLOGY NETWORK SOLUTIONS

Payer ID 58204	PO BOX 723098 ATLANTA, GA 31139	(305) 284-7484 WWW.DERMATOLOGYNETWORKSOLUTIONS.COM

DESERET MUTUAL

Payer ID UH105	PO BOX 45530 SALT LAKE CITY, UT 84145-0530	(801) 578-5600 (800) 777-3622 WWW.DMBA.COM/PROVIDER/DEFAULT.ASPX

DETROIT MEDICAL CENTER

Payer ID 56240	PO BOX 44290 DETROIT, MI 48244	(800) 543-0161 WWW.DMC-CARE.ORG

DIAMOND PLAN

Payer ID 25131	6310 HILLSIDE COURT STE 100 COLUMBIA, MD 21046	(866) 533-5154 HTTP://CHCMEDICAID- MARYLAND.COVENTRYHEALTHCARE.COM/

DINA DENTAL

Payer ID CX090	101 PARKLANE BLVD STE 301 SUGAR LAND, TX 77478	(800) 376-3462 WWW.DINADENTAL.COM

DIRECTORS GUILD OF AMERICA - PRODUCER HEALTH PLAN

Payer ID 23706	PO BOX 48985 LOS ANGELES, CA 90048-8985	(323) 666-2200 (877) 866-2200 WWW.DGAPLANS.ORG/FILINGACLAIM.HTM

D

DISABILITY MANAGEMENT SERVICES, INC

1350 MAIN ST STE 1600
SPRINGFIELD, MA 01103-1641

(413) 747-0990
(800) 804-5342
WWW.DISABILITYMANAGEMENTSERVICES.COM

DIVERSIFIED GROUP BROKERAGE

Payer ID 06102

369 N MAIN ST
MARLBOROUGH, CT 06447-1345
PO BOX 299
MARLBOROUGH, CT 06447

(888) 322-2524
WWW.DGB-ONLINE.COM

DMERC REGION A

Payer ID DMERA

PO BOX 9165
HINGHAM, MA 02043-9165

(866) 419-9458
WWW.MEDICARENHIC.COM/DME/INDEX.ASP

DMERC REGION B

Payer ID DMERB

PO BOX 7027
INDIANAPOLIS, IN 46207-7027

(888) 248-6950
WWW.NGSMEDICARE.COM/WPS/PORTAL/NGSMEDICARE/HOME

DMERC REGION D

Payer ID DMERD

PO BOX 6727
FARGO, ND 58108-6727

(877) 320-0390
WWW.NORIDIANMEDICARE.COM/DME/CLAIMS/

DONLEY AND COMPANY

Payer ID DNLY1

4735 STATESMEN DR STE A
INDIANAPOLIS, IN 46250-4276

(317) 849-3282
(800) 382-5220
WWW.DONLEYBENEFITS.COM

DRISCOLL CHILDRENS HEALTH PLAN

Payer ID 74284

PO BOX 3668
CORPUS CHRISTI, TX 78463-3668

(877) 324-3627
WWW.DCHPKIDS.COM

DSCC - DIVISION OF SPECIALIZED CARE FOR CHILDREN

Payer ID 37600

3135 OLD JACKSONVILLE RD
SPRINGFIELD, IL 62704-6488

(800) 322-3722
HTTP://INTERNET.DSCC.UIC.EDU/DSCCROOT/PROVIDERS/PROVIDERS.ASP

DUNN & ASSOCIATES

Payer ID 35186

PO BOX 2369
COLUMBUS, IN 47203

(812) 378-9960
WWW.DUNNBENEFIT.COM

E.S. BEVERIDGE AND ASSOCIATES

Payer ID 34108

PO BOX 636
MANSFIELD, OH 44901

(419) 525-3961
HTTP://ESBEVERIDGE.COM/HL_PROVIDERS.PHP

EARLY INTERVENTION CENTRAL BILLING

Payer ID 36434

PO BOX 19485
SPRINGFIELD, IL 62794-9485

(800) 634-8540
WWW.EICBO.INFO/PROVIDERS/PROVIDERS.HTM

EAST BAY MEDICAL NETWORK

Payer ID IP130

PO BOX 255125
SACREMENTO, CA 95865

(800) 470-0071
WWW.SUTTERHEALTH.ORG

EAST CAROLINA BEHAVIORAL HEALTH

Payer ID 56089

144 COMMUNITY COLLEGE ROAD
AHOSKIE, NC 27910

(877) 685-2416
WWW.ECBHLME.ORG/

EASTERN ALLIANCE INSURANCE GROUP

Payer ID WB198

25 RACE AVE
LANCASTER, PA 17603
PO BOX 83777
LANCASTER, PA 17608

(717) 396-7095
WWW.EAINS.COM

EASY CHOICE HEALTH PLAN OF NEW YORK

Payer ID 13853

PO BOX 15215
TAMPA, FL 33684

(866) 747-8422
HTTP://COMMERCIAL.EASYCHOICENY.COM/BROKERS.ASP

EBMS

Payer ID 81039

PO BOX 21367
BILLINGS, MT 59104

(406) 245-3575
(800) 777-3575
WWW.EBMS.COM/DEFAULT.ASPX?CID=9

ECOMPPO

Payer ID 75277

8350 N CENTRAL EXPRESSWAY STE 600
DALLAS, TX 75206-1601

(866) 326-6776
WWW.ECOMPPO.COM

EDS HEALTHCHOICE

Payer ID 22521

PO BOX 24870
OKLAHOMA, OK 73124

(800) 782-5218
WWW.OK.GOV/SIB/PROVIDERS/INDEX.HTML

EDUCATORS MUTUAL (EMI)

Payer ID SX110

852 E ARROWHEAD LN
MURRAY, UT 84107-5298

(801) 262-7475
(800) 662-5851
WWW.EDUCATORSMUTUAL.COM/WEB/DEFAULT.ASPX?C=31

EHI (EMPLOYERS HEALTH INSURANCE)

Payer ID 73288

PO BOX 14601
LEXINGTON, CT 40512-4601

(800) 558-4444
WWW.HUMANA.COM/PROVIDERS/

EL PASO FIRST - CHIP

Payer ID EPF03

PO BOX 971370
EL PASO, TX 79997

(915) 532-3778
(877) 532-3778
HTTP://EPFIRST.COM/PROVIDERS.HTML

EL PROYECTO DEL BARRIO

Payer ID MPM04

8902 WOODMAN AVE
ARLETA, CA 91331-6401

(818) 830-7133
WWW.ELPROYECTO.US

ELDER HEALTH MARYLAND HMO INC.

Payer ID 52192
PO BOX 981706
EL PASO, TX 79998
(800) 291-0396
WWW.BRAVOHEALTH.COM/PROVIDERS

ELDERPLAN

Payer ID 31625
PO BOX 73111
NEWNAN, GA 30271-3111
(800) 353-3765
HTTP://ELDERPLAN.ORG/FOR-PROVIDERS/

ELECTRIC INSURANCE CO

Payer ID WX574
75 SAM FONZO DR
BEVERLY, MA 01915
PO BOX 9147
CHELSEA, MA 02150
(800) 342-5342
WWW.ELECTRICINSURANCE.COM

E

ELLIS CONSULTANTS INC

Payer ID ECISF
5909 W LOOP S STE 660
BELLAIRE, TX 77401-2407
(713) 592-0207

ELMCARE

Payer ID NAELM
PO BOX 7759
WESTCHESTER, IL 60154-7759
(708) 432-4050
WWW.ELMCARE.ORG

ELMCO

Payer ID 37253
1905 N MAIN ST
SANTA ANA, CA 92706
(714) 973-1436
HTTP://ELMCOINSURANCE.COM/INDEX.HTML

EMBLEM HEALTH

Payer ID 13551
PO BOX 2830
NEW YORK, NY 10116-2830
(866) 447-9717
WWW.EMBLEMHEALTH.COM/
PROVIDERS.ASPX

EMERALD HEALTH NETWORK, INC

Payer ID 34167
PO BOX 53010
LUBBOCK, TX 79453
(800) 346-3141
HTTP://HEALTHSMART.COM/
HEALTHSMARTCUSTOMERS/PROVIDERS.ASPX

EMPIRE PHYSICIAN'S MEDICAL GROUP

Payer ID EMP01
PO BOX 1389
CORONA, CA 92878
(760) 699-6388
(800) 414-5678
WWW.EMPIREPHYSICIANS.COM

EMPIRE PLAN

Payer ID 87726
PO BOX 1600
KINGSTON, NY 12402-1600
(877) 769-7447
WWW.EMPIREPLANPROVIDERS.COM

EMPLOYEE BENEFIT ADMINISTRATION & MANAGEMENT (EBA&M)

Payer ID 95288
PO BOX 5079
WESTLAKE VILLAGE, CA 91359-5079
(800) 249-8440
WWW.EBAM.COM/PROVIDERS/

EMPLOYEE BENEFIT CONCEPTS

Payer ID 38241
PO BOX 2365
FARMINGTON HILLS, MI 48333-2365
(248) 855-8040
WWW.EMPLOYEEBENEFITCONCEPTS.COM

EMPLOYEE BENEFIT CONSULTANTS, INC.

Payer ID CALL
PO BOX 928
FINDLAY, OH 45839
(440) 262-1160
(866) 296-4002
WWW.EBCTPA.COM/DEFAULT.ASPX
?PAGEID=PROVIDERS

EMPLOYEE BENEFIT CORPORATION

Payer ID 37215
PO BOX 44347
MADISON, WI 53744-4347
(800) 346-2126
WWW.EBCFLEX.COM

EMPLOYEE BENEFIT MANAGEMENT CORP.

Payer ID 31074

4789 RINGS RD
DUBLIN, OH 43017

(614) 766-5800
(877) 304-0761
WWW.EBMCONLINE.COM

EMPLOYEE BENEFIT SERVICES OF LOUISIANA

Payer ID 41198

PO BOX 70100
SHREVEPORT, LA 71137-0100

(800) 256-2657
WWW.MERITAIN.COM

EMPLOYEE BENEFIT SERVICES OF SAN ANTONIO

Payer ID EBSSA

5198 N SUMMIT MAIL STOP 600
TOLEDO, OH 43611

(210) 738-1414
(800) 299-3539
WWW.EBSINCORPORATED.COM

EMPLOYEE BENEFIT SYSTEMS

Payer ID 37216

214 N MAIN ST
BURLINGTON, IA 52601
PO BOX 1053
BURLINGTON, IA 52601-1053

(319) 752-3200
(800) 373-1327
WWW.EBS-TPA.COM/PROVIDERS.SHTML

EMPLOYEE BENEFITS PLAN ADMINISTRATION, INC. (EBPA)

Payer ID 03036

PO BOX 2000
EXETER, NH 03833-2000

(603) 778-7106
(800) 578-3272
WWW.EBPABENEFITS.COM/PROVIDERS/
DEFAULT.ASPX

EMPLOYEE CLAIM ADJUDICATION SERVICES

Payer ID 75184

1415 W 22ND ST
OAK BROOK, IL 60523-2009

(630) 299-7370
(877) 528-1683
WWW.MEDVALUEBPO.COM

EMPLOYEE PLANS, LLC

Payer ID 35112

PO BOX 2362
FORT WAYNE, IN 46801

(260) 625-7500
(800) 395-8601
WWW.OLDNATIONALINS.COM

EMPLOYEE SECURITY, INC

Payer ID 54098

7125 THOMAS EDISON DR STE 105
COLUMBIA, MD 21046

(410) 997-3300
(800) 638-1134
WWW.ESICLAIMS.COM

EMPLOYER PLAN SERVICES, INC

Payer ID 74212

2180 N LOOP W STE 400
HOUSTON, TX 77018

(713) 932-8917
(800) 447-6588
WWW.EPSIBENEFITSINC.COM

EMPLOYERS COALITION ON HEALTH (ECOH)

Payer ID 36335

PO BOX 3428
OAK BROOK, IL 60522-3428

(800) 990-3204
WWW.ECOH.COM/HEALTHCARE/

EMPLOYERS DIRECT HEALTH - EMPLOYEE PLAN

Payer ID 75236

5050 SPRING VALLEY RD
DALLAS, TX 75244-3909

(800) 550-8009
WWW.EDH.COM

EMPLOYERS DIRECT HEALTH - FL

Payer ID 75235

5050 SPRING VALLEY RD
DALLAS, TX 75244-3909

(800) 550-8009
WWW.EDH.COM

EMPLOYERS DIRECT HEALTH - SF

Payer ID 75233

5050 SPRING VALLEY RD
DALLAS, TX 75244-3909

(972) 458-9934
(800) 550-8009
WWW.EDH.COM

EMPLOYERS GENERAL INSURANCE GROUP

Payer ID 24147

1700 PACIFIC AVE #1630
DALLAS, TX 75201
PO BOX 219010
DALLAS, TX 75221-9010

(214) 665-6100
(800) 658-6484

EMPLOYERS HEALTH COOPERATIVE

Payer ID 27008

PO BOX 34585
SEATTLE, WA 98124

(509) 241-7206
(888) 767-4670
HTTPS://PROVIDER.GHC.ORG/OPEN/INDEX.JHTML

EMPLOYERS INSURANCE GROUP

Payer ID WB199

10375 PROFESSIONAL CIR
RENO, NV 89521

(888) 682-6671
WWW.EMPLOYERS.COM

EMPLOYERS MUTUAL, INC. (FLORIDA PROVIDERS ONLY)

Payer ID 59298

700 CENTRAL PARKWAY
STUART, FL 34994-3967

(800) 431-2221
WWW.EMI-TPA.COM

ENCORE HEALTH NETWORK

Payer ID 35206

8520 ALLISON POINTE BLVD STE 200
INDIANAPOLIS, IN 46250-4299

(317) 621-4250
(888) 574-8180
WWW.ENCORECONNECT.COM

ENH MEDICAL GROUP IPA

Payer ID 36364

2650 RIDGE AVE
EVANSTON, IL 60202-1718

(847) 570-2000
WWW.NORTHSHORE.ORG

ENSTAR NATURAL GAS - GRP# P61

Payer ID 91136

PO BOX 190288
ANCHORAGE, AK 99519-0288

(907) 277-5551
(877) 907-9767
WWW.ENSTARNATURALGAS.COM

ENTERPRISE GROUP PLANNING, INC

5910 HARPER RD
SOLON, OH 44139

(440) 349-2210
(800) 229-2210
WWW.EGP-INC.COM

ENTRUST

PO BOX 441588
HOUSTON, TX 77244-1588

(800) 436-8787
WWW.4ENTRUST.COM

EPN - SETON HEALTH PLAN EXCLUSIVE

Payer ID EPNSH

PO BOX 15445
AUSTIN, TX 78761

(512) 421-5667
HTTP://SETONHEALTHPLAN.COM/PROVIDERS/

EQUITABLE PLAN SERVICES, INC

Payer ID 73126

12312 ST ANDREWS DR
OKLAHOMA CITY, OK 73120
PO BOX 720460
OKLAHOMA CITY, OK 73172

(405) 755-2929
(800) 749-2631
WWW.EPSTPA.COM

ERIE INSURANCE GROUP

Payer ID WB169

100 ERIE INSURANCE PL
ERIE, PA 16530-1699

(814) 451-5000
(877) 771-3743
WWW.ERIEINSURANCE.COM

ERIN GROUP ADMINISTRATORS, INC

Payer ID 23250

PO BOX 7777
LANCASTER, PA 17604-7777

(717) 581-1300
(800) 433-3746
HTTP://SIGNIFICABENEFITS.COM/PROVIDERS/DEFAULT.ASPX

ERISA ADMINISTRATIVE SERVICES, INC

Payer ID 74234

13706 RESEARCH BLVD STE 308
AUSTIN, TX 78750

(512) 250-9397

ESIS

Payer ID WS030

PO BOX 6569
SCRANTON, PA 18505-6569

(800) 654-5374
WWW.ESIS.COM

ESKENAZI MEDICAL GROUP

Payer ID SX172

PO BOX 68970
INDIANAPOLIS, IN 46268

(317) 871-8811

ESSENCE HEALTHCARE

Payer ID 57082

PO BOX 12488
ST LOUIS, MO 63132

(866) 597-9560
WWW.ESSENCEHEALTHCARE.COM/PROVIDER/MAIN.ASPX

ESURANCE INSURANCE

Payer ID WA057

PO BOX 5262
SIOUX FALLS, SD 57117

(800) 378-7262
WWW.ESURANCE.COM

EVERCARE STAR PLUS

Payer ID 87726

PO BOX 31361
SALT LAKE CITY, UT 84131-0361

(877) 842-3210
HTTP://EVERCAREHEALTHPLANS.COM

EVERENCE

Payer ID MNM99

PO BOX 483
GOSHEN, IN 46527

(800) 348-7468
WWW.EVERENCE.COM

EVEREST HEALTHPLAN ADMINISTRATORS

PO BOX 19002
PROVO, UT 84605-9002

(800) 286-4160
WWW.EVHEALTH.COM

EVEREST NATIONAL INSURANCE

Payer ID WX666

PO BOX 830
LIBERTY CORNER, NJ 07938-0830

(800) 269-6660
WWW.EVERESTREGROUP.COM

EVERGREEN HEALTH PLAN

Payer ID 58233

12040 NE 128TH ST
KIRKLAND, VA 98034-3013

(425) 899-1600
WWW.EVERGREENHEALTHCARE.ORG

EVOLUTIONS HEALTHCARE SYSTEMS

Payer ID 59313

PO BOX 5001
NEW PORT RICHEY, FL 34656

(727) 938-2222
(800) 308-2749
WWW.EHSPPO.COM/EHSCLAIMSTATUS.ASPX?TYPE=PROVIDER

EXAM WORKS

2501 SW FIRST AVE STE 400
PORTLAND, OR 97201-4726

(503) 796-2775
(888) 822-3866
WWW.EXAMWORKS.COM/LOCAL_OFFICES.HTM

E

EXCEPTIONAL CARE MEDICAL

Payer ID IP080

PO BOX 260830
ENCINO, CA 91426

(818) 461-5055
(888) 445-0062
WWW.CAPCMS.COM/DEFAULT.ASPX

EXPLORER INSURANCE COMPANY

Payer ID WB425

PO BOX 906
SANTA CLARITA, CA 91380-9006

(877) 849-4678
WWW.EXPLORER-INSURANCE.COM

EYE MANAGEMENT INC

Payer ID 65062

PO BOX 2307
HALLANDALE, FL 33008

(305) 861-5400

EYE MED VISION CARE LLC

Payer ID 31165

PO BOX 8504
MASON, OH 45040-7111

(866) 939-3633
WWW.EYEMEDVISIONCARE.COM

EYE SPECIALISTS

Payer ID BVES1

9393 ELKRIDGE LANDING RD STE 200
LINTHICUM, MD 21090

(602) 912-9393
(888) 273-2121
WWW.EYESPEC.COM/ES4000.ASP

EYEMED VISION CARE

4000 LUXOTTICA PL
MASON, OH 45040

(888) 581-3648
WWW.EYEMEDVISIONCARE.COM

FACEY MEDICAL FOUNDATION

Payer ID 95432	PO BOX 9605 MISSION HILLS, CA 91346	(818) 837-5624 WWW.FACEY.COM/ FORPROVIDERS_HOME.PHP

FACS GROUP

Payer ID 37300	9111 DUKE BLVD MASON, OH 45040-8999 PO BOX 850958 RICHARDSON, TX 75085-0958	(800) 234-6229

FAIRMONT SPECIALTY INSURANCE

Payer ID WZ924	10350 RICHMOND AVE STE 300 HOUSTON, TX 77042 PO BOX 2807 HOUSTON, TX 77252-2807	(713) 954-8100 (800) 392-1970 WWW.FAIRMONTSPECIALTY.COM

FAIRPAY SOLUTONS

Payer ID FAIR1	14295 MIDWAY RD STE 300 ADDISON, TX 75001	(888) 475-5215 WWW.FAIRPAYSOLUTIONS.COM

FALLON COMMUNITY HEALTH PLAN, INC

Payer ID 22254	PO BOX 15121 WORCESTER, MA 01615-0121	(866) 275-3247 WWW.FCHP.ORG/PROVIDERS.ASPX

FAMILY CARE MEDICAID

Payer ID FCD01	11111 RICHMOND AVE STE 200 HOUSTON, TX 77082-6602	(800) 323-4057 WWW.FAMILYCARECARD.COM

FAMILY CARE MEDICARE

Payer ID FCR01	825 NE MULTNOMAH STE 300 PORTLAND, OR 97232	(866) 798-2273 WWW.FAMILYCAREINC.ORG/

FAMILY CARE MILWAUKEE WISCONSIN

Payer ID 60995	PO BOX 7460 MADISON, WI 53707-7460	(414) 287-7600 WWW.FAMILYCAREMILWAUKEECOUNTY.COM

FAMILY CHOICE MEDICAL

Payer ID IP080	PO BOX 261040 ENCINO, CA 91426	(818) 461-5055 (888) 445-0062 WWW.FAMILYCHOICEMEDICALGROUP.COM

FAMILY HEALTH ALLIANCE

Payer ID IP080	PO BOX 261040 ENCINO, CA 91426	(818) 461-5055 (888) 445-0062 WWW.CAPCMS.COM/DEFAULT.ASPX

FAMILY HEALTH PARTNERS/MC+MISSOURI

Payer ID 43173	PO BOX 411806 KANSAS CITY, MO 64141-1806	(800) 347-9363 WWW.FHP.ORG/PROVIDER/INDEX.ASP

FARA BENEFIT SERVICES, INC.

Payer ID 37289	1625 W CAUSEWAY APPROACH MANDEVILLE, LA 70471	(985) 624-8383 (800) 259-8388 WWW.FARA.COM/SERVICES-CLAIMS.PHP

FARM BUREAU FINANCIAL SERVICES

Payer ID 13773	5400 UNIVERSITY AVE WEST DES MOINES, IA 50266-5997	(800) 226-6383 WWW.FBFS.COM

FARM FAMILY

Payer ID 14140

PO BOX 22091
ALBANY, NY 12201

(800) 948-3276
WWW.FARMFAMILY.COM/PUB/PUBLICSITE.NSF/CLAIMS.XSP

FARMERS INSURANCE EXCHANGE

Payer ID 21652

PO BOX 372660
DENVER, CO 80237

(602) 375-6800
(800) 419-9150
WWW.FARMERSINSURANCE.COM

FCCI INSURANCE GROUP

Payer ID WB200

6300 UNIVERSITY PARKWAY
SARASOTA, FL 34240

(800) 226-3224
WWW.FCCI-GROUP.COM/DEFAULT.ASP

FCE BENEFIT ADMINISTRATORS

Payer ID 33033

4615 WALZEM RD STE 300
SAN ANTONIO, TX 78218-1610

(800) 899-9355
WWW.FCEBENEFITS.COM/CMS/PAGES/CARE-PAGE-HEALTH-OVERVIEW.HTML

FEDERAL EMPLOYEE PROGRAM (CONNECTICUT)

Payer ID C2BLS

PO BOX 105557
ATLANTA, GA 30348-5557

(800) 438-5356
WWW.FEPBLUE.ORG

FEDERATED MUTUAL INSURANCE CO

Payer ID 41041

PO BOX 991
OWATONNA, MN 55060-0328

(800) 533-0472
WWW.FEDERATEDINSURANCE.COM

FHP OF COLORADO

Payer ID COFHP

PO BOX 17470
DENVER, CO 80217-0470

(303) 751-9051
(800) 414-6198
WWW.CHPPLUSPROVIDERS.COM/CLAIMS.ASP

FIDELIS CARE NEW YORK

Payer ID 11315

PO BOX 806
AMHERST, NY 14226

(888) 343-3547
WWW.FIDELISCARE.ORG/PROVIDERS/INDEX.ASPX

FIDELIS SECURE CARE

Payer ID 77054

PO BOX 3597
SCANTON, PA 18505

(877) 372-8085
WWW.FIDELISSC.COM/PROVIDERS/INDEX.ASP

FIRE & CASUALTY INSURANCE COMPANY OF CONNECTICUT

Payer ID 24880

9 FARM SPRINGS DR
FARMINGTON, CT 06032

(800) 547-7830

FIRST ADMINISTRATORS

Payer ID FAMR1

PO BOX 9900
SIOUX CITY, IA 51102-4709

(800) 206-0827
WWW.FIRSTADMINISTRATORS.COM/PROVIDERS/INDEX.ASPX

FIRST AGENCY

Payer ID FSTAG

5071 WEST H AVE
KALAMAZOO, MI 49009

(269) 381-6630
WWW.1STAGENCY.COM/INDEX.PHP

FIRST CAROLINA CARE

Payer ID 56196

PO BOX 381686
BIRMINGTON, AL 35238

(800) 811-3298
(800) 574-8556
WWW.FIRSTCAROLINACARE.COM/PROVIDERS/INDEX.HTM

FIRST CHOICE HEALTH NETWORK

Payer ID 91131	PO BOX 2289 SEATTLE, WA 98111-2289	(800) 231-6935 WWW.FCHN.COM/FORPROVIDERS.ASPX

FIRST CHOICE OF MIDWEST

Payer ID 75138	PO BOX 5078 SIOUX FALLS, SD 57117-5078	(605) 332-5955 (888) 246-9949 WWW.1CHOICEM.COM

FIRST COMMUNITY SENIOR SELECT

	699-A GALLATIN ST STE A2 HUNTSVILLE, AL 35801-4912	(256) 532-2780 (800) 734-7826 WWW.FIRSTCOMM.ORG

FIRST GREAT WEST LIFE & ANNUITY

Payer ID 80705	PO BOX 1700 DENVER, CO 80201	(800) 537-2033 WWW.GREATWEST.COM/

FIRST HEALTH

Payer ID 73159	PO BOX 5190 TAMPA, FL 33675	(800) 937-6824 HTTP:// FIRSTHEALTH.COVENTRYHEALTHCARE.COM/ PROVIDERS/INDEX.HTM

FIRST PRIORITY

Payer ID 23241	PO BOX 69699 HARRISBURG, PA 17106-9699	(800) 822-8752 WWW.BCNEPA.COM/PROVIDERS/

FIRSTCARE

Payer ID 94999	12940 N HWY 183 AUSTIN, TX 78750-3203	(800) 431-7737 (888) 249-7366 WWW.TPABENEFITS.COM/FIRSTCARE/LOGON/ PROVIDER/PROVIDER.ASP

FIRSTCARE STAR MEDICAID

Payer ID 94998	12940 N HWY 183 AUSTIN, TX 78750-3203	(800) 431-7798 WWW.TPABENEFITS.COM/FIRSTCARE/LOGON/ PROVIDER/PROVIDER.ASP

FIRSTCOMP

Payer ID WX798	P.O. BOX 3009 OMAHA, NE 68103	(888) 500-3344 WWW.FIRSTCOMP.COM

FIRSTIER

Payer ID WB201	800 N RAINBOW BLVD STE 141 LAS VEGAS, NV 89107 PO BOX 35499 LAS VEGAS, NV 89133-5499	(877) 906-7944 WWW.FIRSTIERGA.COM

FITZHARRIS & COMPANY

Payer ID 11244	PO BOX 9182 FARMINGDALE, NY 11735	(800) 635-5651 WWW.FITZHARRISINC.COM

FLEXCARE

Payer ID 68241	300 DELEWARE AVE STE 205 BUFFALO, NY 14202	(716) 848-2955 HTTP://FLEXCAREBENEFITS.COM/INDEX.ASP

FLORIDA HEALTH CARE PLAN

Payer ID 59322	PO BOX 9910 DAYTONA BEACH, FL 32120-9910	(877) 615-4022 WWW.FHCP.COM/PROVIDERS/ ANNOUNCEMENTS/ANNOUNCEMENTS.HTM

FLORIDA HOSPITAL HEALTHCARE SYSTEMS

Payer ID 59321

PO BOX 536847
ORLANDO, FL 32853

(407) 741-4808
(800) 741-4808
WWW.FHHSONLINE.COM

FLORIDA HOSPITAL WATERMAN

Payer ID 48116

1000 WATERMAN WAY
TAVARES, FL 32778-5266

(352) 253-3333
WWW.FHWAT.ORG

FLORIDA LEAGUE OF CITIES, INC

Payer ID 59698

PO BOX 530065
ORLANDO, FL 32853-0065

(407) 425-9142
(800) 445-6248
WWW.FLCITIES.COM

FLORIDA MEDICAID HMO (FLORIDA HEALTH PARTNERS)

PO BOX 12699-FL
NORFOLK, VA 23541-0699

(888) 563-9022
WWW.FLORIDAHEALTHPARTNERS.COM/PROVIDERS.HTM

FLORIDA MEDICAID HMO (HEALTHY PALM BEACHES)

Payer ID 95827

2601 10TH AVE N STE 302
PALM SPRINGS, FL 33461-3186

(866) 930-0035
HTTP://VITAHEALTH.ORG/INDEX.ASPX?PAGE=364

FLORIDA MEDICAID HMO (HUMANA)

Payer ID 61101

PO BOX 14601
LEXINGTON, KY 40512-4601

(800) 448-6262
WWW.HUMANA.COM/PROVIDERS

FLORIDA MEDICAID HMO (WELLCARE)

Payer ID 14163

P.O. BOX 31372
TAMPA, FL 33631-3372

(866) 687-8878
WWW.WELLCARE.COM/MEDICAID/FLORIDA_HEALTHEASE

FLORIDA NETPASS

Payer ID 65063

PO BOX 22812
LONG BEACH, CA 90801

(866) 472-4585
WWW.MOLINAHEALTHCARE.COM/MEDICAID/PROVIDERS/FL/PAGES/HOME.ASPX

FLORIDA TRUE HEALTH

Payer ID 26492

PO BOX 7337
LONDON, KY 40742

(888) 358-0904
WWW.FLTRUEBLUE.COM/PROVIDER/INDEX.ASPX

FLORIDIANCARE

Payer ID APBPN

51 S FEDERAL HWY
BOCA RATON, FL 33432

(561) 542-8478
HTTP://FLORIDIANCARE.MOONFRUIT.COM/#/HEALTH/4555302505

FMH BENEFITS

Payer ID 48117

PO BOX 25946
OVERLAND PARK, KS 66225

(913) 685-4740
(800) 990-9058
WWW.F-M-H.COM/PROVIDERS.HTML

FOREIGN SERVICE BENEFIT PLAN / MUTUAL OF OMAHA

1716 N ST NW
WASHINGTON, DC 20036-2907

(202) 833-4910
HTTP://AFSPA.ORG/PRODUCTS-SERVICES/FSBP/

FORMAX, INC

Payer ID 87066

9150 191ST ST
MOKENA, IL 60448

(708) 479-3500
WWW.PROVISUR.COM

FOX VALLEY MEDICINE SITE 199

Payer ID FVMCH	30 N LINCOLN ST BATAVIA, IL 60510	(630) 482-9701 WWW.FVMEDICINE.COM

FOX-EVERETT, INC

Payer ID 64067	12260 INTRAPLEX PARKWAY GULFPORT, MS 39503	(800) 667-5737 (800) 218-4230 WWW.FOXEVERETT.COM

FRANK GATES MANAGED CARE SERVICES

Payer ID 10061	PO BOX 1549 DUBLIN, OH 43017	(877) 847-5459 WWW.FRANKGATESMCS.COM

FREEDOM BLUE HHIC

Payer ID 71768	PO BOX 60007 LOS ANGELES, CA 90060	(877) 811-3107 WWW.ANTHEM.COM

FREEDOM HEALTH PLAN

Payer ID 41212	PO BOX 151348 TAMPA, FL 33648	(888) 796-0946 WWW.FREEDOMHEALTH.COM/PROVIDERS

FREEDOM LIFE INSURANCE COMPANY

Payer ID 62324	801 CHERRY ST UNIT 33 FORT WORTH, TX 76102-6801	(800) 387-9027 HTTPS://PROVIDER.USHEALTHGROUP.COM/

FREMONT COMPENSATION INSURANCE GROUP

Payer ID WB241	500 N BRAND BLVD GLENDALE, CA 91203-3943	(818) 549-4600 WWW.FREMONTCOMP.COM

FRESENIUS MEDICAL CARE

Payer ID TH118	920 WINTER ST WALTHAM, MA 02451-1457	(781) 699-9000 (800) 662-1237 WWW.FMCNA.COM

FRINGE BENEFIT COORDINATORS

Payer ID 59204	PO BOX 5249 GAINESVILLE, FL 32627-5249	(352) 377-1239 (800) 654-1452 WWW.FBC-INC.COM

FRONTPATH HEALTH COALITION

Payer ID 34171	PO BOX 5810 TROY, MI 48007-5810	(419) 891-5206 WWW.FRONTPATHCOALITION.COM

GATEWAY HEALTH PLAN

Payer ID 25169

PO BOX 69360
HARRISBURG, PA 17106-9360

(800) 685-5205
WWW.GATEWAYHEALTHPLAN.COM/PROVIDERS/PA/MEDICARE.ASPX

Payer ID 25169

PO BOX 69359
HARRISBURG, PA 17106-9359

(800) 392-1145
WWW.GATEWAYHEALTHPLAN.COM

GEHA

Payer ID 44054

PO BOX 4665
INDEPENDENCE, MO 64051-4665

(800) 821-6136
WWW.GEHA.COM

GEISINGER HEALTH PLAN

Payer ID 75273

PO BOX 8200
DANVILLE, PA 17821-8200

(800) 876-5357
WWW.THEHEALTHPLAN.COM/PROVIDERS_US/INDEX.CFM

GEMCARE (GOLDEN EMPIRE MANAGED CARE SYSTEM)

Payer ID MCS01

4550 CALIFORNIA AVE STE 500
BAKERSFIELD, CA 93309

(616) 716-7100
WWW.MANAGEDCARESYSTEMS.COM/

GENERAL CASUALTY COMPANY OF WISCONSIN

1 GENERAL DR
SUN PRAIRIE, WI 53596

(608) 837-4440
(800) 362-5448
WWW.GENERALCASUALTY.COM

GENESIS HEALTHCARE

Payer ID IP087

101 E STATE ST
KENNETT SQUARE, PA 19348

(610) 444-6350
WWW.GENESISHCC.COM

GENEX

Payer ID TP059

440 EAST SWEDESFORD ROAD
WAYNE, PA 19087

(888) 464-3639
WWW.GENEXSERVICES.COM

GEORGIA MEDICAID HMO (AMERIGROUP)

Payer ID 27514

PO BOX 61010
VIRGINIA BEACH, VA 23466-1010

(800) 454-3730
WWW.AMERIGROUPCORP.COM/PROVIDERS

GEORGIA MEDICAID HMO (PEACH STATE HEALTH PLAN)

PO BOX 3030
FARMINGTON, MO 63640

(866) 874-0633
WWW.PSHPGEORGIA.COM/FOR-PROVIDERS/

GEORGIA MEDICAID HMO (WELLCARE)

Payer ID 14163

PO BOX 31224
TAMPA, FL 33631-3224

(866) 231-1821
HTTP://GEORGIA.WELLCARE.COM/PROVIDER/DEFAULT

GEORGIA POWER MEDICAL BENEFITS PLAN

Payer ID 61271

PO BOX 9907
COLUMBUS, GA 31908

(877) 271-2904
WWW.BCBSGA.COM

GEORGIA STATE HEALTH BENEFIT PLAN

Payer ID GABLS

PO BOX 1990
ATLANTA, GA 30301-1990

(800) 610-1863
HTTP://DCH.GEORGIA.GOV/

GETTING US COVERED

Payer ID CHCNT

PO BOX 3559
ENGLEWOOD, CO 80155-3559

(877) 397-1109
WWW.GETTINGUSCOVERED.ORG

GETTYSBURG HEALTH

Payer ID 23274	PO BOX 1060 GETTYSBURG, PA 17325	(800) 497-4474 WWW.GETTHEALTH.COM/GHA/PROVIDER/INDEX/

GHI

Payer ID 25531	PO BOX 2845 NEW YORK, NY 10016	(877) 244-4466 WWW.GHI.COM/PROVIDERS.ASPX

GHI MEDICARE PART B

Payer ID GHMCR	PO BOX 2870 NEW YORK, NY 10116	(877) 868-7965 (646) 458-6721 WWW.TEST.GHI.DFFCO.COM/INDEX.PHP

GHI MEDICARE PART B OF NEW YORK

Payer ID 13551	PO BOX 2832 NEW YORK, NY 10116-2832	(877) 244-4466 WWW.GHI.COM/PROVIDERS.ASPX

GHI-MEDICARE PPFS (PRIVATE FEE FOR SERVICE)

Payer ID 22937	PO BOX 2830 NEW YORK, NY 10116	(866) 557-7300 WWW.GHI.COM/PROVIDERS.ASPX

GHP (GROUP HEALTH PLAN)

Payer ID 25133	PO BOX 7374 LONDON, KY 40742-7374	(800) 613-7721 HTTP:// CHCMISSOURI.COVENTRYHEALTHCARE.COM/

GILSBAR, INC

Payer ID 07205	PO BOX 2947 COVINGTON, LA 70434-2947	(800) 445-7227 WWW.GILSBAR.COM

GLASSWORKERS & GLAZIERS HEALTH & WELFARE FUND TRUST

Payer ID 91136	PO BOX 188004 CHATTANOOGA, TN 37422	(303) 745-1941 WWW.CIGNA.COM/CUSTOMER_CARE/UNIONS/ MEMBERACCESS/PROFESSIONALS.HTM

GLOBAL CARE INC

Payer ID 07689	6875 SHILOH RD EAST ALPHARETTA, GA 30005-8372	(678) 341-1999 (800) 860-1111 WWW.GLOBALCARE.NET/

GLOBAL CARE MEDICAL GROUP IPA

Payer ID MPM05	PO BOX 571420 TARZANA, CA 91357	(877) 452-5472 WWW.GLOBALCAREMED.COM

GLOBAL EXCEL MANAGEMENT

Payer ID GEM01	PO BOX 10 BEEBE PLAIN, VT 05823	(866) 566-3830 WWW.GLOBALEXCELUSA.COM

GLOBAL HEALTH

Payer ID GHOKC	12904 SW 133RD CT MIAMI, FL 33186-5806	(305) 278-2853 WWW.GLOBALHEALTHCLAIMS.COM

GM SOUTHWEST

Payer ID 75246	PO BOX 6000 (COLLEGE CLAIMS) FRISCO, TX 75034-8060	(800) 477-4415 WWW.GMSOUTHWEST.COM
Payer ID 75246	PO BOX 4000 (K-12 CLAIMS) FRISCO, TX 75034-8040	(800) 477-4517 WWW.GMSOUTHWEST.COM

G

GOLD COAST HEALTH PLAN

P.O. BOX 9152
OXNARD, CA 93031-9152

(888) 301-1228
WWW.GOLDCOASTHEALTHPLAN.ORG/PROVIDERS/WELCOME-PROVIDERS.ASPX

GOLDEN DENTAL PLANS

29377 HOOVER RD
WARREN, MI 48093

(800) 451-5918
WWW.GOLDENDENTALPLANS.COM

GOLDEN RULE INSURANCE CO

Payer ID 37602

712 11TH ST
LAWRENCEVILLE, IL 62439-2395

(800) 322-8814
WWW.GOLDENRULE.COM

Payer ID 37602

PO BOX 31374
SALT LAKE CITY, UT 84131-0374

(800) 657-8205
WWW.GOLDENRULE.COM/

GOLDEN WEST DENTAL & VISION

5171 VERDUGO WAY
CAMARILLO, CA 93012

(866) 947-9398
WWW.GOLDENWESTDENTAL.COM/PROVIDER/INDEX.HTML

GOOD SAMARITAN MEDICAL PRACTICE ASSOCIATION (GSMPA)

Payer ID IP086

4909 LAKEWOOD BLVD STE 200
LAKEWOOD, CA 90712

(562) 602-1563
WWW.COASTHEALTHCARE.NET/1_GSMPA.HTM

GOOD SHEPHERD HOSPICE

320 W MAIN ST
LAKELAND, FL 33815

(863) 682-0027
(800) 464-3994
WWW.CHAPTERSHEALTH.ORG/HOME

GOVERNMENT EMPLOYEES HOSPITAL ASSOCIATION,INC. (GEHA)

PO BOX 4665
INDEPENDENCE, MO 64051-4665

(800) 821-6136
WWW.GEHA.COM/INDEX.HTML

GRAND VALLEY HEALTH PLAN

829 FOREST HILLS AVE SE
GRAND RAPIDS, MI 49546-2325

(616) 949-2410
WWW.GVHP.COM/PROVIDERS/

GRAY INSURANCE CO

Payer ID WC134

PO BOX 6202
METAIRIE, LA 70009-6202

(504) 888-7790
WWW.GRAYINSCO.COM

GREAT LAKES HEALTH PLAN

Payer ID 95467

PO BOX 2127
SOUTHFIELD, MI 48037-2127

(800) 903-5253
WWW.GLHP.COM

GREAT WEST (SF)

Payer ID 80705

1 FRONT ST STE 900
SAN FRANCISCO, CA 94111

(877) 457-9321
(800) 573-2033
WWW.GREATWEST.COM

GREAT WEST CASUALTY CO

Payer ID 11371

2950 E GOLDSTONE DR
MERIDIAN, ID 83642
PO BOX 8007
BOISE, ID 83707

(208) 898-3500
(800) 628-4415
WWW.GWCCNET.COM

Payer ID 11371

1100 W 29TH ST
SOUTH SIOUX CITY, NE 68776
PO BOX 277
SOUTH SIOUX CITY, NE 68776-0277

(402) 494-2411
(800) 228-8602
WWW.GWCCNET.COM

Payer ID 11371	2030 FALLING WATER RD STE 300 KNOXVILLE, TN 37922-5892 PO BOX 31289 KNOXVILLE, TN 37930	(865) 670-8850 (800) 998-9288 WWW.GWCCNET.COM
Payer ID 11371	624 SIX FLAGS DR STE 250 ARLINGTON, TX 76011-6370 PO BOX 5408 ARLINGTON, TX 76005	(817) 633-1747 (800) 257-8757 WWW.GWCCNET.COM

GREAT WEST DENVER & WASHINGTON

Payer ID 80705	PO BOX 1700 DENVER, CO 80201	(800) 537-2033 WWW.GREATWEST.COM

GREAT WEST HEALTHCARE

Payer ID 80705	1000 GREAT WEST DR KENNETT, MO 63857-3749	(800) 663-8081 WWW.GREATWESTHEALTHCARE.COM

GREAT WEST LIFE & ANNUITY

Payer ID 63665	PO BOX 1700 DENVER, CO 80201	(800) 573-2033 WWW.GREATWEST.COM

GREAT WEST LIFE ASSURANCE

Payer ID 80705	255 DUFFERIN AVE LONDON, ON NGA 4K1	(800) 957-9777 WWW.GREATWESTLIFE.COM
Payer ID 80705	PLACE BONAVENTURE STE 5800 800 DE LA GUACHETIERE W MONTREAL, QC H5A 1B9	(800) 957-9777 WWW.GREATWESTLIFE.COM
Payer ID 80705	PO BOX 3050 STN MAIN WINNEPEG, MB R3C 0E6	(800) 957-9777 WWW.GREATWESTLIFE.COM
Payer ID 80705	PO BOX 4408 REGINA, SK S4P 3W7	(800) 957-9777 WWW.GREATWESTLIFE.COM
Payer ID 80705	PO BOX 4076 STATION A TORONTO, ON M5W 3A3	(800) 957-9777 WWW.GREATWESTLIFE.COM

GREATER COVINA MEDICAL GROUP

Payer ID GCMG1	605 E BADILLO ST STE 300 COVINA, CA 91723	(626) 974-0440 WWW.WCPIPA.COM/

GREENTREE ADMINISTRATORS

Payer ID 78521	PO BOX 7306 BEAUMONT, TX 77726-7306	(409) 832-2335 (800) 825-2117 WWW.GREENTREEADMIN.COM/PROVIDERS.ASP

GRINNELL MUTUAL REINSURANCE

	PO BOX 790 GRINNELL, IA 50112	(877) 467-2252 WWW.GRINNELLMUTUAL.COM

GROUP & PENSION ADMINISTRATORS

Payer ID 48143	PO BOX 749075 DALLAS, TX 75371-9075	(800) 827-7223 WWW.GPATPA.COM/PROVIDERS.HTM

GROUP ADMINISTRATORS LTD.

Payer ID 36338	915 NATIONAL PKWY STE F SCHAUMBURG, IL 60173-5149	(800) 323-1683 WWW.GROUPADMINISTRATORS.COM

GROUP BENEFIT ADMINISTRATORS

	PO BOX 30749 SALT LAKE CITY, UT 84130	(801) 972-1177 (800) 657-5377 WWW.GBACLAIMS.COM

GROUP HEALTH COOPERATIVE

Payer ID 91051	PO BOX 34585 SEATTLE, WA 98109	(888) 901-4636 WWW.GHC.ORG

GROUP HEALTH COOPERATIVE OF EAU CLAIRE

Payer ID 95192	PO BOX 3217 EAU CLAIRE, WI 54702-3217	(715) 552-4300 (888) 203-7770 WWW.GROUP-HEALTH.COM/LOGIN.ASPX

GROUP HEALTH COOPERATIVE OF SOUTH CENTRAL WISCONSIN CLAIMS

Payer ID 39167	PO BOX 44971 MADISON, WI 53717-1962	(608) 251-4526 (800) 605-4327 WWW.GHCSCW.COM

GROUP HEALTH COOPERATIVE OF SOUTH CENTRAL WISCONSIN ENCOUNTERS

Payer ID 39168	1265 JOHN Q HAMMONS DR MADISON, WI 53717	(608) 251-4526 WWW.GHCSCW.COM

GROUP HEALTH INCORPORATED (GHI) (NEW YORK)

Payer ID 13551	PO BOX 3000 NEW YORK, NY 10016-2833	(212) 501-4444 (800) 223-9870 WWW.EMBLEMHEALTH.COM

GROUP HEALTH INSURANCE

Payer ID 61101	PO BOX 1086 JANESVILLE, WI 53547	(877) 279-7959 WWW.GROUPHEALTHINSURANCE.COM

GROUP HEALTH MANAGERS

	26205 FIVE MILE RD REDFORD, MI 48239-3154	(313) 535-7100

GROUP INSURANCE SERVICE CENTER

Payer ID 37276	PO BOX 9120 MARSHFIELD, MA 02050-9120	(781) 829-8595 WWW.GISCINC.COM

GUARANTEE INSURANCE

Payer ID WB203	401 E LAS OLAS BLVD STE 1540 FORT LAUDERDALE, FL 33301	(877) 886-4334 WWW.GUARANTEEINS.COM

GUARANTEE TRUST LIFE

	1275 MILWAKEE AVE GLENVIEW, IL 60025	(800) 338-7452 WWW.GTLIC.COM

GUARDIAN LIFE INSURANCE CO OF AMERICA

Payer ID 64246	PO BOX 26210 LEHIGH VALLEY, PA 18002	(888) 482-7342 WWW.GLIC.COM

GUIDEONE INSURANCE

Payer ID WZ590	1111 ASHWORTH RD WEST DES MOINES, IA 50265-3538	(877) 448-4331 WWW.GUIDEONE.COM

GULF COAST PROVIDER NETWORK

	1991 MAIN ST STE 147 SARASOTA, FL 34236-5914	(941) 917-4004 WWW.GULFCOASTPROVIDER.NET

GUNDERSEN LUTHERAN HEALTH PLAN

Payer ID 39180

1836 SOUTH AVE
LA CROSSE, WI 54601-5494

(800) 897-1923
WWW.GLHEALTHPLAN.ORG

G

HAA PREFERRED PARTNERS

Payer ID 65101

PO BOX 981603
EL PASO, TX 79998

(305) 893-5151
HTTP://HAAPP.COM/

HANOVER INSURANCE GROUP

440 LINCOLN STREET
WORCESTER, MA 01653-0002
PO BOX 15145
WORCESTER, MA 01615-0145

(508) 855-1000
(800) 853-0456
WWW.HANOVER.COM

HARBOR AMERICA

Payer ID WB204

21977 E WALLIS DR
PORTER, TX 77365

(281) 999-5544
(800) 845-5695
WWW.HAPEO.COM

HARLEYSVILLE INSURANCE

Payer ID WZ591

355 MAPLE AVE
HARLEYSVILLE, PA 19438-2297

(215) 256-3300
(800) 523-6344
WWW.HARLEYSVILLEGROUP.COM

HARMONY HEALTH PLAN OF ILLINOIS

Payer ID 36406

PO BOX 31372
TAMPA, FL 33631-3372

(800) 504-2766
WWW.HARMONYHPI.COM/PROVIDER/
DEFAULT

HARRINGTON BENEFIT SERVICES

Payer ID 95266

PO BOX 16789
COLUMBUS, OH 43216-6789

(800) 228-3564
HTTPS://HB.UMR.COM/PROVIDER/
PROVIDERHOME.HTML

HARRINGTON HEALTH

Payer ID 75196

PO BOX 2697
WICHITA, KS 67201-2697

(316) 264-5311
(800) 235-7160
WWW.HARRINGTONHEALTH.COM

HARTFORD ACCIDENT AND INSURANCE COMPANY

Payer ID 22357

ONE HARTFORD PLAZA T 16 85
HARTFORD, CT 06115

(860) 547-4497
WWW.THEHARTFORD.COM

HARVARD PILGRIM HEALTH CARE

Payer ID 04271

PO BOX 699183
QUINCY, MA 02269-9183

(800) 708-4414
WWW.HARVARDPILGRIM.ORG

HARVARD PILGRIM PASSPORT CONNECT

Payer ID 87726

PO BOX 699183
QUINCY, MA 02269-9183

(866) 844-4864
(800) 708-4414
WWW.HARVARDPILGRIM.ORG

HARVARD UNIVERSITY GROUP HEALTH PROGRAM

PO BOX 986030
BOSTON, MA 02298

(617) 495-2008
WWW.HUGHP.HARVARD.EDU

HAWAII MANAGEMENT ALLIANCE ASSOCIATION

Payer ID 48330

PO BOX 32580
HONOLULU, HI 96803

(800) 434-1002
WWW.HMAA.COM

HAWAII MEDICAID HMO (ALOHA CARE)

CLAIMS-1357 KAPIOLANI BLVD STE 1250
HONOLULU, HI 96814

(800) 830-7222
WWW.ALOHACARE.ORG/PROVIDERS/
DEFAULT.ASPX

HAWAII MEDICAID HMO (WELLCARE)

Payer ID 14163

PO BOX 31372
TAMPA, FL 33631-3372

(888) 846-4262
WWW.OHANAHEALTHPLAN.COM

HAWAII MEDICAL ASSURANCE ASSOCIATION

737 BISHOP STREET, SUITE 1200
HONOLULU, HI 96813

(888) 941-4622
WWW.HMAA.COM

HCH ADMINISTRATION

Payer ID 37111

PO BOX 1986
PEORIA, IL 61656-1986

(800) 447-3227
WWW.HCHADMIN.COM/FORPROVIDERS.HTML

HCHA ALBQ - SELF FUNDED

Payer ID 37329

PO BOX 1986
PEORIA, IL 61656-1986

(800) 322-1516
WWW.HCHADMIN.COM/FORPROVIDERS.HTML

HCSC INSURANCE SERVICES COMPANY

Payer ID 84980

300 E RANDOLPH ST
CHICAGO, IL 60601-7314

(312) 653-6000
WWW.HCSC.COM

HDM BENEFIT SOLUTIONS

Payer ID HDMCO

PO BOX 542020
OMAHA, NE 68154-2020

(402) 951-4530
(800) 667-4824
WWW.HDMCORP.COM

HDPC ALLIANCE PHYSICIANS

Payer ID 20257

17095 MAIN ST
HESPERIA, CA 92345-6004

(760) 948-6606
WWW.HDPCMG.COM

HDPC PREMIER HEALTHCARE

Payer ID 90023

17095 MAIN ST
HESPERIA, CA 92345-6004

(760) 241-6666
WWW.HDPCMG.COM

HEALTH ADVANTAGE HMO PARTNERS

PO BOX 8069
LITTLE ROCK, AR 72203

(800) 843-1329
WWW.HEALTHADVANTAGE-HMO.COM/PROVIDERS/

HEALTH ADVANTAGE OF ARKANSAS

Payer ID ARBLS

PO BOX 8069
LITTLE ROCK, AR 72203-8069

(866) 254-3969
WWW.HEALTHADVANTAGE-HMO.COM/PROVIDERS/

HEALTH ALLIANCE

Payer ID 77950

PO BOX 6003
URBANA, IL 61803

(800) 851-3379
WWW.HEALTHALLIANCE.ORG/CONTENT/CUSTOMER_CENTER/HCPROFESSIONALS

HEALTH ALLIANCE MEDICAL PLANS OF ILLINOIS

Payer ID 77950

PO BOX 6003
URBANA, IL 61803

(800) 851-3379
WWW.HEALTHALLIANCE.ORG/CONTENT/CUSTOMER_CENTER/HCPROFESSIONALS

HEALTH ALLIANCE PLAN OF MICHIGAN

Payer ID 38224

2850 W GRAND BLVD
DETROIT, MI 48202-2692

(313) 664-8075
(800) 688-0040
WWW.HAP.ORG

HEALTH AMERICA INC.

Payer ID 25133

PO BOX 7088
LONDON, KY 40742-7088

(800) 735-4404
HTTP://HEALTHAMERICA.COVENTRYHEALTHCARE.COM/

HEALTH CARE DISTRICT PALM BEACH

PO BOX 3045
WEST PALM BEACH, FL 33402-3045

(866) 930-0035
WWW.HCDPBC.ORG

HEALTH CHOICE GENERATIONS

Payer ID 62180

410 N 44TH ST STE 510
PHOENIX, AZ 85008-6572

(800) 322-8670
WWW.HCGENERATIONS.COM/INDEX.ASP?PAGE=CLAIM.ASP&F=PROVIDERS

HEALTH CHOICE OF AZ

Payer ID 62179

410 N 44TH ST STE 510
PHOENIX, AZ 85008-6572

(800) 322-8670
WWW.HEALTHCHOICEAZ.COM/GENERALPROVIDERS/

HEALTH CHOICE ORLANDO HEALTH

102 W PINELOCH AVE STE 23
ORLANDO, FL 32806

(407) 481-7100
(800) 635-4345
WWW.HEALTHCHOICEORLANDO.ORG

HEALTH CLAIMS SERVICE

Payer ID 82018

PO BOX 1067
BOISE, ID 83701-1067

(208) 388-4567
(888) 427-9732
WWW.HEALTHCLAIMSERVICE.COM/

HEALTH COST SOLUTIONS

Payer ID 62111

PO BOX 1439
HENDERSONVILLE, TN 37077-1439

(615) 822-0483
(800) 526-3919
WWW.MANAGEBENEFITS.COM/

HEALTH DESIGN PLUS

Payer ID 34158

1755 GEORGETOWN RD
HUDSON, OH 44236-4057

(330) 656-1072
(800) 549-9114
WWW.HDPLUS.COM/

HEALTH ECONOMICS CORP

Payer ID 75196

1050 UNIVERSITY AVE STE A
ROCHESTER, NY 14607-1618

(585) 241-9500
(800) 666-6690
WWW.HEGINC.COM

HEALTH EXCHANGE

Payer ID 20356

2800 ROCKCREEK CORPORATION
KANSAS CITY, MO 64117

(816) 221-1024
WWW.CERNER.COM

HEALTH FIRST HEALTH PLANS

Payer ID 95019

PO BOX 69355
HARRISBURG, PA 17106-9333

(800) 356-1511
(800) 716-7737
WWW.HEALTH-FIRST.ORG/HEALTH_PLANS/PROVIDERS/INDEX.CFM

HEALTH FIRST-TYLER, TX

Payer ID 75234

PO BOX 130217
TYLER, TX 75713-0217

(800) 477-2287
WWW.HFTPA.COM/

HEALTH FUTURE, LLC

Payer ID 30946

777 MURPHY RD
MEDFORD, OR 97504-8425

(541) 772-3062
(800) 452-2558
WWW.HEALTHFUTURE.ORG

HEALTH INSURANCE PLAN OF NEW YORK

PO BOX 2830
NEW YORK, NY 10116

(646) 447-5000
(800) 447-8255
WWW.HIPUSA.COM

HEALTH MANAGEMENT ASSOCIATES

Payer ID 86066

PO BOX 22009
TEMPE, AZ 85285

(480) 921-0469
(800) 448-3585
WWW.IMXINC.COM

HEALTH MANAGEMENT SOLUTIONS

Payer ID 10006

2545 FARMERS DR STE 400
COLUMBUS, OH 43235-2705

(888) 202-3515
WWW.HMSSOLUTIONS.COM/

HEALTH NET NATIONAL

PO BOX 870140
SURFSIDE BEACH, SC 29587-9759

(877) 874-2273
WWW.HNFS.COM

HEALTH NET OF ARIZONA

Payer ID AZHNT

PO BOX 14225
LEXINGTON, KY 40512-4225

(800) 289-2818
WWW.HEALTHNET.COM

HEALTH NET OF CALIFORNIA

Payer ID 95567

PO BOX 14702
LEXINGTON, KY 40512-4702

(800) 861-7214
WWW.HEALTHNET.COM/

HEALTH NET OREGON

Payer ID 22340

PO BOX 14130
LEXINGTON, KY 40512-4130

(888) 802-7001
WWW.HEALTHNET.COM

HEALTH NETWORK ONE

Payer ID 65062

PO BOX 4107
HALLANDALE, FL 33008

(800) 595-9631
HTTP://HEALTHNETWORKONE.COM

HEALTH NEW ENGLAND

Payer ID 04286

ONE MONARCH PL STE 1500
SPRINGFIELD, MA 01144-1500

(413) 787-4000
(800) 842-4464
WWW.HNE.COM/HNE_PROVIDERS/
INDEX.HTML

HEALTH OPTIONS OF FLORIDA

Payer ID FLHLT

PO BOX 1798
JACKSONVILLE, FL 32231-0014

(800) 727-2227
WWW.BCBSFL.COM/

HEALTH OPTIONS OF ILLINOIS

Payer ID NAHOI

PO BOX 355
SPARTA, IL 62286

(618) 443-1155
(866) 699-4573
HTTP://HEALTHOPTIONSPARTA.COM

HEALTH PARTNERS - JACKSON, TN

Payer ID 62157

PO BOX 3490
JACKSON, TN 38303-3490

(731) 512-1500
(800) 694-7888
WWW.HPTPA.COM

HEALTH PARTNERS, PA

Payer ID 80142

PO BOX 1220
PHILADELPHIA, PA 19105-1220

(215) 991-4350
(888) 991-9023
WWW.HEALTHPART.COM/PROVIDERS.ASP

HEALTH PAYMENT SYSTEMS

Payer ID 20270

PO BOX 510620
MILWAUKEE, WI 53203

(414) 271-5700
(888) 477-7968
WWW.HPS.MD

HEALTH PLAN

Payer ID 34150	PO BOX 4816 MASSILLON, OH 44648	(888) 830-4370 WWW.HEALTHPLAN.ORG/INDEX.PHP/PROVIDERS

HEALTH PLAN OF MICHIGAN

Payer ID 83253	1001 WOODWARD AVE STE 510 DETROIT, MI 48226	(888) 773-2647 WWW.MHPLAN.COM/MI/PROVIDERS/INDEX.PHP?LOCATION=PROVIDER&PAGE=HOME

HEALTH PLAN OF NEVADA, INC

Payer ID 76343	PO BOX 15645 LAS VEGAS, NV 89114-5645	(702) 242-7300 (800) 777-1840 WWW.HEALTHPLANOFNEVADA.COM/BODY.CFM?ID=9

HEALTH PLAN OF SAN JOAQUIN

Payer ID 68035	PO BOX 839 EL CERRITO, CA 94530	(209) 942-6340 WWW.HPSJ.COM/ENGLISH/PROVIDERS/DEFAULT.ASPX

HEALTH PLAN OF SAN MATEO

Payer ID HPSM1	701 GATEWAY BLVD STE 400 SOUTH SAN FRANCISCO, CA 94080-7041	(650) 616-2106 WWW.HPSM.ORG/PROVIDERS/PROVIDER-RESOURCES/CLAIMS.ASPX

H

HEALTH PLAN OF THE UPPER OHIO VALLEY

	52160 NATIONAL RD E ST CLAIRSVILLE, OH 43950	(877) 847-7901 WWW.HEALTHPLAN.ORG/CONTENT.ASPX/WELCOME-PROVIDERS

HEALTH PLAN SERVICES

Payer ID 59140	PO BOX 30474 TAMPA, FL 33630	(800) 545-6441 HTTPS://SECURE.HEALTHPLAN.COM

HEALTH PLANS INC.

Payer ID 44273	PO BOX 5199 WESTBOROUGH, MA 01581	(800) 532-7575 WWW.HEALTHPLANSINC.COM/PROVIDERS/DEFAULTPROV.ASPX

HEALTH PLUS OF MICHIGAN

Payer ID 38216	PO BOX 1700 FLINT, MI 48501-1700	(800) 332-9161 WWW.HEALTHPLUS.ORG/PROVIDERS.ASPX

HEALTH PLUS PHSP

Payer ID 27514	PO BOX 61010 VIRGINIA BEACH, VA 23466-1010	(800) 450-8753 HTTPS://PROVIDERS.AMERIGROUP.COM/PAGES/NY.ASPX

HEALTH SCOPE BENEFITS

Payer ID 71063	PO BOX 16203 LUBBOCK, TX 79490	(915) 581-8182 (800) 854-2339 WWW.HEALTHSCOPEBENEFITS.COM/PROVIDER/PROVIDER_MAIN.PHP

HEALTH SELECT IPA

Payer ID M3IL1	18410 S CROSSING DR STE A TINLEY PARK, IL 60487-9276	(708) 633-1234 WWW.MED3000.COM

HEALTH SERVICES BENEFITS ADMINISTRATORS

	4160 DUBLIN BLVD STE 400 DUBLIN, CA 94568-7756	(925) 833-7300 WWW.HSBA.COM

HEALTH SERVICES FOR CHILDREN WITH SPECIAL NEEDS (HSCSN)

Payer ID 37290
PO BOX 29055
WASHINGTON, DC 20017
(202) 467-2737
WWW.HSCSN-NET.ORG/NODE/37

HEALTH SERVICES MANAGEMENT, INC

Payer ID HSM01
7805 HUDSON RD STE 190
ST PAUL, MN 55125-1592
(651) 501-9635
(800) 432-3640
WWW.HSMINC.COM/READARTICLE.ASP?ARTICLEID=19

HEALTH SPECIAL RISK, INC

4100 MEDICAL PKWY
CARROLLTON, TX 75007-1517
(972) 512-5600
(800) 328-1114
WWW.HSRI.COM/THIRD-PARTY-CLAIMS.JSP

HEALTH SYSTEMS INTERNATIONAL

PO BOX 91250
MILWAUKEE, WI 53209
(317) 806-2000
(800) 962-6831
WWW.US-HSI.COM

HEALTH VALUE MANAGEMENT, INC

PO BOX 14601
LEXINGTON, KY 40512-4601
(502) 580-1000
(800) 626-2741

HEALTHCARE ALLIANCE

Payer ID 68241
PO BOX 17497
HATTIESBURG, MS 39404-7497
(601) 288-8188
(800) 503-5980
WWW.HEALTHCAREALLIANCE.MS/

HEALTHCARE LA, IPA

Payer ID MPM06
PO BOX 570590
TARZANA, CA 91357
(818) 702-0100
WWW.MEDPOINTMANAGEMENT.COM

HEALTHCARE MANAGEMENT ADMINISTRATORS, INC.

Payer ID HMA01
PO BOX 85008
BELLEVUE, WA 98015-8508
(800) 869-7093
WWW.ACCESSHMA.COM/PROVIDERS/

HEALTHCARE PARTNERS

Payer ID HCP01
PO BOX 6099
TORRANCE, CA 90504
(310) 354-4200
WWW.HEALTHCAREPARTNERS.COM

HEALTHCARE PARTNERS, IPA

Payer ID 11328
501 FRANKLIN AVE STE 300
GARDEN CITY, NY 11530
(888) 746-2200
WWW.HCPIPA.COM/CLAIMS/DEFAULT.ASPX

HEALTHCARE PROVIDER RESOURCES

Payer ID 94254
BISHOP RANCH 3 2603 CAMINO RAMON STE 200
SAN RAMON, CA 94583
(800) 878-9920
HTTP://HPRINSURANCE.COM/HOME.HTML

HEALTHCARE RESOURCES NW

Payer ID 56731
PO BOX 33470
PORTLAND, OR 97292
(503) 251-6890
WWW.HEALTHCARERESOURCESNW.COM/PROVIDERS.PHP

HEALTHCARE SOLUTIONS GROUP

Payer ID 73147
PO BOX 1309
MUSKOGEE, OK 74402
(918) 687-1261
(800) 749-1422
WWW.HSG.COM/

HEALTHCARE USA

Payer ID 00550

10 S BROADWAY STE 1200
ST LOUIS, MO 63102-1704

(800) 295-6888
HTTP://CHCMEDICAID-MISSOURI.COVENTRYHEALTHCARE.COM/FOR-PROVIDERS/INDEX.HTM

HEALTHCOMP

Payer ID 85729

PO BOX 45018
FRESNO, CA 93718-5018

(559) 499-2450
(800) 442-7247
WWW.HEALTHCOMP.COM/PROVIDERS/TABID/119/LANGUAGE/EN-US/DEFAULT.ASPX

HEALTHEASE FLORIDA

Payer ID 59608

PO BOX 31372
TAMPA, FL 33631-3372

(800) 278-0656
WWW.FLORIDA.WELLCARE.COM

HEALTHEDGE ADMINISTRATORS

Payer ID 95213

PO BOX 11210
BAKERSFIELD, CA 93389

(661) 327-7581
WWW.HEALTHEDGEINC.COM

HEALTHEZ

Payer ID 41178

PO BOX 398220
MINNEAPOLIS, MN 55439-8220

(952) 896-4872
(888) 409-2273
WWW.HEALTHEZ.COM/PROVIDER.ASPX

HEALTHFIRST TPA OF AUSTIN

Payer ID 75289

PO BOX 130217
TYLER, TX 75713

(800) 477-2287
WWW.HFTPA.COM

HEALTHFIRST, INC.

Payer ID 80141

PO BOX 958438
LAKE MARY, FL 32795

(888) 801-1660
WWW.HEALTHFIRSTNY.ORG/PROVIDERSERVICES

HEALTHKEEPER HMO

Payer ID VABLS

PO BOX 27401
RICHMOND, VA 23279

(800) 552-6989
(800) 533-1120
WWW.ANTHEM.COM

HEALTHLINK HMO OF ILLINOIS

Payer ID 96475

PO BOX 411580
ST LOUIS, MO 63141

(877) 660-2472
WWW.HEALTHLINK.COM/HOME_PHYSICIAN_HOSPITAL.ASP

HEALTHLINK PPO

Payer ID 90001

PO BOX 419104
ST LOUIS, MO 63141

(877) 660-2472
WWW.HEALTHLINK.COM/HOME_PHYSICIAN_HOSPITAL.ASP

HEALTHMARKETS

PO BOX 809066
DALLAS, TX 75380-9066

(800) 733-8880
(800) 527-2845
WWW.HEALTHMARKETS.COM

HEALTHNOW ADMINISTRATIVE SERVICES

Payer ID 51037

PO BOX 211034
EAGAN, MN 55121

(866) 442-3022
WWW.HNAS.COM

HEALTHNOW NY, INC

	PO BOX 80 257 W GENESEE ST BUFFALO, NY 14240-1199	(800) 945-0556 (800) 856-0480 HTTPS://SECUREWS.HEALTHNOWNY.COM/WPS/PORTAL/HNNY/PROVIDERSHOME

HEALTHPARTNERS MN

	PO BOX 297 MINNEAPOLIS, MN 55440-0297	(952) 883-5000 (800) 883-2177 WWW.HEALTHPARTNERS.COM

HEALTHPARTNERS OF MINNESOTA

Payer ID 94267	PO BOX 1289 MINNEAPOLIS, MN 55440-1289	(800) 444-4558 WWW.HEALTHPARTNERS.COM

HEALTHPLUS OF LOUISIANA

Payer ID 95009	PO BOX 69316 HARRISBURG, PA 17106-9316	(318) 212-8520 (800) 331-5055 WWW.WKHEALTHPLUS.COM/WEBSITE/PROVIDERHOME.ASPX

HEALTHSMART

Payer ID HSPC1	PO BOX 53010 LUBBOCK, TX 79453-3010	(214) 574-3546 (800) 687-0500 WWW.HEALTHSMART.COM/HEALTHSMARTCUSTOMERS/PROVIDERS.ASPX

HEALTHSMART ACCEL

Payer ID 75237	PO BOX 94807 LUBBOCK, TX 79493	(877) 212-2235 WWW.HEALTHSMART.COM/HEALTHSMARTCUSTOMERS/PROVIDERS.ASPX

HEALTHSMART PREFERRED CARE

Payer ID 75250	PO BOX 53010 LUBBOCK, TX 79453-3010	(800) 687-0500 WWW.HEALTHSMART.COM/HEALTHSMARTCUSTOMERS/PROVIDERS.ASPX

HEALTHSOURCE

	PO BOX 182223 CHATTANOOGA, TN 37422	(800) 244-6224 HTTPS://CIGNAFORHCP.CIGNA.COM/

HEALTHSOURCE, MASS

Payer ID 02041	PO BOX 2083 CONCORD, NH 03302	(508) 798-8667 HTTPS://CIGNAFORHCP.CIGNA.COM/

HEALTHSPAN NETWORK

Payer ID HSPAN	225 PICTORIA DR STE 320 CINCINNATI, OH 45246-1614	(513) 551-1440 (888) 914-7726 WWW.HEALTHSPANNETWORK.COM/PROVIDERS/DEFAULT.ASPX

HEALTHSPRING

Payer ID 63092	PO BOX 981804 EL PASO, TX 79998-1804	(615) 291-7000 (800) 888-7647 WWW.HEALTHSPRING.COM/PROVIDERS

HEALTHSUN

Payer ID HESUN	PO BOX 330968 MIAMI, FL 33233-0968	(305) 234-9292 (877) 207-4900 WWW.HEALTH-SUN.COM/

H

HEALTHWAVE OF KANSAS

Payer ID 31472

PO BOX 3571
TOPEKA, KS 66601-3571

(800) 933-6593
WWW.KMAP-STATE-KS.US/PUBLIC/PROVIDER.ASP

HEALTHWAYS WHOLEHEALTH NETWORKS

Payer ID 58213

PO BOX 3192
MILWAUKEE, WI 53201-3192

(866) 430-8647
WWW.WHOLEHEALTHPRO.COM

HEALTHY PALM BEACHES, INC.

Payer ID 95827

PO BOX 3045
WEST PALM BEACH, FL 33402

(866) 930-1002
WWW.HEALTHYPALMBEACHES.ORG/

HEART OF AMERICA HEALTH PLAN

810 S MAIN AVE
RUGBY, ND 58368

(701) 776-5848
(800) 525-5661
WWW.HOAHP.COM

HELIX FAMILY CHOICE

10201 N PORT WASHINGTON RD
MEQUON, WI 53092

(800) 261-3371
WWW.MEDSTARFAMILYCHOICE.COM

HELMSMAN MANAGEMENT SERVICES, INC

Payer ID WZ549

330 N BRAN BLVD STE 500
GLENDALE, CA 91203
PO BOX 29073
GLENDALE, CA 91209

(800) 653-7893
WWW.LIBERTYMUTUAL.COM

HERITAGE CONSULTANTS

Payer ID 59230

PO BOX 1730
AUBURNDALE, FL 33823-1730

(863) 967-4139
WWW.FLORIDATPA.COM/

HERITAGE IPA

Payer ID HERO1

8510 BALBOA BLVD STE 285
NORTHRIDGE, CA 91325-3503

(714) 908-5608
WWW.HERITAGEPROVIDERNETWORK.COM

HERITAGE PHYSICIAN NETWORK

Payer ID ENCTR

PO BOX 10749
BAKERSFIELD, CA 93389

(661) 846-4726
(800) 763-7732
WWW.BFMC.COM/

HFN, INC

Payer ID 36335

PO BOX 3428
OAK BROOK, IL 60522

(630) 954-1232
(800) 295-5444
HTTP://HFNINC.COM

HI DESERT MEDICAL

Payer ID HERZ0

PO BOX 7014
LANCASTER, CA 93539

(661) 726-3821
(800) 266-4364
WWW.HDMG.NET

HIGH DESERT PRIMARY CARE

Payer ID 33069

17095 MAIN ST
HESPERIA, CA 92345-6004

(760) 241-6666
WWW.HDPCMG.COM

HIGHLINE MEDICAL SERVICES MOLINA

PO BOX 22612
LONG BEACH, CA 90801

(888) 665-4621
WWW.MOLINAHEALTHCARE.COM

HIGHMARK - KEY FAMILY

Payer ID 35145	PO BOX 890062 CAMP HILL, PA 17089-0062	(412) 544-7000 (866) 975-5054 WWW.HIGHMARK.COM

HILL PHYSICIANS MEDICAL GROUP

Payer ID HIL01	PO BOX 8001 PARK RIDGE, IL 60068-8001	(925) 820-8300 (800) 445-5747 WWW.HILLPHYSICIANS.COM/PROVIDERS/PAGES/DEFAULT.ASPX

HINSDALE PHYSICIANS HEALTHCARE

Payer ID NAHIN	PO BOX 7789 WESTCHESTER, IL 60154-7789	(708) 432-4000 HTTP://HINSDALEPHYSICIANSHEALTHCARE.COM/

HISPANIC PHYSICIANS IPA

Payer ID HPIPA	PO BOX 10718 BEVERLY HILLS, CA 90213	(213) 637-0925

HMA (SERVICING HI, AZ AND NV)

	5811 PELICAN BAY BLVD STE 500 NAPLES, FL 34108	(239) 598-3131 WWW.HMA.COM

HMO OF COLORADO

Payer ID COHMO	PO BOX 5747 DENVER, CO 80217-5747	(866) 628-3097 WWW.ANTHEM.COM

HNA/TRIVERSIS

	745 HOPE RD TINTON FALLS, NJ 07724-9713	(732) 676-2630 (800) 332-7772 WWW.HEALTHNETWORKAMERICA.COM

HOLLYWOOD PRESBYTERIAN

Payer ID IP080	PO BOX 260890 ENCINO, CA 91436	(213) 413-3000 WWW.HOLLYWOODPRESBYTERIAN.COM

HOME STATE HEALTH PLAN

	PO BOX 4050 FARMINGTON, MO 63640-3829	(855) 694-4663 WWW.HOMESTATEHEALTH.COM

HOMETOWN HEALTH PLAN NEVADA

Payer ID 88023	PO BOX 981703 EL PASO, TX 79998-1703	(800) 336-0123 WWW.HOMETOWNHEALTH.COM/BODY.CFM?ID=10

HOMETOWN HEALTH PLAN OF OHIO

Payer ID 30757	52160 NATIONAL RD E ST CLAIRSVILLE, OH 43950-9365	(740) 695-3585 (800) 624-6961 WWW.HEALTHPLAN.ORG/INDEX.PHP/PROVIDERS

HOMETOWN HEALTH PROVIDERS

Payer ID 88537	PO BOX 981703 EL PASO, TX 79998-1703	(800) 336-0123 WWW.HOMETOWNHEALTH.COM/BODY.CFM?ID=10

HORACE MANN LIFE INSURANCE

Payer ID HMLIC	ONE HORRACE MANN PLAZA SPRINGFIELD, IL 62715	(800) 999-1030 WWW.HORACEMANN.COM/CLAIMS

H

HORIZON BLUE CROSS BLUE SHIELD OF NEW JERSEY

Payer ID 22099

PO BOX 820
NEWARK, NJ 07101-0820

(800) 624-1110
WWW.HORIZON-BCBSNJ.COM/PROVIDERS.HTML
?WT.SVL=HOMETAB

HOSPITAL BENEFITS, INC

PO BOX 162148
ALTAMONTE SPRINGS, FL 32716

(800) 759-7422
WWW.HBIFL.COM

HOTEL EMPLOYEES & RESTAURANT EMPLOYEES HEALTH TRUST

Payer ID 91136

PO BOX 34203
SEATTLE, WA 98124-1203

(206) 728-2326
(800) 735-7053
WWW.WPAS-INC.COM/HERE/

HOTEL EMPLOYEES & RESTAURANT EMPLOYEES INT'L UNION WELFARE PENSION FUNDS

PO BOX 6020
AURORA, IL 60598

(630) 236-5100
(800) 841-3380
WWW.HEREIUFUND.COM

HUDSON HEALTH PLAN

Payer ID 13335

303 S BROADWAY STE 321
TARRYTOWN, NY 10591-5410

(800) 247-6550
WWW.HUDSONHEALTHPLAN.ORG/

HUMANA MILITARY TRICARE

Payer ID 61125

PO BOX 7031
CAMDEN, SC 29020-7031

(800) 403-3950
WWW.HUMANA-MILITARY.COM/SOUTH/
PROVIDER/PROVIDER.ASP

HUMANA VA HERO PROGRAM

Payer ID 61160

PO BOX 7062
CAMDEN, SC 29021

(866) 458-6630
WWW.HUMANA-VETERANS.COM/PROVIDERS/
DEFAULT.ASP

HUMANA VETERANS HEALTHCARE SERVICES

PO BOX 7062
CAMDEN, SC 29021

(866) 458-6630
WWW.HUMANA-VETERANS.COM

HUMANA, CLAIMS ONLY

Payer ID 61101

PO BOX 14601
LEXINGTON, KY 40512-4601

(800) 448-6262
WWW.HUMANA.COM/PROVIDERS/

HUMANA, ENCOUNTERS ONLY

Payer ID 61102

PO BOX 14605
LEXINGTON, KY 40512-4605

(800) 448-6262
WWW.HUMANA.COM/PROVIDERS/

HUNT INSURANCE GROUP, INC.

Payer ID 37260

PO BOX 12909
TALLAHASSEE, FL 32317

(800) 763-4868
WWW.WILLIS.COM

HUNTINGTON PARK MISSION MEDICAL GROUP

Payer ID IP080

PO BOX 261040
ENCINO, CA 91426

(818) 461-5055
(888) 445-0062
WWW.CAPCMS.COM

I. E. SHAFFER

Payer ID 22175
PO BOX 1028
WEST TRENTON, NJ 08628
(800) 792-3666
WWW.IESHAFFER.COM

IBEW WESTERN UTILITIES OR LOCAL 57

Payer ID 74234
PO BOX 30261
SALT LAKE CITY, UT 84130-0261
(800) 424-2080
WWW.IBEW-WEST.COM

IBI INTERMOUNTAIN BUSINESS INSURANCE

Payer ID 41124
899 W BAXTER DR
SOUTH JORDAN, UT 84095-8506
(801) 304-9949
WWW.IBIAGENCY.COM

ICARE

Payer ID 11695
PO BOX 547
BUCKEYSTOWN, MD 21717
(474) 231-1029
(800) 777-4376
WWW.ICARE-WI.ORG/PROVIDERS/

ICON BENEFIT ADMINISTRATORS

Payer ID 75185
PO BOX 53010
LUBBOCK, TX 79453
(806) 473-3000

ICW GROUP

Payer ID WP976
11455 EL CAMNIO REAL
SAN DIEGO, CA 92130-2045
PO BOX 85563
SAN DIEGO, CA 92186-5563
(858) 350-2400
(800) 877-1111
WWW.ICWGROUP.COM

IDAHO TRUE BLUE BCBS

Payer ID TRUEB
PO BOX 7408
BOISE, ID 83707
(866) 482-2250
WWW.BCIDAHO.COM/MEDICARE/TRUE-BLUE/INDEX.ASP

IDS PROPERTY CASUALTY INSURANCE

Payer ID WA055
3500 PACKERLAND
DEPERE, WI 54115
(920) 330-5100
(800) 535-2001

IHC HEALTH SOLUTIONS

PO BOX 21456
EAGAN, MN 55121-0456
(800) 843-3106
WWW.HPAINSURANCE.COM

IHN

Payer ID 35204
PO BOX 6051
INDIANAPOLIS, IN 46206
(888) 446-6670
WWW.IHNPPO.COM

ILLINICARE

Payer ID 68065
PO BOX 4020
FARMINGTON, MO 63640-4402
(866) 329-4701
WWW.ILLINICARE.COM/FOR-PROVIDERS/

ILLINOIS MEDICAID HMO (WELLCARE)

Payer ID 14163
PO BOX 31372
TAMPA, FL 33631-3372
(800) 504-2766
WWW.HARMONYHPI.COM/PROVIDER/DEFAULT

IMA OF LOUISIANA

Payer ID 72091
PO BOX 71120
BOSSIER CITY, LA 71171
(800) 742-9944
WWW.IMALA.COM

IMC

Payer ID 37624
PO BOX 144090
ARECIBO, PR 00614-4090
(787) 878-6909
WWW.INTERMEDPR.COM

IMCARE

Payer ID 41600 | PO BOX 830912, BIRMINGHAM, AL 35283-0912 | (800) 843-9536, WWW.IMCARE.ORG

INDECS CORPORATION

Payer ID 40585 | PO BOX 435, EAST RUTHERFORD, NJ 07073 | (800) 225-0324, WWW.INDECSCORP.COM

INDEPENDENCE ADMINISTRATORS

Payer ID TA720 | 602 OFFICE CTR DR STE 350, FORT WASHINGTON, PA 19034 | (888) 356-7899, WWW.IBXTPA.COM/PROVIDERS

INDEPENDENCE BLUE CROSS

Payer ID SX083 | PO BOX 41474, PHILADELPHIA, PA 19101 | (800) 275-2583, WWW.IBX.COM/PROVIDERS/

INDEPENDENCE CASUALTY AND SURETY

Payer ID WB426 | 11455 EL CAMINO REAL, SAN DIEGO, CA 92130 | (800) 877-1111, WWW.ICWGROUP.COM

INDEPENDENCE MEDICAL GROUP

Payer ID MHM01 | PO BOX 1560, BAKERSFIELD, CA 93302-1560 | (866) 814-4476, WWW.INDMEDGROUP.COM/PROVIDERS.PHP

INDEPENDENT HEALTH

Payer ID 95308 | 511 FARBER LAKES DR, BUFFALO, NY 14221; PO BOX 9066, BUFFALO, NY 14231 | (800) 736-5771, WWW.INDEPENDENTHEALTH.COM

INDIANA PROHEALTH NETWORK

Payer ID 35161 | PO BOX 50407, INDIANAPOLIS, IN 46250 | (317) 621-7581, WWW.ECOMMUNITY.COM/PROHEALTH

INDIANA TEAMSTERS HEALTH BENEFIT FUND

Payer ID 35107 | PO BOX 47130, OAK PARK, MI 48237 | (888) 531-1159, WWW.LOCAL135.COM

INETICO

Payer ID 43471 | 400 N ASHLEY DR, TAMPA, FL 33602 | (877) 601-2200, WWW.INETICO.COM

INFORMED UHC COMPASS ROSE

Payer ID 50946 | PO BOX 141501, NASHVILLE, TN 37214 | (877) 531-1159, WWW.COMPASSROSEBENEFITS.COM

INGALLS PROVIDER GROUP

Payer ID NAING | 4415 W HARRISON ST STE 300, HILLSIDE, IL 60162 | (708) 432-4052

INHEALTH

Payer ID 31112 | ONE YONGE ST STE 1801, TORONTA, CANADA, ON M5E1W7 | (416) 364-6688, WWW.INHEALTH.CA

INLAND EMPIRE HEALTH PLAN

Payer ID IEHP1 | PO BOX 19026, SAN BERNARDINO, CA 92423 | (909) 890-2054, WW2.IEHP.ORG/IEHP/PROVIDERS/

INNOVATIVE RISK MANAGEMENT

Payer ID WE073 | 1431 GREENWAY DR #620, IRVING, TX 75038 | (972) 518-1577, WWW.INNOVATIVE-RISK.COM

INNOVATIVE RISK SOLUTIONS

Payer ID WE091

3330 BARGAINTOWN RD STE 2
EGGHARBOR TOWNSHIP, NJ 08234

(609) 927-7475
WWW.IRSTEAM.COM

INSERVCO

Payer ID WB207

2 N 2ND ST #2
HARRISBURG, PA 17101

(717) 230-8300
(800) 356-0438
WWW.INSERVCO.NET

INSURANCE & RISK MANAGEMENT

PO BOX 80159
INDIANAPOLIS, IN 46240

(317) 706-9500
(800) 860-1977
WWW.EMPLOYEEPLANSLLC.COM

INSURANCE ADMINISTRATIVE SOLUTIONS

8545 126TH AVE N STE 200
LARGO, FL 33773-1502

(727) 584-0007
WWW.IASADMIN.COM

INSURANCE ADMINISTRATOR OF AMERICA

Payer ID 37279

PO BOX 5082
MT LAUREL, NJ 08054

(800) 283-2524
WWW.IAATPA.COM

INSURANCE COMPANY OF THE WEST

Payer ID WB205

11455 EL CAMINO REAL
SAN DIEGO, CA 92130

(800) 877-1111
WWW.ICWGROUP.COM

INSURANCE DESIGN ADMINISTRATORS

Payer ID 13315

PO BOX 690
OAKLAND, NJ 07436-0690

(800) 225-1345
WWW.IDATPA.COM

INSURANCE MANAGEMENT ADMINISTRATORS OF LOUISIANA

Payer ID 72091

PO BOX 71120
BOSSIER CITY, LA 71171-1120

(318) 747-0577
(800) 742-9944
WWW.IMALA.COM/FILE-CLAIMS.PHP

INSURANCE MANAGEMENT SERVICES OF TEXAS

Payer ID IMSMS

PO BOX 15688
AMARILLO, TX 79105-5688

(800) 687-5944
WWW.IMSTPA.COM

INSURANCE SERVICE OF LUBBOCK

Payer ID ISL11

4601 66TH ST STE C
LUBBOCK, TX 79414-4839

(806) 784-0141

INSURICA CLAIMS MANAGEMENT

5105 N CLASSEN STE 300
OKLAHOMA CITY, OK 73118

(405) 523-2100
WWW.INSURICA.COM

INTEGRA ADMINISTRATIVE GROUP, INC.

Payer ID 51020

110 S SHIPLEY ST
SEAFORD, DE 19973-3714

(800) 959-3518
WWW.INTEGRATPA.COM

INTEGRAL QUALITY CARE

Payer ID 23229

PO BOX 61415
PHOENIX, AZ 85082-1415

(866) 258-4326
WWW.INTEGRALQUALITYCARE.COM

INTEGRITY BENEFIT NETWORK

PO BOX 4537
MARIETTA, GA 30061-4537

(770) 428-1604
WWW.IBNTPA.COM

INTEGRITY MUTUAL INSURANCE CO

Payer ID WA059

2121 E CAPITOL DR
APPLETON, WI 54911
PO BOX 539
APPLETON, WI 54912-0539

(920) 734-4511
(800) 348-1741
WWW.INTEGRITYINSURANCE.COM

INTER VALLEY HEALTH PLAN

PO BOX 6002
POMONA, CA 91769-6002

(800) 251-8191
(888) 711-4984
WWW.IVHP.COM

INTER-AMERICAS INSURANCE

PO BOX 9510
WICHITA, KS 67277

(316) 794-2200
(800) 333-2525
WWW.IAI-ONLINE.COM

INTERACTIVE MEDICAL SYSTEMS

Payer ID 56132

PO BOX 1349
WAKE FOREST, NC 27588

(800) 426-8739
WWW.IMS-TPA.COM/MEDICAL.HTML

INTERCARE

Payer ID 37227

PO BOX 2550
SACRAMENTO, CA 95812

(800) 307-5454
WWW.INTERCAREINS.COM

INTERCOMMUNITY HEALTH NETWORK

Payer ID INCHN

PO BOX 887
CORVALLIS, OR 97339

(541) 768-5207
(888) 435-2396
WWW.SAMHEALTH.ORG/HEALTHPLANS/
COMMUNITY/PAGES/ABOUT.ASPX

INTERFACE EAP

Payer ID 60280

PO BOX 421879
HOUSTON, TX 77242-1879

(800) 324-4327
WWW.IEAP.COM/PROVIDER%20FORMS.HTML

INTERGROUP SERVICES CORPORATION

Payer ID 23287

101 LINDENWOOD DR STE 150
MALVERN, PA 19355-1738

(800) 537-9389
WWW.IGS-PPO.COM/
AREYOU_FOR_PROVIDERS.ASP

INTERMOUNTAIN HEALTH CARE

Payer ID UH107

5381 GREEN ST
MURRAY, UT 84123-4661

(801) 442-5442
(800) 538-5038
HTTP://INTERMOUNTAINHEALTHCARE.ORG

INTERMOUNTAIN IRONWORKERS TRUST FUND

Payer ID 74234

PO BOX 30124
SALT LAKE CITY, UT 84130-0124

(801) 606-2425
(888) 867-9510
HTTPS://IIW.COMPUSYSUT.COM

INTERNATIONAL EDUCATIONAL EXCHANGE SERVICES, INC

Payer ID 16158

PO BOX 4930
ITHACA, NY 14852-4930

(607) 272-2707
(866) 433-7462
WWW.IEES.COM

INTERNATIONAL MEDICAL GROUP, INC

Payer ID IMGIN

PO BOX 88500
INDIANAPOLIS, IN 46208-0500

(800) 628-4664
WWW.IMGLOBAL.COM

INTERNATIONAL UNION OPERATING ENGINEERS

Payer ID 37269

PO BOX 34203
SEATTLE, WA 98124-1203

(800) 735-7053
WWW.WPAS-INC.COM

Payer ID 37269	PO BOX 93870 ANCHORAGE, AK 99509	(800) 735-7053 WWW.WPAS-INC.COM

INTERPLAN HEALTH GROUP

	PO BOX 6743 LUBBOCK, TX 79493	(866) 511-4757 WWW.INTERPLANHEALTH.COM

IPMG

Payer ID 36342	225 SMITH RD ST CHARLES, IL 60174	(800) 423-1841 WWW.TOTALBROKERBENEFITS.COM/ BSSIWEBS.NSF/SERVICEPROVIDER?OPENFORM

I

J P FARLEY CORPORATION

Payer ID 34136	PO BOX 458022 WESTLAKE, OH 44145-8022	(440) 250-4300 (800) 634-0173 WWW.JPFARLEY.COM

JAS, INC

	4885 S 900 E STE 202 SALT LAKE CITY, UT 84117-5725	(801) 266-3256 (800) 345-3248 WWW.JASBENEFITS.COM

JF MOLLOY

Payer ID 61271	PO BOX 39710 COLORADO SPRINGS, CO 80949-3910	(866) 317-3113 (317) 879-4040

JFP BENEFIT MANAGEMENT

	PO BOX 189 JACKSON, MI 49204-0189	(517) 784-0535 (800) 589-7660

JI SPECIALTY SERVICES, INC.

Payer ID JISSP	PO BOX 26655 AUSTIN, TX 78755-0655	(512) 427-2300 (800) 580-5477 WWW.JICOMPANIES.COM

JMH HEALTH PLAN

Payer ID 05014	1801 NW 9TH AVE MIAMI, FL 33136	(305) 575-3640 (800) 721-2993 WWW.JMHHP.COM

JOHN ALDEN LIFE INS

Payer ID 41099	PO BOX 2877 CLINTON, IA 52733-2877	(800) 553-7654 WWW.ASSURANTHEALTH.COM

JOHN DEERE HEALTHCARE: UNITEDHEALTHCARE RIVER VALLEY

Payer ID 95378	PO BOX 5230 KINGSTON, NY 12402-5230	(800) 747-1446 (800) 224-6602 WWW.UHCRIVERVALLEY.COM

JOHN MUIR HEALTH NETWORK

Payer ID JMH01	PO BOX 5107 WALNUT CREEK, CA 94596	(925) 952-2887 WWW.JOHNMUIRHEALTH.COM

JOHN MUIR MT. DIABLO HEALTH SYSTEM

Payer ID 68036	1400 TREAT BLVD WALNUT CREEK, CA 94596-2142	(925) 939-3000 WWW.JOHNMUIRHEALTH.COM

JOHN P PEARL & ASSOCIATES

Payer ID 37215	1200 E GLEN AVE PEORIA HEIGHTS, IL 61616	(800) 447-4982 WWW.PEARLINSURANCE.COM

JOHNS HOPKINS (USFHP)

Payer ID 52123	PO BOX 33 GLEN BURNIE, MD 21060-0033	(888) 819-1043 (800) 261-2393 WWW.HOPKINSMEDICINE.ORG/USFHP/

JOHNS HOPKINS HEALTHCARE (EHP/PP)

Payer ID 52189	6704 CURTIS CT GLEN BURNIE, MD 21060	(888) 819-1043 (800) 261-2393 WWW.HOPKINSMEDICINE.ORG

JPS PREFERRED CARE

Payer ID MWP01	PO BOX 60027 FT WORTH, TX 76115	(888) 924-8852 WWW.JPSHEALTHNET.ORG

JSL ADMINISTRATORS

Payer ID 37272

PO BOX 2857
FAYETTEVILLE, NC 28302

(910) 480-3100
(800) 337-6288
HTTP://WFIS.WELLSFARGO.COM/TPA

J

KAISER FOUNDATION HEALTH PLAN OF GEORGIA

Payer ID 21313	PO BOX 190849 ATLANTA, GA 31119	(404) 261-2825 (888) 895-5813 HTTP://PROVIDERS.KP.ORG/GA/

KAISER FOUNDATION HEALTH PLAN OF NORTHERN CA

Payer ID KS003	1950 FRANKLIN ST 1ST FL OAKLAND, CA 94612	(800) 337-0115 HTTPS://HEALTHY.KAISERPERMANENTE.ORG/ HTML/KAISER/INDEX.SHTML

KAISER FOUNDATION HEALTH PLAN OF OHIO

Payer ID NG007	PO BOX 5316 CLEVELAND, OH 44101	(800) 686-7100 HTTP://PROVIDERS.KP.ORG/OH/

KAISER FOUNDATION HEALTH PLAN OF SOUTHERN CA REGION

Payer ID 94134	PO BOX 7004 DOWNEY, CA 90241-7004	(800) 390-3510 HTTP://PROVIDERS.KP.ORG/SCAL/INDEX.HTML

KAISER MID ATLANTIC

Payer ID 52095	PO BOX 6233 ROCKVILLE, MD 20849	(800) 810-4766 HTTP://PROVIDERS.KP.ORG/MAS/INDEX.HTML

KAISER NW REGION

Payer ID NG009	500 NE MULTNOMAH ST STE 100 PORTLAND, OR 97232-2012	(800) 464-4000 HTTP://PROVIDERS.KP.ORG/

KAISER PERMANENTE

Payer ID 94320	450 N LAKE AVE PASADENA, CA 91101-1216	(216) 623-8765 (800) 441-9742 HTTP://PROVIDERS.KP.ORG/NATIONAL/ INDEX.HTML

KAISER PERMANENTE (COLORADO PLANS ONLY)

Payer ID 91617	PO BOX 372910 DENVER, CO 80237	(303) 338-3600 (800) 681-7878 HTTP://PROVIDERS.KP.ORG/COD/

KAISER PPO

Payer ID 94320	PO BOX 75026 PLANO, TX 75026	(800) 464-4000 HTTP://PROVIDERS.KP.ORG/

KANAWHA HEALTHCARE SOLUTIONS

Payer ID 57038	PO BOX 514587 WALTHAM, MA 02454	(800) 260-2162 WWW.KMGAMERICA.COM

KANCARE

Payer ID 96385	PO BOX 3571 TOPEKA, KS 66601-3571	(800) 933-6593 WWW.KANCARE.KS.GOV/ PROVIDER_BILLING_INFORMATION.HTM

KANSAS CITY LIFE INSURANCE CO

Payer ID 44030	PO BOX 219425 KANSAS CITY, MO 64121-9325	(800) 821-6164 WWW.KCLIFE.COM

KANSAS MEDICAID HMO (CHILDREN'S MERCY FAMILY HEALTH PARTNERS)

Payer ID 31472	PO BOX 411806 KANSAS CITY, MO 64141-1806	(877) 347-9363 WWW.FHP.ORG/PROVIDER/ KS_PROVIDERRESOURCE.ASP

KEENAN & ASSOCIATES

	PO BOX 2744 TORRANCE, CA 90510	(800) 654-8102 WWW.KEENAN.COM/PROVIDER

KELSEY SEYBOLD

Payer ID KELSE
PO BOX 300368
HOUSTON, TX 77230
(713) 442-5440
WWW.KELSEY-SEYBOLD.COM

KEMPER INSURANCE COMPANIES

Payer ID WZ926
PO BOX 2847
CLINTON, IA 52733-2847
(888) 252-2799
WWW.KEMPER.COM

KEMPTON GROUP

Payer ID 73100
PO BOX 54889
OKLAHOMA CITY, OK 73154-1889
(405) 521-1711
(800) 521-1711
WWW.KEMPTONGROUP.COM

KENTUCKY HEALTH ADMINISTRATORS

Payer ID 27215
2331 FORTUNE DR STE 185
LEXINGTON, KY 40509
(859) 263-2382
HTTP://KENTUCKYHEALTHADMIN.COM/PROVIDER-LOGIN-PAGE

KENTUCKY MEDICAID HMO (PASSPORT HEALTH PLAN)

Payer ID 61129
PO BOX 7114
LONDON, KY 40742
(800) 578-0775
WWW.PASSPORTHEALTHPLAN.COM/PROVIDER/INDEX.ASPX

KENTUCKY SPIRIT HEALTH PLAN

Payer ID 68069
PO BOX 4001
FARMINGTON, MO 63640
(866) 643-3153
WWW.KENTUCKYSPIRITHEALTH.COM

KERN COUNTY CDCR

Payer ID 28021
1115 TRUXTUN AVE 5TH FL
BAKERSFIELD, CA 93301
(661) 868-3140
WWW.CO.KERN.CA.US/

KERN HEALTH SYSTEMS

Payer ID 77039
PO BOX 25003
BAKERSFIELD, CA 93311
(661) 664-5146
WWW.KERNHEALTHSYSTEMS.COM/PROVIDERS/

KEY BENEFIT ADMINISTRATORS

Payer ID 37217
PO BOX 55210
INDIANAPOLIS, IN 46205-0210
(317) 284-7111
(800) 331-4757
WWW.KEYBENEFIT.COM

KEY HEALTH PLAN

Payer ID 39026
30699 RUSSELL RANCH RD STE 175
WEST LAKE VILLAGE, CA 91362
(877) 633-5436
WWW.KEYHEALTH.NET

KEY INSURANCE GROUP

Payer ID KEYIP
PO BOX 781
TEXARKANA, TX 75504
(903) 792-0085
WWW.KEYINSURANCEGROUP.NET

KEY INSURANCE PLAN

PO BOX 25237
TAMPA, FL 33622
(877) 539-2911
WWW.AVMED.ORG/PROVIDERS/INDEX.ASPX

KEY MEDICAL GROUP

Payer ID IP082
3335 S FAIRWAY
VISALIA, CA 93277-7781
(559) 734-2801
WWW.KEYMEDICAL.ORG/INDEXEF73.HTML?ID=33

KEY SELECT

Payer ID 37321
PO BOX 639
FORT MILLS, SC 29716-0639
(866) 387-3402
WWW.KEYBENEFITRESOURCES.COM/KEYSELECT

KEYCARE PPO

Payer ID VABLS	PO BOX 27401 RICHMOND, VA 23279-7401	(800) 451-1527 WWW.ANTHEM.COM/HOME-PROVIDERS.HTML

KEYSTONE FIRST HEALTH PLAN

Payer ID 23284	PO BOX 7115 LONDON, KY 40742	(800) 521-6007 (800) 521-6860 WWW.KEYSTONEFIRSTPA.COM

KEYSTONE HEALTH PLAN CENTRAL

	PO BOX 779503 HARRISBURG, PA 17177-9503	(800) 874-8433 WWW.CAPBLUECROSS.COM

KINDRED HEALTHCARE

Payer ID 73288	680 SOUTH FOURTH STREET LOUISVILLE, KY 40202-2407	(502) 596-7300 (800) 991-6171 WWW.KINDREDHEALTHCARE.COM

KLAIS & COMPANY, INC

Payer ID 34145	1867 W MARKET ST AKRON, OH 44313-6977	(800) 331-1096 WWW.KLAIS.COM

KPS HEALTH PLANS

Payer ID KPS01	PO BOX 339 BREMERTON, WA 98337-0039	(360) 478-6796 (800) 552-7114 WWW.KPSHEALTHPLANS.COM/PROVIDERS/INDEX.SHTML

LA CARE

PO BOX 811580
LOS ANGELES, CA 90081

(866) 522-2736
WWW.LACARE.ORG/PROVIDERS

LA CARE HEALTH PLAN

Payer ID LACAR

PO BOX 811580
LOS ANGELES, CA 90081

(866) 522-2736
WWW.LACARE.ORG

LAFAYETTE CONSOLIDATED GOVERNMENT

Payer ID 71037

PO BOX 5007
DE PERE, WI 54115

(337) 291-8292
WWW.LAFAYETTELA.GOV

LAKESIDE HEALTH SERVICES

Payer ID 95415

PO BOX 371390
RESEDA, CA 91337

(585) 395-6049
(866) 654-3471
WWW.LAKESIDEHEALTH.ORG

LAKESIDE MEDICAL GROUP INC

Payer ID LMG11

PO BOX 371390
RESEDA, CA 91337

(888) 472-7787
WWW.LAKESIDECOMMUNITYHEALTHCARE.COM

LANCASTER GENERAL HEALTH GROUP

PO BOX 3555
LANCASTER, PA 17604-3555

(717) 544-4953
WWW.LANCASTERGENERALHEALTH.ORG

LANDMARK HEALTHCARE INC

Payer ID LNDMK

1750 HOWE AVE STE 300
SACRAMENTO, CA 95825

(800) 638-4557
WWW.LANDMARKHEALTHCARE.COM

LASALLE MEDICAL ASSOCIATES

1680 S CARFIELD AVE. SUITE 205
ALHAMBRA, CA 91801-5413

(909) 890-0407
WWW.LASALLEMEDICALASSOCIATES.COM

LAWNDALE CHRISTIAN HEALTH CENTER

Payer ID 36333

3860 W OGDEN AVE
CHICAGO, IL 60623

(773) 650-3232
WWW.LAWNDALE.ORG

LAWRENCE E. SMITH & ASSOCIATES, INC

PO BOX 411216
ST LOUIS, MO 63141-1216

(636) 532-1660
(800) 325-1350
WWW.LESMITH.NET

LBA HEALTH PLANS

Payer ID 52193

PO BOX 981801
EL PASO, TX 79998-1801

(800) 858-4468
WWW.LBAX.COM

LEON MEDICAL CENTER HEALTH PLAN

Payer ID 37316

PO BOX 659006
MIAMI, FL 33265

(305) 631-5337
WWW.LMCHEALTHPLANS.COM

LEWER AGENCY, INC

4534 WORNALL RD
KANSAS CITY, MO 64111

(800) 821-7715
WWW.LEWER.COM

LIBERTY AMERICAN SELECT INSURANCE COMPANY

Payer ID WZ672

7785 66TH ST N
PINELLAS PARK,, FL 33780
PO BOX 8080
PINELLAS PARK, FL 33780

(800) 299-8911

LIBERTY MUTUAL INSURANCE COMPANY

Payer ID 11123
PO BOX 7203
LONDON, KY 40742
(877) 384-1071
WWW.LIBERTYMUTUALPROVIDERSUPPORT.COM

LIFE & HEALTH INS CO OF AMERICA

11720 KATY FREEWAY STE 1700
HOUSTON, TX 77079
(800) 713-4680

LIFE INSURANCE CO OF ALABAMA

302 BROAD ST
GADSDEN, AL 35901-3716
PO BOX 349
GADSDEN, AL 35902-0349
(256) 543-2022
(800) 226-2371
WWW.LICOA.COM

LIFE INVESTORS INS CO OF AMERICA

Payer ID LIICA
4333 EDGEWOOD RD N
CEDAR RAPIDS, IA 52499
(319) 398-8511
(866) 745-3545
WWW.TRANSAMERICA.COM

LIFE TRAC

Payer ID 41136
11100 WAYZATA BLVD STE 350
MINNETONKA, MN 55305-1544
(800) 968-8722
WWW.LIFETRACNETWORK.COM

LIFEPRINT

Payer ID LIFE1
PO BOX 46770
LAS VEGAS, NV 89114-6770
(877) 370-2845
WWW.LIFEPRINTHEALTH.COM

LIFEWELL HEALTH PLANS

PO BOX 2920
CLINTON, IA 52733-2920
(770) 420-1500
(877) 543-3935
WWW.LWHP.COM

LIFEWISE A PREMIER HEALTH PLAN

Payer ID 93093
PO BOX 7709
BEND, OR 97708-7709
(800) 596-3440
WWW.LIFEWISEOR.COM

LIFEWISE HEALTH PLAN OF WASHINGTON A PREMIER HEALTH PLAN

Payer ID 91049
PO BOX 91059
SEATTLE, WA 98111-9159
(800) 592-6804
WWW.LIFEWISEWA.COM

LIHP (LOW INCOME HEALTH PROGRAM)

Payer ID MS077
PO BOX 23667
SAN DIEGO, CA 92193
(800) 587-8118
WWW.DHCS.CA.GOV/PROVGOVPART/PAGES/DEFAULT.ASPX

LINDEN OAKS BEHAVIORAL HEALTH

Payer ID LOBH1
PO BOX 3135
NAPERVILLE, IL 60566-7135
(630) 527-6800
HTTP://WWW.EDWARD.ORG/LINDENOAKS

LIPA/AGATE RESOURCES

Payer ID LIPA1
PO BOX 11740
EUGENE, OR 97403-1740
(541) 485-2155
(877) 600-5472
WWW.LIPA.NET

LITTLE COMPANY OF MARY

Payer ID 4725P
2800 W 95 ST
EVERGREEN PARK, IL 60805
(708) 499-8500
(708) 422-6200
WWW.LCMH.ORG

LOCAL CHOICE

Payer ID VABLS
101 N 14TH ST 13TH FL
RICHMOND, VA 23219-3603
(804) 786-6460
WWW.THELOCALCHOICE.STATE.VA.US

LOCKARD & WILLIAMS

PO BOX 1688
PASCAGOULA, CA 39568-1688

(228) 762-2500
WWW.LOCKARDANDWILLIAMS.COM/TESTJOOMLA/INDEX.PHP/EN/

LONDON HEALTH ADMINISTRATORS

Payer ID 37226

40 COMMERCIAL WAY
EAST PROVIDENCE, RI 02914-1006

(800) 343-2236
WWW.LONDONHEALTHUSA.COM

LONE STAR TPA

PO BOX 601749
DALLAS, TX 75360-1749

(903) 617-6706
(855) 820-2047
WWW.LONESTARTPA.COM/INDEX.PHP

LOOMIS COMPANY

Payer ID 23223

PO BOX 7011
WYOMISSING, PA 19610

(610) 374-4040
WWW.LOOMISCO.COM

LOUISIANA HEALTHCARE CONNECTIONS

Payer ID 68069

PO BOX 4040
FARMINGTON, MO 63640-3826

(866) 595-8133
WWW.LOUISIANAHEALTHCONNECT.COM/FOR-PROVIDERS

LOVELACE HEALTH PLAN, INC

Payer ID 90328

PO BOX 549
BUCKEYSTOWN, MD 21717

(505) 727-5456
(800) 808-7363
WWW.LOVELACEHEALTHPLAN.COM

LUBA CASUALTY INSURANCE COMPANY

Payer ID WB237

PO BOX 98082
BATON ROUGE, LA 70898-9082

(225) 389-5822
(888) 884-5822
WWW.LUBAWC.COM

LUCENT INSURANCE

Payer ID WB378

3319 CALICO AVENUE
SAN JOSE, CA 95124

(408) 348-8930
WWW.LUCENTINSURANCESERVICES.COM

LUMBERMANS UNDERWRITING ALLIANCE

Payer ID 23108

1905 NW CORPORATE BLVD
BOCA RATON, FL 33431

(561) 994-1900
(800) 327-0515
WWW.LUMBERMENSUNDERWRITING.COM/

MACHINIST DISTRICT 9 WELFARE

Payer ID 37292

PO BOX 419104
ST LOIUS, MO 63141

(800) 624-2356
WWW.HEALTHLINK.COM/
HOME_PHYSICIAN_HOSPITAL.ASP

MACNEAL HEALTH PROVIDERS - CHS

Payer ID 36334

PO BOX 9006
OAKBROOK, IL 60522

(708) 783-9100
WWW.MACNEAL.COM

MAGELLAN BEHAVIORAL HEALTH

Payer ID 60054

14100 MAGELLAN PLAZA
MARYLAND HEIGHTS, MO 63043
PO BOX 1958
MARYLAND HEIGHTS, MO 63043

(800) 450-7281
WWW.MAGELLANPROVIDER.COM/
MAGELLANPROVIDER/DO/LOADHOME

MAGNACARE

Payer ID 11303

PO BOX 1001
GARDEN CITY, NY 11530

(800) 235-7267
WWW.MAGNACARE.COM/PROVIDERS/
PROVIDERS.ASPX

MAGNOLIA MISSISSIPPI

Payer ID 68062

PO BOX 3090
FARMINGTON, MO 63640-3825

(866) 912-6285
WWW.MAGNOLIAHEALTHPLAN.COM/FOR-
PROVIDERS/

MAIL HANDLERS BENEFIT PLAN

Payer ID 62413

PO BOX 8402
LONDON, KY 40742

(800) 410-7778
WWW.MHBP.COM

MAINE-NEBRASKA

301 CENTENNIAL MALL S
LINCOLN, NE 68508-2529
PO BOX 95026
LINCOLN, NE 68509-5026

(402) 471-3121
(877) 255-3092
WWW.HHS.STATE.NE.US

MAINE-NORTH DAKOTA

600 E BLVD AVE DEPT 325
BISMARK, ND 58505-0250

(701) 328-2321
WWW.ND.GOV/DHS

MAJESTACARE

Payer ID 26372

PO BOX 63545
PHOENIX, AZ 85082

(866) 996-9140
WWW.MAJESTACARE.COM/PROVIDERS/

MAKSIN MANAGEMENT CORPORATION

Payer ID 22195

PO BOX 2648
CAMDEN, NJ 08101

(800) 547-9646
WWW.STUDENTINSURANCE.COM/
VIEWPROVIDERS.ASP

MANAGED CARE AMERICA

Payer ID 25160

1910 COCHRAN RD STE 605 MANOR OAK TWO
PITTSBURGH, PA 15220

(717) 652-8040
(800) 762-8316
WWW.MCOA.COM

MANAGED CARE SYSTEMS

Payer ID MCS02

PO BOX 940
BAKERSFIELD, CA 93302

(661) 716-7100
WWW.MANAGEDCARESYSTEMS.COM/

MANAGED HEALTH NETWORKS

Payer ID 22771

PO BOX 14621
LEXINGTON, KY 40512-4621

(800) 444-4281
WWW.MHN.COM/PROVIDER/START.DO

MANAGED HEALTH SERVICES INDIANA

Payer ID 39186 | PO BOX 3002, FARMINGTON, MO 63640 | (317) 684-9478, (877) 647-4848, WWW.MHSINDIANA.COM/FOR-PROVIDERS/

MANAGED HEALTH SERVICES OF WISCONSIN

Payer ID 39187 | PO BOX 3001, FARMINGTON, MO 63640-3901 | (800) 222-9831, WWW.MHSWI.COM/FOR-PROVIDERS/PROVIDER-RESOURCES/

MANAGED HEALTHCARE NORTHWEST

422 E BURNSIDE ST #215, PORTLAND, OR 97208; PO BOX 4629, PORTLAND, OR 97208 | (503) 413-5800, WWW.MHNINC.COM/FOR_PHYSICIANS.HTM

MANAGED PHYSICAL NETWORK

Payer ID 41159 | PO BOX 8200, KINGSTON, NY 12402-8200 | (800) 236-9921, WWW.UNITEDHEALTHCAREONLINE.COM

MANHATTAN INSURANCE GROUP

PO BOX 925309, HOUSTON, TX 77292-5309 | (800) 669-9030, WWW.MANHATTANLIFE.COM

MAPCO INC.

Payer ID 75258 | 427 W CEVALLOS, SAN ANTONIO, TX 78204 | (210) 444-9711, WWW.MAPCOINC.NET

MARIAN IPA

Payer ID IPO97 | PO BOX 940, BAKERSFIELD, CA 93302 | (877) 509-9072

MARICOPA HEALTHPLAN

PO BOX 37169, PHOENIX, AZ 85069 | (502) 874-5290, (800) 582-8686, WWW.MHPAZ.COM

MARION POLK HEALTH PLAN

Payer ID MPCHA | PO BOX 5490, SALEM, OR 97304 | (888) 236-2496, WWW.PHYSICIANSCHOICEPLANS.COM/

Payer ID MPCHP | PO BOX 5490, SALEM, OR 97304 | (888) 236-2496, WWW.PHYSICIANSCHOICEPLANS.COM/

MARRIOTT CLAIMS SERVICES

Payer ID 68241 | PO BOX 29210, HOT SPRINGS, AR 71903-9210 | (714) 545-5261

MARTIN'S POINT HEALTH CARE

Payer ID MPHC2 | PO BOX 11410, PORTLAND, ME 04104 | (888) 732-7364, WWW.MARTINSPOINT.ORG

MARYLAND MEDICAID HMO (MARYLAND PHYSICIANS CARE)

Payer ID 22348 | PO BOX 61778, PHOENIX, AZ 85082-1778 | (800) 953-8854, WWW.MARYLANDPHYSICIANSCARE.COM

MARYLAND MEDICAID HMO (MEDSTAR FAMILY CHOICE)

Payer ID 0243 | CLAIMS-10201 N PORT WASHINGTON RD, MEQUON, WI 53092 | (800) 261-3371, WWW.MEDSTARFAMILYCHOICE.NET

MARYLAND MEDICAID HMO (PRIORITY PARTNERS)

6704 CURTIS COURT
GLEN BURNIE, MD 21060-6406

(410) 762-5385
(888) 895-4998
WWW.PPMCO.ORG

MARYLAND PHYSICIANS CARE

Payer ID 22348

PO BOX 61778
PHOENIX, AZ 85082-1778

(800) 953-8852
WWW.MARYLANDPHYSICIANSCARE.COM/PROVIDERS.ASPX

MARYLAND PMHS VALUEOPTIONS

Payer ID 77063

PO BOX 1950
LATHAM, NY 12110

(800) 888-1965
HTTP://MARYLAND.VALUEOPTIONS.COM/INDEX.HTM

MASSACHUSETTS MEDICAID HMO (NEIGHBORHOOD HEALTH PLAN)

Payer ID 4293

253 SUMMER ST
BOSTON, MA 02210
PO BOX 10
NUTTING LAKE, MA 01865-0010

(800) 462-5449
WWW.NHP.ORG

MASSACHUSETTS MEDICAID HMO (NETWORK HEALTH)

Payer ID 4332

101 STATION LANDING 4TH FL
MEDFORD, MA 02155
PO BOX 390310
CAMBRIDGE, MA 02139

(888) 257-1985
WWW.NETWORK-HEALTH.ORG

MASSACHUSETTS MUTUAL

Payer ID 80314

1295 STATE ST
SPRINGFIELD, MA 01111-0001

(413) 788-8411
(800) 272-2216
WWW.MASSMUTUAL.COM

MASTERS, MATES AND PILOTS PLAN

Payer ID MMPHB

700 MARITIME BLVD STE A
LINTHICUM HEIGHTS, MD 21090-1996

(410) 850-8500
(877) 667-5522
WWW.BRIDGEDECK.ORG

MATRIX ABSENCE MANAGEMENT

Payer ID WA045

11221 N 28TH DR
PHOENIX, AZ 85029

(602) 866-2333
WWW.MATRIXCOS.COM

MAYO MANAGEMENT SERVICES, INC.

Payer ID 41154

4001 41ST STREET NW
ROCHESTER, MN 55901-8901

(800) 635-6671
WWW.MMSISERVICES.COM

MBA

Payer ID 83028

PO BOX 57340
MURRAY, UT 84157

(801) 268-3334
(800) 877-3727
WWW.MBA.TO/

MBA OF MD, INC.

Payer ID 37298

PO BOX 950
FOREST HILL, MD 21050

(410) 877-2002
(888) 532-3467
WWW.MBAMARYLAND.COM

MBA OF WYOMING

Payer ID 87065

PO BOX 98
WORLAND, WY 82401

(800) 246-4622
WWW.MBAWYOMING.COM

MCLAREN

Payer ID 38338

PO BOX 1511
FLINT, MI 48501

(888) 327-0671
WWW.MCLARENHEALTHPLAN.ORG

MCS

Payer ID 6197P

PO BOX 9026547
SAN JUAN, PR 00902-3547

(888) 758-1616
WWW.MCS.COM.PR/ES/PROVEEDORES/PAGINAS/DEFAULT.ASPX

MD CARE HEALTH PLAN

PO BOX 92919
LONG BEACH, CA 90809

(888) 285-9676
WWW.MDCAREHEALTHPLAN.COM/PROVIDERS.HTML

MDWISE HOOSIER ALLIANCE

Payer ID 20475

PO BOX 7303
LONDON, KY 40742-7303

(800) 581-2488
WWW.HOOSIERALLIANCE.ORG/PROVIDER/

MDWISE SELECT HEALTH NETWORK

Payer ID MWSHN

PO BOX 853921
RICHARDSON, TX 75085-3921

(800) 356-1204
WWW.MDWISE.ORG/PROVIDERS.HTML

MDWISE- HIP

Payer ID MDWIS

PO BOX 78310
INDIANAPOLIS, IN 46278

(317) 630-2831
(800) 356-1204
WWW.MDWISE.ORG/PROVIDERS.HTML

MDX HAWAII

500 ALA MOANA BLVD STE 2-200
HONOLULU, HI 96813

(808) 522-7560
WWW.MDXHAWAII.COM

MEADOWBROOK INSURANCE GROUP

Payer ID WZ927

26255 AMERICAN DR
SOUTHFIELD, MI 48034-6112

(248) 358-1100
(800) 482-2726
WWW.MEADOWBROOK.COM

MED-PAY

Payer ID 00130

PO BOX 10909
SPRINGFIELD, MO 65808

(800) 777-9087
WWW.MED-PAY.COM/HEALTHCARE.PHP?ID=8

MED3000 COVENTRY HEALTHY KIDS

Payer ID EM521

PO BOX 10948
PENSACOLA, FL 32524

(805) 438-4487
WWW.HFNI.COM

MED3000 HEALTHSPRING

Payer ID EM216

PO BOX 11547
PENSACOLA, FL 32524

(805) 438-4487
WWW.HFNI.COM

MED3000 PEDICARE TITLE 19

Payer ID EM039

PO BOX 981713
EL PASO, TX 79998

(866) 376-2456
WWW.PEDICARE.PEDS.UFL.EDU/

MED3000 PEDICARE TITLE 21

Payer ID EM522

PO BOX 981717
EL PASO, TX 79998

(866) 376-2456
WWW.PEDICARE.PEDS.UFL.EDU/

MEDADMIN SOL INC

Payer ID 58204

1995 N PARK PL STE 150
ATLANTA, GA 30339

(770) 810-3700
WWW.MEDADMINSOLUTIONS.COM/

MEDCO HEALTH, LLC

PO BOX 7247
PHILADELPHIA, PA 19170-0304

(800) 251-7690
WWW.MEDCOHEALTH.COM

MEDCOST, INC.

Payer ID 56162	PO BOX 25307 WINSTON-SALEM, NC 27114-5307	(800) 824-7406 WWW.MEDCOST.COM/ PHYSICIANS_MAIN.HTM

MEDFOCUS

Payer ID 95321	2811 WILSHIRE BLVD STE 900 SANTA MONICA, CA 90403-4801	(800) 398-8999 WWW.MEDFOCUS.NET

MEDI-CAL

Payer ID MDCAL	PO BOX 15700 SACRAMENTO, CA 95852-1700	(916) 636-1200 WWW.MEDI-CAL.CA.GOV
Payer ID MDCAL	PO BOX 15507 SACRAMENTO, CA 95852-1507	(916) 636-1200 WWW.MEDI-CAL.CA.GOV

MEDICA

Payer ID 94265	PO BOX 30990 SALT LAKE CITY, UT 84130	(800) 458-5512 HTTP://PROVIDER.MEDICA.COM/ DEFAULT.ASPX

MEDICA HEALTH CARE PLAN, INC

Payer ID 78857	PO BOX 141368 CORAL GABLES, FL 33114	(305) 460-0650 (800) 348-5548 WWW.MEDICAPLANS.COM/

MEDICAID-ALABAMA

Payer ID ALMCD	PO BOX 5624 MONTGOMERY, AL 36103-5624	(334) 242-5000 (800) 362-1504 WWW.MEDICAID.ALABAMA.GOV

MEDICAID-ALASKA

Payer ID AKMCD	PO BOX 240769 ANCHORAGE, AK 99524-0769	(907) 644-6800 (800) 770-5650 WWW.MEDICAIDALASKA.COM

MEDICAID-ARIZONA

Payer ID AZMCD	801 E JEFFERSON PHOENIX, AZ 85034-2217	(602) 417-4000 (800) 523-0231 WWW.AZAHCCS.GOV

MEDICAID-ARKANSAS

Payer ID ARMCD	PO BOX 8036 LITTLE ROCK, AR 72203-8036	(501) 376-2211 WWW.MEDICAID.STATE.AR.US

MEDICAID-CALIFORNIA

Payer ID MDCAL	PO BOX 997413 MS 4400 SACREMENTO, CA 95899-7413	(916) 445-4171 (800) 541-5555 WWW.DHCS.CA.GOV/PROVGOVPART/PAGES/ DEFAULT.ASPX

MEDICAID-COLORADO

Payer ID COMCD	PO BOX 30 DENVER, CO 80201	(303) 534-0146 (800) 237-0757 WWW.COLORADO.GOV/CS/SATELLITE/HCPF/ HCPF/1197364127336

MEDICAID-CONNECTICUT

Payer ID CTMCD	25 SIGOURNEY ST HARTFORD, CT 06106-5001	(860) 269-2028 WWW.CTDSSMAP.COM/CTPORTAL/PROVIDER/ TABID/45/DEFAULT.ASPX

MEDICAID-DELAWARE

Payer ID DEMCD	PO BOX 909 NEW CASTLE, DE 19720-0909	(302) 454-7154 (800) 999-3371 WWW.DMAP.STATE.DE.US

MEDICAID-DISTRICT OF COLUMBIA

Payer ID DCMCD	PO BOX 34768 WASHINGTON, DC 20043-4768	(866) 407-2005 WWW.DC-MEDICAID.COM

MEDICAID-FLORIDA

Payer ID FLMCD	PO BOX 7072 TALLAHASSEE, FL 32314-7072	(800) 239-7560 WWW.MYMEDICAID-FLORIDA.COM

MEDICAID-GEORGIA

Payer ID GAMCD	PO BOX 5000 MCRAE, GA 31055	(800) 766-4456 WWW.MMIS.GEORGIA.GOV

MEDICAID-HAWAII

Payer ID HIMCD	PO BOX 1220 HONOLULU, HI 96807-1220	(808) 327-4970 (800) 235-4378 WWW.MED-QUEST.US

MEDICAID-IDAHO

Payer ID IDMCD	PO BOX 70084 BOISE, ID 83707	(208) 334-5747 WWW.HEALTHANDWELFARE.IDAHO.GOV

MEDICAID-ILLINOIS

Payer ID ILMCD	PO BOX 19105 SPRINGFIELD, IL 62794-9105	(800) 842-1461 WWW.HFS.ILLINOIS.GOV

MEDICAID-INDIANA

Payer ID INMCD	PO BOX 7269 INDIANAPOLIS, IN 46207-7269	(317) 233-4455 (800) 738-6770 WWW.INDIANAMEDICAID.COM

MEDICAID-IOWA

Payer ID IAMCD	PO BOX 150001 DES MOINES, IA 50315	(515) 256-4609 (800) 338-7752 WWW.IME.STATE.IA.US

MEDICAID-KANSAS

Payer ID KSMCD	PO BOX 3571 TOPEKA, KS 66601-3571	(800) 933-6593 WWW.KMAP-STATE-KS.US

MEDICAID-KENTUCKY

Payer ID KYMCD	PO BOX 2108 FRANKFORT, KY 40602	(800) 807-1232 HTTP://CHFS.KY.GOV/PROVIDERS/

MEDICAID-LOUISIANA

Payer ID LAMCD	PO BOX 91020 BATON ROUGE, LA 70821	(800) 473-2783 WWW.LAMEDICAID.COM

MEDICAID-MAINE

Payer ID MEMCD	MAINE CARE CLAIMS PROCESSING M-500 AUGUSTA, ME 04332	(866) 690-5585 HTTPS://MAINECARE.MAINE.GOV/ PROVIDERHOMEPAGE.ASPX

MEDICAID-MARYLAND

Payer ID MDMCD	PO BOX 1935 BALTIMORE, MD 21203	(410) 767-5503 (800) 445-1159 HTTP://MMCP.DHMH.MARYLAND.GOV/

MEDICAID-MASSACHUSETTS

Payer ID MAMCD | PO BOX 9118 HINGHAM, MA 02043 | (800) 841-2900 WWW.MASS.GOV/MASSHEALTH

MEDICAID-MICHIGAN

Payer ID MIMCD | PO BOX 30043 LANSING, MI 48909-7979 | (800) 292-2550 WWW.MICHIGAN.GOV/MEDICAIDPROVIDERS

MEDICAID-MINNESOTA

Payer ID MNMCD | PO BOX 64975 ST PAUL, MN 55164 | (651) 431-2700 (800) 366-5411 WWW.DHS.STATE.MN.US/

MEDICAID-MISSISSIPPI

Payer ID MSMCD | PO BOX 23076 JACKSON, MS 39225-3076 | (601) 206-3000 (800) 884-3222 WWW.MEDICAID.MS.GOV

MEDICAID-MISSOURI

Payer ID MOMCD | PO BOX 5600 JEFFERSON CITY, MO 65102 | (573) 635-8908 WWW.DSS.MO.GOV

MEDICAID-MONTANA

Payer ID MTMCD | PO BOX 8000 HELENA, MT 59604 | (406) 442-1837 (800) 624-3958 WWW.MEDICAIDPROVIDER.HHS.MT.GOV

MEDICAID-NEBRASKA

Payer ID NEMCD | PO BOX 95026 LINCOLN, NE 68509-5026 | (402) 471-9128 (877) 255-3092 HTTP://DHHS.NE.GOV/MEDICAID/PAGES/MED_PROVHOME.ASPX

MEDICAID-NEVADA

Payer ID NVMCD | PO BOX 30042 RENO, NV 89520-3042 | (800) 942-6511 (877) 638-3472 WWW.MEDICAID.NV.GOV/PROVIDERS

MEDICAID-NEW HAMPSHIRE

Payer ID NHMCD | PO BOX 2001 CONCORD, NH 03302 | (603) 224-1747 (800) 423-8303 WWW.NHMEDICAID.COM

MEDICAID-NEW JERSEY

Payer ID NJMCD | PO BOX 4808 TRENTON, NJ 08650-4808 | (800) 776-6334 WWW.NJMMIS.COM

MEDICAID-NEW MEXICO

Payer ID NMMCD | PO BOX 27418 ALBUQUERQUE, NM 87125-7418 | (505) 246-2219 (800) 820-6901 WWW.HSD.STATE.NM.US

MEDICAID-NEW YORK

Payer ID NYMCD | PO BOX 4601 RENSSELAER, NY 12144-4601 | (800) 343-9000 WWW.EMEDNY.ORG

MEDICAID-NORTH CAROLINA

Payer ID NCMCD | PO BOX 30968 RALEIGH, NC 27622 | (800) 723-4337 WWW.DHHS.STATE.NC.US/DMA

MEDICAID-NORTH DAKOTA

Payer ID NDMCD	600 E BLVD AVE DEPT 325 BISMARK, ND 58505-0250	(701) 328-2321 WWW.ND.GOV/DHS

MEDICAID-OHIO

Payer ID OHMCD	PO BOX 7965 AKRON, OH 44306	(800) 686-1516 HTTP://JFS.OHIO.GOV/OHP/PROVIDER.STM

MEDICAID-OKLAHOMA

Payer ID OKMCD	PO BOX 18506 OKLAHOMA CITY, OK 73154	(405) 522-6205 (800) 522-0114 WWW.OKHCA.ORG

MEDICAID-OREGON

Payer ID ORMCD	PO BOX 14955 SALEM, OR 97309-4957	(503) 945-5772 (800) 336-6016 WWW.OREGON.GOV/DHS/HEALTHPLAN/

MEDICAID-PENNSYLVANIA

Payer ID PAMCD	PO BOX 8297 HARRISBURG, PA 17105	(800) 537-8862 WWW.DPW.STATE.PA.US/PROVIDER/ INDEX.HTM

MEDICAID-RHODE ISLAND

Payer ID RIMCD	PO BOX 2010 WARWICK, RI 02887-2010	(401) 784-8100 (800) 964-6211 WWW.DHS.RI.GOV

MEDICAID-SOUTH CAROLINA

Payer ID SCMCD	PO BOX 1412 COLUMBIA, SC 29202-1412	(888) 289-0709 WWW.SCDHS.GOV

MEDICAID-SOUTH DAKOTA

Payer ID SDMCD	700 GOVERNERS DR PIERRE, SD 57501-2237	(605) 773-3165 HTTP://DSS.SD.GOV/SDMEDX/ PROVIDERS.ASPX

MEDICAID-TENNESSEE

Payer ID TNMCD	PO BOX 460 NASHVILLE, TN 37202	(800) 852-2683 WWW.TN.GOV/TENNCARE/PROVIDERS.SHTML

MEDICAID-TEXAS

Payer ID TXMCD	PO BOX 200555 AUSTIN, TX 78720-0555	(512) 424-6500 (800) 925-9126 WWW.TMHP.COM

MEDICAID-UTAH

Payer ID UTMCD	PO BOX 143106 SALT LAKE CITY, UT 84114-3106	(801) 538-6155 (800) 662-9651 HTTP://HEALTH.UTAH.GOV/MEDICAID/ PROVHTML/PROVIDER.HTML

MEDICAID-VERMONT

Payer ID VTMCD	PO BOX 777 WILLISTON, VT 05495-0777	(802) 878-7871 HTTP://OVHA.VERMONT.GOV/

MEDICAID-VIRGINIA

Payer ID VAMCD	PO BOX 27444 RICHMOND, VA 23261-7444	(804) 965-9732 (800) 772-9996 WWW.DMAS.VIRGINIA.GOV

MEDICAID-WASHINGTON

Payer ID WAMCD

PO BOX 9248
OLYMPIA, WA 98507-9248

(800) 562-3022
HTTP://HRSA.DSHS.WA.GOV

MEDICAID-WEST VIRGINIA

Payer ID WVMCD

PO BOX 3767
CHARLESTON, WV 25337

(888) 483-0793
WWW.DHHR.WV.GOV/BMS/PAGES/DEFAULT.ASPX

MEDICAID-WISCONSIN

Payer ID WIMCD

313 BLETTNER BLVD
MADISON, WI 53784

(800) 947-9627
WWW.DHS.WISCONSIN.GOV/PARTNERS.HTM

MEDICAID-WYOMING

Payer ID WYMCD

PO BOX 547
CHEYENNE, WY 82003-0547

(800) 251-1268
HTTP://WYEQUALITYCARE.ACS-INC.COM

MEDICAL ASSOCIATES HEALTH PLANS AND HEALTH CHOICES

1605 ASSOCIATES DR STE. 101
DUBUQUE, IA 52004-5002

(563) 556-8070
(800) 747-8900
WWW.MAHEALTHCARE.COM

MEDICAL BENEFIT ADMINISTRATION, INC.

Payer ID 68041

900 E MAIN ST STE 301
GRASS VALLEY, CA 95945

(530) 271-3200
(866) 537-5755
WWW.E-MBAINC.COM/

MEDICAL BENEFITS MUTUAL

Payer ID 74323

1975 TAMARACK RD
NEWARK, OH 43058

(800) 423-3151
WWW.MEDBEN.COM

MEDICAL DEVELOPMENT INTERNATIONAL

Payer ID 52181

90 FORT WADE RD
PONTE VEDRA, FL 32081

(904) 473-1200
WWW.MEDINT.COM

MEDICAL MUTUAL OF OHIO

Payer ID 29076

PO BOX 6018
CLEVELAND, OH 44101-1018

(800) 362-1279
WWW.PROVIDER.MEDMUTUAL.COM/

M

MEDICAL NETWORK OF COLORADO SPRINGS

Payer ID CSMED

PO BOX 828
COLORADO SPRINGS, CO 80901

(800) 207-1018
WWW.MYMEDNET.COM

MEDICAL PARTNERS OF AMERICA

Payer ID 80026

90 FORT WADE RD
PONTE VEDRA, FL 32081-5102

(904) 473-1200
WWW.MEDINT.COM

MEDICAL RESOURCE NETWORK

Payer ID 58203

5285 MEADOWS RD STE 181
LAKE OSWEGO, OR 97035-3253

(503) 452-1748
WWW.MEDRES.NET

MEDICAL SERVICES INITIATIVE

Payer ID 12057

PO BOX 30248
LONG BEACH, CA 90853

(800) 206-6591
WWW.OCHEALTHINFO.COM/PHS/SERVICES/HCR/MSI

MEDICARE BLUE ADVANTAGE OF SOUTH CAROLINA

Payer ID SCBLS

PO BOX 100300
COLUMBIA, SC 29202

(803) 736-1576
(800) 334-2583
WWW.SOUTHCAROLINABLUES.COM

MEDICARE PART B GHI

Payer ID GHMCR

PO BOX 2870
NEW YORK, NY 10116

(877) 868-7965
(646) 458-6721
HTTP://TEST.GHI.DFFCO.COM/INDEX.PHP

MEDICARE RAILROAD

Payer ID RRWMC

PO BOX 10066
AUGUSTA, GA 30999

(888) 355-9165
WWW.PALMETTOGBA.COM

MEDICARE SUPPLEMENTAL

Payer ID VABLS

PO BOX 27401
RICHMOND, VA 23279

(888) 445-8916
WWW.MEDICARE-ANTHEM.COM

MEDICARE-DME MAC-ALABAMA

Payer ID 86033

PO BOX 20010
NASHVILLE, TN 37202

(866) 270-4909
WWW.CGSMEDICARE.COM

MEDICARE-DME MAC-ALASKA

PO BOX 6727
FARGO, ND 58108-6727

(877) 320-0390
WWW.NORIDIANMEDICARE.COM

MEDICARE-DME MAC-ARIZONA

PO BOX 6727
FARGO, ND 58108-6727

(877) 320-0390
WWW.NORIDIANMEDICARE.COM

MEDICARE-DME MAC-ARKANSAS

Payer ID 86033

PO BOX 20010
NASHVILLE, TN 37202

(866) 270-4909
WWW.CGSMEDICARE.COM

MEDICARE-DME MAC-CALIFORNIA

PO BOX 6727
FARGO, ND 58108-6727

(877) 320-0390
WWW.NORIDIANMEDICARE.COM

MEDICARE-DME MAC-COLORADO

Payer ID 86033

PO BOX 20010
NASHVILLE, TN 37202

(866) 270-4909
WWW.CGSMEDICARE.COM

MEDICARE-DME MAC-CONNECTICUT

PO BOX 9165
HINGHAM, MA 02043-9165

(866) 590-6731
WWW.MEDICARENHIC.COM

MEDICARE-DME MAC-DELAWARE

PO BOX 9165
HINGHAM, MA 02043-9165

(866) 590-6731
WWW.MEDICARENHIC.COM

MEDICARE-DME MAC-DISTRICT OF COLUMBIA

PO BOX 9165
HINGHAM, MA 02043-9165

(866) 590-6731
WWW.MEDICARENHIC.COM

MEDICARE-DME MAC-FLORIDA

Payer ID 86033

PO BOX 20010
NASHVILLE, TN 37202

(866) 270-4909
WWW.CGSMEDICARE.COM

MEDICARE-DME MAC-GEORGIA

Payer ID 86033

PO BOX 20010
NASHVILLE, TN 37202

(866) 270-4909
WWW.CGSMEDICARE.COM

MEDICARE-DME MAC-GUAM

PO BOX 6727
FARGO, ND 58108-6727

(877) 320-0390
WWW.NORIDIANMEDICARE.COM

MEDICARE-DME MAC-HAWAII

PO BOX 6727
FARGO, ND 58108-6727

(877) 320-0390
WWW.NORIDIANMEDICARE.COM

MEDICARE-DME MAC-IDAHO

PO BOX 6727
FARGO, ND 58108-6727

(877) 320-0390
WWW.NORIDIANMEDICARE.COM

MEDICARE-DME MAC-ILLINOIS

PO BOX 7027
INDIANAPOLIS, IN 46207-7027

(866) 590-6727
WWW.NGSMEDICARE.COM

MEDICARE-DME MAC-INDIANA

PO BOX 7027
INDIANAPOLIS, IN 46207-7027

(866) 590-6727
WWW.NGSMEDICARE.COM

MEDICARE-DME MAC-IOWA

PO BOX 6727
FARGO, ND 58108-6727

(877) 320-0390
WWW.NORIDIANMEDICARE.COM

MEDICARE-DME MAC-KANSAS

PO BOX 6727
FARGO, ND 58108-6727

(877) 320-0390
WWW.NORIDIANMEDICARE.COM

MEDICARE-DME MAC-KENTUCKY

PO BOX 7027
INDIANAPOLIS, IN 46207-7027

(866) 590-6727
WWW.NGSMEDICARE.COM

MEDICARE-DME MAC-LOUISIANA

Payer ID 86033

PO BOX 20010
NASHVILLE, TN 37202

(866) 270-4909
WWW.CGSMEDICARE.COM

MEDICARE-DME MAC-MONTANA

PO BOX 6727
FARGO, ND 58108-6727

(877) 320-0390
WWW.NORIDIANMEDICARE.COM

MEDICARE-DME MAC-MAINE

PO BOX 9165
HINGHAM, MA 02043-9165

(866) 590-6731
WWW.MEDICARENHIC.COM

MEDICARE-DME MAC-MARYLAND

PO BOX 9165
HINGHAM, MA 02043-9165

(866) 590-6731
WWW.MEDICARENHIC.COM

MEDICARE-DME MAC-MASSACHUSETTS

PO BOX 9165
HINGHAM, MA 02043-9165

(866) 590-6731
WWW.MEDICARENHIC.COM

MEDICARE-DME MAC-MICHIGAN

PO BOX 7027
INDIANAPOLIS, IN 46207-7027

(866) 590-6727
WWW.NGSMEDICARE.COM

MEDICARE-DME MAC-MINNESOTA

PO BOX 7027
INDIANAPOLIS, IN 46207-7027

(866) 590-6727
WWW.NGSMEDICARE.COM

MEDICARE-DME MAC-MISSISSIPPI

Payer ID 86033

PO BOX 20010
NASHVILLE, TN 37202

(866) 270-4909
WWW.CGSMEDICARE.COM

MEDICARE-DME MAC-MISSOURI

PO BOX 6727
FARGO, ND 58108-6727

(877) 320-0390
WWW.NORIDIANMEDICARE.COM

MEDICARE-DME MAC-NEBRASKA

PO BOX 6727
FARGO, ND 58108-6727

(877) 320-0390
WWW.NORIDIANMEDICARE.COM

MEDICARE-DME MAC-NEVADA

PO BOX 6727
FARGO, ND 58108-6727

(877) 320-0390
WWW.NORIDIANMEDICARE.COM

MEDICARE-DME MAC-NEW HAMPSHIRE

PO BOX 9165
HINGHAM, MA 02043-9165

(866) 590-6731
WWW.MEDICARENHIC.COM

MEDICARE-DME MAC-NEW JERSEY

PO BOX 9165
HINGHAM, MA 02043-9165

(866) 590-6731
WWW.MEDICARENHIC.COM

MEDICARE-DME MAC-NEW MEXICO

Payer ID 86033

PO BOX 20010
NASHVILLE, TN 37202

(866) 270-4909
WWW.CGSMEDICARE.COM

MEDICARE-DME MAC-NEW YORK

PO BOX 9165
HINGHAM, MA 02043-9165

(866) 590-6731
WWW.MEDICARENHIC.COM

MEDICARE-DME MAC-NORTH CAROLINA

Payer ID 86033

PO BOX 20010
NASHVILLE, TN 37202

(866) 270-4909
WWW.CGSMEDICARE.COM

MEDICARE-DME MAC-NORTH DAKOTA

PO BOX 6727
FARGO, ND 58108-6727

(877) 320-0390
WWW.NORIDIANMEDICARE.COM

MEDICARE-DME MAC-OHIO

PO BOX 7027
INDIANAPOLIS, IN 46207-7027

(866) 590-6727
WWW.NGSMEDICARE.COM

MEDICARE-DME MAC-OKLAHOMA

Payer ID 86033

PO BOX 20010
NASHVILLE, TN 37202

(866) 270-4909
WWW.CGSMEDICARE.COM

MEDICARE-DME MAC-OREGON

PO BOX 6727
FARGO, ND 58108-6727

(877) 320-0390
WWW.NORIDIANMEDICARE.COM

MEDICARE-DME MAC-PENNSYLVANIA

PO BOX 9165
HINGHAM, MA 02043-9165

(866) 590-6731
WWW.MEDICARENHIC.COM

MEDICARE-DME MAC-PUERTO RICO

Payer ID 86033

PO BOX 20010
NASHVILLE, TN 37202

(866) 270-4909
WWW.CGSMEDICARE.COM

MEDICARE-DME MAC-RHODE ISLAND

PO BOX 9165
HINGHAM, MA 02043-9165

(866) 590-6731
WWW.MEDICARENHIC.COM

MEDICARE-DME MAC-SOUTH CAROLINA

Payer ID 86033 | PO BOX 20010, NASHVILLE, TN 37202 | (866) 270-4909, WWW.CGSMEDICARE.COM

MEDICARE-DME MAC-SOUTH DAKOTA

PO BOX 6727, FARGO, ND 58108-6727 | (877) 320-0390, WWW.NORIDIANMEDICARE.COM

MEDICARE-DME MAC-TENNESSEE

Payer ID 86033 | PO BOX 20010, NASHVILLE, TN 37202 | (866) 270-4909, WWW.CGSMEDICARE.COM

MEDICARE-DME MAC-TEXAS

Payer ID 86033 | PO BOX 20010, NASHVILLE, TN 37202 | (866) 270-4909, WWW.CGSMEDICARE.COM

MEDICARE-DME MAC-UTAH

PO BOX 6727, FARGO, ND 58108-6727 | (877) 320-0390, WWW.NORIDIANMEDICARE.COM

MEDICARE-DME MAC-VERMONT

PO BOX 9165, HINGHAM, MA 02043-9165 | (866) 590-6731, WWW.MEDICARENHIC.COM

MEDICARE-DME MAC-VIRGIN ISLANDS

Payer ID 86033 | PO BOX 20010, NASHVILLE, TN 37202 | (866) 270-4909, WWW.CGSMEDICARE.COM

MEDICARE-DME MAC-VIRGINIA

Payer ID 86033 | PO BOX 20010, NASHVILLE, TN 37202 | (866) 270-4909, WWW.CGSMEDICARE.COM

MEDICARE-DME MAC-WASHINGTON

PO BOX 6727, FARGO, ND 58108-6727 | (877) 320-0390, WWW.NORIDIANMEDICARE.COM

MEDICARE-DME MAC-WEST VIRGINIA

Payer ID 86033 | PO BOX 20010, NASHVILLE, TN 37202 | (866) 270-4909, WWW.CGSMEDICARE.COM

MEDICARE-DME MAC-WISCONSIN

PO BOX 7027, INDIANAPOLIS, IN 46207-7027 | (866) 590-6727, WWW.NGSMEDICARE.COM

MEDICARE-DME MAC-WYOMING

PO BOX 6727, FARGO, ND 58108-6727 | (877) 320-0390, WWW.NORIDIANMEDICARE.COM

MEDICARE-HOME HEALTH & HOSPICE-ALABAMA

AG-600 PO BOX 100238, COLUMBIA, SC 29202-3238 | (866) 830-3925, WWW.PALMETTOGBA.COM

MEDICARE-HOME HEALTH & HOSPICE-ALASKA

PO BOX 7150, INDIANAPOLIS, IN 46207-7150 | (866) 590-6724, WWW.NGSMEDICARE.COM

MEDICARE-HOME HEALTH & HOSPICE-ARIZONA

PO BOX 7150, INDIANAPOLIS, IN 46207-7150 | (866) 590-6724, WWW.NGSMEDICARE.COM

MEDICARE-HOME HEALTH & HOSPICE-ARKANSAS

AG-600 PO BOX 100238
COLUMBIA, SC 29202-3238
(866) 801-5301
WWW.PALMETTOGBA.COM

MEDICARE-HOME HEALTH & HOSPICE-CALIFORNIA

PO BOX 7150
INDIANAPOLIS, IN 46207-7150
(866) 590-6724
WWW.NGSMEDICARE.COM

MEDICARE-HOME HEALTH & HOSPICE-COLORADO

PO B OX 20019
NASHVILLE, TN 37202
(877) 299-4500
WWW.CGSMEDICARE.COM

MEDICARE-HOME HEALTH & HOSPICE-CONNECTICUT

PO BOX 9201
HINGHAM, MA 02044
(877) 757-7783
WWW.MEDICARENHIC.COM

MEDICARE-HOME HEALTH & HOSPICE-DELAWARE

PO BOX 20019
NASHVILLE, TN 37202
(877) 299-4500
WWW.CGSMEDICARE.COM

MEDICARE-HOME HEALTH & HOSPICE-DISTRICT OF COLUMBIA

PO BOX 20019
NASHVILLE, TN 37202
(877) 299-4500
WWW.CGSMEDICARE.COM

MEDICARE-HOME HEALTH & HOSPICE-FLORIDA

AG-600 PO BOX 100238
COLUMBIA, SC 29202-3238
(866) 801-5301
WWW.PALMETTOGBA.COM

MEDICARE-HOME HEALTH & HOSPICE-GEORGIA

AG-600 PO BOX 100238
COLUMBIA, SC 29202-3238
(866) 801-5301
WWW.PALMETTOGBA.COM

MEDICARE-HOME HEALTH & HOSPICE-GUAM

PO BOX 7150
INDIANAPOLIS, IN 46207-7150
(866) 590-6724
WWW.NGSMEDICARE.COM

MEDICARE-HOME HEALTH & HOSPICE-HAWAII

PO BOX 7150
INDIANAPOLIS, IN 46207-7150
(866) 590-6724
WWW.NGSMEDICARE.COM

MEDICARE-HOME HEALTH & HOSPICE-IDAHO

PO BOX 7150
INDIANAPOLIS, IN 46207-7150
(866) 590-6724
WWW.NGSMEDICARE.COM

MEDICARE-HOME HEALTH & HOSPICE-ILLINOIS

AG-600 PO BOX 100238
COLUMBIA, SC 29202-3238
(866) 830-3925
WWW.PALMETTOGBA.COM

MEDICARE-HOME HEALTH & HOSPICE-INDIANA

AG-600 PO BOX 100238
COLUMBIA, SC 29202-3238
(866) 801-5301
WWW.PALMETTOGBA.COM

MEDICARE-HOME HEALTH & HOSPICE-IOWA

PO BOX 20019
NASHVILLE, TN 37202
(877) 299-4500
WWW.CGSMEDICARE.COM

MEDICARE-HOME HEALTH & HOSPICE-KANSAS

PO BOX 20019
NASHVILLE, TN 37202
(877) 299-4500
WWW.CGSMEDICARE.COM

MEDICARE-HOME HEALTH & HOSPICE-KENTUCKY

PO BOX 20019
NASHVILLE, TN 37202
(877) 299-4500
WWW.NGSMEDICARE.COM

MEDICARE-HOME HEALTH & HOSPICE-LOUISIANA

AG-600 PO BOX 100238
COLUMBIA, SC 29202-3238
(866) 801-5301
WWW.PALMETTOGBA.COM

MEDICARE-HOME HEALTH & HOSPICE-MAINE

PO BOX 9201
HINGHAM, MA 02044
(877) 757-7783
WWW.MEDICARENHIC.COM

MEDICARE-HOME HEALTH & HOSPICE-MARYLAND

PO BOX 20019
NASHVILLE, TN 37202
(877) 299-4500
WWW.CGSMEDICARE.COM

MEDICARE-HOME HEALTH & HOSPICE-MASSACHUSETTS

PO BOX 9201
HINGHAM, MA 02044
(877) 757-7783
WWW.MEDICARENHIC.COM

MEDICARE-HOME HEALTH & HOSPICE-MICHIGAN

PO BOX 7150
INDIANAPOLIS, IN 46207-7150
(866) 590-6728
WWW.NGSMEDICARE.COM

MEDICARE-HOME HEALTH & HOSPICE-MINNESOTA

PO BOX 7150
INDIANAPOLIS, IN 46207-7150
(866) 590-6728
WWW.NGSMEDICARE.COM

MEDICARE-HOME HEALTH & HOSPICE-MISSISSIPPI

AG-600 PO BOX 100238
COLUMBIA, SC 29202-3238
(866) 801-5301
WWW.PALMETTOGBA.COM

MEDICARE-HOME HEALTH & HOSPICE-MISSOURI

PO BOX 20019
NASHVILLE, TN 37202
(877) 299-4500
WWW.CGSMEDICARE.COM

MEDICARE-HOME HEALTH & HOSPICE-MONTANA

PO BOX 20019
NASHVILLE, TN 37202
(877) 299-4500
WWW.CGSMEDICARE.COM

MEDICARE-HOME HEALTH & HOSPICE-NEBRASKA

PO BOX 20019
NASHVILLE, TN 37202
(877) 299-4500
WWW.CGSMEDICARE.COM

MEDICARE-HOME HEALTH & HOSPICE-NEVADA

PO BOX 7150
INDIANAPOLIS, IN 46207-7150
(866) 590-6724
WWW.NGSMEDICARE.COM

MEDICARE-HOME HEALTH & HOSPICE-NEW HAMPSHIRE

PO BOX 9201
HINGHAM, MA 02044
(877) 757-7783
WWW.MEDICARENHIC.COM

MEDICARE-HOME HEALTH & HOSPICE-NEW JERSEY

PO BOX 7091
INDIANAPOLIS, IN 46207-7150
(866) 590-6728
WWW.NGSMEDICARE.COM

MEDICARE-HOME HEALTH & HOSPICE-NEW MEXICO

AG-600 PO BOX 100238
COLUMBIA, SC 29202-3238
(866) 801-5301
WWW.PALMETTOGBA.COM

MEDICARE-HOME HEALTH & HOSPICE-NEW YORK

PO BOX 7091
INDIANAPOLIS, IN 46207-7150
(866) 590-6728
WWW.NGSMEDICARE.COM

MEDICARE-HOME HEALTH & HOSPICE-NORTH CAROLINA

AG-600 PO BOX 100238
COLUMBIA, SC 29202-3238
(866) 801-5301
WWW.PALMETTOGBA.COM

MEDICARE-HOME HEALTH & HOSPICE-NORTH DAKOTA

PO BOX 20019
NASHVILLE, TN 37202
(877) 299-4500
WWW.CGSMEDICARE.COM

MEDICARE-HOME HEALTH & HOSPICE-OHIO

AG-600 PO BOX 100238
COLUMBIA, SC 29202-3238
(866) 801-5301
WWW.PALMETTOGBA.COM

MEDICARE-HOME HEALTH & HOSPICE-OKLAHOMA

AG-600 PO BOX 100238
COLUMBIA, SC 29202-3238
(866) 801-5301
WWW.PALMETTOGBA.COM

MEDICARE-HOME HEALTH & HOSPICE-OREGON

PO BOX 7150
INDIANAPOLIS, IN 46207-7150
(866) 590-6724
WWW.NGSMEDICARE.COM

MEDICARE-HOME HEALTH & HOSPICE-PENNSYLVANIA

PO BOX 20019
NASHVILLE, TN 37202
(877) 299-4500
WWW.CGSMEDICARE.COM

MEDICARE-HOME HEALTH & HOSPICE-PUERTO RICO

PO BOX 7150
INDIANAPOLIS, IN 46207-7150
(866) 590-6728
WWW.NGSMEDICARE.COM

MEDICARE-HOME HEALTH & HOSPICE-RHODE ISLAND

PO BOX 9201
HINGHAM, MA 02044
(877) 757-7783
WWW.MEDICARENHIC.COM

MEDICARE-HOME HEALTH & HOSPICE-SOUTH CAROLINA

AG-600 PO BOX 100238
COLUMBIA, SC 29202-3238
(866) 801-5301
WWW.PALMETTOGBA.COM

MEDICARE-HOME HEALTH & HOSPICE-SOUTH DAKOTA

PO BOX 20019
NASHVILLE, TN 37202
(877) 299-4500
WWW.CGSMEDICARE.COM

MEDICARE-HOME HEALTH & HOSPICE-TENNESSEE

AG-600 PO BOX 100238
COLUMBIA, SC 29202-3238
(866) 801-5301
WWW.PALMETTOGBA.COM

MEDICARE-HOME HEALTH & HOSPICE-TEXAS

AG-600 PO BOX 100238
COLUMBIA, SC 29202-3238
(866) 801-5301
WWW.PALMETTOGBA.COM

MEDICARE-HOME HEALTH & HOSPICE-UTAH

PO BOX 20019
NASHVILLE, TN 37202
(877) 299-4500
WWW.CGSMEDICARE.COM

MEDICARE-HOME HEALTH & HOSPICE-VERMONT

PO BOX 9201
HINGHAM, MA 02044
(877) 757-7783
WWW.MEDICARENHIC.COM

MEDICARE-HOME HEALTH & HOSPICE-VIRGIN ISLANDS

PO BOX 7150
INDIANAPOLIS, IN 46207-7150
(866) 419-9462
WWW.NGSMEDICARE.COM

MEDICARE-HOME HEALTH & HOSPICE-VIRGINIA

PO BOX 20019
NASHVILLE, TN 37202
(877) 299-4500
WWW.CGSMEDICARE.COM

MEDICARE-HOME HEALTH & HOSPICE-WASHINGTON

PO BOX 7150
INDIANAPOLIS, IN 46207-7150
(866) 590-6724
WWW.NGSMEDICARE.COM

MEDICARE-HOME HEALTH & HOSPICE-WEST VIRGINIA

PO BOX 20019
NASHVILLE, TN 37202
(877) 299-4500
WWW.CGSMEDICARE.COM

MEDICARE-HOME HEALTH & HOSPICE-WISCONSIN

PO BOX 7150
INDIANAPOLIS, IN 46207-7150
(866) 590-6728
WWW.NGSMEDICARE.COM

MEDICARE-HOME HEALTH & HOSPICE-WYOMING

PO BOX 20019
NASHVILLE, TN 37202
(877) 299-4500
WWW.CGSMEDICARE.COM

MEDICARE-PART A-ALABAMA

PO BOX 830139
BIRMINGHAM, AL 35283-0139
(877) 467-7516
WWW.CAHABAGBA.COM

MEDICARE-PART A-ALASKA

PO BOX 6720
FARGO, ND 57108-6720
(866) 497-7857
WWW.NORIDIANMEDICARE.COM

MEDICARE-PART A-ARIZONA

PO BOX 6730
FARGO, ND 57108-6730
(866) 497-7857
WWW.NORIDIANMEDICARE.COM

MEDICARE-PART A-ARKANSAS

PO BOX 890103
CAMP HILL, PA 17089
(855) 262-8782
WWW.NOVITAS-SOLUTIONS.COM

MEDICARE-PART A-CALIFORNIA

PO BOX 6726
FARGO, ND 57108
(866) 497-7857
WW.NORIDIANMEDICARE.COM

MEDICARE-PART A-COLORADO

PO BOX 890113
CAMP HILL, PA 17089
(855) 252-8782
WWW.NOVITAS-SOLUTIONS.COM

MEDICARE-PART A-CONNECTICUT

PO BOX 7091
INDIANAPOLIS, IN 46207-7091
(888) 855-4356
WWW.NGSMEDICARE.COM

MEDICARE-PART A-DELAWARE

PO BOX 890417
CAMP HILL, PA 17089-0417
(877) 235-8073
WWW.NOVITAS-SOLUTIONS.COM

MEDICARE-PART A-DISTRICT OF COLUMBIA

PO BOX 890385
CAMP HILL, PA 17089-0385
(877) 235-8073
WWW.NOVITAS-SOLUTIONS.COM

MEDICARE-PART A-FLORIDA

PO BOX 2711
JACKSONVILLE, FL 32232-5087
(888) 664-4112
WWW.FCSO.COM

MEDICARE-PART A-GEORGIA

PO BOX 830867
BIRMINGHAM, AL 35283-0867
(877) 467-7516
WWW.CAHABAGBA.COM

MEDICARE-PART A-GUAM

PO BOX 6726
FARGO, ND 57108
(866) 497-7857
WW.NORIDIANMEDICARE.COM

MEDICARE-PART A-HAWAII

PO BOX 6772
FARGO, ND 57108
(866) 497-7857
WW.NORIDIANMEDICARE.COM

MEDICARE-PART A-IDAHO

PO BOX 6726
FARGO, ND 57108-6726
(866) 497-7857
WWW.NORIDIANMEDICARE.COM

MEDICARE-PART A-ILLINOIS

PO BOX 7138
INDIANAPOLIS, IN 46207-7138
(877) 702-0990
WWW.NGSMEDICARE.COM

MEDICARE-PART A-INDIANA

PO BOX 8805
MARION, IL 62959
(855) 765-5378
WWW.WPSMEDICARE.COM

MEDICARE-PART A-IOWA

PO BOX 7665
MADISON, WI 53707-7665
(866) 518-3285
WWW.WPSMEDICARE.COM

MEDICARE-PART A-KANSAS

PO BOX 7576
MADISON, WI 53707-7576
(866) 518-3285
WWW.WPSMEDICARE.COM

MEDICARE-PART A-KENTUCKY

AG-600 PO BOX 100112
COLUMBIA, SC 29202
(866) 590-6703
WWW.CGSMEDICARE.COM

MEDICARE-PART A-LOUISIANA

PO BOX 890103
CAMP HILL, PA 17089
(877) 235-8073
WWW.NOVITAS-SOLUTIONS.COM

MEDICARE-PART A-MAINE

PO BOX 9201
HINGHAM, MA 02044
(877) 757-7783
WWW.MEDICARENHIC.COM

MEDICARE-PART A-MARYLAND

PO BOX 890385
CAMP HILL, PA 17089-0385
(877) 235-8037
WWW.NOVITAS-SOLUTIONS.COM

MEDICARE-PART A-MASSACHUSETTS

PO BOX 9201
HINGHAM, MA 02044
(877) 757-7783
WWW.MEDICARENHIC.COM

MEDICARE-PART A-MICHIGAN

PO BOX 8800
MARION, IL 62959
(855) 765-5378
WWW.WPSMEDICARE.COM

MEDICARE-PART A-MINNESOTA

PO BOX 7150
INDIANAPOLIS, IN 46207

(877) 309-4290
WWW.NGSMEDICARE.COM

MEDICARE-PART A-MISSISSIPPI

PO BOX 890103
CAMP HILL, PA 17089

(877) 235-8073
WWW.NOVITAS-SOLUTIONS.COM

MEDICARE-PART A-MISSOURI

PO BOX 8890
MADISON, WI 53708-8890

(866) 518-3285
WWW.WPSMEDICARE.COM

MEDICARE-PART A-MONTANA

PO BOX 6732
FARGO, ND 57108-6732

(866) 497-7857
WWW.NORIDIANMEDICARE.COM

MEDICARE-PART A-NEBRASKA

P.O. BOX 8667
MADISON, WI 53708-8799

(866) 518-3285
WWW.WPSMEDICARE.COM

MEDICARE-PART A-NEVADA

PO BOX 6726
FARGO, ND 57108

(866) 497-7587
WW.NORIDIANMEDICARE.COM

MEDICARE-PART A-NEW HAMPSHIRE

PO BOX 9201
HINGHAM, MA 02044

(877) 757-7783
WWW.MEDICARENHIC.COM

MEDICARE-PART A-NEW JERSEY

PO BOX 890385
CAMP HILL, PA 17089-0385

(877) 235-8073
WWW.NOVITAS-SOLUTIONS.COM

MEDICARE-PART A-NEW MEXICO

PO BOX 890113
CAMP HILL, PA 17089

(855) 252-8782
WWW.NOVITAS-SOLUTIONS.COM

MEDICARE-PART A-NEW YORK

PO BOX 7091
INDIANAPOLIS, IN 46207-7091

(888) 855-4356
WWW.NGSMEDICARE.COM

MEDICARE-PART A-NORTH CAROLINA

AG-620 PO BOX 100238
COLUMBIA, SC 29202-3238

(866) 830-3455
WWW.PALMETTOGBA.COM

MEDICARE-PART A-NORTH DAKOTA

PO BOX 6709
FARGO, ND 57108-6709

(866) 497-7857
WWW.NORIDIANMEDICARE.COM

MEDICARE-PART A-OHIO

AG-600 PO BOX 100112
COLUMBIA, SC 29202

(866) 590-6703
WWW.CGSMEDICARE.COM

MEDICARE-PART A-OKLAHOMA

PO BOX 890114
CAMP HILL, PA 17089

(855) 252-8782
WWW.NOVITAS-SOLUTIONS.COM

MEDICARE-PART A-OREGON

PO BOX 6726
FARGO, ND 57108-6726

(866) 497-7857
WWW.NORIDIANMEDICARE.COM

MEDICARE-PART A-PENNSYLVANIA

PO BOX 890385
CAMP HILL, PA 17089-0385
(877) 235-8073
WWW.NOVITAS-SOLUTIONS.COM

MEDICARE-PART A-PUERTO RICO

PO BOX 2711
JACKSONVILLE, FL 32232-5087
(888) 664-4112
WWW.FCSO.COM

MEDICARE-PART A-RHODE ISLAND

PO BOX 9201
HINGHAM, MA 02044
(877) 757-7783
WWW.MEDICARENHIC.COM

MEDICARE-PART A-SOUTH CAROLINA

AG-620 PO BOX 100238
COLUMBIA, SC 29202-3238
(866) 830-3455
WWW.PALMETTOGBA.COM

MEDICARE-PART A-SOUTH DAKOTA

PO BOX 6733
FARGO, ND 57108-6733
(866) 497-7857
WWW.NORIDIANMEDICARE.COM

MEDICARE-PART A-TENNESSEE

PO BOX 830139
BIRMINGHAM, AL 35202-0139
(877) 467-7516
WWW.CAHABAGBA.COM

MEDICARE-PART A-TEXAS

PO BOX 890113
CAMP HILL, PA 17089
(855) 252-8782
WWW.NOVITAS-SOLUTIONS.COM

MEDICARE-PART A-UTAH

PO BOX 6724
FARGO, ND 57108-6724
(866) 497-7857
WWW.NORIDIANMEDICARE.COM

MEDICARE-PART A-VERMONT

PO BOX 9201
HINGHAM, MA 02044
(877) 757-7783
WWW.MEDICARENHIC.COM

MEDICARE-PART A-VIRGIN ISLANDS

PO BOX 45071
JACKSONVILLE, FL 32232-5071
(888) 664-4112
WWW.FCSO.COM

MEDICARE-PART A-VIRGINIA

AG-620 PO BOX 100238
COLUMBIA, SC 29202-3238
(866) 830-3455
WWW.PALMETTOGBA.COM

MEDICARE-PART A-WASHINGTON

PO BOX 6720
FARGO, ND 57108-6720
(866) 497-7857
WWW.NORIDIANMEDICARE.COM

MEDICARE-PART A-WEST VIRGINIA

AG-260 PO BOX 100238
COLUMBIA, SC 29202-3238
(866) 830-3455
WWW.PALMETTOGBA.COM

MEDICARE-PART A-WISCONSIN

PO BOX 7150
INDIANAPOLIS, IN 46207-7150
(877) 702-0990
WWW.NGSMEDICARE.COM

MEDICARE-PART A-WYOMING

PO BOX 6734
FARGO, ND 57108-6734
(866) 497-7857
WWW.NORIDIANMEDICARE.COM

MEDICARE-PART B-ALABAMA

Payer ID ALMCR | PO BOX 830140
BIRMINGHAM, AL 35283-0140 | (877) 567-7271
WWW.CAHABAGBA.COM

MEDICARE-PART B-ALASKA

Payer ID AKMCR | PO BOX 6703
FARGO, ND 58108-6703 | (877) 908-8431
WWW.NORIDIANMEDICARE.COM

MEDICARE-PART B-AMERICAN SAMOA

Payer ID HIMCR | PO BOX 1051
AUGUSTA, GA 30903-1051 | (866) 931-3901
WWW.PALMETTOGBA.COM

MEDICARE-PART B-ARIZONA

Payer ID AZMCR | PO BOX 6704
FARGO, ND 58108-6704 | (877) 908-8431
WWW.NORIDIANMEDICARE.COM

MEDICARE-PART B-ARKANSAS

Payer ID ARMCR | PO BOX 890098
CAMP HILL, PA 17089 | (855) 252-8782
WWW.NOVITAS-SOLUTIONS.COM

MEDICARE-PART B-CALIFORNIA

Payer ID CNMCR | PO BOX 1051
AUGUSTA, GA 30903-1051 | (866) 931-3901
WWW.PALMETTOGBA.COM

MEDICARE-PART B-COLORADO

Payer ID COMCR | PO BOX 890107
CAMP HILL, PA 17089 | (855) 252-8782
WWW.NOVITAS-SOLUTIONS.COM

MEDICARE-PART B-CONNECTICUT

Payer ID CTMCR | PO BOX 6185
INDIANAPOLIS, IN 46206-6185 | (866) 837-0241
WWW.NGSMEDICARE.COM

MEDICARE-PART B-DELAWARE

Payer ID 00902 | PO BOX 890397
CAMP HILL, PA 17089-0397 | (877) 235-8073
WWW.NOVITAS-SOLUTIONS.COM

MEDICARE-PART B-DISTRICT OF COLUMBIA

Payer ID 00903 | PO BOX 890396
CAMP HILL, PA 17089-0396 | (877) 235-8073
WWW.NOVITAS-SOLUTIONS.COM

MEDICARE-PART B-FLORIDA

Payer ID FLMCR | PO BOX 2525
JACKSONVILLE, FL 32231-0019 | (866) 454-9007
WWW.FCSO.COM

MEDICARE-PART B-GEORGIA

Payer ID GAMCR | PO BOX 12847
BIRMINGHAM, AL 35202-2847 | (877) 567-7217
WWW.CAHABAGBA.ORG

MEDICARE-PART B-GUAM

Payer ID HIMCR | PO BOX 1051
AUGUST, GA 30903 | (866) 931-3901
WWW.PALMETTOGBA.COM

MEDICARE-PART B-HAWAII

Payer ID HIMCR | PO BOX 1051
AUGUSTA, GA 30903 | (866) 931-3901
WWW.PALMETTOGBA.COM

MEDICARE-PART B-IDAHO

Payer ID IDMCR | PO BOX 6701
FARGO, ND 58108-6701 | (877) 908-8431
WWW.NORIDIANMEDICARE.COM

MEDICARE-PART B-ILLINOIS

Payer ID ILMCR	PO BOX 1030 MARION, IL 62959-7530	(866) 234-7340 WWW.WPSMEDICARE.COM

MEDICARE-PART B-INDIANA

Payer ID INMCR	PO BOX 6160 INDIANAPOLIS, IN 46206-6160	(866) 276-8129 WWW.NGSMEDICARE.COM

MEDICARE-PART B-IOWA

Payer ID IAMCR	PO BOX 8550 MADISON, WI 53708-8550	(866) 503-3807 WWW.WPSMEDICARE.COM

MEDICARE-PART B-KANSAS

Payer ID KSMCR	PO BOX 7238 MADISON, WI 53707-7238	(866) 503-3807 WWW.WPSMEDICARE.COM

MEDICARE-PART B-KENTUCKY

Payer ID KYMCR	PO BOX 20019 NASHVILLE, TN 37202	(866) 276-9558 WWW.CGSMEDICARE.COM

MEDICARE-PART B-LOUISIANA

Payer ID LAMCR	PO BOX 890097 CAMP HILL, PA 17089	(855) 252-8782 WWW.NOVITAS-SOLUTIONS.COM

MEDICARE-PART B-MAINE

Payer ID MEMCR	PO BOX 2323 HINGHAM, PA 02044	(866) 801-5304 WWW.MEDICARENHIC.COM

MEDICARE-PART B-MARYLAND

Payer ID 00901	PO BOX 890398 CAMP HILL, PA 17089-0398	(877) 235-8073 WWW.NOVITAS-SOLUTIONS.COM

MEDICARE-PART B-MASSACHUSETTS

Payer ID MAMCR	PO BOX 1212 HINGHAM, MA 02044	(866) 801-5304 WWW.MEDICARENHIC.COM

MEDICARE-PART B-MICHIGAN

Payer ID MIMCR	PO BOX 5555 MARION, IL 62959-0967	(866) 234-7331 WWW.WPSMEDICARE.COM

MEDICARE-PART B-MINNESOTA

Payer ID MNMCR	8120 PENN AVE S STE 200 BLOOMINGTON, MN 55431-1318	(866) 359-1598 WWW.WPSMEDICARE.COM

MEDICARE-PART B-MISSISSIPPI

Payer ID MSMCR	PO BOX 890129 CAMP HILL, PA 17089	(855) 252-8782 WWW.NOVITAS-SOLUTIONS.COM

MEDICARE-PART B-MISSOURI

Payer ID MOMCR	PO BOX 14260 MADISON, WI 53707-0260	(866) 503-3807 WWW.WPSMEDICARE.COM

MEDICARE-PART B-MONTANA

Payer ID MTMCR	PO BOX 6735 FARGO, ND 58108-6735	(877) 908-8431 WWW.NORIDIANMEDICARE.COM

MEDICARE-PART B-NEBRASKA

Payer ID NEMCR	PO BOX 8667 MADISON, WI 53708-8667	(866) 503-3807 WWW.WPSMEDICARE.COM

MEDICARE-PART B-NEVADA

Payer ID NVMCR | PO BOX 1051, AGUSTA, GA 30903 | (866) 931-3901, WWW.PALMETTOGBA.COM

MEDICARE-PART B-NEW HAMPSHIRE

Payer ID NHMCR | PO BOX 1717, HINGHAM, MA 02044 | (866) 801-5304, WWW.MEDICARENHIC.COM

MEDICARE-PART B-NEW JERSEY

Payer ID NJMCR | PO BOX 890030, CAMP HILL, PA 17089-0030 | (877) 235-8073, WWW.NOVITAS-SOLUTIONS.COM

MEDICARE-PART B-NEW MEXICO

Payer ID NMMCR | PO BOX 890107, CAMP, PA 17089 | (855) 252-8782, WWW.NOVITAS-SOLUTIONS.COM

MEDICARE-PART B-NEW YORK (DOWNSTATE)

Payer ID NYMCR | PO BOX 6178, INDIANAPOLIS, IN 46206 | (866) 837-0241, WWW.NGSMEDICARE.COM

MEDICARE-PART B-NEW YORK (QUEENS)

Payer ID GHMCR | PO BOX 6239, INDIANAPOLIS, IN 46206 | (866) 837-0241, WWW.NGSMEDICARE.COM

MEDICARE-PART B-NEW YORK (UPSTATE)

Payer ID N1MCR | PO BOX 6189, INDIANAPOLIS, IN 46206 | (866) 837-0241, WWW.NGSMEDICARE.COM

MEDICARE-PART B-NORTH CAROLINA

Payer ID NDMCR | AG-600 PO BOX 100190, COLUMBIA, SC 29202-3190 | (866) 830-3043, WWW.PALMETTOGBA.COM

MEDICARE-PART B-NORTH DAKOTA

Payer ID NDMCR | PO BOX 6706, FARGO, ND 58108-6706 | (877) 908-8431, WWW.NORIDIANMEDICARE.COM

MEDICARE-PART B-NORTHERN MARIANA ISLANDS

Payer ID HIMCR | PO BOX 1051, AUGUSTA, GA 30903-1051 | (866) 931-3901, WWW.PALMETTOGBA.COM

MEDICARE-PART B-OHIO

Payer ID OHMCR | PO BOX 20019, NASHVILLE, TN 37202 | (866) 276-9558, WWW.CGSMEDICARE.COM

MEDICARE-PART B-OKLAHOMA

Payer ID OKMCR | PO BOX 890107, CAMP HILL, PA 17089 | (855) 252-8782, WWW.NOVITAS-SOLUTIONS.COM

MEDICARE-PART B-OREGON

Payer ID ORMCR | PO B OX 6702, FARGO, ND 58108-6702 | (877) 908-8431, WWW.NORIDIANMEDICARE.COM

MEDICARE-PART B-PENNSYLVANIA

Payer ID PAMCR | PO BOX 890418, CAMP HILL, PA 17089-0418 | (877) 235-8073, WWW.NOVITAS-SOLUTIONS.COM

MEDICARE-PART B-PUERTO RICO

Payer ID PRMCR | PO BOX 45036, JACKSONVILLE, FL 32232-5036 | (877) 715-1921, WWW.FCSO.COM

M

MEDICARE-PART B-RHODE ISLAND

Payer ID RIMCR | PO BOX 9203, HINGHAM, MA 02044 | (866) 801-5304, WWW.MEDICARENHIC.COM

MEDICARE-PART B-SOUTH CAROLINA

Payer ID SCMCR | AG-600 PO BOX 100190, COLUMBIA, SC 29202-3190 | (866) 830-3043, WWW.PALMETTOGBA.COM

MEDICARE-PART B-SOUTH DAKOTA

Payer ID SDMCR | PO BOX 6707, FARGO, ND 58108-6707 | (877) 908-8431, WWW.NORIDIANMEDICARE.COM

MEDICARE-PART B-TENNESSEE

Payer ID TNMCR | PO BOX 12086, BIRMINGHAM, AL 35202-2086 | (877) 567-7271, WWW.CAHABAGBA.COM

MEDICARE-PART B-TEXAS

Payer ID TXMCR | PO BOX 89018, CAMP HILL, PA 17089 | (855) 252-8782, WWW.NOVITAS-SOLUTIONS.COM

MEDICARE-PART B-UTAH

Payer ID UTMCR | PO BOX 6725, FARGO, ND 58108-6725 | (877) 908-8431, WWW.NORIDIANMEDICARE.COM

MEDICARE-PART B-VERMONT

Payer ID VTMCR | PO BOX 7777, HINGHAM, MA 02044 | (866) 801-5304, WWW.MEDICARENHIC.COM

MEDICARE-PART B-VIRGIN ISLANDS

Payer ID 09302 | PO BOX 45098, JACKSONVILLE, FL 32232-5098 | (866) 454-9007, WWW.FCSO.COM

MEDICARE-PART B-VIRGINIA

Payer ID VAMCR | AG-600 PO BOX 100190, COLUMBIA, SC 29202-3190 | (866) 830-3043, WWW.PALMETTOGBA.COM

MEDICARE-PART B-WASHINGTON

Payer ID WAMCR | PO BOX 6700, FARGO, ND 58108-6700 | (877) 908-8431, WWW.NORIDIANMEDICARE.COM

MEDICARE-PART B-WEST VIRGINIA

Payer ID WVMCR | AG-600 PO BOX 100190, COLUMBIA, SC 29202-3190 | (866) 830-3043, WWW.PALMETTOGBA.COM

MEDICARE-PART B-WISCONSIN

Payer ID WIMCR | PO BOX 1787, MADISON, WI 53701-1787 | (866) 359-1599, WWW.WPSMEDICARE.COM

MEDICARE-PART B-WYOMING

Payer ID WYMCR | PO BOX 6708, FARGO, ND 58108-6708 | (877) 908-8431, WWW.NORIDIANMEDICARE.COM

MEDICINA FAMILIAR MEDICAL GROUP

Payer ID IP080 | PO BOX 261040, ENCINO, CA 91426 | (818) 461-5000, (800) 445-0062, WWW.CAPCMS.COM

MEDICO INSURANCE COMPANY

Payer ID HDM04 | PO BOX 3477, OMAHA, NE 68103 | (402) 398-0881, WWW.GOMEDICO.COM/HEALTHCARE_PRO.HTM

M

MEDIGOLD

Payer ID 95655

PO BOX 69318
HARRISBURG, PA 17106-9318

(800) 240-3851
WWW.MEDIGOLD.COM/PROVIDERS

MEDIMPACT HEALTHCARE SYSTEMS INC

10680 TREENA ST 5TH FL
SAN DIEGO, CA 92131

(858) 566-2727
WWW.MEDIMPACT.COM

MEDIPRIME

Payer ID 94254

401 BARTOW RD
LAKELAND, FL 33801-5461

(800) 741-1511
WWW.MEDI-HEALTHCARE.COM

MEDPARTNERS ADMINISTRATIVE SERVICES

Payer ID 35205

6920 POINTE INVERNESS WAY STE 200
FORT WAYNE, IN 46804-7900

(800) 258-0974
WWW.MEDPARTNERSONLINE.COM

MEDSAVE

Payer ID 59276

3035 LAKELAND HILLS BLVD
LAKELAND, FL 33805

(800) 226-3155
WWW.MEDSAVEADMIN.COM/PAGES/
PROVIDERS.SHTML

MEDSOLUTIONS, INC

Payer ID 62160

PO BOX 981612
EL PASO, TX 79998

(888) 693-3296
WWW.MEDSOLUTIONSONLINE.COM

MEDSTAR FAMILY CHOICE

Payer ID 00243

10201 N PORT WASHINGTON RD
MEQUON, WI 53092-5752

(410) 933-3069
(800) 261-3371
WWW.MEDSTARFAMILYCHOICE.NET/BODY.CFM
?ID=14

MEDSTAR PHYSICIAN PARTNERS

Payer ID 00243

PO BOX 418865
BOSTON, MA 02241-8861

(800) 423-3507
WWW.MPPDOCS.ORG

MEGA LIFE & HEALTH

Payer ID 97055

PO BOX 1606
EL PASO, TX 79998

(800) 359-4440
(888) 757-0703
WWW.MEGAINSURANCE.COM

MEGA LIFE AND HEALTH INSURANCE COMPANY-OKC

Payer ID 59221

PO BOX 305009
NASHVILLE, TN 37230-5009

(866) 215-5343
WWW.MEGAINSURANCE.COM

MEMIC

Payer ID 01047

PO BOX 11409
PORTLAND, ME 04104

(800) 660-1306
WWW.MEMIC.COM

MEMORIAL CLINICAL ASSOCIATES

Payer ID MCA11

PO BOX 741107
EL PASO, TX 77274-1107

(888) 800-0760
WWW.MEMORIALDOCS.COM

MEMORIAL HERMANN HEALTH NETWORK

Payer ID MHHNP

7737 SW FREEWAY STE C 97
HOUSTON, TX 77074

(713) 338-6535
WWW.MEMORIALHERMANN.ORG

MEMORIAL INTEGRATED HEALTHCARE

Payer ID CALL

PO BOX 849029
PEMBROKE PINES, FL 33084

(954) 276-3131
WWW.MHS.NET

MENDOTA INSURANCE

Payer ID WA062	PO BOX 64586 ST. PAUL, MN 55164-0586	(800) 422-0793 WWW.MENDOTA-INSURANCE.COM

MENNONITE MUTUAL AID

Payer ID MNM99	1110 N MAIN ST GOSHEN, IN 46527 PO BOX 483 GOSHEN, IN 46527	(800) 348-7468 WWW.EVERENCE.COM

MENTAL HEALTH NETWORK

Payer ID 74289	PO BOX 14621 LEXINGTON, KY 40512	(800) 444-4281 WWW.MHN.COM

MERCY CARE PLAN OF AZ

Payer ID 86052	PO BOX 52089 PHOENIX, AZ 85072-2089	(602) 453-6098 (800) 624-3879 WWW.MERCYCAREPLAN.COM
Payer ID M3433	PO BOX 52089 PHOENIX, AZ 85072-2089	(602) 453-6098 (800) 624-3879 WWW.MERCYCAREPLAN.COM

MERCY HEALTH PLAN OF NEW JERSEY

Payer ID 22326	PO BOX 820 NEWARK, NJ 07101-0820	(800) 624-1110 WWW.HORIZON-BCBSNJ.COM

MERCYCARE INSURANCE CO

	PO BOX 2770 JANESVILLE, WI 53547	(800) 895-2421 HTTP://MERCYCAREHEALTHPLANS.COM

MERIDIAN HEALTH PLAN

Payer ID 13189	1001 WOODWARD AVE STE 510 DETROIT, MI 48226	(312) 705-2900 (866) 606-3700 WWW.MHPLAN.COM

METLIFE DENTAL

	PO BOX 981282 EL PASO, TX 79998-1282	(800) 942-0854 WWW.METLIFE.COM/DENTAL

METRO PLUS HEALTH PLAN

Payer ID 13265	PO BOX 1966 NEW YORK, NY 10116-1966	(800) 303-9626 WWW.METROPLUS.ORG

MGIS COMPANIES

	PO BOX 16110 SALT LAKE CITY, UT 84116-0110	(801) 990-2400 (800) 969-6447 WWW.MGIS.COM/PHYSICIANS.ASPX

MHNET

	PO BOX 7802 LONDON, KY 40742	(866) 992-5246 WWW.MHNET.COM/PROVIDERS/TABID/73/ DEFAULT.ASPX

MICHAEL EDWARDS DIRECT INC

	1 TOWER LANE STE 2375 OAK BROOK TERRACE, IL 60181	(630) 570-4400 WWW.MICHAELEDWARDS-DIRECT.COM

MICHIGAN BLUE CARE HMO

Payer ID MIBCN	PO BOX 2500 DETROIT, MI 48231	(800) 662-6667 WWW.BCBSM.COM/PROVIDER/

MICHIGAN EMPLOYEE BENEFIT SERVICES

3809 LAKE EASTBROOK BLVD
GRAND RAPIDS, MI 49546

(800) 968-6327
WWW.MEBS.COM

MICHIGAN MEDICAID HMO (CARESOURCE)

Payer ID 38325

PO BOX 1511
FLINT, MI 48501

(800) 390-7102
WWW.CARESOURCE.COM

MICHIGAN MEDICAID HMO (GREAT LAKES HEALTH PLAN)

Payer ID 95467

PO BOX 2127
SOUTHFIELD, MI 48037

(800) 903-5253
HTTP://UHCGREATLAKES.COM/

MICHIGAN MEDICAID HMO (HEALTH PLAN OF MICHIGAN)

Payer ID A0915

CLAIMS DEPT, 777 WOODWARD AVE, SUITE 600
DETROIT, MI 48226

(888) 773-2647
WWW.HPMICH.COM

MICHIGAN MEDICAID HMO (HEALTHPLUS)

PO BOX 1700
FLINT, MI 48501-1700

(800) 332-9161
WWW.HEALTHPLUS.ORG

MICHIGAN MEDICAID HMO (MOLINA HEALTHCARE)

Payer ID 38334

PO BOX 22668
LONG BEACH, CA 90801

(888) 898-7969
WWW.MOLINAHEALTHCARE.COM

MICHIGAN MEDICARE PLUS BLUE

Payer ID MIMPB

PO BOX 32593
DETROIT, MI 48232-0593

(800) 662-6667
WWW.BCBSM.COM/PROVIDER

MICRON TECH

Payer ID 96598

PO BOX 7406
SIOUX FALLS, SD 57117-7406

(866) 551-8022
HTTP://ID.MICRONHEALTH.COM/HEALTH-RESOURCES/

MID ATLANTIC PSYCHIATRIC SERVICES, INC.

Payer ID 52149

PO BOX 934
FEDERICK, MD 21705-0934

(800) 342-3289
WWW.MAMSIUNITEDHEALTHCARE.COM

M

MID-AMERICA ASSOCIATES

Payer ID 37281

PO BOX 71507
MADISON HEIGHTS, MI 48071

(800) 482-0945
WWW.LIBERTYUNIONLIFE.COM/PROVIDERS.ASP

MID-AMERICAN BENEFITS, INC

5310 N 99TH ST STE 1
OMAHA, NE 68134

(402) 571-6224
(800) 364-9505
WWW.MID-AMERICANBENEFITS.COM

MID-WEST NATIONAL LIFE INSURANCE CO. OF TENNESSEE

Payer ID 59224

PO BOX 981606
EL PASO, TX 79998

(888) 756-3534
WWW.MIDWESTLIFE.COM

MID-WEST UNITED LIFE (STUDENT DIVISION)

Payer ID 74227

PO BOX 809025
DALLAS, TX 75380

(800) 767-0700
WWW.UHCSR.COM

MIDLAND NATIONAL LIFE INS CO

Payer ID 90956

ONE SAMMONS PLZ
SIOUX FALLS, SD 57193-0002

(605) 335-5700
WWW.MNLIFE.COM

MIDLANDS CHOICE

Payer ID 47080

PO BOX 5809
TROY, MI 48007-5809

(800) 605-8259
WWW.MIDLANDSCHOICE.COM

MIDWEST FAMILY MUTUAL

Payer ID 23574

PO BOX 9425
MINNEAPOLIS, MN 55440

(800) 225-5636
WWW.MIDWESTFAMILY.COM/

MIDWEST GROUP BENEFITS

Payer ID 61146

PO BOX 408
DECORAH, IA 52101-0408

(563) 382-9611
WWW.MGBTA.COM

MIDWEST HEALTH PLANS, INC.

Payer ID MHP77

4700 SCHAEFER RD STE 340
DEARBORN, MI 48126

(888) 654-2200
WWW.MIDWESTHEALTHPLAN.COM

MIDWEST INSURANCE COMPANY

Payer ID 10895

300 S BRADFORDTON RD
SPRINGFIELD, IL 62711

(217) 726-6811
(800) 293-0616
WWW.MIDINS.COM/

MILLS PENISULA MEDICAL GROUP

Payer ID MPMG1

PO BOX 4348
BURLINGAME, CA 94011-4348

(650) 240-8059
WWW.MPMG.COM

MILWAUKEE CASUALTY INSURANCE COMPANY

Payer ID 26662

12790 MERIT DR
DALLAS, TX 75265
PO BOX 650771
DALLAS, TX 75265

(214) 360-8000
(800) 777-2249

MINNESOTA MEDICAID HMO (MEDICA)

Payer ID 94265

PO BOX 30990
SALT LAKE CITY, UT 84130

(800) 458-5512
HTTP://PROVIDER.MEDICA.COM

MINNESOTA MEDICAID HMO (UCARE)

PO BOX 70
MINNEAPOLIS, MN 55440

(888) 531-1493
WWW.UCARE.ORG

MISSION COMMUNITY IPA MED GRP

Payer ID MPM07

PO BOX 571270
TARZANA, CA 91357

(818) 702-0100
WWW.MEDPOINTMANAGEMENT.COM

MISSION HOSPITAL AFFILIATES

Payer ID STJOE

PO BOX 25666
ANAHEIM, CA 92825-5666

(949) 364-4854
WWW.MISSION4HEALTH.COM/

MISSIONARY MEDICAL

PO BOX 45730
SALT LAKE CITY, UT 84145

(800) 777-1647
WWW.DMBA.COM/NSC/DMBA/
CONTACTUS.ASPX

MISSISSIPPI PHYSICIANS CARE NETWORK

Payer ID 64084

PO BOX 1530
RIDGELAND, MS 39158

(800) 931-8533
WWW.MPCN-MS.COM

MISSISSIPPI SELECT HEALTHCARE

Payer ID 64088

PO BOX 3209
GULFPORT, MS 39505

(228) 214-0561
(800) 847-6621
WWW.SELECTADMINISTRATIVESERVICES.COM

MISSOULA COUNTY MEDICAL BENEFITS

Payer ID 37275
200 W BROADWAY
MISSOULA, MT 59802
(406) 523-4876
WWW.CO.MISSOULA.MT.US

MISSOURI CARE

Payer ID 43179
PO BOX 61625
PHOENIX, AZ 85082-1625
(800) 322-6027
WWW.MISSOURICARE.COM/PROVIDERS.ASPX

MISSOURI MEDICAID HMO (HEALTHCARE USA)

Payer ID 87043
PO BOX 7401
LONDON, KY 40742
(800) 627-6406
HTTP://CHCMEDICAID-MISSOURI.COVENTRYHEALTHCARE.COM

MISSOURI MEDICAID HMO (MOLINA HEALTHCARE)

Payer ID 71079
PO BOX 22676
LONG BEACH, CA 90801
(800) 875-0679
WWW.MOLINAHEALTHCARE.COM

MISSOURI MEDICAID HMO (WELLCARE)

Payer ID 14163
PO BOX 31372
TAMPA, FL 33631-3372
(866) 822-1340
WWW.HARMONYHPM.COM

MMM (MEDICARE Y MUCHO MAS)

Payer ID 88600
PO BOX 71114
SAN JUAN, PR 00936-8014
(866) 620-2377
WWW.MMM-PR.COM/MEMBERS/PROVIDERS/INDEX.HTML

MOBILECARE 2U LLC

8500 W 110TH ST STE 450
OVERLAND PARK, KS 66210-1808
(888) 384-8996
WWW.MOBILECARE2U.COM

MOLINA HEALTHCARE OF CALIFORNIA

Payer ID 38333
PO BOX 22702
LONG BEACH, CA 90801
(888) 665-4621
WWW.MOLINAHEALTHCARE.COM/MEDICAID/PROVIDERS/CA/PAGES/HOME.ASPX

MOLINA HEALTHCARE OF FLORIDA

Payer ID 51062
PO BOX 22812
LONG BEACH, CA 90801
(866) 472-4585
WWW.MOLINAHEALTHCARE.COM/MEDICAID/PROVIDERS/FL/PAGES/HOME.ASPX

MOLINA HEALTHCARE OF MICHIGAN

Payer ID 38334
PO BOX 22668
LONG BEACH, CA 90801
(888) 898-7969
WWW.MOLINAHEALTHCARE.COM/MEDICAID/PROVIDERS/NM/PAGES/HOME.ASPX

MOLINA HEALTHCARE OF MISSOURI

Payer ID 71079
PO BOX 22676
LONG BEACH, CA 90801
(800) 875-0679
WWW.MOLINAHEALTHCARE.COM/MEDICAID/PROVIDERS/MO/PAGES/HOME.ASPX

MOLINA HEALTHCARE OF NEW MEXICO

Payer ID NM505
PO BOX 22801
LONG BEACH, CA 90801
(505) 828-9594
(800) 377-9594
WWW.MOLINAHEALTHCARE.COM

MOLINA HEALTHCARE OF OHIO

Payer ID 20149
PO BOX 22712
LONG BEACH, CA 90801
(800) 642-4168
WWW.MOLINAHEALTHCARE.COM

MOLINA HEALTHCARE OF TEXAS

Payer ID 20554

PO BOX 22719
LONG BEACH, CA 90801-5719

(866) 449-6849
WWW.MOLINAHEALTHCARE.COM/MEDICAID/PROVIDERS/TX/PAGES/HOME.ASPX

MOLINA HEALTHCARE OF UTAH

Payer ID SX109

PO BOX 22811
LONG BEACH, CA 90801

(888) 483-0760
WWW.MOLINAHEALTHCARE.COM/MEDICAID/PROVIDERS/UT/PAGES/HOME.ASPX

MOLINA HEALTHCARE OF WASHINGTON

Payer ID 38336

PO BOX 22612
LONG BEACH, CA 90801

(800) 869-7165
WWW.MOLINAHEALTHCARE.COM

MONARCH HEALTHCARE IPA

Payer ID IP095

CLAIMS MS 31 11 TECHNOLOGY DR
IRVINE, CA 92618-2302

(888) 767-2222
WWW.MONARCHHEALTHCARE.COM

MONTEFIORE CONTRACT MANAGEMENT ORGANIZATION

Payer ID 13174

200 CORPORATE DR
YONKERS, NY 10701

(914) 377-4400
WWW.MONTEFIORE.ORG

MONTGOMERY MUTUAL INSURANCE CO

Payer ID WB172

13830 BALLANTYNE CORP. PLACE STE 300
CHARLOTTE, NC 28277-2711
PO BOX 49130
CHARLOTTE, NC 28277-9130

(704) 759-7661
WWW.MONTGOMERY-INS.COM

MONUMENTAL LIFE INS CO.

Payer ID MMLIC

PO BOX 97
SCRANTON, PA 18504-0097

(501) 277-1284
(800) 752-9797
WWW.MEDSUPPINFO.COM

MOTION PICTURE INDUSTRY HEALTH PLAN

Payer ID MPI01

PO BOX 1999
STUDIO CITY, CA 91614-0999

(818) 769-0007
WWW.MPIPHP.ORG

MOTOROLA (SEND CLAIMS TO LOCAL BCBS PLAN)

Payer ID 36111

PO BOX 105187
ATLANTA, GA 30348-5187

(866) 645-4135
WWW.ANTHEM.COM/MOT-SOLUTIONS

MOUNTAIN STATES ADMINISTRATIVE SERVICES, INC.

Payer ID 86040

PO BOX 981693
EL PASO, TX 79998-1693

(520) 722-0811
(800) 866-4731
WWW.MYMSAS.COM

MPE EMPLOYEE BENEFIT SERVICES

Payer ID 37233

PO BOX 784
BUCKEYSTOWN, MD 21717-0784

(800) 311-1573
WWW.MPEEBS.COM

MS ADMINISTRATORS

PO BOX 45073
BOISE, ID 83711-5073

(208) 343-2964
WWW.MSADMIN.COM/PROVIDERS.CFM

MT. CARMEL

Payer ID 95655

PO BOX 931068
CLEVELAND, OH 44193-0004

(614) 234-6000
WWW.MOUNTCARMELHEALTH.COM/MEDICAL-PROFESSIONALS.HTML

MULTIPLAN

115 FIFTH AVE
NEW YORK, NY 10003

(800) 950-7040
WWW.MULTIPLAN.COM

MULTIPLAN WISCONSIN PREFERRED PROVIDER NETWORK

Payer ID 34080

PO BOX 6090
DEPERE, WI 54115-6090

(920) 337-6550
WWW.HEALTHEOS.COM

MUTUAL ASSURANCE ADMINISTRATORS

Payer ID 37256

PO BOX 42096
OKLAHOMA CITY, OK 73123-3005

(800) 825-3540
WWW.MAA-TPA.COM/PROVIDERS

MUTUAL HEALTH SERVICES

Payer ID 34178

PO BOX 5700
CLEVELAND, OH 44101

(800) 367-3762
WWW.MUTUALHEALTHSERVICES.COM/PROVIDER/MAIN.ASPX

MUTUAL MEDICAL PLANS

416 MAIN ST STE 1025
PEORIA, IL 61602
PO BOX 689
PEORIA, IL 61652

(800) 448-4689
WWW.MUTUALMEDICAL.COM

MUTUAL OF OMAHA

Payer ID 71412

MUTUAL OF OMAHA PLZ
OMAHA, NE 68175

(800) 775-1000
WWW.MUTUALOFOMAHA.COM

MVP HEALTH CARE

PO BOX 2207
SCHENECTADY, NY 12301

(585) 325-3920
(800) 933-3920
WWW.MVPHEALTHCARE.COM/PROVIDER/INDEX.HTML

MVP HEALTH PLAN OF NY

Payer ID 14165

PO BOX 2207
SCHENECTADY, NY 12301-2207

(800) 777-4793
WWW.MVPHEALTHCARE.COM/PROVIDER/INDEX.HTML

MYERS STEVENS

26101 MARGUERITE PKWY
MISSION VIEJO, CA 92692-3203

(949) 348-0656
(800) 827-4695
WWW.MYERS-STEVENS.COM

N.W. IRONWORKERS HEALTH & SECURITY TRUST FUND - GRP#F15

Payer ID 91136
PO BOX 34464
SEATTLE, WA 98124
(206) 441-7226
(800) 331-6158

N.W. ROOFERS & EMPLOYERS HEALTH & SECURITY TRUST FUND - GRP#F14

Payer ID 91136
PO BOX 34498
SEATTLE, WA 98124-1498
(800) 735-7053
WWW.WPAS-INC.COM/NORTHWESTROOFERS/

NAA (NORTH AMERICA ADMINISTRATORS)

Payer ID 65085
PO BOX 1984
NASHVILLE, TN 37202
(800) 411-3650
HTTP://NAA-LP.COM/PROVIDER.HTM

NAPERVILLE HEALTH CARE ASSOCIATES

Payer ID NHCA1
PO BOX 3135
NAPERVILLE, IL 60566-7135
(630) 527-6800
WWW.EDWARD.ORG

NAPHCARE

2090 COLUMBIANA RD
BIRMINGHAM, AL 35216
(205) 536-8400
(800) 834-2420
WWW.NAPHCARE.COM

NATIONAL AMERICAN INSURANCE CO.

1010 MANVEL AVE
CHANDLER, OK 74834
PO BOX 38
CHANDLER, OK 74834
(405) 236-1751
(800) 822-7802
WWW.NAICO.COM

NATIONAL ASSOCIATION OF LETTER CARRIERS

Payer ID 53011
PO BOX 188004
CHATTANOOGA, TN 37422-8004
(888) 636-6252
WWW.NALC.ORG

NATIONAL BENEFITS ADMINISTRATORS - NORTH CAROLINA

Payer ID 56176
PO BOX 690903
CHARLOTTE, NC 28227
(704) 844-2966
(800) 482-6736
HTTP://NATIONALBENEFITS.BIZ/

NATIONAL CAPITAL AREA

Payer ID NCABS
PO BOX 14116
LEXINGTON, KY 40512-4116
(800) 842-5975
HTTPS://PROVIDER.CAREFIRST.COM

NATIONAL CAPITAL PREFERRED PROVIDER ORGANIZATION

Payer ID 90001
PO BOX 419104
ST LOUIS, MO 63141
(800) 272-5911
WWW.HEALTHLINK.COM/HOME_PHYSICIAN_HOSPITAL.ASP

NATIONAL CASUALTY COMPANY

Payer ID 11991
8877 NORTH GAINEY CENTER DR
SCOTTSDALE, AZ 85258
(480) 365-4000
(800) 423-7675
WWW.SCOTTSDALEINS.COM/PUBLIC/INDEX.JSP

NATIONAL CLAIMS ADMINISTRATIVE SOURCES

Payer ID 75190
6201 FAIRVIEW RD STE 300
CHARLOTTE, NC 28210-3296
PO BOX 220789
CHARLOTTE, NC 28222-0789
(800) 666-2100
WWW.NCAS.COM

Payer ID 75190
3928 PENDER DR STE 100
FAIRFAX, VA 22030-6028
PO BOX 1227
FAIRFAX, VA 22030-1227
(703) 934-6200
(800) 423-9791
WWW.NCAS.COM

NATIONAL CONTINENTAL INSURANCE COMPANY

Payer ID 10243

PO BOX 89490
CLEVELAND, OH 44101

(440) 461-5000
(800) 776-4737
WWW.PROGRESSIVE.COM

NATIONAL FOUNDATION LIFE INSURANCE CO

Payer ID 98205

PO BOX 650474
DALLAS, TX 75265-0474

(800) 387-9027
(800) 221-9039
HTTPS://PROVIDER.USHEALTHGROUP.COM/

NATIONAL HEALTH ADMINISTRATORS

Payer ID NHAIN

425 EAGLE ROCK AVE
ROSELAND, NJ 07068-1712

(888) 679-2400
(888) 335-0133
HTTP://NHAI.NET

NATIONAL HEALTH BENEFTIS CORP (NHBC)

Payer ID 88050

17851 N 85TH ST STE 105
SCOTTSDALE, AZ 85255-6309

(888) 621-7900
WWW.NHBC.COM/
MEDICAL_CLAIMS_PROCESSING.PHP

NATIONAL IMAGING ASSOCIATES

Payer ID NIA11

6950 COLUMBIA GATEWAY DR
COLUMBIA, MD 21046

(800) 642-7820
WWW1.RADMD.COM/CLAIMS.ASPX

NATIONAL RURAL ELECTRIC

Payer ID 52132

PO BOX 6249
LINCOLN, NE 68506

(866) 673-2299
WWW.NRECA.ORG/

NATIONAL SECURITY INSURANCE CO

661 E DAVIS ST
ELBA, AL 36323

(800) 239-2358
WWW.NATIONALSECURITYGROUP.COM

NATIONAL TEACHERS ASSOCIATION (NTA)

Payer ID NTA11

PO BOX 2369
ADDISON, TX 75001-2369

(888) 671-6771
WWW.NTALIFE.COM/CLAIMS.HTML

NATIONAL TELECOMMUNICATIONS COOPERATIVE ASSOCIATION (NTCA)

Payer ID 52103

30 TOWN SQUARE BLVD STE 300
ASHEVILLE, NC 28803

(828) 252-9776
WWW.NTCA.ORG/HEALTH-CARE-PROVIDERS/
HEALTH-CARE-PROVIDERS.HTML

NATIONWIDE HEALTH PLANS

Payer ID 31417

PO BOX 182690
COLUMBUS, OH 43218-2690

(800) 372-0713
WWW.NATIONWIDEHEALTHPLANS.COM

NATIONWIDE SPECIALTY HEALTH

Payer ID 31417

PO BOX 420
SPRINGFIELD, MA 01101

(800) 525-8669
WWW.NATIONWIDE.COM/ACCIDENT-MEDICAL-
INSURANCE-HI.JSP

NEA GROUP INSURANCE PROGRAM

Payer ID 19988

PO BOX 10424
DES MOINES, IA 50306-0424

(800) 541-4119
WWW.NEAMB.COM

NEIGHBORHOOD HEALTH PARTNERSHIP OF FLORIDA

Payer ID 95123

PO BOX 5210
KINGSTON, NY 12402

(877) 972-8845
WWW.MYNHP.COM/PROVIDERS/

NEIGHBORHOOD HEALTH PLAN

Payer ID 04293	PO BOX 10 NUTTING LAKE, MA 01865-0010	(617) 772-5517 (800) 462-5449 WWW.NHP.ORG/PAGES/ PROVIDERS_HOME.ASPX

NEIGHBORHOOD HEALTH PLAN OF RHODE ISLAND

Payer ID 05047	299 PROMENADE ST PROVIDENCE, RI 02908-5720	(401) 459-6030 (800) 459-6019 WWW.NHPRI.ORG

NEIGHBORHOOD HEALTH PROVIDERS

Payer ID 11325	PO BOX 6008 HAUPPAUGE, NY 11788-9007	(800) 558-7970 WWW.GETNHP.COM/PROVIDERS.HTML

NESIKA HEALTH GROUP

Payer ID 37255	2360 NE STEPHENS ROSEBURG, OR 97470-1372	(541) 677-5508 (800) 284-9917 WWW.COWCREEK.COM/ECONOMIC- DEVELOPMENT/522-NESIKA-HEALTH-GROUP

NETCARE LIFE AND HEALTH INSURANCE (GUAM)

Payer ID 66055	424 W OBREIEN DR STE 200 HAGATNA, GU 96910-0000	(671) 472-3610 WWW.NETCARELIFEANDHEALTH.COM/ PROVIDER/PROVIDER.HTML

NETWORK HEALTH

Payer ID 04332	PO BOX 390310 CAMBRIDGE, MA 02139	(617) 806-8104 (888) 257-1985 WWW.NETWORK-HEALTH.ORG/PROVIDERS

NETWORK HEALTH INSURANCE CORP - MEDICARE

Payer ID 77076	PO BOX 3687 SCRANTON, PA 18505	(800) 378-5234 HTTP://NPPDRUGPLANS.COM

NETWORK HEALTH PLAN OF WISCONSIN, INC.

Payer ID 39144	PO BOX 568 MENASHA, WI 54952	(920) 720-1506 (800) 826-0940 WWW.NETWORKHEALTH.COM

NETWORK HEALTH PPO

Payer ID AMS01	PO BOX 568 MENASHA, WI 54952	(800) 826-0940 WWW.NETWORKHEALTH.COM

NETWORK SYNERGY GROUP

Payer ID NSG99	4631 WOODLAND CORPORATE BLVD STE 310 TAMPA, FL 33614	(813) 207-0727 (888) 533-0727 WWW.NETWORK-SYNERGY.COM

NEW AVENUES, INC.

	PO BOX 360 SOUTH BEND, IN 46624	(866) 925-5730 WWW.NEWAVENUESONLINE.COM/PROVIDERS

NEW CENTURY HEALTH - VISTA CARDIOLOGY

Payer ID NCH09	675 PLACENTIA AVE STE 300 BREA, CA 92821	(888) 999-7713 WWW.NEWCENTURYHEALTH.COM/ PHYSICIANS.HTML

NEW ENGLAND FINANCIAL/ONE HEALTH

Payer ID 66893	PO BOX 24146 SEATLE, WA 98124	(800) 654-1731 WWW.HEALTHPLAN.COM

NEW ERA LIFE INSURANCE CO

Payer ID 75281
PO BOX 4884
HOUSTON, TX 77210-4884
(800) 552-7879
WWW.NEWERALIFE.COM

NEW JERSEY MEDICAID HMO (HORIZON NJ HEALTH)

PO BOX 7117
LONDON, KY 40702
(800) 682-9091
HTTP://HORIZONNJHEALTH.COM/FOR-PROVIDERS

NEW MEXICO DISTRICT COUNCIL OF CARPENTERS

Payer ID 74234
PO BOX 17973
LOS ANGELES, CA 90017-0973
(877) 359-9644
WWW.ANTHEM.COM

NEW MEXICO MEDICAID HMO (LOVELACE HEALTH PLAN)

Payer ID SX159
PO BOX 549
BUCKEYSTOWN, MD 21717
(800) 808-7363
WWW.LOVELACEHEALTHPLAN.COM/PROVIDERS

NEW MEXICO MEDICAID HMO (PRESBYTERIAN HEALTH PLAN)

PO BOX 27489
ALBURQUERQUE, NM 87125-7489
(888) 923-5757
HTTPS://DS.PHS.ORG/PRESLOGIN/INDEX.JSP?EXT

NEW MEXICO PAINTERS AND ALLIED TRADES LOCAL NO 823

Payer ID 74234
5701 BALLOON FIESTA PKWY NE
ALBUQUERQUE, NM 87113
(505) 291-3500
(888) 349-3706
WWW.BCBSNM.COM/PROVIDER/

NEW WEST HEALTH PLAN

Payer ID 84141
PO BOX 548
KALISPELL, MT 59903-0548
(888) 500-3355
WWW.NEWWESTHEALTH.COM/HOME/PROVIDERS

NEW YORK LIFE - LONG TERM CARE

Payer ID NYL11
PO BOX 559005
AUSTIN, TX 78755
(800) 224-4582
WWW.NEWYORKLIFE.COM

NEW YORK MEDICAID HMO (AFFINITY HEALTH PLAN)

Payer ID 13334
PO BOX 981726
EL PASO, TX 79998
(866) 247-5678
WWW.AFFINITYPLAN.ORG/AFFINITY/PROVIDERS/PROVIDERS.ASPX

N

NEW YORK MEDICAID HMO (EXCELLUS)

PO BOX 22999
ROCHESTER, NY 14692
(800) 920-8889
WWW.EXCELLUSBCBS.COM/WPS/PORTAL/XL/PRV/

NEW YORK MEDICAID HMO (FIDELIS CARE)

Payer ID 11315
PO BOX 898
AMHERST, NY 14226-0898
(888) 343-3547
WWW.FIDELISCARE.ORG/PROVIDERS/INDEX.ASPX

NEW YORK MEDICAID HMO (HEALTH FIRST)

Payer ID 80141
PO BOX 958438
LAKE MARY, FL 32795-8438
(866) 463-6743
WWW.HEALTHFIRSTNY.ORG/PROVIDERSERVICES

NEW YORK MEDICAID HMO (HEALTH PLUS)

Payer ID 27514
PO BOX 61599
VIRGINIA BEACH, VA 23466-1599
(800) 454-3730
HTTPS://PROVIDERS.AMERIGROUP.COM/PAGES/NY.ASPX

NEW YORK MEDICAID HMO (METROPLUS)

Payer ID 13265 | PO BOX 1966
NEW YORK, NY 10116-1966 | (800) 303-9626
WWW.METROPLUS.ORG/PROVIDERS_CLAIMS.PHP

NEW YORK MEDICAID HMO (NEIGHBORHOOD HEALTH)

Payer ID 11325 | PO BOX 6008
HAUPPAUGE, NY 11788-9007 | (800) 558-7970
WWW.GETNHP.COM/PROVIDERS.HTML

NEW YORK MEDICAID HMO (WELLCARE)

Payer ID 14163 | PO BOX 31372
TAMPA, FL 33631-3372 | (800) 278-5155
WWW.WELLCARE.COM/PROVIDER/DEFAULT

NEW YORK MEDICAL IMAGING-MVP

Payer ID 14179 | 165 E 84TH ST
NEW YORK, NY 10028 | (212) 535-9770
WWW.NYMIASSOCIATES.COM

NEW YORK NETWORK MANAGEMENT IPA

Payer ID 11334 | PO BOX 620
LAKE KATRINE, NY 12449 | (718) 748-7316
(888) 511-5208
WWW.NYNMONLINE.COM

NEW YORK PRESBYTERIAN SYSTEM SELECT HEALTH

Payer ID 24819 | PO BOX 6023
HAUPPAUGE, NY 11788 | (866) 469-7774
(800) 630-3717
HTTP://NYP.ORG/SELECTHEALTH/

NGS AMERICAN, INC

Payer ID 38225 | PO BOX 2310
MT CLEMENS, MI 48046 | (586) 779-7676
(800) 521-1555
WWW.NGS.COM/PROVIDERS.ASPX

NHC HEALTH BENEFIT PLAN

Payer ID 62124 | PO BOX 1398
MURFREESBORO, TN 37133-7036 | (615) 278-1230
(615) 890-2020
WWW.NHCCARE.COM

NIPPON LIFE INSURANCE COMPANY

Payer ID 81264 | PO BOX 25951
SHAWNEE MISSION, KS 66225 | (800) 374-1835
WWW.NLIA.COM

NJ CARPENTERS HEALTH FUND (BCBS NEW JERSEY)

Payer ID 22603 | PO BOX 1609
NEWARK, NJ 07101 | (732) 417-3900
(800) 624-3096
WWW.NJCF.ORG

NM BLUE MEDICARE PPO

Payer ID 00790 | PO BOX 27630
ALBUQUERQUE, NM 87125 | (888) 349-3706
WWW.BCBSNM.COM/PROVIDER

NOBLE COMMUNITY MEDICAL ASSOCIATES

Payer ID IP080 | 11631 VICTORY BLVD STE 101
N HOLLYWOOD, CA 91606 | (818) 508-2201

NOITU INSURANCE TRUST FUND

148-06 HILLSIDE AVE
JAMAICA, NY 11435 | (718) 291-3434
WWW.NOITU.ORG

NORTH AMERICA ADMINISTRATORS, LP

Payer ID 64157 | PO BOX 1984
NASHVILLE, TN 37202-1984 | (800) 411-3650
WWW.NAA-LP.COM/PROVIDER.HTM

N

NORTH AMERICAN BENEFITS COMPANY

530 E SWEDESFORD RD STE 100
WAYNE, PA 19087

(610) 995-0169
(800) 537-4565
WWW.NABENEFITS.COM

NORTH AMERICAN MEDICAL MANAGEMENT

Payer ID IP079

PO BOX 6903
RANCHO CUCAMONGA, CA 91729-6903

(800) 956-8000
WWW.NAMMCAL.COM

NORTH SHORE PHYSICIANS ASSOCIATES

Payer ID 36392

PO BOX 331719
CORPUS CHRISTI, TX 78463

(866) 233-7601
WWW.VALENCEHEALTH.COM

NORTH SUBURBAN ASSOCIATED PHYSICIANS (VALENCE HEALTH)

Payer ID 36392

600 W JACKSON BLVD STE 800
CHICAGO, IL 60661-5601
PO BOX 331719
CORPUS CHRISTI, TX 78463

(866) 233-7601
WWW.VALENCEHEALTH.COM

NORTHERN ILLINOIS HEALTH PLAN

Payer ID 36347

PO BOX 880
FREEPORT, IL 61032-0210

(815) 599-7050
(800) 723-0202
HTTPS://SECURE1.NIHP.COM/NIHPWEB/MAINHOMEPAGE.HTML#

NORTHERN NEVADA TRUST FUNDS

Payer ID 88027

PO BOX 11337
RENO, NV 89510

(775) 826-7200

NORTHLAND INSURANCE CO

Payer ID WB161

385 WASHINGTON ST
ST PAUL, MN 55102-1309
PO BOX 64816
ST PAUL, MN 55164-0816

(651) 310-4100
(800) 237-9334
WWW.NORTHLANDINS.COM

NORTHRIDGE MEDICAL GROUP

Payer ID NMG01

PO BOX 6099
TORRANCE, CA 90504

(818) 444-5271
(866) 604-3334
WWW.HEALTHCAREPARTNERS.COM

NORTHWEST ADMINISTRATORS

2323 E LAKE AVE E STE 400
SEATTLE, WA 98102-3305
PO BOX 32403
SEATTLE, WA 98124-1203

(206) 329-4900
(800) 443-0425
WWW.NWADMIN.COM

NORTHWEST COMMUNITY HEALTH PARTNERS

Payer ID NANWC

PO BOX 50890
INDIANAPOLIS, IN 46250

(708) 432-4054
WWW.NCH.ORG

NORTHWEST PHYSICIANS NETWORK

1304 S FAWCETT AVE STE 200
TACOMA, WA 98402

(253) 207-4348
WWW.NPNWA.NET/INDEX.PHP

NORTHWEST SUBURBAN IPA (IL)

Payer ID 36346

630 E JEFFERSON ST
ROCKFORD, IL 61107-4026

(888) 747-2264
WWW.USESAGE.COM/LOGIN/PROVIDERLOGIN.ASPX

NORTHWESTERN NATIONAL LIFE (ING)

Payer ID PH018

20 WASHINGTON AVE
MINNEAPOLIS, MN 55480

(877) 884-5050
WWW.ING.COM

NOVA CASUALTY COMPANY

Payer ID 16114	5 WATERSIDE CROSSING STE 201 WINDSOR, CT 06095-1567	(860) 683-4250 (866) 633-6945 WWW.AIXGROUP.COM

NOVA HEALTHCARE ADMINISTRATORS

Payer ID 16644	PO BOX 9050 BUFFALO, NY 14231	(877) 929-3767 WWW.NOVAHEALTHCARE.COM

NOVANET

Payer ID 06226	3500 PARKWAY LANE STE 700 NORCROSS, GA 30092	(770) 729-1997 (800) 513-7177 WWW.NOVANETPPO.COM/PROVIDERS.ASP

NOVASYS HEALTH NETWORK

Payer ID 71080	PO BOX 25228 LITTLE ROCK, AR 72221	(501) 219-4444 (800) 294-3557 WWW.NOVASYSHEALTH.COM/ PROVIDER_ONLY.HTML

NY CENTRAL FEP (FEDERAL EMPLOYEE PROGRAM) BLUE SHIELD

	333 BUTTERNUT DR SYRACUSE, NY 13214	(800) 252-2209 WWW.FEPBLUE.ORG/INDEX.JSP

NYS DOH UCP

Payer ID 14142	PO BOX 4611 RENSSELAER, NY 12144	(518) 474-3575 (800) 342-3005 WWW.EMEDNY.ORG

N

OCHSNER HEALTH PLAN

Payer ID 72127

1514 JEFFERSON ST
NEW ORLEANS, LA 70121

(800) 231-5257
WWW.OCHSNER.ORG

ODS COMPANIES

Payer ID 13350

PO BOX 40384
PORTLAND, OR 97240-0384

(877) 664-4762
WWW.ODSCOMPANIES.COM

OGDEN BENEFITS ADMINISTRATION

PO BOX 90548
HENDERSON, NV 89009-0548

(714) 549-7052
(800) 222-2184
WWW.OBATPA.COM

OHIO BUREAU OF WORKERS' COMPENSATION

30 WEST SPRING ST.
COLUMBUS, OH 43215-2256

(740) 353-2187
(800) 644-6292
WWW.OHIOBWC.COM

OHIO CASUALTY GROUP

Payer ID WB214

9450 SEWARD RD
FAIRFIELD, OH 45014
PO BOX 188060
FAIRFIELD, OH 45018

(513) 603-2400
(800) 843-6446
WWW.OHIOCASUALITY-INS.COM

OHIO HEALTH CHOICE PPO

Payer ID 34189

PO BOX 2090
AKRON, OH 44309-2090

(800) 554-0027
WWW.OHIOHEALTHCHOICE.COM/
PROVIDER.ASP

OHIO MEDICAID HMO (AMERIGROUP)

Payer ID 27514

PO BOX 61010
VIRGINIA BEACH, VA 23466-1010

(800) 454-3730
WWW.AMERIGROUPCORP.COM/PROVIDERS

OHIO MEDICAID HMO (CARESOURCE)

Payer ID 31114

PO BOX 8730
DAYTON, OH 45401-8730

(800) 488-0134
WWW.CARESOURCE.COM

OHIO MEDICAID HMO (MOLINA HEALTHCARE)

Payer ID 20149

PO BOX 22712
LONG BEACH, CA 90801

(800) 642-4168
WWW.MOLINAHEALTHCARE.COM/MEDICAID/
PROVIDERS/OH

OHIO MEDICAID HMO (WELLCARE)

Payer ID 14163

PO BOX 31224
TAMPA, FL 33631-3224

(800) 951-7719
HTTP://OHIO.WELLCARE.COM

OLD GUARD-WESTFIELD INSURANCE

Payer ID WZ886

ONE PARK CIR
WESTFIELD CENTER, OH 44251
PO BOX 5001
WESTFIELD CENTER, OH 44251

(800) 243-0210
(866) 937-2663
WWW.WESTFIELDINSURANCE.COM

OLYMPIC HEALTH MANAGEMENT SYSTEMS

Payer ID 91150

PO BOX 5348
BELLINGHAM, WA 98227-5348

(888) 858-8544
WWW.OHMSYSTEMS.COM

OMNICARE HEALTH PLAN

Payer ID 25150

PO BOX 7150
LONDON, KY 40742

(866) 314-3784
WWW.OMNICAREHEALTHPLAN.COM

ONE BEACON INSURANCE

Payer ID WB173	601 CARLSON PKWY # 700 MINNETONKA, MN 55305	(952) 852-2431 (877) 248-3455 WWW.ONEBEACON.COM

ONE CALL MEDICAL

Payer ID 22321	20 WATERVIEW BLVD PARSIPPANY, NJ 07054-1219 PO BOX 614 PARSIPPANY, NJ 07054	(800) 872-2875 WWW.ONECALLMEDICAL.COM

ONENET PPO, LLC

Payer ID 52149	PO BOX 934 FREDERICK, MD 21705-0934	(800) 342-3289 WWW.ONENETPPO.COM

OPERATING ENGINEERS LOCAL 302 & 612

Payer ID 91136	PO BOX 34684 SEATTLE, WA 98124-1684	(877) 441-1212

OPTICARE EYE HEALTH NETWORK

Payer ID 56190	PO BOX 7548 ROCKY MOUNT, NC 27804	(800) 334-3937 WWW.OPTICARE.COM

OPTICARE OF UTAH, INC

	1901 W PARKWAY BLVD SALT LAKE CITY, UT 84119-2001	(800) 363-0950 WWW.OPTICAREOFUTAH.COM

OPTIMA HEALTH (SENTARA)

	PO BOX 5028 TROY, MI 48007	(800) 229-8822 WWW.OPTIMAHEALTH.COM

OPTIMA HEALTH PLAN

	PO BOX 5028 TROY, MI 48007-5028	(800) 229-8822 WWW.OPTIMAHEALTH.COM

OPTIMUM HEALTHCARE, INC

Payer ID 20133	PO BOX 151258 TAMPA, FL 33684	(813) 506-6151 (866) 245-5360 WWW.YOUROPTIMUMHEALTHCARE.COM

OPTUMHEALTH BEHAVIOR SOLUTIONS

Payer ID 87726	PO BOX 30755 SALT LAKE CITY, UT 84130-0755	(800) 333-8724 WWW.UBHONLINE.COM

OPTUMHEALTH CARE SOLUTIONS

Payer ID 41161	PO BOX 212 MINNEAPOLIS, MN 55440	(800) 873-4575 WWW.OPTUMHEALTH.COM

OPTUMHEALTH MANAGED TRANSPLANT PROGRAM

Payer ID 52190	PO BOX 30758 SALT LAKE CITY, UT 84130	(800) 847-2050 WWW.MYOPTUMHEALTHCOMPLEXMEDICAL.COM/ GATEWAY/PUBLIC/WELCOME.JSP

OPTUMHEALTH NEW MEXICO

Payer ID 87726	PO BOX 3137 ALBUQUERQUE, NM 87190	(866) 660-7185 WWW.OPTUMHEALTHNEWMEXICO.COM

ORANGE COUNTY FOUNDATION FOR MEDICAL CARE

Payer ID OCFMC	PO BOX 11210 BAKERSFIELD, CA 93389	(800) 345-8643 WWW.OCFMC.COM

ORTHONET CORPORATION

Payer ID 13381	1311 MAMARONECK AVE STE 240 WHITE PLAINS, NY 10605-5202	(888) 678-4663 WWW.ORTHONET-ONLINE.COM

ORTHONET-AETNA

Payer ID 13383	PO BOX 5034 WHITE PLAINS, NY 10605-5202	(888) 391-3040 WWW.ORTHONET-ONLINE.COM

ORTHONET-HEALTHNET

Payer ID 25681	PO BOX 5042 WHITE PLAINS, NY 10605-5202	(800) 413-8695 WWW.ORTHONET-ONLINE.COM

OSF HEALTH PLANS (HUMANA)

Payer ID 61101	PO BOX 14601 LEXINGTON, KY 40512-4601	(800) 673-8868 WWW.HUMANA.COM

OXFORD HEALTH PLANS

Payer ID 06111	PO BOX 7082 BRIDGEPORT, CT 06601-7082	(800) 666-1353 WWW.OXHP.COM

O

PA PREFERRED HEALTH

Payer ID CALL	50 COMMERCE DR WYOMISSING, PA 19610	(610) 743-6054 (888) 898-7746 WWW.PPHN.COM/

PACIFIC BEHAVIORAL HEALTH

Payer ID 33053	PO BOX 30602 SALT LAKE CITY, UT 84130	(800) 999-9585 WWW.UBHONLINE.COM

PACIFIC HEALTH MFO

	820 S GARFIELD AVE STE 201 ALHAMBRA, CA 91801	(626) 782-6202 WWW.MEDPOINTMANAGEMENT.COM

PACIFIC SOURCE HEALTH PLANS

Payer ID 93029	PO BOX 7068 SPRINGFIELD, OR 97475-0068	(888) 977-9299 WWW.PACIFICSOURCE.COM

PACIFICSOURCE MEDICARE

Payer ID 20377	PO BOX 7068 SPRINGFIELD, OR 97401	(888) 863-3637 HTTP://MEDICARE.PACIFICSOURCE.COM/ PARTNERS/PROVIDERS/DEFAULT.ASPX

PACIFICSOURCE OHP

	PO BOX 5729 BEND, OR 97708-5729	(541) 382-5920 (800) 431-4135 WWW.COMMUNITYSOLUTIONS.PACIFICSOURCE.COM

PALLADIAN MUSCULAR SKELETAL HEALTH

Payer ID 37268	PO BOX 270 LANCASTER, NY 14086	(888) 266-9041 WWW.PALLADIANHEALTH.COM

PALMETTO TRICARE

Payer ID 38520	NORTH - PO BOX 870140 SURFSIDE BEACH, SC 29587-9740	(877) 874-2273 WWW.MYTRICARE.COM/INTERNET/TRIC/TRI/ MTC_NPROV.NSF
Payer ID 38520	SOUTH - PO BOX 7031 CAMDEN, SC 29020-7031	(877) 874-2273 WWW.MYTRICARE.COM/INTERNET/TRIC/TRI/ MTC_SPROV.NSF

PAN AMERICAN LIFE INSURANCE CO

	601 POYDRAS ST NEW ORLEANS, LA 70130 PO BOX 60219 NEW ORLEANS, LA 70160-0219	(504) 566-1300 (877) 939-4550 WWW.PANAMERICANLIFE.COM

PAN-AMERICAN HEALTH

Payer ID 81240	PO BOX 99007 LUBBOCK, TX 79490-9007	(877) 939-4550 WWW.PALIG.COM

PARAGON BENEFITS, INC

Payer ID 58174	PO BOX 12288 COLUMBUS, GA 31917	(800) 277-9218 WWW.PARAGONBENEFITS.COM/ PROVIDERS.ASPX

PARAMOUNT HEALTH

Payer ID SX158	PO BOX 497 TOLEDO, OH 43697-0497	(419) 887-2564 (888) 891-2564 WWW.PARAMOUNTHEALTHCARE.COM/ PROVIDERS

PARKLAND COMMUNITY HEALTH PLAN

Payer ID 66917
PO BOX 61088
PHOENIX, AZ 85082
(888) 672-2277
WWW.PARKLANDHMO.ORG

PARTNERS BEHAVIORAL HEALTH

901 S. NEW HOPE RD
GASTONIA, NC 28054
(704) 884-2501
WWW.PARTNERSBHM.ORG/PROVIDERS

PARTNERS NATIONAL HEALTH PLANS OF NORTH CAROLINA

Payer ID 56152
PO BOX 35
DURHAM, NC 27702
(800) 214-4844
(888) 296-9790
WWW.BCBSNC.COM/CONTENT/PROVIDERS/INDEX.HTM

PARTNERSHIP HEALTH PLAN

Payer ID PHP02
PO BOX 1368
SUISSUN, CA 94585
(707) 863-4130
(800) 863-4144
WWW.PARTNERSHIPHP.ORG/PROVIDER/PROVIDER.HTM

PASADENA PRIMARY CARE PHYSICIANS

Payer ID IP080
PO BOX 260830
ENCINO, CA 91426
(818) 461-5055
(888) 445-0062
WWW.CAPCMS.COM

PASSPORT ADVANTAGE

Payer ID 76569
PO BOX 152107
TAMPA, FL 33684
(800) 578-0775
WWW.PASSPORTHEALTHPLAN.COM/PROVIDER/INDEX.ASPX

PASSPORT HEALTH PLAN

Payer ID 61129
PO BOX 7114
LONDON, KY 40742
(800) 578-0775
WWW.PASSPORTHEALTHPLAN.COM/PROVIDER/INDEX.ASPX

PATIENT ADVOCATES, LLC

Payer ID 10525
PO BOX 1959
GRAY, ME 04039-1959
(800) 290-8559
WWW.PATIENTADVOCATESLLC.COM/PROVIDERS

PATIENT SERVICES, INC.

PO BOX 5930
MIDLOTHIAN, VA 23112
(800) 366-7741
WWW.UNEEDPSI.ORG

PATRIOT GENERAL INSURANCE COMPANY

Payer ID WB138
1800 NORTH POINT DR
STEVENS POINT, WI 54481
(800) 833-2244

PCA HUMANA

Payer ID 61101
P.O. BOX 14601
LEXINGTON, KY 40512
(877) 845-3480
WWW.HUMANA.COM/PROVIDER

PEACH STATE HEALTH PLAN

Payer ID 68050
PO BOX 3030
FARMINGTON, MO 63640-3812
(866) 874-0633
(800) 704-1463
WWW.PSHPGEORGIA.COM/FOR-PROVIDERS/

PEDIATRIC ASSOCIATES

Payer ID 20472
4620 N ST RD 7 STE 316 BLDG H
LAUDERDALE LAKES, FL 33319
(954) 967-6400
WWW.PEDIATRICASSOCIATES.COM

PEERLESS INSURANCE CO

Payer ID WB174	62 MAPLE AVE KEENE, NH 03431	(603) 352-3221 (800) 542-5385 WWW.PEERLESS-INS.COM
Payer ID WB174	PO BOX 507 KEENE, NH 03431	(603) 352-3221 (800) 542-5385

PEHP

Payer ID SX106	560 E 200 S SALT LAKE CITY, UT 84102-2004	(801) 366-7555 (800) 765-7347 WWW1.PEHP.ORG/PROVIDERS/PAGES/ HOME.ASPX

PENINSULA HEALTHCARE

Payer ID VABLS	PO BOX 27401 RICHMOND, VA 23279	(800) 533-1120 WWW.ANTHEM.COM

PENN MILLERS INSURANCE CO

	72 N FRANKLIN ST WILKES-BARRE, PA 18773-0016 PO BOX P WILKES-BARRE, PA 18773-0016	(570) 822-8111 (800) 233-8347 WWW.PENNMILLERS.COM

PENN NATIONAL INSURANCE

Payer ID WB215	PO BOX 2361 HARRISBURG, PA 17105	(800) 388-4764 WWW.PENNNATIONALINSURANCE.COM

PENN WESTERN BENEFITS, INC

	PO BOX 7834 GREENSBORO, NC 27417-0834	(336) 665-9400 (888) 792-7828 WWW.PENNWESTERN.COM

PENNSYLVANIA KEYSTONE HEALTH PLAN CENTRAL

Payer ID PKCCL	PO BOX 779503 HARRISBURG, PA 17177-9503	(800) 874-8433 WWW.CAPBLUECROSS.COM/PROVIDERS/

PENNSYLVANIA KEYSTONE HEALTH PLAN EAST

Payer ID PCBLS	PO BOX 69353 HARRISBURG, PA 17106-9353	(800) 275-2583 WWW.IBX.COM/PROVIDERS/

PENNSYLVANIA LIFE INSURANCE

Payer ID 23130	PO BOX 130 PENSACOLA, FL 32591-0130	(800) 275-7366 WWW.PENNLIFE.COM

PENNSYLVANIA MEDICAID HMO (AETNA)

	PO BOX 62198 PHOIENIX, AZ 85082-2198	(866) 638-1232 WWW.AETNABETTERHEALTH.COM

PENNSYLVANIA MEDICAID HMO (GATEWAY HEALTH PLAN)

Payer ID 25169	PO BOX 69359 HARRISBURG, PA 17106-9359	(800) 685-5205 WWW.GATEWAYHEALTHPLAN.COM

PENNSYLVANIA MEDICAID HMO (HEALTH PARTNERS OF PHILADELPHIA)

Payer ID 80142	PO BOX 1220 PHILADELPHIA, PA 19105-1220	(215) 991-4350 (800) 991-9023 WWW.HEALTHPART.COM

PENNSYLVANIA MEDICAID HMO (KEYSTONE MERCY HEALTH PLAN)

Payer ID 23284	PO BOX 7115 LONDON, KY 40742	(800) 521-6007 WWW.KEYSTONEMERCY.COM23284

P

PENNSYLVANIA MEDICAID HMO (UPMC HEALTH PLAN)

Payer ID 23281	PO BOX 2995 PITTSBURGH, PA 15230-2995	(866) 918-1595 (800) 286-4242 WWW.UPMCHEALTHPLAN.COM

PEOPLES HEALTH NETWORK

Payer ID 72126	3838 N CAUSEWAY BLVD STE 2200 METAIRIE, LA 70002	(504) 849-4500 (800) 631-8443 WWW.PEOPLESHEALTH.COM

PERSONAL INSURANCE ADMINISTRATORS

Payer ID 95397	PO BOX 6040 AGOURA HILLS, CA 91376-6040	(800) 468-4343 WWW.PIACLAIMS.COM

PERSONALCARE

Payer ID 25133	PO BOX 7141 LONDON, KY 40742	(800) 562-5792 HTTP:// CHCILLINOIS.COVENTRYHEALTHCARE.COM/

PHCS SAVILITY

Payer ID 13306	PO BOX 211532 EAGAN, MN 55121	(877) 728-4548 WWW.PHCSSAVILITY.COM/PROVIDERS/

PHIFER WIRE INSURANCE

	PO BOX 1700 TUSCALOOSA, AL 35401-7042	(205) 345-2120 WWW.PHIFER.COM

PHILLIPS ADMINISTRATIVE SERVICES

	PO BOX 218 ALBANY, OR 97321	(541) 928-1717 (800) 356-9822 WWW.PAS-BENEFITS.COM

PHOENIX HEALTH PLAN

Payer ID 03440	PO BOX 81000 PHOENIX, AZ 85069-1000	(602) 824-3700 (800) 747-7997 WWW.PHOENIXHEALTHPLAN.COM/ PROVIDERS.ASPX

PHOENIX LIFE

Payer ID 67814	PO BOX 8027 BOSTON, MA 02266-8027	(800) 814-3692 WWW.PHOENIXWM.PHL.COM

PHOENIX LIFE INSURANCE

Payer ID 67814	PO BOX 5056 HARTFORD, CT 06102-5056	(800) 814-3692 WWW.PHOENIXWM.COM

PHP HEALTH PLAN

	PO BOX 30377 LANSING, MI 48909	(800) 562-6197 WWW.PHPMM.ORG

PHYSICIAN HEALTH PARTNERS

Payer ID PHPMC	PO BOX 1738 DENVER, CO 80201	(303) 256-1703 WWW.PHPMCS.COM

PHYSICIAN HEALTHWAYS IPA

Payer ID PHIPA	1540 BRIDGEGATE DR DIAMOND BAR, CA 91765	(626) 388-2300 WWW.PHWIPA.ORG

PHYSICIAN UNITED PLAN

Payer ID 10775	9102 SOUTHPARK CENTER LOOP STE 200 ORLANDO, FL 32819	(877) 978-7776 (866) 427-9152 WWW.UASKPUP.COM

PHYSICIANS CARE NETWORK

Payer ID 38265
630 E JEFFERSON ST
ROCKFORD, IL 61107-4026
(815) 963-6699
WWW.USESAGE.COM/LOGIN/PROVIDERLOGIN.ASPX

PHYSICIANS CORPORATION OF AMERICA

Payer ID 65018
PO BOX 14601
LEXINGTON, KY 40512-4601
(800) 448-6262
WWW.HUMANA.COM/PROVIDERS

PHYSICIANS HEALTH CHOICE-CLAIMS

Payer ID PHCS1
PO BOX 29429
SAN ANTONIO, TX 78229
(866) 550-4736
WWW.PHCCARES.COM/DOCTORS/

PHYSICIANS HEALTH CHOICE-ENCOUNTERS

Payer ID PHCEN
PO BOX 29429
SAN ANTONIO, TX 78229
(866) 550-4736
WWW.PHCCARES.COM

PHYSICIANS HEALTH PLAN OF MID MICHIGAN

Payer ID 37330
PO BOX 30377
LANSING, MI 48909-7877
(800) 562-6197
WWW.PHPMM.ORG/FORPROVIDERS/TABID/3343/DEFAULT.ASPX

PHYSICIANS HEALTH PLAN OF NORTHERN INDIANA

Payer ID 12399
PO BOX 2359
FORT WAYNE, IN 46801-2359
(800) 982-6257
WWW.PHPNI.COM/PROVIDERS.ASPX

PHYSICIANS HEALTHWAYS IPA

1540 BRIDGEGATE DR
DIAMOND BAR, CA 91765
(626) 388-2300
(877) 749-9297
WWW.PHWIPA.ORG

PHYSICIANS MUTUAL INSURANCE CO

Payer ID 47027
PO BOX 2018
OMAHA, NE 68103-2018
(866) 477-7878
WWW.PHYSICIANSMUTUAL.COM

PHYSICIANS PLUS INSURANCE CORP

Payer ID 39156
PO BOX 269017
PLANO, TX 75026-9017
(608) 282-8900
(800) 545-5015
WWW.PPLUSIC.COM/PROVIDERS

PIEDMONT BEHAVIORAL HEALTH

Payer ID 06607
4855 MILESTONE AVE
KANNAPOLIS, NC 28081
(704) 721-7000
WWW.PBHSOLUTIONS.ORG/PROVIDERS

PINAL GILA LONG TERM CARE

Payer ID PGLTC
PO BOX 7186
BOISE, ID 83707
(520) 866-6775
(888) 431-1311
HTTP://PINALCOUNTYAZ.GOV/PAGES/HOME.ASPX

PINNACOL ASSURANCE

Payer ID CCIA1
PO BOX 469013
DENVER, CO 80246-9013
(800) 873-7242
WWW.PINNACOL.COM/PROVIDER/

PIONEER PROVIDER NETWORK

PO BOX 1682
BELLFLOWER, CA 90706
(562) 867-8681
WWW.PIONEERMEDICALGROUP.COM

PIPE INDUSTRY HEALTH AND WELFARE FUND OF COLORADO (CIGNA)

Payer ID COMPU
PO BOX 182223
CHATTANOOGA, TN 37422
(800) 882-4462
WWW.CIGNA.COM

PIPEFITTERS LOCAL 597

Payer ID 59700
45 N OGDEN AVE
CHICAGO, IL 60607-1813
(312) 633-0597
WWW.PF597.ORG

PIPELINE INDUSTRY BENEFIT FUND

Payer ID 73074
PO BOX 470950
TULSA, OK 74147-0950
(918) 280-4800
WWW.PIBF.ORG

PITTMAN AND ASSOCIATES

Payer ID 37224
ONE PRESCOTT SOUTH
MEMPHIS, TN 38111-4618
(800) 238-1344
WWW.PA-TPA.COM/ELG-CLAIM-LOOKUP.ASPX

PLANNED ADMINISTRATORS, INC.

Payer ID 37287
PO BOX 6927
COLUMBIA, SC 29260-6927
(800) 768-4375
WWW.PAISC.COM/HEALTHCAREPROVIDERS.ASPX

PMA INSURANCE GROUP

Payer ID WB175
PO BOX 3031
BLUE BELL, PA 19422
(800) 227-2749
WWW.PMAGROUP.COM

PMG OF SAN JOSE

Payer ID PMGSJ
75 E SANTA CLARA STE 950
SAN JOSE, CA 95113
(408) 937-3612
WWW.PMGMD.COM/PROVLOGIN.ASP

PODIATRY FIRST

Payer ID PDFST
20 GREENWAY PLAZA STE 1000
HOUSTON, TX 77046
(713) 797-0050
(866) 458-6076
WWW.GLOBALHCA.COM

POMCO

Payer ID 16111
PO BOX 6329
SYRACUSE, NY 13217-6329
(314) 437-9518
(800) 766-2687
WWW.POMCOGROUP.COM

POMONA VALLEY MEDICAL GROUP

Payer ID IP057
PO BOX 2399
RANCHO CUCAMONGA, CA 91729
(909) 932-1045
WWW.PROMEDHEALTH.COM/HCNDOCS/PROMEDHCN.HTML

PPO PLUS, LLC

Payer ID 72148
PO BOX 90802
LUBBOCK, TX 79408-8802
(504) 680-4499
(888) 965-7718
WWW.PPOPLUS.COM/PROVIDER

PPONEXT

Payer ID 36332
25500 COMMERCENTRE DR
LAKE FOREST, CA 92630-8855
(800) 877-1444
WWW.BEECHSTREET.COM/PROVIDERS/INDEX.HTML

PRACTICARE

Payer ID 04334
4567 CROSSROADS PARK DR
LIVERPOOL, NY 13088-3589
(315) 295-2100
WWW.PRACTICARE.NET

PRAIRIE STATES ENTERPRISES, INC

Payer ID 36373
PO BOX 23
SHEBOYGAN, WI 53082-0023
(800) 615-7020
WWW.PRAIRIEONTHEWEB.COM/PRAIRIE2/WEB-BUILD/1.3_PROVIDERS.HTML

PREFERRED ADMINISTRATORS

Payer ID EPF10

PO BOX 18263
TAMPA, FL 33679-8263

(877) 276-7198
WWW.PREFERREDADMIN.NET/PROVIDERS.HTML

PREFERRED BENEFIT ADMINISTRATORS

Payer ID 53476

PO BOX 916188
LONGWOOD, FL 32791-6188

(407) 786-2777
(888) 524-2777
HTTP://PREFERREDCORP.NETRECALL.COM/

PREFERRED CARE PARTNERS

Payer ID 59291

PO BOX 56-5790
MIAMI, FL 33256-6420

(305) 670-8440
(866) 725-9334
WWW.MYPREFERREDPROVIDERS.COM

PREFERRED CARE PARTNERS (MIAMI, FL)

PO BOX 56-5790
MIAMI, FL 33256-5790

(866) 725-9334
WWW.MYPREFERREDPROVIDER.COM/MEDICAID/EN/PROVIDER-RESOURCES/HOME.ASPX

PREFERRED COMMUNITY CHOICE

Payer ID 73145

PO BOX 3270
TULSA, OK 74101

(918) 594-5323
(800) 884-4776
WWW.CCOK.COM/PROVIDERS

PREFERRED HEALTH CARE

Payer ID CALL

480 NEW HOLLAND AVE STE 7203
LANCASTER, PA 17602

(717) 560-9290
WWW.PHCUNITY.COM/PROVIDERS/INDEX.PHP

PREFERRED HEALTH CHOICES

1605 ASSOCIATES DR STE 101
DUBUQUE, IA 52002
PO BOX 5003
DUBUQUE, IA 52002

(563) 584-4783
WWW.PREFERREDHEALTHCHOICES.COM

PREFERRED HEALTH NETWORK

Payer ID 35173

PO BOX 49288
WICHITA, KS 67201-9318

(877) 609-2467
WWW.PHSYSTEMS.COM/PROVIDERS/PAGES/PROVIDERSLANDINGPAGE.ASPX

PREFERRED HEALTH PLAN

Payer ID 61106

PO BOX 437017
LOUISVILLE, KY 40253

(800) 832-8212
WWW.PHPINC.COM

PREFERRED HEALTH SYSTEMS INSURANCE

Payer ID 60110

PO BOX 7109
LONDON, KY 40742

(316) 609-2467
(877) 609-2467
WWW.PHSYSTEMS.COM/PROVIDERS/PAGES/PROVIDERSLANDINGPAGE.ASPX

PREFERRED IPA

Payer ID PFIPA

PO BOX 4449
CHATSWORTH, CA 91313-4449

(800) 874-2091
WWW.PREFERREDIPA.COM/PROVIDERS.HTML

PREFERRED MENTAL HEALTH MANAGEMENT

401 E. DOUGLAS, SUITE 505
WITCHITA, KS 67202

(800) 776-4357
WWW.PMHM.COM/PROVIDERS.HTML

PREFERRED NETWORK ACCESS

Payer ID 36401

1510 W 75TH ST STE 250
DARIEN, IL 60561-4407

(630) 493-0905
WWW.PNA-USA.COM

PREFERRED ONE

Payer ID 41147
PO BOX 1527
MINNEAPOLIS, MN 55440-1527
(800) 451-9597
WWW.PREFERREDONE.COM/PROVIDERS.ASPX

PREMIER EYE CARE

Payer ID CALL
4205 W ATLANTIC AVE STE 401
DELRAY BEACH, FL 33455
(800) 738-1889
HTTP://PREMIEREYECARE.NET

PREMIER HEALTH PLAN

Payer ID 43166
1235 E CHEROKEE ST
SPRINGFIELD, MO 65890
(417) 820-3870
WWW.MERCYHEALTHPLANS.COM

PREMIER PHYSICIANS NETWORK

Payer ID CAPMN
PO BOX 261580
ENCINO, CA 91426
(818) 461-5055
(888) 445-0062
WWW.CAPCMS.COM

PRESBYTERIAN HEALTH PLAN

Payer ID PREHP
PO BOX 27489
ALBUQUERQUE, NM 87125-7489
(888) 923-5757
WWW.PHS.ORG/PHS/HOSPITALS/PHYSICIANS

PRESBYTERIAN SALUD

Payer ID PRESA
PO BOX 27489
ALBUQUERQUE, NM 87125-7489
(888) 923-5757
WWW.PHS.ORG/PHS/HOSPITALS/PHYSICIANS

PRESTIGE HEALTH CHOICE

Payer ID 45056
PO BOX 6018
HAUPPAUGE, NY 11749
(800) 617-5727
WWW.PRESTIGEHEALTHCHOICE.COM

PREVEA HEALTH INSURANCE PLAN

Payer ID 39185
PO BOX 11625
GREEN BAY, WI 54307-1625
(920) 490-6900
(888) 711-1444
WWW.WECAREFORWISCONSIN.COM/PROVIDERS

PRIMARY CHOICE

Payer ID 60054
PO BOX 981106
EL PASO, TX 79998
(888) 632-3862
WWW.AETNA.COM

PRIMARY HEALTH NETWORK

Payer ID 82048
PO BOX 716
SHARON, PA 16146
(724) 342-5313
WWW.PRIMARY-HEALTH.NET

PRIMARY HEALTH PLAN

Payer ID PRIME
PO BOX 7068
SPRINGFIELD, OR 97475
(800) 688-5008
WWW.PACIFICSOURCE.COM/PROVIDER/WHATS-NEW.ASPX

PRIMARY PHYSICIANCARE, INC

Payer ID 56144
PO BOX 11088
CHARLOTTE, NC 28220-1088
(800) 446-5439
WWW.PRIMARYPC.COM/PROVIDERS/INDEX.CFM?

PRIME WEST HEALTH PLAN

Payer ID 61604
PO BOX 69348
HARRISBURG, PA 17106
(866) 431-0802
(888) 588-4420
WWW.PRIMEWEST.ORG/PROVIDERS/DEFAULT.ASPX

PRIMECARE HEALTH PLAN, INC

Payer ID IP079
PO BOX 6903
RANCHO CUCAMONGA, CA 91729
(800) 956-8000
WWW.PRIMECARE.COM

PRIMESOURCE HEALTH NETWORK

Payer ID 23266	PO BOX 2347 YORK, PA 17405	(717) 851-6800 (800) 842-1768 WWW.PRIMESOURCEHEALTHNETWORK.COM/PROVIDERS.ASPX

PRINCIPAL MUTUAL LIFE INSURANCE COMPANY

Payer ID 61271	PO BOX 10357 DES MOINES, IA 50306	(800) 247-4695 WWW.PRINCIPAL.COM/PARTNERS/PROVIDERS/

PRIORITY HEALTH

Payer ID 38217	PO BOX 232 GRAND RAPIDS, MI 49501-0232	(800) 942-4765 WWW.PRIORITYHEALTH.COM/PROVIDER

PRIORITY HEALTHCARE

	5719 HWY 25 STE 203 FLOWOOD, MS 39232	(769) 257-5685 WWW.PRIORITYHC.COM/INDEX.PHP

PRISM UNIVERA

Payer ID 37315	PO BOX 23000 ROCHESTER, NY 14692	(716) 857-4444 (800) 617-1114 WWW.UNIVERAHEALTHCARE.COM/WPS/PORTAL/UV/PRV/

PROCARE HEALTH PLAN MEDICAID

Payer ID 70259	PO BOX 441970 DETROIT, MI 48244-1970	(313) 925-1668 (877) 255-3055 WWW.PROCAREHP.COM

PRODUCER'S EXCHANGE

Payer ID PEBSI	15305 N DALLAS PKWY #100 COLONNADE III ADDISON, TX 75001	(972) 774-110 (800) 443-2595 WWW.PEBSI.COM

PROFESSIONAL ADMINISTRATORS, INC

	PO BOX 1730 AUBURNDALE, FL 33823	(407) 896-0521 WWW.PROFADMIN.COM

PROFESSIONAL BENEFIT ADMINISTRATORS, INC

Payer ID 36331	PO BOX 4687 OAK BROOK, IL 60523	(800) 435-5694 WWW.PBACLAIMS.COM/PROVIDER_LOGIN.HTM

PROFESSIONAL BENEFITS ADMINISTRATORS

Payer ID 59296	PO BOX 5409 WINTER PARK, FL 32793	(407) 671-7331 (800) 762-4130 WWW.PBA-FL.COM

PROFESSIONAL RISK MANAGEMENT

Payer ID 34134	PO BOX 853921 RICHARDSON, TX 75085	(800) 331-7620 WWW.PRMTPA.COM/LIN-LOGIN1.HTM

PROSPECT MEDICAL GROUP

Payer ID PROSP	1920 E 17TH ST STE 200 SANTA ANA, CA 92705	(800) 708-3230 WWW.PROSPECTMEDICAL.COM/PROVIDERS/INDEX.HTML

PROTECTIVE LIFE INSURANCE COMPANY

Payer ID 37309	PO BOX 12687 BIRMINGHAM, AL 35202-6687	(800) 866-9933 WWW.PROTECTIVE.COM

PROVIDENCE HEALTH PLANS

Payer ID PHP01

PO BOX 3125
PORTLAND, OR 97208

(503) 574-7500
(800) 793-9338
WWW.PROVIDENCE.ORG

PROVIDENCE PREFERRED PPO

Payer ID PHP00

PO BOX 3236
PORTLAND, OR 97208

(800) 878-4445
WWW.PROVIDENCE.ORG

PROVIDENT LIFE & ACCIDENT INSURANCE COMPANY

Payer ID 68195

PO BOX 100158
COLUMBIA, SC 29202

(800) 799-4455
WWW.UNUM.COM

PROVIDRS CARE NETWORK

Payer ID 48100

1102 S HILLSIDE
WICHITA, KS 67211

(316) 683-4111
(800) 801-9772
WWW.PROVIDRSCARE.NET/PROVIDERS.HTM

PRUDENTIAL INSURANCE COMPANY OF AMERICA

PO BOX 89436
CLEVELAND, OH 44101

(800) 828-0153
WWW.PRUDENTIAL.COM

PSN-FLORIDA MEDICAID

Payer ID 09822

1801 NW 9 AVE STE 100
MIAMI, FL 33136

(305) 575-3680
WWW.JMHHP.COM/PROVIDERS/
PROVIDERS.ASP

PSYCHCARE, LLC

Payer ID 51052

10200 SUNSET DR
MIAMI, FL 33173

(800) 221-5487
WWW.PSYCHCARE.COM/INDEX.PHP?ID=8

PUERTO RICO MEDICAID HMO (HUMANA HEALTH PLANS)

Payer ID 61101

PO BOX 14601
LEXINGTON, KY 40512-4601

(800) 626-2741
WWW.HUMANA.COM/PROVIDERS

PUGET SOUND BENEFITS TRUST

Payer ID 91136

PO BOX 34711
SEATTLE, WA 98124-1711

(866) 314-4239
WWW.WPAS-INC.COM

PUGET SOUND ELECTRICAL WORKERS TRUST - GRP#33

Payer ID 91136

PO BOX 34970
SEATTLE, WA 98124-1970

(866) 314-4239
WWW.WPAS-INC.COM

PUGET SOUND HEALTH PARTNERS, INC.

Payer ID 42172

PO BOX 4537
FEDERAL WAY, WA 98063

(866) 789-7747
HTTP://SOUNDPATHHEALTH.COM/
PHYSICIANS.ASPX

PYRAMID LIFE

1001 HEATHROW PARK LN STE 5001
LAKE MARY, FL 32746-5586
PO BOX 12922
PENSACOLA, FL 32591

(800) 444-0321
(800) 777-1126
WWW.UNIVERSALAMERICANINSURANCEPLANS.COM/
COMPANIES/PYRAMID-LIFE/

QUAD CITY COMMUNITY HEALTHCARE

	PO BOX 389 DUBUQUE, IA 52004-0389	(563) 322-8995 (888) 498-7224 HTTP://QCCHEALTH.COM

QUADMED

Payer ID 39197	555 S 108TH ST WEST ALLIS, WI 53214-1100	(414) 566-6800 (800) 937-2230 WWW.QUADMEDICAL.COM

QUAL CHOICE OF ARKANSAS

Payer ID 35174	PO BOX 25610 LITTLE ROCK, AR 72211-5610	(501) 228-7111 (800) 235-7111 WWW.QUALCHOICE.COM

QUAL CHOICE OF OHIO

Payer ID 01250	6000 PARKLAND BLVD CLEVELAND, OH 44124-6120	(800) 460-4677 WWW.QUALCHOICE.COM/

QUALCARE

Payer ID 23342	PO BOX 820 PISCATAWAY, NJ 08855	(732) 562-0833 (800) 992-6613 WWW.QUALCAREINC.COM

QUALITY CARE PARTNERS

	2806 BELL ST ZANESVILLE, OH 43701	(740) 455-5199 (888) 258-7621 WWW.QUALITYCAREPARTNERS.COM/ PROVIDERS.HTML

QUANTUM CARE LLC

	8211 W BROWARD BLVD STE 400 PLANTATION, FL 33324	(877) 801-9541 WWW.QUANTUMCARETPA.COM/INDEX.HTML

QUICKTRIP CORPORATION

Payer ID 73067	PO BOX 3475 TULSA, OK 74101-3475	(918) 615-7700 WWW.QUIKTRIP.COM/

QVI RISK SOLUTIONS, INC.

Payer ID 57117	PO BOX 7199 BEND, OR 97708	(541) 312-8512 (800) 408-9717 WWW.QVIRISK.COM

RAM MUTUAL INSURANCE COMPANY

Payer ID WZ890
PO BOX 308
ESKO, MN 55733
(890) 218-8793
WWW.RAMMUTUAL.COM

RAPID CITY REGIONAL HOSPITAL

Payer ID 37306
PO BOX 6000
RAPID CITY, SD 57709
(605) 719-5510
WWW.REGIONALHEALTH.COM

REDLANDS IPA

Payer ID SYMED
PO BOX 2002
MONTEREY, CA 91754
(213) 406-2830
(877) 963-7633
WWW.SYNERMEDCONNECT.COM/

REGAL MEDICAL GROUP

Payer ID REGAL
PO BOX 371330
RESEDA, CA 91337-1330
(866) 654-3471
WWW.REGALMED.COM

REGENCE BLUE SHIELD OF WASHINGTON

Payer ID RGBLS
PO BOX 1071
PORTLAND, OR 97207
(800) 458-3523
WWW.WA.REGENCE.COM

REGIONAL CARE, INC

Payer ID 47076
905 W 27TH ST
SCOTTSBLUFF, NE 69361-1545
(800) 795-7772
WWW.REGIONALCARE.COM

REHN AND ASSOCIATES

Payer ID REHNA
PO BOX 5433
SPOKANE, WA 99205
(509) 534-0600
(800) 872-8979
WWW.REHNONLINE.COM

RELIASTAR

Payer ID PH018
PO BOX 5050
MINOT, ND 58702-5050
(877) 884-5050
WWW.ING-USA.COM

RENAISSANCE PHYSICIANS ORGANIZATION

Payer ID 76066
PO BOX 2888
HOUSTON, TX 77252-2888
(832) 553-3300
(800) 280-8888
WWW.MYRPO.COM

REPUBLIC FRANKLIN INSURANCE

Payer ID WP746
2600 CORPORATE EXCHANGE #200
COLUMBUS, OH 43231
(800) 274-1914
WWW.UTICANATIONAL.COM

REPUBLIC INDEMNITY CO OF AMERICA

Payer ID WR618
PO BOX 20036
ENCINO, CA 91416
(818) 990-9860
(800) 821-4520
WWW.REPUBLICINDEMNITY.COM

REPUBLIC WESTERN INSURANCE COMPANY

Payer ID WZ620
2721 NORTH CENTRAL AVE
PHOENIX, AZ 85004
PO BOX 24181
PHOENIX, AZ 85074-4181
(877) 528-5674
WWW.REPWEST.COM

RESERVE NATIONAL INSURANCE CO

Payer ID 73066
PO BOX 26620
OKLAHOMA CITY, OK 73126
(800) 654-9106
WWW.RESERVENATIONAL.COM

RESOLVE HEALTH PLAN ADMINISTRATORS

Payer ID 20481
PO BOX 724
BUCKEYSTOWN, MD 21717
(866) 977-4872
WWW.RESOLVEHEALTHPLAN.COM

RESOURCEONE

Payer ID 37278 | PO BOX 489, BUCKEYSTOWN, MD 21717-0489 | (800) 967-2077, WWW.ROATPA.COM

RESTAT, LLC

11900 W LAKE PARK DR, MILWAUKEE, WI 53224-3013 | (800) 248-1062, WWW.RESTAT.COM

RESURRECTION HEALTH CARE

Payer ID 37277 | 1021 W ADAMS ST FL 3, CHICAGO, IL 60607-2937 | (773) 572-8300, WWW.RESHEALTH.ORG

RESURRECTION PHYSICIAN GROUP

Payer ID RPPG1 | 5860 W HIGGINS AVE, CHICAGO, IL 60630-2036 | (773) 695-4800, WWW.RESURRECTIONPHYSICIANS.COM

RIGHT CARE FROM SCOTT AND WHITE PLAN

Payer ID 74205 | PO BOX 3757, CORPUS CHRISTI, TX 78463-3757 | (855) 897-4448, WWW.RIGHTCARE.SWHP.ORG/HOMEPAGE/RIGHTCARE

RIGHTCHOICE BENEFITS ADMINISTRATORS

Payer ID 37331 | 1831 CHESTNUT ST, ST LOUIS, MO 63103-2231 | (314) 821-3957, (800) 365-9036, WWW.RCTPA.COM

RISING MEDICAL

Payer ID WB216 | 325 N LA SALLE ST #600, CHICAGO, IL 60654 | (312) 599-8445, WWW.RISINGMS.COM

RISK ENTERPRISE MANAGEMENT

Payer ID TO578 | 2540 ROUTE 130 STE 109, CRANBURY, NJ 05412 | (800) 208-3431, WWW.REMLTD.COM

RIVERSIDE FAMILY HEALTH MED GRP IPA

Payer ID MPM08 | PO BOX 571450, TARZANA, CA 91357 | (818) 702-0100, WWW.MEDPOINTMANAGEMENT.COM

RMSCO, INC

Payer ID 16117 | PO BOX 6309, SYRACUSE, NY 13217 | (800) 356-1029, WWW.RMSCOINC.COM

ROCKY MOUNTAIN HEALTH PLANS

Payer ID RMHMO | PO BOX 10600, GRAND JUNCTION, CO 81502 | (970) 243-7050, (800) 854-4558, WWW.RMHP.ORG

ROYAL HEALTH NEIGHBOR

PO BOX 5265, HAUPPAUGE, NY 11788 | (212) 808-4775, WWW.ROYALHC.COM

ROYAL STATE GROUP

819 S BERETANIA ST STE 100, HONOLULU, HI 96813-2501 | (808) 539-1600, WWW.ROYALSTATE.COM

RUSH PRUDENTIAL HEALTH PLANS

Payer ID 36389 | 120 MONUMENT CIR, INDIANAPOLIS, IN 46204-2904 | (317) 532-6000, WWW.WELLPOINT.COM

RX OPTIONS

2181 E AURORA RD STE 201
TWINSBURG, OH 44087-1923

(800) 361-4542
WWW.ENVISIONRX.COM

S & S HEALTHCARE STRATEGIES

Payer ID 31441
1385 KEMPER MEADOW DR
CINCINNATI, OH 45240
(800) 717-2872
WWW.SS-HEALTHCARE.COM/

SAFECO INSURANCE CO OF AMERICA

Payer ID WR746
1001 4TH AVE
SEATTLE, WA 98154
(206) 545-5000
(800) 332-3226
WWW.SAFECO.COM

SAFEGAURD

Payer ID SFG99
PO BOX 981987
EL PASO, TX 79998
(800) 880-1800
WWW.SAFEGUARD.NET

SAGAMORE HEALTH NETWORK

Payer ID 35164
PO BOX 6051
INDIANPOLIS, IN 46206-6051
(317) 580-8060
(800) 320-0015
WWW.SAGAMOREHN.COM

SAGE TECHNOLOGIES - PBS

Payer ID 37137
630 E JEFFERSON ST
ROCKFORD, IL 61107-4026
(888) 227-8904
WWW.USESAGE.COM

SAGICOR LIFE

Payer ID 65067
PO BOX 52121
PHOENIX, AZ 85072
(800) 531-5067
WWW.SAGICORLIFEUSA.COM

SAINT MARYS HEALTH PLAN

Payer ID 88029
1510 MEADOW WOOD LN
RENO, NV 89502
(775) 770-6278
WWW.SAINTMARYSHEALTHPLANS.COM

SAMARITAN ADVANTAGE

Payer ID SAMAD
PO BOX 1510
CORVALLIS, OR 97339
(541) 768-5207
(888) 435-2396
WWW.SAMHEALTH.ORG

SAMARITAN CHOICE PLAN

Payer ID SAMCP
PO BOX 336
CORVALLIS, OR 97339
(541) 768-5207
(888) 435-2396
WWW.SAMHEALTH.ORG

SAMARITAN HEALTH KIDSCONNECT

Payer ID SAMHK
PO BOX 1310
CORVALLIS, OR 97339
(888) 435-2396
WWW.SAMHEALTH.ORG

SAMARITAN SELECT

Payer ID SAMSE
PO BOX 1310
CORVALLIS, OR 97339
(541) 768-5207
(888) 435-2396
WWW.SAMHEALTH.ORG

SAMBA

PO BOX 188007
CHATTANOOGA, TN 37422
(301) 984-1440
(800) 638-6589
WWW.SAMBAPLANS.COM

SAN DIEGO COUNTY MEDICAL SERVICES (CMS)

Payer ID MS011
CMS PROGRAM CLAIMS DEPT.
PO BOX 939016
SAN DIEGO, CA 92193
(858) 495-1333
WWW.SDCOUNTY.CA.GOV/HHSA/PROGRAMS/SSP/COUNTY_MEDICAL_SERVICES/

SAN DIEGO COUNTY PHYSICIAN EMERGENCY SERVICES

Payer ID MS022	PO BOX 939000 SAN DIEGO, CA 92193	(858) 495-1333 WWW.SDCOUNTY.CA.GOV/HHSA/PROGRAMS/ SSP/DOCUMENTS/PHYSICIANERSERVICES.PDF

SAN DIEGO COUNTY PRIMARY CARE SERVICES

Payer ID MS044	PO BOX 939016 SAN DIEGO, CA 92193	(858) 495-1333 WWW.SDCOUNTY.CA.GOV/HHSA/PROGRAMS/ SSP/DOCUMENTS/PCCHANDBOOK.PDF

SANDHILLS CENTER

Payer ID SHC30	1120 SEVEN LAKES DR WEST END, NC 27376	(855) 777-4652 WWW.SANDHILLSCENTER.ORG/ PROVIDERS.HTM

SANFORD HEALTH PLAN

Payer ID 91184	PO BOX 91110 SIOUX FALLS, SD 57109-1110	(605) 328-6877 WWW.SANFORDHEALTH.ORG

SANTA CLARA FAMILY HEALTH PLANS

Payer ID 24077	210 E HACIENDA AVE CAMPBELL, CA 95008-6617	(408) 874-1788 WWW.SCFHP.COM

SANTE HEALTH SYSTEMS

Payer ID 77038	PO BOX 1507 FRESNO, CA 93716-1507	(559) 228-5410 WWW.SANTEHEALTH.NET

SARATOGA COUNTY SELF INSURANCE PLANS

Payer ID WB533	40 MCMASTER ST BALLSTON SPA, NY 12020	(518) 885-2234 WWW.SARATOGACOUNTYNY.GOV

SAV-RX PRESCRIPTION SERVICES

	224 N PARK AVE FREMONT, NE 68025-4964	(800) 228-3108 WWW.SAVRX.COM

SC BLUE CROSS FEP

Payer ID SC402	PO BOX 600601 COLUMBIA, SC 29260	(800) 444-0025 WWW.SOUTHCAROLINABLUES.COM/ EMPLOYERS/PRODUCTSSERVICES/ FEDERALEMPLOYEESFEP.ASPX
Payer ID SC402	PO BOX 31457 CHARLESTON, SC 29417	(800) 444-4325 WWW.SOUTHCAROLINABLUES.COM/ PROVIDERS.ASPX

SCAN HEALTH PLAN

Payer ID 72261	PO BOX 22698 LONG BEACH, CA 90801	(562) 989-5100 (877) 235-7226 WWW.SCANHEALTHPLAN.COM

SCAN HEALTH PLAN ARIZONA

Payer ID 73172	PO BOX 61450 PHOENIX, AZ 85082-1450	(877) 235-7226 WWW.SCANHEALTHPLAN.COM

SCAN LONG TERM CARE

Payer ID 20460	PO BOX 61450 PHOENIX, AZ 85082	(888) 540-7226 WWW.SCANHEALTHPLAN.COM

SCHC TOTAL CARE

Payer ID 16146	PO BOX 11507 SYRACUSE, NY 13218-1507	(800) 223-7242 WWW.TOTALCARENY.COM

SCOTT & WHITE HEALTH PLAN

Payer ID 88030

PO BOX 21800
EAGAN, MN 55121-0800

(800) 321-7947
WWW.SWHP.ORG

SCRIPVENTURES GROUP LTD

5629 FM 1960 W STE 234
HOUSTON, TX 77069

(800) 451-0133
HTTP://LUSCINIAHEALTH.COM

SECURA INSURANCE COMPANIES

Payer ID WZ082

PO BOX 819
APPLETON, WI 54912-0819

(920) 739-3161
(800) 558-3405
WWW.SECURA.NET

SECURE HEALTH OF GEORGIA

Payer ID 28530

PO BOX 13447
MACON, GA 31208-3447

(478) 314-2400
WWW.SHPG.COM

SECURE HEALTH PLANS

PO BOX 13447
MACON, GA 31208

(478) 314-2400
(800) 648-7563
WWW.SHPG.COM

SECURE HORIZONS OF CO

Payer ID COFHP

PO BOX 52064
PHOENIX, AZ 85072-2064

(800) 643-4845
WWW.SECUREHORIZONS.COM

SECURITY HEALTH PLAN

Payer ID 39045

PO BOX 8000
MARSHFIELD, WI 54449-8000

(800) 472-2363
WWW.SECURITYHEALTH.ORG

SEDGWICK CLAIM MANAGEMENT SERVICES

Payer ID TP097

1100 RIDGEWAY LOOP RD
MEMPHIS, TN 38120-4053
PO BOX 14423
MEMPHIS, TN 40512

(901) 415-7400
(866) 856-4805
WWW.SEDGWICKCMS.COM/PROVIDERS.ASPX

SEECHANGE

Payer ID 77024

PO BOX 14326
READING, PA 19612

(415) 229-4640
WWW.SEECHANGEHEALTH.COM

SELECT BENEFIT ADMINISTRATORS

Payer ID 42137

PO BOX 65887
WEST DES MOINES, IA 50265

(800) 397-0427
WWW.AMERICANADMINISTRATORS.COM

SELECT BENEFIT ADMINISTRATORS OF AMERICA

Payer ID 37282

PO BOX 440
ASHLAND, WI 54806-0440

(800) 497-3699
WWW.SYMETRA.COM

SELECT BENEFIT ADMINISTRATORS, INC.

Payer ID 93031

PO BOX 70088
SPRINGFIELD, OR 97475-0105

(541) 225-1950
(888) 532-5332
HTTP://TPA.PACIFICSOURCE.COM

SELECT CHOICE

Payer ID 60054

155 N RIVERVIEW STE 308
ANAHEIM, CA 92808-1225

(714) 769-9141
WWW.SELECTCHOICENOW.COM

SELECT HEALTH

Payer ID UH107

4646 W LAKE PARK BLVD
SALT LAKE CITY, UT 84120
PO BOX 30192
SALT LAKE CITY, UT 84130-0192

(800) 538-5038
WWW.SELECTHEALTH.ORG

SELECT HEALTH OF SOUTH CAROLINA

Payer ID 23285 | PO BOX 7120, LONDON, KY 40742-7120 | (800) 575-0418, WWW.SELECTHEALTHOFSC.COM

SELECTCARE OF OK - TRIBUTE

Payer ID SCOK1 | PO BOX 744947, HOUSTON, TX 77274 | (800) 817-3515, WWW.UNIVERSALAMERICAN.COM

SELECTCARE OF TEXAS (HPN) HERITAGE PHYSICIANS NETWORK

Payer ID 76045 | PO BOX 741107, HOUSTON, TX 77274 | (800) 958-2707, WWW.UNIVERSALAMERICAN.COM

SELECTCARE OF TX (BEAUMONT)

Payer ID GTPA1 | PO BOX 741107, HOUSTON, TX 77274 | (800) 958-2707, WWW.UNIVERSALAMERICAN.COM/

SELECTCARE OF TX (HOUSTON)

Payer ID HPN11 | PO BOX 741107, HOUSTON, TX 77274 | (800) 958-2707, WWW.UNIVERSALAMERICAN.COM/

SELECTCARE OF TX (KELSEY-SEYBOLD)

Payer ID KLSY1 | PO BOX 741107, HOUSTON, TX 77274 | (800) 958-2707, WWW.UNIVERSALAMERICAN.COM/

SELF FUNDING ADMINISTRATORS

PO BOX 6596, ANNAPOLIS, MD 21401-0596 | (410) 757-4200, (800) 424-8611, WWW.SELF-FUNDING-ADMIN.COM

SELF INSURED BENEFIT ADMINISTRATORS

Payer ID 59111 | 2600 MCCORMICK DR STE 370, CLEARWATER, FL 33759-1025 | (727) 532-0400, (800) 683-7422, WWW.SIBATPA.COM

SELF INSURED PLANS, LLC

Payer ID 36404 | 14710 TAMIAMI TRAIL N STE 201, NAPLES, FL 34110 | (239) 403-7884, WWW.SELFINSUREDPLANS.COM

SELF-FUNDED PLANS (IL, PA, OH)

Payer ID 34131 | 1432 HAMILTON AVE, CLEVELAND, OH 44114-1146 | (800) 722-7374, WWW.SFPI.COM

SELMAN & CO

6110 PARKLAND BLVD, CLEVELAND, OH 44124-4187 | (440) 646-9336, (800) 735-6262, WWW.SELMANCO.COM

SENDERO HEALTH PLANS

Payer ID 36426 | PO BOX 3869, CORPUS CHRISTI, TX 78463 | (855) 526-7388, WWW.SENDEROHEALTH.COM/EN/

SENIOR CARE

Payer ID 68241 | PO BOX 9910, DAYTONA BEACH, FL 32120-0910 | (800) 352-9824, WWW.FHCP.COM

SENIOR CARE PARTNERS

Payer ID NANPR | PO BOX 7550, WESTCHESTER, IL 60154 | (866) 785-4118, WWW.MYSENIORCAREPARTNERS.COM/DEFAULT.ASPX

SENIOR CHOICE (AETNA HP - NY/NJ)

Payer ID 60054	151 FARMINGTON AVE HARTFORD, CT 06156	(800) 624-0756 WWW.AETNA.COM

SENIOR SMART CHOICE

Payer ID 95444	1776 N MERIDIAN ST STE 300 INDIANAPOLIS, IN 46202-1404	(317) 963-9700 (800) 455-9776

SENIOR WHOLE HEALTH

Payer ID 83035	PO BOX 425027 CAMBRIDGE, MA 02142	(617) 494-5353 WWW.SENIORWHOLEHEALTH.COM

SENTARA FAMILY PLAN

Payer ID 54154	PO BOX 5028 TROY, MI 48007-5028	(800) 229-8822 WWW.OPTIMAHEALTH.COM

SENTARA HEALTH MANAGEMENT

Payer ID 54154	PO BOX 5028 TROY, MI 48007-5028	(757) 552-7200 WWW.OPTIMAHEALTH.COM

SENTINEL MANAGEMENT SERVICES

Payer ID 23249	PO BOX 8377 LANCASTER, PA 17604-8377	(800) 432-8877 HTTP://SENTINEL4HEALTH.COM

SENTRY CASUALTY COMPANY

Payer ID WB140	1800 NORTHPOINT DR STEVENS POINT, WI 54481	(715) 346-6000 (800) 373-6879 WWW.SENTRY .COM

SENTRY INSURANCE MUTUAL CO

Payer ID 39033	PO BOX 8025 STEVENS POINT, WI 54481	(800) 426-7234 WWW.SENTRYINSURANCE.COM

SENTRY LLOYDS OF TEXAS

Payer ID WB142	1800 NORTH POINT DR STEVENS POINT, WI 54481	(512) 238-3164

SENTRY SELECT INSURANCE CO

Payer ID WB143	4400 E 53RD ST DAVENPORT, IA 52807 PO BOX 8023 DAVENPORT, IA 52808	(800) 447-0633 WWW.SENTRYINSURANCE.COM

SETON CHIP

Payer ID SHPCH	PO BOX 15507 AUSTIN, TX 78761-5445	(800) 749-7624 WWW.SETONHEALTHPLAN.COM

SETON EMPLOYEE PLAN

Payer ID SHEBP	PO BOX 15445 AUSTIN, TX 78761	(512) 324-3125 WWW.SETONHEALTHPLAN.COM

SETON MAP PROGRAM - MEDIVIEW

Payer ID SHMAP	PO BOX 14447 AUSTIN, TX 78761	(512) 324-3125 WWW.SETONHEALTHPLAN.COM

SETON STAR

	6937 N IH35 STE 500 AUSTIN, TX 78752	(877) 451-5601 WWW.SETONHEALTHPLAN.COM/PROVIDERS/

SEVEN CORNERS

Payer ID 25404

303 CONGRESSIONAL BLVD
CARMEL, IN 46032-5631

(800) 335-0611
WWW.SEVENCORNERS.COM

SHARP HEALTH PLAN

PO BOX 939036
SAN DIEGO, CA 92193

(800) 359-2002
WWW.SHARPHEALTHPLAN.COM

SHASTA ADMINISTRATIVE SERVICES

Payer ID 75280

PO BOX 1747
REDMOND, OR 97756

(800) 441-4518
WWW.SHASTATPA.COM

SHEAKLEY UNICOMP (OH BWC)

Payer ID 10002

ONE SHEAKLEY WAY
CINCINNATI, OH 45246

(888) 743-2559
(800) 877-2053
WWW.SHEAKLEY.COM

SHEET METAL WORKERS LOCAL 104

Payer ID 38238

PO BOX 1917
SAN RAMON, CA 94583

(800) 548-1771
WWW.SMW104.ORG

SHEFFIELD OLSON & MCQUEEN, INC

2145 FORD PKY STE 300
ST PAUL, MN 55116-1912

(651) 695-2500
(800) 486-7664
WWW.SOMI.COM

SHENANDOAH LIFE INSURANCE CO

2301 BRAMBLETON AVE SW
ROANOKE, VA 24015
PO BOX 12847
ROANOKE, VA 24029-2847

(540) 985-4400
(800) 848-5433
WWW.SHENLIFE.COM

SHERMAN CHOICE

Payer ID SC359

PO BOX 239
ELGIN, IL 60121

(224) 783-8933
WWW.SHERMANHEALTH.COM

SIERRA HEALTH & LIFE INSURANCE CO, INC

Payer ID 76342

2724 N TENAYA WY
LAS VEGAS, NV 89128-0424
PO BOX 15645
LAS VEGAS, NV 89114-5645

(702) 242-7000
(800) 962-8074
WWW.SIERRAHEALTHANDLIFE.COM

SIGNATURE HEALTH ALLIANCE

Payer ID 62159

PO BOX 22419
NASHVILLE, TN 37202-2419

(800) 264-3060
WWW.SIGNATUREHEALTH.COM

SIGNIFICA BENEFIT SERVICES, INC

Payer ID 23250

PO BOX 7777
LANCASTER, PA 17604-7777

(717) 581-1300
(800) 433-3746
WWW.SIGNIFICABENEFITS.COM

SIHO

Payer ID NTWKS

P.O. BOX 1787
COLUMBUS, IN 47202-1787

(812) 378-7070
(800) 443-2980
WWW.SIHO.ORG/EN/PROVIDERS/

SIMPLIFI

Payer ID 55438

3600 AMERICAN BLVD STE 750
BLOOMINGTON, MN 55431

(800) 824-3882
WWW.SIMPLIFIESO.COM

SIMPLY HEALTHCARE PLANS

Payer ID 27094 | PO BOX 21535
EAGAN, MN 55121 | (800) 887-6888
WWW.SIMPLYHEALTHCAREPLANS.COM/

SINCLAIR HEALTH PLAN

Payer ID 84076 | PO BOX 30827
SALT LAKE CITY, UT 84130-0827 | (888) 800-2230

SISCO (SELF INSURED SERVICES COMPANY)

Payer ID 00540 | PO BOX 389
DUBUQUE, IA 52004-0389 | (800) 457-4726
WWW.CB-SISCO.COM

SMA HEALTH PLAN

Payer ID 72112 | PO BOX 15645
LAS VEGAS, NV 89114-5645 | (702) 877-5111
WWW.SMALV.COM

SMITH ADMINISTRATORS

Payer ID SMITH | PO BOX 853937
RICHARDSON, TX 75085 | (800) 261-5511
WWW.SMITHADMIN.COM

SOUND HEALTH

Payer ID 91131 | PO BOX 2265
SEATTLE, WA 98111 | (206) 282-4500
(800) 225-7620
WWW.SOUNDHEALTHWELLNESS.COM

SOUTH CENTRAL PREFERRED

PO BOX 2347
YORK, PA 17405-2347 | (717) 851-6800
(800) 842-1768
WWW.SCP-PPO.COM

SOUTH COUNTY HEALTH ALLIANCE

P.O. BOX 4014
ROCHESTER, MN 55903 | (800) 995-4543
WWW.MNSCHA.ORG

SOUTH DAKOTA CHIROPRACTIC (SANFORD HEALTH PLAN)

Payer ID CASD2 | 2301 RESEARCH PARK WAY STE 221
BROOKINGS, SD 57006 | (800) 658-2214
WWW.CASD.US

SOUTHCARE / HEALTHCARE PREFERRED

Payer ID 25147 | 6705 ROCKLEDGE DR STE 900
BETHESDA, MD 20817 | (301) 581-0600
(800) 937-6824
HTTP://COVENTRYHEALTHCARE.COM/

SOUTHEASTERN INDIANA HEALTH ORGANIZATION

PO BOX 1787
COLUMBUS, IN 47202-1787 | (812) 378-7000
(800) 443-2980
WWW.SIHO.ORG

SOUTHERN BENEFIT ADMINISTRATORS, INC

PO BOX 1449
GOODLETTSVILLE, TN 37070-1449 | (615) 859-0131
(800) 831-4914
WWW.SOUTHERNBENEFIT.COM

SOUTHERN BENEFIT SERVICES

Payer ID 37318 | 2400 VETERANS BLVD, SUITE 140
KENNER, LA 70062 | (504) 323-7500
WWW.SBSTPA.COM/PAGES/BASICWEBP/
HOME.ASPX

SOUTHERN CAL PHYSICIANS MANAGED CARE SERVICES

Payer ID SCP01 | 6760 TOP GUN ST 100
SAN DIEGO, CA 92121-4152 | (858) 824-7000
WWW.SCPMCS.ORG

SOUTHERN GROUP ADMINISTRATORS, INC

Payer ID 56131

200 S MARSHALL ST
WINSTON-SALEM, NC 27101-5251

(336) 728-7111
(800) 334-8159
WWW.SGROUPADMIN.COM

SOUTHERN HEALTH SERVICES, INC.

Payer ID 25128

PO BOX 7704
LONDON, KY 40742

(804) 747-3700
HTTP://
CHCVIRGINIA.COVENTRYHEALTHCARE.COM/

SOUTHWEST ADMINISTRATORS

PO BOX 1121
ALHAMBRA, CA 91802-1121

(626) 284-4792
(877) 350-4792
WWW.SWADMIN.COM

SOUTHWEST BUSINESS CORP

PO BOX 795027
SAN ANTONIO, TX 78729-5027

(210) 525-1241
(800) 527-0066
WWW.SWBC.COM

SOUTHWEST CARPENTERS HEALTH & WELFARE TRUST

PO BOX 17973
LOS ANGELES, CA 90017-0973

(213) 385-0551
(800) 252-9255
WWW.CARPENTERSSW.ORG

SOUTHWEST SERVICE ADMINISTRATORS, INC

Payer ID 53589

2400 W DUNLAP AVE 250
PHOENIX, AZ 85021

(602) 249-3582
(800) 432-6636
WWW.SOUTHWESTSERVICETPA.COM

SOUTHWEST SERVICE LIFE

Payer ID 37266

PO BOX 982005
FORT WORTH, TX 76182-8005

(817) 284-4888
WWW.SOUTHWESTSERVICELIFE.COM

SPECTERA

6220 OLD DOBBIN LANE STE 200
COLUMBIA, MD 21045-5801
PO BOX 30978
SALT LAKE CITY, UT 84130

(800) 638-3120
WWW.SPECTERA.COM

SPECTRUM ADMINISTRATORS

Payer ID 23253

2166 S 12TH ST
ALLENTOWN, PA 18103-4752
PO BOX 1830
ALLENTOWN, PA 18105-1830

(610) 969-0410
(800) 925-8459
WWW.SPECTRUMTPA.COM

SRC SERVICES, INC

PO BOX 14079
LEXINGTON, KY 40512

(888) 772-9682
WWW.SRC-WEB.COM

ST JOSEPH HERITAGE MEDICAL GROUP

Payer ID IP106

2501 E CHAPMAN AVE
ORANGE, CA 92869
P.O. BOX 4138
FULLERTON,, CA 92834-4138

(714) 712-3398
(888) 313-4373
WWW.SJHMG.COM

ST. BARNABAS SYSTEM HEALTH PLAN

Payer ID 22240

PO BOX 1120
PISCATAWAY, NJ 08855-1120

(800) 578-1440
WWW.SAINTBARNABAS.COM

ST. JOHN'S CLAIMS ADMINISTRATION

Payer ID 37264	PO BOX 14230 SPRINGFIELD, MO 65814	(877) 875-7700 WWW.STJOHNS.COM

STAR HRG

Payer ID 59225	PO BOX 55270 PHOENIX, AZ 85078-5270	(800) 308-5948 WWW.CIGNAVOLUNTARY.COM

STARMARK

Payer ID 61425	PO BOX 2942 CLINTON, IA 52733-2942	(800) 522-1246 WWW.STARMARKINC.COM

STARMARK - 4MOST/STRATOSE

Payer ID 06057	PO BOX 13519 CHARLESTON, WV 25360	(888) 258-6477 WWW.4MOSTHEALTH.COM

STATE EMPLOYEES GROUP BENEFITS

Payer ID 72087	7389 FLORIDA BLVD STE 400 BATON ROUGE, LA 70806-4637	(800) 215-1093 WWW.GROUPBENEFITS.ORG

STATE FARM GROUP MEDICAL & IND HEALTH INS CO

Payer ID 31053	PO BOX 805107 CHICAGO, IL 60680-4112	(888) 652-4013 WWW.BCBSIL.COM/STATEFARM

STATE FUND MUTUAL INSURANCE

	(CORVEL) 3001 NE BROADWAY ST STE 620 MINNEAPOLIS, MN 55413 PO BOX 9416 MINNEAPOLIS, MN 55440-9416	(612) 436-2579 (866) 706-5434 WWW.SFMIC.COM

STATE MERIT GA

Payer ID GABLS	PO BOX 9907 COLUMBUS, GA 31908	(404) 842-8000 (800) 441-2273 WWW.BCBSGA.COM

STATE OFFICE OF RISK MANAGEMENT TEXAS

Payer ID WB125	PO BOX 13777 AUSTIN, TX 78711	(512) 475-1440 WWW.SORM.STATE.TX.US

STAYWELL

Payer ID SWELL	430 WEST SOLEDAD AVE HAGATNA, GU 96910	(671) 477-5091 WWW.STAYWELLGUAM.COM

STERLING

Payer ID 91151	PO BOX 5348 BELLINGHAM, WA 98227-5348	(888) 858-8551 WWW.STERLINGHEALTH.COM

STERLING BENEFIT SOLUTIONS

	PO BOX 26103 OVERLAND PARK, KS 66225	(913) 498-9090 (877) 292-6037 WWW.AMERICANSTERLING.COM

STERLING MEDICARE ADVANTAGE

Payer ID 67829	PO BOX 269003 PLANO, TX 75026-9003	(888) 839-9052 WWW.WINDSORHEALTHPLAN.COM

STIRLING & STIRLING

Payer ID 06089	20 ARMORY LN MILFORD, CT 06460	(800) 447-6689 WWW.STIRLINGBENEFITS.COM

STONEBRIDGE INSURANCE CO

	2700 W PLANO PKWY PLANO, TX 75075-8205	(800) 692-5246 WWW.STONEBRIDGELIFE.COM

STONER & ASSOCIATES

Payer ID 31121	205 W 4TH ST 225 CINCINNATI, OH 45202-4813	(800) 832-7113 WWW.STONERANDASSOCIATES.COM

STONES RIVER REGIONAL IPA - WINDSOR

Payer ID 15752	1370 GATEWAY BLVD STE 130 MURFREESBORO, TN 37129	(615) 869-0030 WWW.STONESRIVERIPA.COM

STUDENT INSURANCE - BOSTON MUTUAL LIFE INSURANCE COMPANY

Payer ID 74227	120 ROYALL ST CANTON, MA 02021	(800) 669-2668 WWW.BOSTONMUTUAL.COM

STUDENT INSURANCE - LIFE INSURANCE COMPANY OF BOSTON AND NEW YORK

Payer ID 74227	PO BOX 34952 OMAHA, NE 68134	(800) 645-2317 WWW.LIFEOFBOSTON.COM

STUDENT INSURANCE - MEGA LIFE & HEALTH INSURANCE COMPANY

Payer ID 74227	PO BOX 982010 NORTHRICHLAND HILLS, TX 76182	(800) 527-5504 WWW.MEGAINSURANCE.COM

STUDENT INSURANCE - MID-WEST NATIONAL LIFE INSURANCE COMPANY OF TENNESSEE

Payer ID 74227	PO BOX 982010 NORTHRICHLAND HILLS, TX 76182	(209) 572-6900 (888) 756-3534 WWW.MIDWESTLIFE.COM

STUDENT INSURANCE - UNITED HEALTHCARE

Payer ID 74227	PO BOX 809025 DALLAS, TX 75380	(800) 767-0700 WWW.UHCSR.COM

SUFFOLK HEALTH PLAN OF NEW YORK

Payer ID 88331	PO BOX 6022 HAUPPAUGE, NY 11788-9007	(800) 556-0674 WWW.SUFFOLKHEALTHPLAN.COM

SUMMA CARE HEALTH PLAN

Payer ID 95202	PO BOX 3620 AKRON, OH 44309	(330) 996-8400 WWW.SUMMACARE.COM

SUMMERLIN LIFE AND HEALTH

Payer ID 86071	PO BOX 22009 TEMPE, AZ 85285	(702) 304-5500 WWW.IMXINC.COM

SUMMIT AMERICA INSURANCE SERVICES, INC.

Payer ID 37301	7400 COLLEGE BLVD STE 100 OVERLAND PARK, KS 66210-1857	(800) 955-1991 WWW.SUMMITAMERICA-INS.COM

SUN HEALTH CORPORATION

Payer ID SX186	525 W BROWN RD MESA, AZ 85201-3202	(623) 977-7211 WWW.BANNERHEALTH.COM

SUNAMERICA LIFE INS CO

Payer ID 90956	PO BOX 54299 LOS ANGELES, CA 90054-0299	(800) 445-7862 WWW.SUNAMERICA.COM

SUNSHINE HEALTH PLAN

Payer ID 68057	PO BOX 3070 FARMINGTON, MO 63640-3823	(866) 796-0530 WWW.SUNSHINESTATEHEALTH.COM

SUPERIOR ADMINISTRATORS, INC.

Payer ID 23218
PO BOX 27730
SANTA ANA, CA 92799
(714) 429-1700
WWW.SUPERIORADMINISTRATORS.COM

SUPERIOR HEALTH PLAN

Payer ID 39188
PO BOX 3003
FARMINGTON, MO 63640-3803
(877) 391-5921
WWW.SUPERIORHEALTHPLAN.COM

SUTTER CONNECT - CENTRAL VALLEY MED GROUP

Payer ID 77035
PO BOX 254789
SACRAMENTO, CA 95865
(866) 681-0747
WWW.SUTTERHEALTH.ORG

SUTTER CONNECT - DELTA - CLAIMS

Payer ID IP100
PO BOX 255427
SACRAMENTO, CA 95865
(925) 779-7200
(800) 470-0071
WWW.SUTTERHEALTH.ORG

SUTTER CONNECT - SOLANO REGIONAL MEDICAL GROUP

Payer ID IP099
PO BOX 255648
SACRAMENTO, CA 95865
(800) 470-0071
WWW.SUTTERHEALTH.ORG

SUTTER CONNECT - SUTTER GOULD MEDICAL FOUNDATION

Payer ID IP091
PO BOX 255708
SACRAMENTO, CA 95865
(916) 733-8800
(800) 470-0071
WWW.SUTTERHEALTH.ORG

SUTTER CONNECT EAST BAY MED FOUNDATION

Payer ID IP130
PO BOX 255125
SACRAMENTO, CA 95865
(866) 681-0745
WWW.SEBMF.ORG

SUTTER CONNECT SUTTER MEDICAL GROUP (SMG,SWMG,SIP)

Payer ID IP092
PO BOX 255187
SACRAMENTO, CA 95865
(916) 854-6960
(800) 611-5191
WWW.SUTTERHEALTH.ORG

SUTTER MEDICAL GROUP OF THE REDWOODS (SMG)

Payer ID HM057
PO BOX 255392
SACREMENTO, CA 95865
(916) 854-6960
(800) 611-5191
WWW.SUTTERHEALTH.ORG

SWEDISH COVENANT HOSPITAL

Payer ID NASWD
5145 N CALIFORNIA AVE
CHICAGO, IL 60625
(773) 878-8200
WWW.SWEDISHCOVENANT.ORG

SWEDISHAMERICAN HEALTH ALLIANCE CORP

1313 E STATE ST
ROCKFORD, IL 61104-2227
(815) 968-4400
WWW.SWEDISHAMERICAN.ORG

T & M FINANCIAL

3706 SW TOPEKA BLVD STE 400
TOPEKA, KS 66609-1292

(785) 266-8333
(800) 550-2377
WWW.T-MFINANCIAL.COM

TALBERT MEDICAL GROUP

Payer ID TALMG

PO BOX 6099
TORRANCE, CA 90504

(800) 241-4347
WWW.TALBERTMEDICAL.COM/PROVIDERS/TABID/123/DEFAULT.ASPX

TALL TREES ADMINISTRATORS

Payer ID 88067

PO BOX 71747
SALT LAKE CITY, UT 84171

(801) 274-8100
(877) 453-4201
WWW.TALLTREEHEALTH.COM/PROVIDER/PROVIDER_LOGIN

TARRANT

Payer ID 37228

PO BOX 961205
FORT WORTH, TX 76161

(817) 740-8400
WWW.TXHEALTHCARE.COM

TBG ADMINISTRATIVE SERVICES

Payer ID 39157

205 E THOMAS ST
WAUSAU, WI 54401-6139
PO BOX 1725
WAUSAU, WI 54402

(800) 826-0012
WWW.TBGASI.COM

TEACHERS HEALTH TRUST

Payer ID 88019

PO BOX 96238
LAS VEGAS, NV 89193-6238

(702) 866-6160
HTTP://TEACHERSHEALTHTRUST.ORG

TEAM HEALTH CARE PARTNERSHIP, INC.

Payer ID 10038

30 W SPRING ST #L11
COLUMBUS, OH 43215-2256

(614) 728-5550
(800) 644-6292
WWW.OHIOBWC.COM/PROVIDER/DEFAULT.ASP

TEAM HEALTH GOLD

Payer ID 75139

265 BROOKVIEW CENTRE WAY STE 400
KNOXVILLE, TN 37919

(865) 693-1000
(800) 342-2898
WWW.TEAMHEALTH.COM

TEAMCARE

Payer ID 36215

PO BOX 5109
DES PLAINES, IL 60017-5109

(800) 323-2190
WWW.CENTRALSTATESFUNDS.ORG

TEAMSTERS BENEFIT TRUST

39420 LIBERTY ST STE 260
FREMONT, CA 94538-2200
PO BOX 5820
FREMONT, CA 94537-5820

(510) 796-4676
(800) 533-0119
WWW.TBTFUND.ORG

TEAMSTERS LOCAL UNION #301

Payer ID 36612

36990 N GREEN BAY RD
WAUKEGAN, IL 60087-3406

(847) 623-5430

TENNCARE

Payer ID TNMCD

PO BOX 460
NASHVILLE, TN 37202

(800) 852-2683
WWW.TN.GOV/TENNCARE

TENNESSEE MEDICAID HMO (AMERIGROUP)

Payer ID 27514	22 CENTURY BLVD STE 310 NASHVILLE, TN 37214-3644 PO BOX 61010 VIRGINIA BEACH, VA 23466-1010	(800) 600-4441 WWW.AMERIGROUPCORP.COM/PROVIDERS

TETHYS HEALTH VENTURES

Payer ID 20212	FOUR N PARK DR STE 104 HUNT VALLEY, MD 21030-1812	(410) 771-0692 WWW.TETHYSHEALTH.COM

TEXAS BUILDERS INSURANCE COMPANY

Payer ID WZ643	11612 RM2244 #1-200 AUSTIN, TX 78738	(512) 708-0148 WWW.TBIC.COM

TEXAS CHILDREN'S HEALTH PLAN

Payer ID 76048	MEDICAID PO BOX 300125 HOUSTON, TX 77230	(832) 828-1004 WWW.TEXASCHILDRENSHEALTHPLAN.ORG

TEXAS CHILDREN'S HEALTH PLAN (CONTINUED)

Payer ID 75228	MEDICAID PO BOX 300125 HOUSTON, TX 77230	(832) 828-1004 WWW.TEXASCHILDRENSHEALTHPLAN.ORG
Payer ID 76048	CHIP PO BOX 300286 HOUSTON, TX 77230	(832) 828-1004 WWW.TEXASCHILDRENSHEALTHPLAN.COM/ PROVIDERS
Payer ID 75228	CHIP PO BOX 300286 HOUSTON, TX 77230	(832) 828-1004 WWW.TEXASCHILDRENSHEALTHPLAN.COM/ PROVIDERS

TEXAS CHILDREN'S STAR MEDICAID

Payer ID TXCSM	PO BOX 300286 HOUSTON, TX 77230-0286	(800) 731-8527 WWW.TEXASCHILDRENSHEALTHPLAN.COM/ PROVIDERS

TEXAS HEALTHCARE FOUNDATION

	1278 FM 407 STE 105 LEWISVILLE, TX 75077	(800) 716-6777 WWW.TEXASHEALTHCAREFOUNDATION.COM

TEXAS HEALTHSPRING

Payer ID THS01	PO BOX 2888 HOUSTON, TX 77252	(888) 501-1115 WWW.HEALTHSPRING.COM/PROVIDERS

TEXAS HOSPITAL INSURANCE EXCHANGE

Payer ID WE040	8310 N CAPITAL OF TEXAS #1-230 AUSTIN, TX 78731	(512) 451-5775 (800) 792-0060 WWW.THIE.COM

TEXAS MEDICAID HMO (AETNA)

Payer ID 38692	PO BOX 60938 PHOENIX, AZ 85026	(800) 248-7767 WWW.AETNAMEDICAID.COM/FAQ3_EN.ASP ?OPTION=PROVIDER

TEXAS MEDICAID HMO (COMMUNITY FIRST)

Payer ID COMMF	CLAIMS-12238 SILICON DR STE 100 SAN ANTONIO, TX 78249	(210) 358-6200 WWW.CFHP.COM

TEXAS MEDICAID HMO (COMMUNITY HEALTH CHOICE)

Payer ID 48145	PO BOX 301404 HOUSTON, TX 77230-1404	(888) 760-2600 WWW.CHCHEALTH.ORG

T

TEXAS MEDICAID HMO (PARKLAND COMMUNITY HEALTH PLAN)

PO BOX 61088
PHOENIX, AZ 85082

(888) 672-2277
WWW.PARKLANDHMO.ORG

TEXAS MEDICAID HMO (SUPERIOR HEALTH PLAN-STAR)

Payer ID 39188

PO BOX 3003
FARMINGTON, MO 63640-3803

(877) 391-5921
WWW.SUPERIORHEALTHPLAN.COM

TEXAS MEDICAID HMO (TEXAS CHILDREN'S HEALTH PLAN)

Payer ID 76048

PO BOX 300286
HOUSTON, TX 77230-0286

(832) 828-1004
WWW.TEXASCHILDRENSHEALTHPLAN.ORG

TEXAS MUNICIPAL LEAGUE GROUP BENEFITS RISK POOL

Payer ID 74214

PO BOX 149190
AUSTIN, TX 78714-1337

(800) 282-5385
HTTP://TMLIEBP.ORG/

TEXAS MUNICIPAL LEAGUE INTERGOVERNMENTAL RISK POOL

Payer ID WA048

1821 RUTHERFORD LANE
AUSTIN, TX 78754

(512) 491-2300
(800) 537-6655
WWW.TMLIRP.ORG

TEXAS MUTUAL INSURANCE COMPANY

Payer ID WX606

PO BOX 12058
AUSTIN, TX 78711-2058

(888) 532-5246
WWW.TEXASMUTUAL.COM

TEXAS POLITICAL SUBDIVISIONS JOINT SELF INSURANCE FUND

Payer ID WE041

15660 N DALLAS PKWY STE 1175
DALLAS, TX 75248

(972) 361-6300
HTTP://TPSPOOL.ORG

TEXAS TRUE CHOICE

Payer ID TH055

PO BOX 250089
PLANO, TX 75025

(800) 683-4856
WWW.TEXASTRUECHOICE.COM/
PROVIDERS.ASP

THE ALLIANCE

Payer ID 88461

PO BOX 44365
MADISON, WI 53744

(608) 276-6630
WWW.THE-ALLIANCE.ORG/PROVIDERS/

THE EMPIRE PLAN

Payer ID 87726

PO BOX 1600
KINGSTON, NY 12402-1600

(877) 769-7447
WWW.EMPIREPLANPROVIDERS.COM

THE INTEGRITY BENEFIT NETWORK

Payer ID 58200

PO BOX 4537
MARIETTA, GA 30061-4537

(770) 428-1604
HTTP://IBNTPA.COM

THE LOOMIS COMPANY

Payer ID 23223

PO BOX 7011
WYOMISSING, PA 19610

(610) 374-4040
WWW.LOOMISCO.COM

THE MEGA LIFE & HEALTH INSURANCE COMPANY

Payer ID 59227

PO BOX 548801
OKLAHOMA CITY, OK 73154

(888) 757-0703
WWW.MEGAINSURANCE.COM

THERAPY REVIEW SYSTEM

Payer ID 75305

6100 BLUE LAGOON DR STE 235
MIAMI, FL 33126-2043

(305) 670-0640
(866) 409-7572
WWW.THERSYS.COM

THOMAS COOPER

Payer ID SC315

PO BOX 22557
CHARLESTON, SC 29413-2557

(800) 815-3314
WWW.THOMASCOOPERINSURANCE.COM

THOMAS M. MURPHY & ASSOCIATES, INC

ONE ENTERPRISE DR STE 210
SHELTON, CT 06484-4637

(203) 924-2994
(800) 243-2534

TIC INTERNATIONAL CORP

11590 N MERIDIAN ST STE 600
CARMEL, IN 46032-4529

(317) 580-8686
(800) 321-3856
WWW.TICI.COM

TIG AMERICAN SPECIALTY INSURANCE

Payer ID WZ648

5205 N O CONNOR BLVD #130
IRVING, TX 75039-3700

(972) 831-5000

TIG INSURANCE COMPANY

Payer ID 25534

250 COMMERCIAL ST STE 5000
MANCHESTER, NH 03101

(255) 346-0365

TIME INSURANCE

Payer ID 39065

PO BOX 2806
CLINTON, IA 52733-2806

(800) 553-7654
WWW.ASSURANTHEALTH.COM/CORP/AH/PROVIDERS/CLAIMSSUBMISSION.HTM

TLC ADVANTAGE IN SIOUX FALLS

Payer ID TLC01

PO BOX 89410
SIOUX FALLS, SD 57109-9410

(877) 893-9685
WWW.TLCADVANTAGE.COM

TMG HEALTH

455 S GULPH RD STE 307
KING OF PRUSSIA, PA 19406

(610) 878-9111
WWW.TMGHEALTH.COM

TODAYS OPTION

Payer ID 48055

PO BOX 742528
HOUSTON, TX 77274

(866) 422-5009
WWW.UNIVERSAL-AMERICAN-MEDICARE.COM

TOKIO MARINE AND FIRE INSURANCE

Payer ID WX603

230 PARK AVE
NEW YORK, NY 10169

(212) 297-6600
(800) 628-2796
WWW.TOKIOMARINE.US

TONGASS TIMBER TRUST

Payer ID 92620

111 STEDMAN ST STE 200
KETCHIKAN, AK 99901-6523

(907) 225-6114
WWW.AKFOREST.ORG

TOTAL CARE OF NY

Payer ID TCARE

PO BOX 11507
SYRACUSE, NY 13218-1507

(800) 223-7242
WWW.TOTALCARENY.COM/DEFAULT.ASPX?PAGEID=817

TOTAL CAROLINA CARE

Payer ID 68055

PO BOX 3050
FARMINGTON, MO 63640-3821

(866) 433-6041
WWW.ABSOLUTETOTALCARE.COM/FOR-PROVIDERS

TOTAL COMMUNITY CARE

Payer ID 31182

904 LAS LOMAS NE
ALBUQUERQUE, NM 87102-2608

(505) 924-2650
WWW.TOTALCOMMUNITYCARE.ORG

T

TOTAL HEALTH CARE, INC

	3011 W GRAND BLVD STE 1600 DETROIT, MI 48202	(313) 871-2000 (800) 826-2862 WWW.TOTALHEALTHCAREONLINE.COM

TOTAL HEALTH CHOICE

Payer ID 38202	PO BOX 21485 EAGAN, MN 55121-0485	(305) 408-5700 (800) 887-6888 WWW.FL.THCONLINE.US/

TOTAL HEALTH MANAGEMENT, LTD

Payer ID 10019	1901 E ALTON AVE STE 200 SANTA ANA, CA 92705-5835	(949) 757-0075 HTTP://THMNET.COM/

TOUCHSTONE HEALTH PSO

Payer ID 11328	501 FRANKLIN AVE STE 300 GARDEN CITY, NY 11530	(888) 777-0350 WWW.TOUCHSTONEH.COM/PROVIDERS/ DEFAULT.ASPX

TOWER GROUP

Payer ID WZ308	120 BROADWAY 31ST FL NEW YORK, NY 10271	(888) 856-5522 WWW.TWRGRP.COM

TOWER LIFE INSURANCE CO

Payer ID 69493	310 S ST MARY ST STE 400 SAN ANTONIO, TX 78205-3113	(800) 880-4576 WWW.TOWERLIFE.COM

TPCIGA

Payer ID WE061	9120 BURNET RD AUSTIN, TX 78758	(512) 345-9335 (800) 856-0298 WWW.TPCIGA.COM

TR PAUL, INC

Payer ID 37230	PO BOX 46511 CINCINNATI, OH 45246	(800) 678-8161 (866) 334-4553 WWW.TRPAUL.COM

TRANSAMERICA LIFE INSURANCE CO

Payer ID TLINS	4333 EDGEWOOD RD NE CEDAR RAPIDS, IA 52499	(800) 852-4678 WWW.MYTRANSAMERICA.COM

TRANSCHOICE - KEY BENEFIT ADMIN

Payer ID 37284	PO BOX 1279 FORT MILLS, SC 29716-1279	(866) 867-6883 WWW.TRANSCHOICEPLUS.COM

TRANSGUARD INSURANCE

Payer ID WX670	PO BOX 2148 WARRENVILLE, IL 60555-9936	(800) 474-2526 WWW.TRANSGUARD.COM

TRANSWESTERN GENERAL AGENCY

Payer ID 74234	PO BOX 1196 SALT LAKE CITY, UT 84110	(801) 521-3310 (800) 453-3156 WWW.TRANSWESTERN.COM

TRANSWESTERN INSURANCE ADMINISTRATORS, INC.

Payer ID TRAN1	PO BOX 45019 FRESNO, CA 93718-5019	(800) 221-8942 WWW.TRANS-WESTERN.COM

TRAVELERS' INSURANCE

Payer ID WP467	1 TOWER SQUARE 8MS HARTFORD, CT 06183	(800) 238-6225 WWW.TRAVELERS.COM

T

TRI STAR RISK MANAGEMENT

100 OCEANGATE STE 700
LONG BEACH, CA 90802-4313
PO BOX 19775
IRVINE, CA 92623-9775

(562) 495-6600
(800) 782-5888
WWW.TRISTARRISK.COM

TRICARE FOR LIFE

Payer ID TDDIR

PO BOX 7890
MADISON, WI 53707-7890

(888) 874-9378
(866) 773-0404
WWW.TRICARE4U.COM/APPS-PORTAL/
TRICAREAPPS-APP/STATIC/PROVIDERS

TRICARE-ALABAMA-SOUTH REGION

PO BOX 7031
CAMDEN, SC 29020-7031

(800) 403-3950
WWW.MYTRICARE.COM

TRICARE-ALASKA-WEST REGION

PO BOX 7064
CAMDEN, SC 29020-7064

(877) 988-9378
WWW.MYTRICARE.COM

TRICARE-ARIZONA-WEST REGION

PO BOX 7064
CAMDEN, SC 29020-7064

(877) 988-9378
WWW.MYTRICARE.COM

TRICARE-ARKANSAS-SOUTH REGION

PO BOX 7031
CAMDEN, SC 29020-7031

(800) 403-3950
WWW.MYTRICARE.COM

TRICARE-CALIFORNIA-WEST REGION

PO BOX 7064
CAMDEN, SC 29020-7064

(877) 988-9378
WWW.MYTRICARE.COM

TRICARE-COLORADO-WEST REGION

PO BOX 7064
CAMDEN, SC 29020-7064

(877) 988-9378
WWW.MYTRICARE.COM

TRICARE-DELAWARE-NORTH REGION

PO BOX 870140
SURFSIDE BEACH, SC 29587-9740

(877) 874-2273
WWW.MYTRICARE.COM

TRICARE-FLORIDA-SOUTH REGION

PO BOX 7031
CAMDEN, SC 29020-7031

(800) 403-3950
WWW.MYTRICARE.COM

TRICARE-GEORGIA-SOUTH REGION

PO BOX 7031
CAMDEN, SC 29020-7031

(800) 403-3950
WWW.MYTRICARE.COM

TRICARE-HAWAII-WEST REGION

PO BOX 7064
CAMDEN, SC 29020-7064

(877) 988-9378
WWW.MYTRICARE.COM

TRICARE-IDAHO-WEST REGION

PO BOX 7064
CAMDEN, SC 29020-7064

(877) 988-9378
WWW.MYTRICARE.COM

TRICARE-ILLINOIS-NORTH REGION

PO BOX 870140
SURFSIDE BEACH, SC 29587-9740

(877) 874-2273
WWW.MYTRICARE.COM

TRICARE-INDIANA-NORTH REGION

PO BOX 870140
SURFSIDE BEACH, SC 29587-9740

(877) 874-2273
WWW.MYTRICARE.COM

TRICARE-IOWA-NORTH REGION

PO BOX 870140
SURFSIDE BEACH, SC 29587-9740

(877) 874-2273
WWW.MYTRICARE.COM

TRICARE-IOWA-WEST REGION

PO BOX 7064
CAMDEN, SC 29020-7064

(877) 988-9378
WWW.MYTRICARE.COM

TRICARE-KANSAS-WEST REGION

PO BOX 7064
CAMDEN, SC 29020-7064

(877) 988-9378
WWW.MYTRICARE.COM

TRICARE-KENTUCKY-NORTH REGION

PO BOX 870140
SURFSIDE BEACH, SC 29587-9740

(877) 874-2273
WWW.MYTRICARE.COM

TRICARE-LOUISIANA-SOUTH REGION

PO BOX 7031
CAMDEN, SC 29020-7031

(800) 403-3950
WWW.MYTRICARE.COM

TRICARE-MAINE-NORTH REGION

PO BOX 870140
SURFSIDE BEACH, SC 29587-9740

(877) 874-2273
WWW.MYTRICARE.COM

TRICARE-MARYLAND-NORTH REGION

PO BOX 870140
SURFSIDE BEACH, SC 29587-9740

(877) 874-2273
WWW.MYTRICARE.COM

TRICARE-MASSACHUSETTS-NORTH REGION

PO BOX 870140
SURFSIDE BEACH, SC 29587-9740

(877) 874-2273
WWW.MYTRICARE.COM

TRICARE-MICHIGAN-NORTH REGION

PO BOX 870140
SURFSIDE BEACH, SC 29587-9740

(877) 874-2273
WWW.MYTRICARE.COM

TRICARE-MINNESOTA-WEST REGION

PO BOX 7064
CAMDEN, SC 29020-7064

(877) 988-9378
WWW.MYTRICARE.COM

TRICARE-MISSISSIPPI-SOUTH REGION

PO BOX 7031
CAMDEN, SC 29020-7031

(800) 403-3950
WWW.MYTRICARE.COM

TRICARE-MISSOURI-NORTH REGION

PO BOX 870140
SURFSIDE BEACH, SC 29587-9740

(877) 874-2273
WWW.MYTRICARE.COM

TRICARE-MISSOURI-WEST REGION

PO BOX 7064
CAMDEN, SC 29020-7064

(877) 988-9378
WWW.MYTRICARE.COM

TRICARE-MONTANA-WEST REGION

PO BOX 7064
CAMDEN, SC 29020-7064

(877) 988-9378
WWW.MYTRICARE.COM

TRICARE-NEBRASKA-WEST REGION

PO BOX 7064
CAMDEN, SC 29020-7064
(877) 988-9378
WWW.MYTRICARE.COM

TRICARE-NEVADA-WEST REGION

PO BOX 7064
CAMDEN, SC 29020-7064
(877) 988-9378
WWW.MYTRICARE.COM

TRICARE-NEW HAMPSHIRE-NORTH REGION

PO BOX 870140
SURFSIDE BEACH, SC 29587-9740
(877) 874-2273
WWW.MYTRICARE.COM

TRICARE-NEW JERSEY-NORTH REGION

PO BOX 870140
SURFSIDE BEACH, SC 29587-9740
(877) 874-2273
WWW.MYTRICARE.COM

TRICARE-NEW MEXICO-WEST REGION

PO BOX 7064
CAMDEN, SC 29020-7064
(877) 988-9378
WWW.MYTRICARE.COM

TRICARE-NEW YORK-NORTH REGION

PO BOX 870140
SURFSIDE BEACH, SC 29587-9740
(877) 874-2273
WWW.MYTRICARE.COM

TRICARE-NORTH CAROLINA-NORTH REGION

PO BOX 870140
SURFSIDE BEACH, SC 29587-9740
(877) 874-2273
WWW.MYTRICARE.COM

TRICARE-NORTH DAKOTA-WEST REGION

PO BOX 7064
CAMDEN, SC 29020-7064
(877) 988-9378
WWW.MYTRICARE.COM

TRICARE-OHIO-NORTH REGION

PO BOX 870140
SURFSIDE BEACH, SC 29587-9740
(877) 874-2273
WWW.MYTRICARE.COM

TRICARE-OKLAHOMA-SOUTH REGION

PO BOX 7031
CAMDEN, SC 29020-7031
(800) 403-3950
WWW.MYTRICARE.COM

TRICARE-OREGON-WEST REGION

PO BOX 7064
CAMDEN, SC 29020-7064
(877) 988-9378
WWW.MYTRICARE.COM

TRICARE-PENNSYLVANIA-NORTH REGION

PO BOX 870140
SURFSIDE BEACH, SC 29587-9740
(877) 874-2273
WWW.MYTRICARE.COM

TRICARE-RHODE ISLAND-NORTH REGION

PO BOX 870140
SURFSIDE BEACH, SC 29587-9740
(877) 874-2273
WWW.MYTRICARE.COM

TRICARE-SOUTH CAROLINA-SOUTH REGION

PO BOX 7031
CAMDEN, SC 29020-7031
(800) 403-3950
WWW.MYTRICARE.COM

PO BOX 7031
CAMDEN, SC 29020-7031
(800) 403-3950
WWW.MYTRICARE.COM

TRICARE-SOUTH DAKOTA-WEST REGION

PO BOX 7064
CAMDEN, SC 29020-7064

(877) 988-9378
WWW.MYTRICARE.COM

TRICARE-TENNESSEE-NORTH REGION

PO BOX 870140
SURFSIDE BEACH, SC 29587-9740

(877) 874-2273
WWW.MYTRICARE.COM

TRICARE-TENNESSEE-SOUTH REGION

PO BOX 7031
CAMDEN, SC 29020-7031

(800) 403-3950
WWW.MYTRICARE.COM

TRICARE-TEXAS-SOUTH REGION

PO BOX 7031
CAMDEN, SC 29020-7031

(800) 403-3950
WWW.MYTRICARE.COM

TRICARE-TEXAS-WEST REGION

PO BOX 7064
CAMDEN, SC 29020-7064

(877) 988-9378
WWW.MYTRICARE.COM

TRICARE-UTAH-WEST REGION

PO BOX 7064
CAMDEN, SC 29020-7064

(877) 988-9378
WWW.MYTRICARE.COM

TRICARE-VERMONT-NORTH REGION

PO BOX 870140
SURFSIDE BEACH, SC 29587-9740

(877) 874-2273
WWW.MYTRICARE.COM

TRICARE-VIRGINIA-NORTH REGION

PO BOX 870140
SURFSIDE BEACH, SC 29587-9740

(877) 874-2273
WWW.MYTRICARE.COM

TRICARE-WASHINGTON, DC-NORTH REGION

PO BOX 870140
SURFSIDE BEACH, SC 29587-9740

(877) 874-2273
WWW.MYTRICARE.COM

TRICARE-WASHINGTON-WEST REGION

PO BOX 7064
CAMDEN, SC 29020-7064

(877) 988-9378
WWW.MYTRICARE.COM

TRICARE-WEST VIRGINIA-NORTH REGION

PO BOX 870140
SURFSIDE BEACH, SC 29587-9740

(877) 874-2273
WWW.MYTRICARE.COM

TRICARE-WISCONSIN-NORTH REGION

PO BOX 870140
SURFSIDE BEACH, SC 29587-9740

(877) 874-2273
WWW.MYTRICARE.COM

TRICARE-WYOMING-WEST REGION

PO BOX 7064
CAMDEN, SC 29020-7064

(877) 988-9378
WWW.MYTRICARE.COM

TRIHEALTH PHYSICIAN SOLUTIONS

Payer ID 31144

619 OAK ST
CINCINNATI, OH 45206

(513) 569-5400
WWW.DATAPAY3.COM/C/TPS01

TRILOGY HEALTH

Payer ID 98514

PO BOX 30544
SALT LAKE CITY, UT 84130

(262) 432-9150
(866) 429-3242
WWW.TRILOGYCARES.COM

T

TRINITY UNIVERSAL INSURANCE COMPANY

Payer ID 19887

2886 N MARBURG AVE
MERIDIAN, ID 83646-8280

(208) 855-0744
WWW.KEMPERCORPORATION.COM

TRIPLE-S SALUD

Payer ID 97300

PO BOX 363628
SAN JUAN, PR 00936-3628

(787) 774-6060
(877) 357-9777
WWW.SSSPR.COM

TRISTAR BENEFIT ADMINISTRATORS

Payer ID 42112

PO BOX 65887
WEST DES MOINES, IA 50265

(800) 456-4584
WWW.TBAHEALTH.COM

TRISTAR RISK MANAGEMENT

Payer ID WE058

100 OCEANGATE #700
LONG BEACH, CA 90802

(562) 495-6601
WWW.TRISTARRISK.COM

TRIWEST WPS

Payer ID WESTR

PO BOX 77028
MADISON, WI 53707-1028

(888) 874-9378
WWW.TRIWEST.COM/EN/PROVIDER

TRUSTEED PLANS SERVICE CORP

Payer ID 91078

PO BOX 2950
TACOMA, WA 98401-1894

(253) 564-5611
(800) 426-9786
WWW.TRUSTEEDPLANS.COM

TRUSTMARK INSURANCE

Payer ID 61425

400 FIELD DR
LAKE FOREST, IL 60045-2586

(847) 615-1500
(800) 877-9077
WWW.TRUSTMARKINS.COM

TUCKER ADMINISTRATORS, INC

3800 ARCO CORPORATE DR STE 450
CHARLOTTE, NC 28273-0001

(704) 525-9666
WWW.TUCKERADMINISTRATORS.COM/
PROVIDERS

TUFTS ASSOCIATED HEALTH

Payer ID 04298

PO BOX 9165
WATERTOWN, MA 02471-9165

(888) 884-2404
WWW.TUFTSHEALTHPLAN.COM/PROVIDERS/
PROVIDER.PHP

TUFTS HEALTH PLAN

Payer ID 04298

PO BOX 9183
WATERTOWN, MA 02471

(888) 880-8699
WWW.TUFTSHEALTHPLAN.COM

T

U-CARE HMO

	PO BOX 70 MINNEAPOLIS, MN 55440	(888) 531-1493 WWW.UCARE.ORG

UCARE MINNESOTA

Payer ID 19991	PO BOX 70 MINNEAPOLIS, MN 55440-0070	(612) 676-3300 (888) 531-1493 WWW.UCARE.ORG/PROVIDERS/PAGES/DEFAULT.ASPX

UFCW LOCAL 400-5205

Payer ID UFC97	911 RIDGEBROOK RD SPARKS, MD 21152-9451	(800) 638-2972 WWW.ASSOCIATED-ADMIN.COM

UHC WEST OF CA

Payer ID 95959	PO BOX 30968 SALT LAKE CITY, UT 84130	(800) 624-8822 WWW.UHCWEST.COM

UHC WEST OF OK

Payer ID 95959	PO BOX 30967 SALT LAKE CITY, UT 84130	(800) 825-9355 WWW.UHCWEST.COM

UHC WEST OF OR

Payer ID 95959	PO BOX 30974 SALT LAKE CITY, UT 84130	(800) 932-3004 WWW.UHCWEST.COM

UHC WEST OF TX

Payer ID 95959	PO BOX 30975 SALT LAKE CITY, UT 84130	(800) 825-9355 WWW.UHCWEST.COM

UHC WEST OF WA

Payer ID 95959	PO BOX 30976 SALT LAKE CITY, UT 84130	(800) 932-3004 WWW.UHCWEST.COM

UMC HEALTH PLAN

Payer ID 75130	4601 W LOOP 289 LUBBOCK, TX 79414-1403	(806) 775-8793 WWW.UMCHEALTHSYSTEM.COM

UMR

	PO BOX 8077 WAUSAU, WI 54402-8077	(877) 233-1800 WWW.UMR.COM/OSS/CMS/UMR/LOGIN/PROVIDERLOGIN.HTML

UMR KANSAS

Payer ID 62061	PO BOX 8077 WAUSAU, WI 54402-8077	(866) 281-2993 WWW.UMR.COM/OSS/CMS/UMR/KANSAS/INDEX.HTML

UMR MIDWEST SECURITIES

Payer ID 79480	2700 MIDWEST DR ONALASKA, WI 54650-8764	(608) 783-7130 (800) 651-8231 HTTPS://FHS.UMR.COM/

UMR WAUSAU/UHIS

Payer ID 39026	PO BOX 30541 SALT LAKE CITY, UT 84130-0541	(800) 826-9781 WWW.UMR.COM

UMWA HEALTH & RETIREMENT FUNDS

Payer ID 52180	PO BOX 99002 LUBBOCK, TX 79490-9002	(888) 865-5290 WWW.UMWAFUNDS.ORG

U

UNDERWRITERS SAFETY & CLAIMS

Payer ID TP108 | PO BOX 23790, LOUISVILLE, KY 40223 | (502) 244-1343, (800) 678-1536, WWW.USCKY.COM

UNICARE HEALTH PLANS OF TEXAS

Payer ID 80314 | PO BOX 139030, DALLAS, TX 75313 | (866) 480-4830, WWW.UNICARE.COM

UNIFIED GROUP SERVICES

Payer ID 35198 | PO BOX 10, PENDLETON, IN 46064 | (800) 291-5837, WWW.UNIFIEDGRP.COM

UNIFIED HEALTH SERVICES

Payer ID 62170 | 6750 LENOX CENTER CT STE 300, MEMPHIS, TN 38115 | (888) 510-2667, WWW.UHSWEB.COM

UNIFIED PHYSICIANS NETWORK

Payer ID 34638 | 5215 OLD ORCHARD RD STE 340, SKOKIE, IL 60077-1042 | (847) 763-1700, WWW.UPNUS.COM/

UNIFORM MEDICAL PLAN

Payer ID 75243 | PO BOX 30271, SALT LAKE CITY, UT 84130-0271 | (888) 849-3681, WWW.UMP.HCA.WA.GOV

UNIFORMED SERVICE FAMILY HEALTH PLAN

Payer ID 13407 | PO BOX 830745, BIRMINGHAM, AL 35283-0745 | (800) 241-4848, WWW.USFHP.NET

UNIMED DIRECT

Payer ID WB223 | 5068 W PLANO PKWY STE 122, PLANO, TX 75093 | (972) 931-5100, WWW.UNIMEDDIRECT.COM

UNINSURED EMPLOYERS BENEFITS TRUST FUND (UEBTF)

Payer ID LM012 | 320 W 4TH ST STE 690, LOS, CA 90013 | (213) 576-7300, WWW.DIR.CA.GOV/DWC/CLAIMS.HTML

UNION HEALTH SERVICE, INC

1634 W POLK ST, CHICAGO, IL 60612-4352 | (312) 423-4200, WWW.UNIONHEALTH.ORG

UNION LABOR LIFE INSURANCE COMPANY

Payer ID 13142 | 1625 EYE STREET, NW, WASHINGTON, DC 20006-4071 | (800) 431-5425, WWW.ULLICO.COM/

UNION PACIFIC RAILROAD EMPLOYEES HEALTH SYSTEMS

Payer ID 87042 | PO BOX 161020, SALT LAKE CITY, UT 84116-1020 | (800) 547-0421, WWW.UPHEALTH.COM

UNISON HEALTH PLAN

Payer ID 25175 | PO BOX 8207, KINGSTON, NY 12402 | (800) 600-9007, WWW.UHCCOMMUNITYPLAN.COM

UNITED AGRICULTURE BENEFIT TRUST

Payer ID UABT1 | 54 CORPORATE PARK, IRVINE, CA 92606-5105 | (800) 223-4590, WWW.UABT.ORG

UNITED AMERICAN INSURANCE CO

PO BOX 8080, MCKINNEY, TX 75070-8080 | (972) 529-5085, WWW.UNITEDAMERICAN.COM

UNITED BEHAVIORAL HEALTH

Payer ID 87726

PO BOX 30755
SALT LAKE CITY, UT 84130-0755

(800) 557-5745
WWW.UBHONLINE.COM

UNITED CONCORDIA DENTAL PLANS

PO BOX 69421
HARRISBURG, PA 17106-9421

(866) 357-3304
WWW.UCCI.COM

UNITED FINANCIAL CASUALTY COMPANY

Payer ID 11770

PO BOX 89490
CLEVELAND, OH 44101

(440) 461-5000
(800) 776-4737

UNITED HEALTHCARE (UHC)

Payer ID 87726

PO BOX 740800
ATLANTA, GA 30374-0800

(877) 842-3210
WWW.UNITEDHEALTHCAREONLINE.COM

UNITED HEALTHCARE OF THE RIVER VALLEY

Payer ID 95378

PO BOX 5230
KINGSTON, NY 12402

(800) 747-1446
WWW.UHCRIVERVALLEY.COM/PROVIDERS/

UNITED MEDICAL ALLIANCE

Payer ID 84132

2021 BATTLECREEK DR STE A
FORT COLLINS, CO 80528-6212

(866) 644-7873
WWW.UNITEDMEDICAL.ORG

UNITED OF OMAHA

Payer ID 71412

MUTUAL OF OMAHA PLAZA
OMAHA, NE 68175

(800) 775-1000
WWW.MUTUALOFOMAHA.COM

UNITED PHYSICIANS OF NORTHERN COLORADO

Payer ID 84132

2021 BATTLECREEK DR STE A
FORT COLLINS, CO 80528-6212

(970) 224-4600
WWW.UNITEDMEDICAL.ORG

UNITED SECURITY LIFE AND HEALTH INSURANCE CO OF ILLINOIS

Payer ID 81108

PO BOX 24655
SEATTLE, WA 91824

(847) 298-1400
(800) 875-4422
WWW.UNITEDSECURITYLIFEANDHEALTH.COM

UNITED SERVICE ASSOCIATION FOR HEALTHCARE

PO BOX 6080-172
MISSION VIEJO, CA 92690

(800) 872-1187
WWW.USAHC.COM

UNITED WISCONSIN INSURANCE COMPANY

Payer ID WX956

PO BOX 3026
MILWAUKEE, WI 53201

(800) 258-2667
WWW.UNITEDHEARTLAND.BIZ

UNITY HEALTH INSURANCE

Payer ID 66705

PO BOX 610
SAUK CITY, WI 53583-0610

(800) 362-3308
WWW.UNITYHEALTH.COM/PROVIDERS/
INDEX.HTM

UNIVERA HEALTHCARE

Payer ID HC001

PO BOX 23000
ROCHESTER, NY 14692

(716) 857-4444
(800) 617-1114
WWW.UNIVERAHEALTHCARE.COM/WPS/PORTAL/
UV/PRV/

UNIVERSAL CARE-CALIFORNIA

Payer ID 33001

PO BOX 93122
LONG BEACH, CA 90809-3122

(562) 424-6200
(800) 635-6668
WWW.UNIVERSALCARE.COM/PROVIDERS/
PROVIDERSWELCOME.ASP?PROVIDERS=5

UNIVERSAL GUARANTY

PO BOX 5147
SPRINGFIELD, IL 62705-5147

(800) 323-0050
WWW.UTGINS.COM/CLAIMS/LIFECLAIM.PHP

UNIVERSAL HEALTH PLAN

PO BOX 294
ST. PETERSBURG, FL 33731

(877) 661-3920
WWW.UNIVHC.COM

UNIVERSAL RX

710 THIRD ST SW
ROANOKE, VA 24016

(540) 777-7179
WWW.UNIVERSALRX.COM

UNIVERSITY FAMILY CARE

Payer ID 09830

PO BOX 35699
PHOENIX, AZ 85069

(800) 582-8686
WWW.UFCAZ.COM/
PROVIDERINFORMATION.ASPX

UNIVERSITY FAMILY CARE-HEALTHCARE GROUP

Payer ID 07503

PO BOX 37279
PHOENIX, AZ 85069

(800) 582-8686
WWW.UFCAZ.COM/
PROVIDERINFORMATION.ASPX

UNIVERSITY FAMILY CARE-MARICOPA HEALTH PLAN

Payer ID 09908

PO BOX 37169
PHOENIX, AZ 85069

(800) 582-8686
WWW.UFCAZ.COM/
PROVIDERINFORMATION.ASPX

UNIVERSITY HEALTH ALLIANCE

Payer ID 99026

700 BISHOP ST STE 300
HONOLULU, HI 96813-4123

(808) 532-4000
WWW.UHAHEALTH.COM/PROVIDERS/
INDEX.ASP

UNIVERSITY OF ARIZONA HEALTH PLANS

PO BOX 35699
PHOENIX, AZ 85069

(800) 582-8686
WWW.UFCAZ.COM/
PROVIDERRESOURCEPAGE.ASPX

UNIVERSITY OF HAWAII HEALTH PLANS

700 BISHOP STREET, SUITE 300
HONOLULU, HI 96813-4100

(808) 532-4006
WWW.UHAHEALTH.COM

UNIVERSITY OF MIAMI BEHAVIORAL HEALTH

Payer ID 92579

1320 S DIXIE HWY STE 400
CORAL GABLES, FL 33146

(800) 294-8642
WWW.UMBH.MED.MIAMI.EDU/X227.XML

UNIVERSITY OF UTAH HEALTH PLANS

Payer ID SX155

PO BOX 45180
SALT LAKE CITY, UT 84145

(888) 271-5870
WWW.UHEALTHPLAN.UTAH.EDU/
FOR_PROVIDERS.HTML

UPMC HEALTH PLAN

Payer ID 23281

PO BOX 2999
PITTSBURGH, PA 15230

(866) 918-1595
WWW.UPMCHEALTHPLAN.COM/PROVIDERS/
INDEX.HTML

UPPER PENINSULA HEALTH PLAN

Payer ID 38337

PO BOX 190
MARQUETTE, MI 49855

(800) 835-2556
WWW.UPHP.COM/PROVIDER/PROVIDER.HTML

US BENEFITS

Payer ID 93092

4660 NE BELKNAP CT STE 209
HILLSBORO, OR 97124-6456

(503) 640-2000
WWW.INTERLINKHEALTH.COM/

US FAMILY HEALTH PLAN (USFHP)

Payer ID USFHP

PO BOX 830745
BIRMINGHAM, AL 35283-0745

(800) 241-4848
WWW.USFHP.NET

US IMAGING NETWORK LLC

PO BOX 21624
EAGAN, MN 55121

(877) 874-6385
HTTP://USIMAGINGNETWORK.COM

USA MANAGED CARE ORGANIZATION INC

7301 N 16TH ST STE 201
PHOENIX, AZ 85020-5224

(800) 872-0020
WWW.USAMCO.COM/PROVIDERCENTER.HTM

USAA LIFE INSURANCE CO

Payer ID 74095

9800 FREDERICKSBURG RD
SAN ANTONIO, TX 78288-0346

(800) 531-8722
WWW.USAA.COM

USAA UNITED SERVICES AUTOMOBILE

Payer ID CQ537

9800 FREDERICKSBURG RD
SAN ANTONIO, TX 78288

(800) 551-8722
WWW.USAA.COM

UTAH CARPENTERS

Payer ID 74234

533 S FREEMONT AVE
LOS ANGELES, CA 90071-1706

(801) 373-7220
WWW.SWCARPENTERS.ORG

UTAH LABORERS

Payer ID 74234

PO BOX 30262
SALT LAKE CITY, UT 84130-0262

(801) 908-5781
HTTPS://UTL.COMPUSYSUT.COM/

UTAH PIPE TRADES

Payer ID 74234

PO BOX 30604
SALT LAKE CITY, UT 84130-0604

(801) 908-5781
HTTPS://UTPIPE.COMPUSYSUT.COM

UTMB HEALTHCARE SYSTEMS

Payer ID UHSCH

PO BOX 15485
AUSTIN, TX 78761

(866) 735-3281
WWW.UTMBHCS.ORG

VA FEE BASIS PROGRAMS

Payer ID 12115

810 VERMONT AVE NW
WASHINGTON, DC 20420

(512) 460-5049
WWW.NONVACARE.VA.GOV/PROVIDERS.ASP

VALLEY BAPTIST HEALTH PLAN

Payer ID VBHP1

12940 N HIGHWAY 183
AUSTIN, TX 78750-3203

(877) 422-4400
WWW.VALLEYBAPTISTHEALTHPLANS.COM

VALLEY HEALTH ADMINISTRATORS

Payer ID VHA11

800 PLZ DR STE 230
BELLE VERNON, PA 15012-4019

(877) 264-8258
WWW.VALEUHEALTH.COM

VALLEY HEALTH PLAN

2480 N FIRST ST STE 200
SAN JOSE, CA 95131

(408) 885-2221
WWW.VALLEYHEALTHPLAN.ORG

VALUE OPTIONS COMMERCIAL CLAIMS

Payer ID 00813

PO BOX 1290
LATHAM, NY 12110

(877) 729-8213
WWW.VALUEOPTIONS.COM/PROVIDERS/
PROVIDERS.HTM

VALUE OPTIONS MASSACHUSETTS BEHAVIORAL HEALTH PARTNERSHIP

Payer ID 00816

100 HIGH ST 3RD FL
BOSTON, MA 02110

(800) 495-0086
WWW.MASSPARTNERSHIP.COM

VALUE OPTIONS TEXAS NORTHSTAR

Payer ID 00818

PO BOX 12450
NORFOLK, VA 23541

(888) 800-6799
WWW.VALUEOPTIONS.COM/NORTHSTAR/
PROVIDERS.HTM

VANLINER INSURANCE CO

Payer ID 21172

ONE PREMIER DR
FENTON, MO 63026
PO BOX 956586
ST. LOUIS, MO 63195-6586

(636) 343-9889
(800) 325-3619
WWW.VANLINER.COM

VANTAGE HEALTH PLAN, INC

Payer ID 72128

130 DESIARD ST STE 300
MONROE, LA 71201

(318) 361-0900
(888) 823-1910
WWW.VHPLA.COM/PROVIDERS

VANTAGE MEDICAL GROUP

Payer ID PPM01

2115 COMPTON AVE STE 301
CORONA, CA 92881

(951) 280-7700
WWW.VANTAGEMEDICALGROUP.COM

VENTURA COUNTY HEALTH CARE PLAN

2220 E GONZALES RD #210-B
OXNARD, CA 93036

(866) 575-4120
WWW.VCHEALTHCAREPLAN.ORG

VERITY NATIONAL GROUP

Payer ID 75256

11467 HUEBNER RD STE 300
SAN ANTONIO, TX 78230-0000

(800) 840-3977
WWW.VERITYNATIONAL.COM

VILLAGECARE MAX

PO BOX 5536
HAUPPAUGE, NY 11788

(855) 769-2500
WWW.VILLAGECAREMAX.ORG

VIPA

Payer ID BVVP1

PO BOX 44077
MILWUAKEE, WI 53214-7077

(800) 883-5747
WWW.VISIONPLANS.COM/PROVIDERS.ASPX

VIRGINIA MEDICAID HMO (OPTIMA FAMILY CARE)

PO BOX 5028
TROY, MI 48007-5028

(800) 229-8822
HTTP://PROVIDERS.OPTIMAHEALTH.COM

VIRGINIA MEDICAID HMO (VIRGINIA PREMIER HEALTH PLAN)

Payer ID 54176

PO BOX 5207
RICHMOD, VA 23220-0207

(804) 819-5151
(800) 727-7536
WWW.VAPREMIER.COM/INDEX.PHP
?PAGE=CLAIMS

VIRGINIA PREMIER HEALTH PLAN

Payer ID 54176

PO BOX 5207
RICHMOND, VA 23220-0307

(804) 819-5151
WWW.VAPREMIER.COM/INDEX.PHP
?PAGE=CLAIMS

VISION SERVICE PLAN

PO BOX 997100
SACRAMENTO, CA 95899-7100

(916) 851-5000
(800) 852-7600
WWW.VSP.COM

VISITING NURSE SERVICE OF NY CHOICE HEALTH PLANS

Payer ID 77073

PO BOX 4498
SCRANTON, PA 18505

(866) 783-0222
HTTP://2013.VNSNYCHOICE.ORG

VISTA HEALTH PLAN

Payer ID 55248

PO BOX 45-9011
SUNRISE, FL 33345-9011

(866) 847-8235
HTTP://
CHCFLORIDA.COVENTRYHEALTHCARE.COM/

VISTA HEALTHPLAN OF SOUTH FLORIDA

Payer ID 59257

PO BOX 45-3219
SUNRISE, FL 33345-3219

(800) 441-5501
HTTP://
CHCFLORIDA.COVENTRYHEALTHCARE.COM/

VIVA HEALTH

Payer ID 63114

PO BOX 55926
BIRMINGHAM, AL 35255

(205) 558-7474
(800) 294-7780
WWW.VIVAPROVIDER.COM/DEFAULT.ASPX

VNS CHOICE MEDICARE

Payer ID 77073

PO BOX 4498
SCRANTON, PA 18505

(866) 783-0222
HTTP://2012.VNSNYCHOICE.ORG/FOR-
PROVIDERS

VOLUSIA HEALTH NETWORK

Payer ID 59266

PO BOX 2814
DAYTONA BEACH, FL 32120

(386) 425-4846
HTTP://VHNONLINE.COM/FOR-PROVIDERS/
DEFAULT.ASPX

VYTRA HEALTHCARE

Payer ID 22264

PO BOX 9091
MELVILLE, NY 11747-9091

(888) 288-9872
WWW.VYTRA.COM/DEFAULT.ASP
?LEVEL1=PROVIDERS

WABASH MEMORIAL HOSPITAL ASSOCIATION

Payer ID 85256

PO BOX 1340
DECATUR, IL 62525-1340

(888) 800-9161
WWW.WABASHCANNONBALL.ORG

WASHINGTON MEDICAID HMO (MOLINA HEALTHCARE)

Payer ID 38336

PO BOX 22612
LONG BEACH, CA 90801

(800) 745-4044
WWW.MOLINAHEALTHCARE.COM

WASHINGTON STATE LABOR AND INDUSTRY

Payer ID WALAI

PO BOX 44269
OLYMPIA, WA 98504-4269

(360) 902-5204
(800) 831-5227
WWW.LNI.WA.GOV/CLAIMSINS/PROVIDERS

WASHINGTON STATE PREMERA BLUE CROSS

Payer ID WABLC

PO BOX 91059
SEATTLE, WA 98111-9159

(877) 342-5258
WWW.PREMERA.COM

WATERSTONE BENEFIT ADMINISTRATORS

Payer ID 73155

4013 NW EXPRESSWAY 575
OKLAHOMA CITY, OK 73116-1623

(405) 440-8888
(888) 440-0971
WWW.WATERSTONEADMINISTRATORS.COM

WATTS HEALTHCARE CORP

Payer ID MPM09

PO BOX 570220
TARZANA, CA 91357

(818) 702-0100
WWW.MEDPOINTMANAGEMENT.COM

WEA TRUST

Payer ID 39151

PO BOX 7338
MADISON, WI 53707-7338

(608) 276-4000
(800) 279-4000
WWW.WEATRUST.COM

WELBORN HEALTH PLANS

101 SE THIRD ST
EVANSVILLE, IN 47708

(812) 426-6600
(800) 521-0265
WWW.WELBORNHEALTHPLANS.COM

WELFARE & PENSION ADMIN SERV

PO BOX 34203
SEATTLE, WA 98124

(206) 441-7574
(800) 331-6158
WWW.WPAS-INC.COM

WELLCARE

Payer ID 14163

PO BOX 31372
TAMPA, FL 33631-3372

(866) 530-9491
WWW.WELLCARE.COM/PROVIDER/DEFAULT

WELLCARE OF CT & NY

Payer ID 14164

PO BOX 31372
TAMPA, FL 33631-3372

(800) 278-5155
WWW.WELLCARE.COM/PROVIDER/DEFAULT

WELLMED

Payer ID WELM2

PO BOX 400066
SAN ANTONIO, TX 78229

(888) 781-9355
WWW.WELLMEDMEDICALGROUP.COM

WELLPATH-COVENTRY HEALTHCARE

Payer ID 25129

PO BOX 7102
LONDON, KY 40742

(800) 889-1947
HTTP://
CHCNORTHCAROLINA.COVENTRYHEALTHCARE.COM/

WENATCHEE VALLEY MEDICAL CENTER

Payer ID 91064

PO BOX 810
WENATCHEE, WA 98801

(509) 663-8711
(888) 499-4801
WWW.WVMEDICAL.COM

WEST BEND MUTUAL INSURANCE CO

Payer ID WZ081	1900 S 18TH AVE WEST BEND, WI 53095	(262) 334-5571 (800) 236-5010 WWW.THESILVERLINING.COM

WEST VIRGINIA MEDICAID HMO (CARELINK)

Payer ID 25140	PO BOX 7373 LONDON, KY 40742-7373	(800) 348-2922 HTTP://CHCWESTVIRGINIA.COM

WEST VIRGINIA MEDICAID HMO (UPPER OHIO VALLEY HEALTH PLAN)

	CLAIMS-52160 NATIONAL RD E ST CLAIRSVILLE, OH 43950	(800) 624-6961 WWW.HEALTHPLAN.ORG

WEST VIRGINIA STATE EMPLOYEES

Payer ID 75196	PO BOX 2451 CHARLESTON, WV 25329-2451	(304) 558-7850 (888) 680-7342 WWW.PEIA.WV.GOV

WESTCO INSURANCE COMPANY

Payer ID 25011	PO BOX 655028 DALLAS, TX 75265	(212) 220-7120 WWW.AMTRUSTGROUP.COM

WESTERN AGRICULTURAL INSURANCE COMPANY

Payer ID 27871	5400 UNIVERSITY AVE WEST DES MOINES, IA 50266	(515) 225-5400

WESTERN AMERICAN INSURANCE COMPANY

	PO BOX 833879 RICHARDSON, TX 75083-3879	(972) 699-2770 WWW.WALIC.COM

WESTERN BENEFITS, INC

Payer ID 93128	14835 SE 82ND DR CLACKAMAS, OR 97015 PO BOX 22185 PORTLAND, OR 97269	(503) 968-2360 (800) 277-8579 WWW.WESTERNBENEFITSINC.COM

WESTERN GROWER'S ASSURANCE TRUST

Payer ID 24735	PO BOX 7240 NEWPORT BEACH, CA 92658	(800) 777-7898 WWW.WGA.COM

WESTERN NATIONAL MUTUAL INSURANCE CO

Payer ID WZ898	5350 W 78TH ST EDINA, MN 55439 PO BOX 1463 MINNEAPOLIS, MN 55440-1463	(952) 835-5350 (800) 862-6070 WWW.WNINS.COM

WESTERN SOUTHERN FINANCIAL GROUP

Payer ID 31048	PO BOX 1399 CINCINNATI, OH 45273-9425	(800) 926-1315 WWW.WESTERNSOUTHERN.COM

WESTFIELD INSURANCE

Payer ID WZ899	1 PARK CIR WESTFIELD CENTER, OH 44251 PO BOX 5001 WESTFIELD CENTER, OH 44521	(866) 937-2663 WWW.WESTFIELDINSURANCE.COM

WESTLAKE FINANCIAL GROUP, INC

Payer ID 90560	PO BOX 981805 EL PASO, TX 79998	(847) 353-6150 WWW.WESTLAKEFG.COM

WILLIAM C EARHART COMPANY, INC

Payer ID 93050

PO BOX 4148
PORTLAND, OR 97208

(503) 282-5581
(800) 547-1314
WWW.WCEARHART.COM

WILLIAM J SUTTON & CO LTD

Payer ID 98010

33 YONGE ST STE 270
TORONTO, ON M5E 1G4

(416) 366-2223
(800) 461-3292
WWW.WJSUTTON.COM

WILSON MUTUAL INSURANCE

Payer ID WZ309

3330 STAHL RD
SHEBOYGAN, WI 53081
PO BOX 1340
SHEBOYGAN, WI 53082-1340

(920) 458-3359
(800) 242-7708
WWW.WILSONMUTUAL.COM

WILSON-MCSHANE

Payer ID 41095

3001 METRO DR STE 500
BLOOMINGTON, MN 55425-1546

(952) 854-0795
(800) 535-6373
WWW.UCWCP.COM

WIN HEALTHCARE

Payer ID 13413

1311 MAMARONECK AVE STE 140
WHTIE PLAINS, NY 10605

(877) 444-4946
WWW.WINHEALTHCARE.ORG

WINDSOR HEALTH PLAN

Payer ID 62153

PO BOX 269025
PLANO, TX 75026

(866) 270-5333
WWW.WINDSORHEALTHPLAN.COM

WINDSOR MEDICARE EXTRA

Payer ID 62153

PO BOX 269025
PLANO, TX 75026

(866) 270-5223
WWW.WINDSORHEALTHPLAN.COM/
PROVIDERS

WINHEALTH PARTNERS MEDICARE PLAN

Payer ID RMWIN

1200 E 20TH ST STE A
CHEYENNE, WY 82001-3949

(307) 773-1300
(800) 868-7670
WWW.WINHEALTHPARTNERS.ORG/
PROVIDERS.HTML

WINHEALTH PARTNERS/WYOMING HEALTH SOLUTIONS

1200 E 20TH ST
CHEYENNE, WY 82001

(307) 773-1330
(800) 868-7670
WWW.WINHEALTHPARTNERS.ORG/
PROVIDERS.HTML

WISCONSIN AUTO & TRUCK DEALERS INSURANCE CORPORATION

Payer ID 39200

PO BOX 5345
MADISON, WI 53705-0345

(608) 251-5577
WWW.WATDA.ORG

WISCONSIN DEPT OF CORRECTIONS

Payer ID VEST1

3099 E. WASHINGTON AVE
MADISON, WI 53707-7925
PO BOX 7925
MADISON, WI 53707-7925

(608) 240-5000
HTTP://DOC.WI.GOV/HOME

WISCONSIN MEDICAID HMO (DEAN HEALTH PLAN)

PO BOX 56099
MADISON, WI 53705

(800) 356-7344
WWW.DEANCARE.COM

WISCONSIN MEDICAID HMO (MANAGED HEALTH SERVICES)

PO BOX 3002
FARMINGTON, MO 63640-3802

(877) 647-4848
WWW.MHSINDIANA.COM

WISCONSIN MEDICAID HMO (NETWORK HEALTH PLAN)

PO BOX 568
MENASHA, WI 54952

(800) 826-0940
WWW.NETWORKHEALTH.COM

WISCONSIN MEDICAID HMO (SECURITY HEALTH PLAN)

PO BOX 8000
MARSHFIELD, WI 54449-8000

(800) 548-1224
WWW.SECURITYHEALTH.ORG

WOODMAN ACCIDENT AND LIFE CO

Payer ID 81949

1700 FARNAM ST
OMAHA, NE 68102-2001

(800) 225-3108
WWW.WOODMEN.ORG

WORKCOMP EDI

Payer ID WCEDI

85 W ALGONQUIN STE 410
ARLINGTON HEIGHTS, IL 60005

(800) 297-6906
(800) 297-6909
WWW.WORKCOMPEDI.COM

WORKFIRST CASUALTY COMPANY

Payer ID WB298

3521 SILVERSIDE RD QUILLEN BLDG STE 2E
WILMINGTON, DE 19810

(302) 477-1710
(877) 772-4667
WWW.WORKFIRSTCASUALTY.COM

WORKFORCE SAFETY & INSURANCE OF NORTH DAKOTA

Payer ID CB001

1600 E CENTURY AVE #1
BISMARK, ND 58503

(800) 777-5033
WWW.WORKFORCESAFETY.COM

WORKSITE BENEFIT SERVICES

Payer ID 20333

PO BOX 707
TIFTON, GA 31794-0707

(229) 386-9779
WWW.WSBENEFIT.COM

WPP ELDERCARE WISCONSIN

Payer ID 77080

PO BOX 6090
DEPERE, WI 54115-6090

(920) 337-6550
WWW.DHS.WISCONSIN.GOV/PARTNERS/PROVIDERS.HTM

WPPA-PROVIDRS CARE NETWORK

Payer ID WP481

1102 S HILSIDE
WICHITA, KS 67211-4004

(316) 683-4111
(800) 801-9772
WWW.PROVIDRSCARE.NET/PROVIDERS.HTM

WPS COMMERCIAL

Payer ID OOWPS

PO BOX 8190
MADISON, WI 53708-8190

(800) 765-4977
WWW.WPSIC.COM/PROVIDERS/INDEX.SHTML

WRITERS' GUILD - INDUSTRY HEALTH PLAN

Payer ID 23710

1015 N HOLLYWOOD WAY
BURBANK, CA 91505-2526

(818) 846-1015
(800) 227-7863
WWW.WGAPLANS.ORG

WYOMING SCHOOL BOARDS ASSOCIATION INSURANCE TRUST

Payer ID WYSCH

PO BOX 3559
ENGLEWOOD, CO 80155

(800) 426-7453
WWW.CNICHS.COM/PROVIDERS.HTML

YALE UNIVERSITY HEALTH PLAN

Payer ID 60646

PO BOX 208237
NEW HAVEN, CT 06520-8237

(203) 432-0246
HTTP://YALEHEALTH.YALE.EDU

YAVAPAI COUNTY

Payer ID 09829

1015 FAIR 2ND FL
PRESCOTT, AZ 86305

(928) 771-3560
WWW.CO.YAVAPAI.AZ.US

ZENITH ADMINISTRATORS

	188661 90TH AVE STE A MOKENA, IL 60448	(312) 649-1200 WWW.ZENITHTPA.COM

ZENITH INSURANCE CO

Payer ID 13269	21255 CALIFA ST WOODLAND HILLS, CA 91367-5005	(818) 713-1000 (800) 448-4356 WWW.THEZENITH.COM

Appendix A: Abbreviations

State and Province Abbreviations

Alabama	AL
Alaska	AK
American Samoa	AS
Arizona	AZ
Arkansas	AR
California	CA
Colorado	CO
Connecticut	CT
Delaware	DE
District of Columbia	DC
Federated States of Micronesia	FM
Florida	FL
Georgia	GA
Guam	GU
Hawaii	HI
Idaho	ID
Illinois	IL
Indiana	IN
Iowa	IA
Kansas	KS
Kentucky	KY
Louisiana	LA
Maine	ME
Marshall Islands	MH
Maryland	MD
Massachusetts	MA
Michigan	MI
Minnesota	MN
Mississippi	MS
Missouri	MO
Montana	MT
Nebraska	NE
Nevada	NV
New Hampshire	NH
New Jersey	NJ
New Mexico	NM
New York	NY
North Carolina	NC
North Dakota	ND
Northern Mariana Islands	MP
Ohio	OH
Oklahoma	OK
Oregon	OR
Palau	PW
Pennsylvania	PA
Puerto Rico	PR
Rhode Island	RI
South Carolina	SC
South Dakota	SD
Tennessee	TN
Texas	TX
Utah	UT
Vermont	VT
Virgin Islands	VI
Virginia	VA
Washington	WA
West Virginia	WV
Wisconsin	WI
Wyoming	WY

Canadian Provinces

Alberta	AB
British Columbia	BC
Manitoba	MB
New Brunswick	NB
Newfoundland and Labrador	NL
Nova Scotia	NS
Northwest Territories	NT
Nunavut	NU
Ontario	ON
Prince Edward Island	PE
Quebec	QC
Saskatchewan	SK
Yukon	YT

Geographic Directional Abbreviations

North	N
East	E
South	S
West	W
Northeast	NE
Southeast	SE
Southwest	SW
Northwest	NW

Regional Abbreviations

All Regions	NATL
Central Region	CR
Eastern Region	ER
Northeast Region	NE
Southern Region	SR
Western Region	WR

Abbreviations for Street Designators

Street Suffix or Suffix Abbrev.	USPS Suffix Abbrev.
allee	aly
alley	aly
ally	aly
anex	anx
annex	anx
annx	anx
arcade	arc
av	ave
aven	ave
avenu	ave
avenue	ave
avn	ave
avnue	ave
bayoo	byu
bayou	byu
beach	bch
bend	bnd
bluf	blf
bluff	blf
bluffs	blf
bot	btm
bottm	btm
bottom	btm
boul	blvd
boulevard	blvd
boulv	blvd
branch	br
brdge	brg
bridge	brg
brnch	br
brook	brk
brooks	brk
burg	bg
burgs	bg
bypa	byp
bypas	byp
bypass	byp

Street Suffix or Suffix Abbrev.	USPS Suffix Abbrev.
byps	byp
camp	cp
canyn	cyn
canyon	cyn
cape	cpe
causeway	cswy
causway	cswy
cen	ctr
cent	ctr
center	ctr
centers	ctr
centr	ctr
circ	cir
circl	cir
circle	cir
crcles	cir
clf	clfs
cliff	clfs
cliffs	clfs
club	clb
cmp	cp
cnter	ctr
cntr	ctr
cnyn	cyn
corner	cor
corners	cors
course	crse
court	ct
courts	cts
cove	cv
coves	cv
crcl	cir
circle	cir
crecent	cres
creek	crk
crest	cres
crescent	cres
cresentv	cres

Street Suffix or Suffix Abbrev.	USPS Suffix Abbrev.
crossing	xing
crscent	cres
crsent	cres
crsnt	cres
crssng	xing
dale	dl
dam	dm
div	dv
divide	dv
driv	dr
drive	dr
drives	dr
drv	dr
dvd	dv
estate	est
estates	est
ests	est
exp	expy
expr	expy
express	expy
expressway	expy
expw	exp
extension	ext
extn	ext
extnsn	ext
exts	ext
falls	fls
ferry	fry
field	fld
fields	flds
flat	flt
flats	flt
flts	flt
ford	frd
fords	frd
forest	frst
forests	frst
forg	frg
forg	frg
forges	frg
fork	frk
forks	frks
fort	ft
freeway	fwy
freewy	fwy
frry	fry
frt	ft
frway	fwy
frwy	fwy
garden	gdns
gardens	gdns
gardn	gdns
gateway	gtwy
Gatewy	gtwy
gatway	gtwy
gdn	gdns
glen	gln
glens	gln
grden	gdns
grdn	gdns
grdns	gdns
green	grn
greens	grn
grov	grv
grove	grv
gtway	gtwy
harb	hbr
harbor	hbr
harbors	hbr
harbr	hbr
haven	hvn
havn	hvn
height	hts
heights	hts
highway	hwy
highwy	hwy

Appendix A: Abbreviations

Street Suffix or Suffix Abbrev.	USPS Suffix Abbrev.
hill	hl
hills	hls
hiway	hwy
hiwy	hwy
hllw	holw
hollow	holw
holws	holw
hrbor	hbr
ht	hts
hway	hwy
inlet	inlt
island	is
islands	iss
isles	isle
islnd	is
islnds	iss
jction	jct
jctn	jct
jctns	jct
jcts	jct
junction	jct
junctn	jct
juncton	jct
keyv	ky
keys	ky
knl	knls
knol	knls
knoll	knls
knolls	knls
kys	ky
lake	lk
lakes	lks
landing	lndg
lane	ln
lanes	ln
ldge	ldg
light	lgt
lights	lgt

Street Suffix or Suffix Abbrev.	USPS Suffix Abbrev.
lndng	lndg
loaf	lf
lock	lcks
locks	lcks
lodg	ldg
lodge	ldg
loops	loop
manor	mnr
manors	mnr
mdw	mdws
meadow	mdws
meadows	mdws
medows	mdws
mill	ml
mills	mls
mission	msn
missn	msn
mnrs	mnr
mnt	mt
mntain	mtn
mntn	mtn
mntns	mtn
mount	mt
mountain	mtn
mountin	mtn
mssn	msn
mtinv	mtn
neck	nck
orchard	orch
orchrd	orch
ovl	oval
parks	park
parkway	pky
parkwy	pky
paths	path
pikes	pike
pine	pnes
pines	pnes

Street Suffix or Suffix Abbrev.	USPS Suffix Abbrev.
pkway	pky
pkwy	pky
pkwys	pky
place	pl
plain	pln
plaines	plns
plaza	plz
plza	plz
point	pt
points	pt
port	prt
ports	prt
prarie	pr
prk	park
prr	pr
prts	prt
pts	pt
rad	radl
radial	radl
radiel	radl
ranches	rnch
rapid	rpds
rapids	rpds
rdge	rdg
rdgs	rdg
rds	rd
rest	rst
ridge	rdg
ridges	rdg
river	riv
rivr	riv
rnchs	rnch
road	rd
roads	rd
route	rt
rpd	rpds
rvr	riv
shoal	shl
shoals	shls
shoar	shr
shoars	shrs
shore	shr
shores	shrs
spng	spg
spngs	spgs
spring	spg
springs	spgs
sprng	spg
sprngs	spgs
spurs	spur
sqr	sq
sqre	sq
squ	sq
square	sq
squares	sq
station	sta
statn	sta
stn	sta
str	st
strav	stra
strave	stra
straven	stra
stravenue	stra
stravn	stra
stream	strm
street	st
streets	st
streme	strm
strt	st
strvn	stra
strvnue	stra
sumit	smt
sumitt	smt
summit	smt
terr	ter
terrace	ter

Appendix A: Abbreviations

Street Suffix or Suffix Abbrev.	USPS Suffix Abbrev.
tpk	tpke
trace	trce
traces	trce
track	trak
tracks	trak
trail	trl
trailer	trlr
trails	trl
trk	trak
trks	trak
trlrs	trlr
trls	trl
trnpk	tpke
tunel	tunl
tunls	tunl
tunnel	tunl
tunnl	tunl
turnpike	tpke
turnpk	tpke
union	un
unions	un
valley	vly
valley	vly
vally	vly
vdct	via
viadct	via
viaduct	via
view	vw
views	vw
vill	vlg
villag	vlg
village	vlg
ville	vl
villg	vlg
villiage	vlg
vist	vis
vista	vis
vlg	vlg
vlgs	vlg
vlly	vly
vlys	vly
vst	vis
vsta	vis
vws	vw
walks	walk
ways	way
well	wls
wells	wls
wy	way

USPS Approved Envelope Addressing Formats

MISS JANICE SMITH
PO BOX 34
DULUTH MN 55803-0034

336543M 80V
MS LOIS SMITH
4653 GEORGIA AVE NW
WASHINGTON DC 22001-7128

H E BROWN
RR 3 BOX 9
CANTON OH 44730-9521

MR STANLEY DOE
LAST NATIONAL BANK
PO BOX 345
NEW YORK NY 10163-0345

MR JAMES F JONES
4417 BROOKS ST NE
WASHINGTON DC 20019-4649

ACME INSURANCE CO
CAREW TOWERS
300 E MAIN ST RM 1121
MEMPHIS TN 38166-1121

B G LIGHT CO
HC 2 BOX 293A
DULUTH MN 55811-9702

PVT WILLARD J SMITH
COMPANY F
167TH INFANTRY REGT
APO NEW YORK NY 09801-1087

MR THOMAS CLARK
17 RUSSELL DRIVE
LONDON WIP 6HQ
ENGLAND

MS HELEN SANDERS
1010 CLEAR ST
OTTAWA ON K1AOB1
CANADA

Appendix A: Abbreviations

Appendix B: Place of Service Codes

The following table indicates the place of service codes and the payment rate for each. (Database updated November 1, 2012)

POS Code	Name	Description
01	PHARMACY	A FACILITY OR LOCATION WHERE DRUGS AND OTHER MEDICALLY RELATED ITEMS AND SERVICES ARE SOLD, DISPENSED, OR OTHERWISE PROVIDED DIRECTLY TO PATIENTS. (EFFECTIVE OCTOBER 1, 2005)
02	UNASSIGNED	N/A
03	SCHOOL	A FACILITY WHOSE PRIMARY PURPOSE IS EDUCATION. (EFFECTIVE JANUARY 1, 2003)
04	HOMELESS SHELTER	A FACILITY OR LOCATION WHOSE PRIMARY PURPOSE IS TO PROVIDE TEMPORARY HOUSING TO HOMELESS INDIVIDUALS (E.G., EMERGENCY SHELTERS, INDIVIDUAL OR FAMILY SHELTERS). (EFFECTIVE JANUARY 1, 2003)
05	INDIAN HEALTH SERVICE FREE-STANDING FACILITY	A FACILITY OR LOCATION, OWNED AND OPERATED BY THE INDIAN HEALTH SERVICE, WHICH PROVIDES DIAGNOSTIC, THERAPEUTIC (SURGICAL AND NON-SURGICAL), AND REHABILITATION SERVICES TO AMERICAN INDIANS AND ALASKA NATIVES WHO DO NOT REQUIRE HOSPITALIZATION. (EFFECTIVE JANUARY 1, 2003)
06	INDIAN HEALTH SERVICE PROVIDER-BASED FACILITY	A FACILITY OR LOCATION, OWNED AND OPERATED BY THE INDIAN HEALTH SERVICE, WHICH PROVIDES DIAGNOSTIC, THERAPEUTIC (SURGICAL AND NON-SURGICAL), AND REHABILITATION SERVICES RENDERED BY, OR UNDER THE SUPERVISION OF, PHYSICIANS TO AMERICAN INDIANS AND ALASKA NATIVES ADMITTED AS INPATIENTS OR OUTPATIENTS. (EFFECTIVE JANUARY 1, 2003)
07	TRIBAL 638 FREE-STANDING FACILITY	A FACILITY OR LOCATION OWNED AND OPERATED BY A FEDERALLY RECOGNIZED AMERICAN INDIAN OR ALASKA NATIVE TRIBE OR TRIBAL ORGANIZATION UNDER A 638 AGREEMENT, WHICH PROVIDES DIAGNOSTIC, THERAPEUTIC (SURGICAL AND NON-SURGICAL), AND REHABILITATION SERVICES TO TRIBAL MEMBERS WHO DO NOT REQUIRE HOSPITALIZATION. (EFFECTIVE JANUARY 1, 2003)
08	TRIBAL 638	A FACILITY OR LOCATION OWNED AND OPERATED BY A PROVIDER-BASED FACILITY FEDERALLY RECOGNIZED AMERICAN INDIAN OR ALASKA NATIVE TRIBE OR TRIBAL ORGANIZATION UNDER A 638 AGREEMENT, WHICH PROVIDES DIAGNOSTIC, THERAPEUTIC (SURGICAL AND NON-SURGICAL), AND REHABILITATION SERVICES TO TRIBAL MEMBERS ADMITTED AS INPATIENTS OR OUTPATIENTS. (EFFECTIVE JANUARY 1, 2003)
09	PRISON/ CORRECTIONAL FACILITY	A PRISON, JAIL, REFORMATORY, WORK FARM, DETENTION CENTER, OR ANY OTHER SIMILAR FACILITY MAINTAINED BY EITHER FEDERAL, STATE OR LOCAL AUTHORITIES FOR THE PURPOSE OF CONFINEMENT OR REHABILITATION OF ADULT OR JUVENILE CRIMINAL OFFENDERS. (EFFECTIVE JULY 1, 2006)
10	UNASSIGNED	
11	OFFICE	LOCATION, OTHER THAN A HOSPITAL, SKILLED NURSING FACILITY (SNF), MILITARY TREATMENT FACILITY, COMMUNITY HEALTH CENTER, STATE OR LOCAL PUBLIC HEALTH CLINIC, OR INTERMEDIATE CARE FACILITY (ICF), WHERE THE HEALTH PROFESSIONAL ROUTINELY PROVIDES HEALTH EXAMINATIONS, DIAGNOSIS, AND TREATMENT OF ILLNESS OR INJURY ON AN AMBULATORY BASIS.
12	HOME	LOCATION, OTHER THAN A HOSPITAL OR OTHER FACILITY, WHERE THE PATIENT RECEIVES CARE IN A PRIVATE RESIDENCE.

POS Code	Name	Description
13	ASSISTED LIVING FACILITY	CONGREGATE RESIDENTIAL FACILITY WITH SELF-CONTAINED LIVING UNITS PROVIDING ASSESSMENT OF EACH RESIDENT'S NEEDS AND ON-SITE SUPPORT 24 HOURS A DAY, 7 DAYS A WEEK, WITH THE CAPACITY TO DELIVER OR ARRANGE FOR SERVICES INCLUDING SOME HEALTH CARE AND OTHER SERVICES. (EFFECTIVE OCTOBER 1, 2003)
14	GROUP HOME *	A RESIDENCE, WITH SHARED LIVING AREAS, WHERE CLIENTS RECEIVE SUPERVISION AND OTHER SERVICES SUCH AS SOCIAL AND/OR BEHAVIORAL SERVICES, CUSTODIAL SERVICE, AND MINIMAL SERVICES (E.G., MEDICATION ADMINISTRATION). (EFFECTIVE OCTOBER 1, 2003)
15	MOBILE UNIT	A FACILITY/UNIT THAT MOVES FROM PLACE-TO-PLACE EQUIPPED TO PROVIDE PREVENTIVE, SCREENING, DIAGNOSTIC, AND/OR TREATMENT SERVICES. (EFFECTIVE JANUARY 1, 2003)
16	TEMPORARY LODGING	A SHORT TERM ACCOMMODATION SUCH AS A HOTEL, CAMP GROUND, HOSTEL, CRUISE SHIP OR RESORT WHERE THE PATIENT RECEIVES CARE, AND WHICH IS NOT IDENTIFIED BY ANY OTHER POS CODE. (EFFECTIVE APRIL 1, 2008)
17	WALK-IN RETAIL HEALTH CLINIC	A WALK-IN HEALTH CLINIC, OTHER THAN AN OFFICE, URGENT CARE FACILITY, PHARMACY OR INDEPENDENT CLINIC AND NOT DESCRIBED BY ANY OTHER PLACE OF SERVICE CODE, THAT IS LOCATED WITHIN A RETAIL OPERATION AND PROVIDES, ON AN AMBULATORY BASIS, PREVENTIVE AND PRIMARY CARE SERVICES. (EFFECTIVE MAY 1, 2010)
18	PLACE OF EMPLOYMENT-WORKSITE	A LOCATION, NOT DESCRIBED BY ANY OTHER POS CODE, OWNED OR OPERATED BY A PUBLIC OR PRIVATE ENTITY WHERE THE PATIENT IS EMPLOYED, AND WHERE A HEALTH PROFESSIONAL PROVIDES ON-GOING OR EPISODIC OCCUPATIONAL MEDICAL, THERAPEUTIC OR REHABILITATIVE SERVICES TO THE INDIVIDUAL. (THIS CODE IS AVAILABLE FOR USE EFFECTIVE JANUARY 1, 2013 BUT NO LATER THAN MAY 1, 2013)
19	UNASSIGNED	N/A
20	URGENT CARE FACILITY	LOCATION, DISTINCT FROM A HOSPITAL EMERGENCY ROOM, AN OFFICE, OR A CLINIC, WHOSE PURPOSE IS TO DIAGNOSE AND TREAT ILLNESS OR INJURY FOR UNSCHEDULED, AMBULATORY PATIENTS SEEKING IMMEDIATE MEDICAL ATTENTION. (EFFECTIVE JANUARY 1, 2003)
21	INPATIENT HOSPITAL	A FACILITY, OTHER THAN PSYCHIATRIC, WHICH PRIMARILY PROVIDES DIAGNOSTIC, THERAPEUTIC (BOTH SURGICAL AND NONSURGICAL), AND REHABILITATION SERVICES BY, OR UNDER, THE SUPERVISION OF PHYSICIANS TO PATIENTS ADMITTED FOR A VARIETY OF MEDICAL CONDITIONS.
22	OUTPATIENT HOSPITAL	A PORTION OF A HOSPITAL WHICH PROVIDES DIAGNOSTIC, THERAPEUTIC (BOTH SURGICAL AND NONSURGICAL), AND REHABILITATION SERVICES TO SICK OR INJURED PERSONS WHO DO NOT REQUIRE HOSPITALIZATION OR INSTITUTIONALIZATION.
23	EMERGENCY ROOM – HOSPITAL	A PORTION OF A HOSPITAL WHERE EMERGENCY DIAGNOSIS AND TREATMENT OF ILLNESS OR INJURY IS PROVIDED.
24	AMBULATORY SURGICAL CENTER	A FREESTANDING FACILITY, OTHER THAN A PHYSICIAN'S OFFICE, WHERE SURGICAL AND DIAGNOSTIC SERVICES ARE PROVIDED ON AN AMBULATORY BASIS.
25	BIRTHING CENTER	A FACILITY, OTHER THAN A HOSPITAL'S MATERNITY FACILITIES OR A PHYSICIAN'S OFFICE, WHICH PROVIDES A SETTING FOR LABOR, DELIVERY, AND IMMEDIATE POST- PARTUM CARE AS WELL AS IMMEDIATE CARE OF NEW BORN INFANTS.
26	MILITARY TREATMENT FACILITY	A MEDICAL FACILITY OPERATED BY ONE OR MORE OF THE UNIFORMED SERVICES. MILITARY TREATMENT FACILITY (MTF) ALSO REFERS TO CERTAIN FORMER U.S. PUBLIC HEALTH SERVICE (USPHS) FACILITIES NOW DESIGNATED AS UNIFORMED SERVICE TREATMENT FACILITIES (USTF).
27-30	UNASSIGNED	N/A
31	SKILLED NURSING FACILITY	A FACILITY WHICH PRIMARILY PROVIDES INPATIENT SKILLED NURSING CARE AND RELATED SERVICES TO PATIENTS WHO REQUIRE MEDICAL, NURSING, OR REHABILITATIVE SERVICES BUT DOES NOT PROVIDE THE LEVEL OF CARE OR TREATMENT AVAILABLE IN A HOSPITAL.
32	NURSING FACILITY	A FACILITY WHICH PRIMARILY PROVIDES TO RESIDENTS SKILLED NURSING CARE AND RELATED SERVICES FOR THE REHABILITATION OF INJURED, DISABLED, OR SICK PERSONS, OR, ON A REGULAR BASIS, HEALTH-RELATED CARE SERVICES ABOVE THE LEVEL OF CUSTODIAL CARE TO OTHER THAN MENTALLY RETARDED INDIVIDUALS.

POS Code	Name	Description
33	**CUSTODIAL CARE FACILITY**	A FACILITY WHICH PROVIDES ROOM, BOARD AND OTHER PERSONAL ASSISTANCE SERVICES, GENERALLY ON A LONG- TERM BASIS, AND WHICH DOES NOT INCLUDE A MEDICAL COMPONENT.
34	**HOSPICE**	A FACILITY, OTHER THAN A PATIENT'S HOME, IN WHICH PALLIATIVE AND SUPPORTIVE CARE FOR TERMINALLY ILL PATIENTS AND THEIR FAMILIES ARE PROVIDED.
35-40	**UNASSIGNED**	N/A
41	**AMBULANCE - LAND**	A LAND VEHICLE SPECIFICALLY DESIGNED, EQUIPPED AND STAFFED FOR LIFESAVING AND TRANSPORTING THE SICK OR INJURED.
42	**AMBULANCE – AIR OR WATER**	AN AIR OR WATER VEHICLE SPECIFICALLY DESIGNED, EQUIPPED AND STAFFED FOR LIFESAVING AND TRANSPORTING THE SICK OR INJURED.
43-48	**UNASSIGNED**	N/A
49	**INDEPENDENT CLINIC**	A LOCATION, NOT PART OF A HOSPITAL AND NOT DESCRIBED BY ANY OTHER PLACE OF SERVICE CODE, THAT IS ORGANIZED AND OPERATED TO PROVIDE PREVENTIVE, DIAGNOSTIC, THERAPEUTIC, REHABILITATIVE, OR PALLIATIVE SERVICES TO OUTPATIENTS ONLY. (EFFECTIVE OCTOBER 1, 2003)
50	**FEDERALLY QUALIFIED HEALTH CENTER**	A FACILITY LOCATED IN A MEDICALLY UNDERSERVED AREA THAT PROVIDES MEDICARE BENEFICIARIES PREVENTIVE PRIMARY MEDICAL CARE UNDER THE GENERAL DIRECTION OF A PHYSICIAN.
51	**INPATIENT PSYCHIATRIC FACILITY**	A FACILITY THAT PROVIDES INPATIENT PSYCHIATRIC SERVICES FOR THE DIAGNOSIS AND TREATMENT OF MENTAL ILLNESS ON A 24-HOUR BASIS, BY OR UNDER THE SUPERVISION OF A PHYSICIAN.
52	**PSYCHIATRIC FACILITY-PARTIAL HOSPITALIZATION**	A FACILITY FOR THE DIAGNOSIS AND TREATMENT OF MENTAL ILLNESS THAT PROVIDES A PLANNED THERAPEUTIC PROGRAM FOR PATIENTS WHO DO NOT REQUIRE FULL TIME HOSPITALIZATION, BUT WHO NEED BROADER PROGRAMS THAN ARE POSSIBLE FROM OUTPATIENT VISITS TO A HOSPITAL-BASED OR HOSPITAL-AFFILIATED FACILITY.
53	**COMMUNITY MENTAL HEALTH CENTER**	A FACILITY THAT PROVIDES THE FOLLOWING SERVICES: OUTPATIENT SERVICES, INCLUDING SPECIALIZED OUTPATIENT SERVICES FOR CHILDREN, THE ELDERLY, INDIVIDUALS WHO ARE CHRONICALLY ILL, AND RESIDENTS OF THE CMHC'S MENTAL HEALTH SERVICES AREA WHO HAVE BEEN DISCHARGED FROM INPATIENT TREATMENT AT A MENTAL HEALTH FACILITY; 24 HOUR A DAY EMERGENCY CARE SERVICES; DAY TREATMENT, OTHER PARTIAL HOSPITALIZATION SERVICES, OR PSYCHOSOCIAL REHABILITATION SERVICES; SCREENING FOR PATIENTS BEING CONSIDERED FOR ADMISSION TO STATE MENTAL HEALTH FACILITIES TO DETERMINE THE APPROPRIATENESS OF SUCH ADMISSION; AND CONSULTATION AND EDUCATION SERVICES
54	**INTERMEDIATE CARE FACILITY/ MENTALLY RETARDED**	A FACILITY WHICH PRIMARILY PROVIDES HEALTH-RELATED CARE AND SERVICES ABOVE THE LEVEL OF CUSTODIAL CARE TO MENTALLY RETARDED INDIVIDUALS BUT DOES NOT PROVIDE THE LEVEL OF CARE OR TREATMENT AVAILABLE IN A HOSPITAL OR SNF.
55	**RESIDENTIAL SUBSTANCE ABUSE TREATMENT FACILITY**	A FACILITY WHICH PROVIDES TREATMENT FOR SUBSTANCE (ALCOHOL AND DRUG) ABUSE TO LIVE-IN RESIDENTS WHO DO NOT REQUIRE ACUTE MEDICAL CARE. SERVICES INCLUDE INDIVIDUAL AND GROUP THERAPY AND COUNSELING, FAMILY COUNSELING, LABORATORY TESTS, DRUGS AND SUPPLIES, PSYCHOLOGICAL TESTING, AND ROOM AND BOARD.
56	**PSYCHIATRIC RESIDENTIAL TREATMENT CENTER**	A FACILITY OR DISTINCT PART OF A FACILITY FOR PSYCHIATRIC CARE WHICH PROVIDES A TOTAL 24-HOUR THERAPEUTICALLY PLANNED AND PROFESSIONALLY STAFFED GROUP LIVING AND LEARNING ENVIRONMENT.
57	**NON-RESIDENTIAL SUBSTANCE ABUSE TREATMENT FACILITY**	A LOCATION WHICH PROVIDES TREATMENT FOR SUBSTANCE (ALCOHOL AND DRUG) ABUSE ON AN AMBULATORY BASIS. SERVICES INCLUDE INDIVIDUAL AND GROUP THERAPY AND COUNSELING, FAMILY COUNSELING, LABORATORY TESTS, DRUGS AND SUPPLIES, AND PSYCHOLOGICAL TESTING. (EFFECTIVE OCTOBER 1, 2003)
58-59	**UNASSIGNED**	N/A
60	**MASS IMMUNIZATION CENTER**	A LOCATION WHERE PROVIDERS ADMINISTER PNEUMOCOCCAL PNEUMONIA AND INFLUENZA VIRUS VACCINATIONS AND SUBMIT THESE SERVICES AS ELECTRONIC MEDIA CLAIMS, PAPER CLAIMS, OR USING THE ROSTER BILLING METHOD. THIS GENERALLY TAKES PLACE IN A MASS IMMUNIZATION SETTING, SUCH AS, A PUBLIC HEALTH CENTER, PHARMACY, OR MALL BUT MAY INCLUDE A PHYSICIAN OFFICE SETTING.

POS Code	Name	Description
61	**COMPREHENSIVE INPATIENT REHABILITATION FACILITY**	A FACILITY THAT PROVIDES COMPREHENSIVE REHABILITATION SERVICES UNDER THE SUPERVISION OF A PHYSICIAN TO INPATIENTS WITH PHYSICAL DISABILITIES. SERVICES INCLUDE PHYSICAL THERAPY, OCCUPATIONAL THERAPY, SPEECH PATHOLOGY, SOCIAL OR PSYCHOLOGICAL SERVICES, AND ORTHOTICS AND PROSTHETICS SERVICES.
62	**COMPREHENSIVE OUTPATIENT REHABILITATION FACILITY**	A FACILITY THAT PROVIDES COMPREHENSIVE REHABILITATION SERVICES UNDER THE SUPERVISION OF A PHYSICIAN TO OUTPATIENTS WITH PHYSICAL DISABILITIES. SERVICES INCLUDE PHYSICAL THERAPY, OCCUPATIONAL THERAPY, AND SPEECH PATHOLOGY SERVICES.
63-64	**UNASSIGNED**	N/A
65	**END-STAGE RENAL DISEASE TREATMENT FACILITY**	A FACILITY OTHER THAN A HOSPITAL, WHICH PROVIDES DIALYSIS TREATMENT, MAINTENANCE, AND/OR TRAINING TO PATIENTS OR CAREGIVERS ON AN AMBULATORY OR HOME-CARE BASIS.
66-70	**UNASSIGNED**	N/A
71	**PUBLIC HEALTH CLINIC**	A FACILITY MAINTAINED BY EITHER STATE OR LOCAL HEALTH DEPARTMENTS THAT PROVIDES AMBULATORY PRIMARY MEDICAL CARE UNDER THE GENERAL DIRECTION OF A PHYSICIAN.
72	**RURAL HEALTH CLINIC**	A CERTIFIED FACILITY WHICH IS LOCATED IN A RURAL MEDICALLY UNDERSERVED AREA THAT PROVIDES AMBULATORY PRIMARY MEDICAL CARE UNDER THE GENERAL DIRECTION OF A PHYSICIAN.
73-80	**UNASSIGNED**	N/A
81	**INDEPENDENT LABORATORY**	A LABORATORY CERTIFIED TO PERFORM DIAGNOSTIC AND/OR CLINICAL TESTS INDEPENDENT OF AN INSTITUTION OR A PHYSICIAN'S OFFICE.
82-98	**UNASSIGNED**	N/A
99	**OTHER PLACE OF SERVICE**	OTHER PLACE OF SERVICE NOT IDENTIFIED ABOVE.
* REVISED, EFFECTIVE APRIL 1, 2004		

Appendix C: Glossary

5010. Transaction standard for electronic submission of health care claims, replacing the current X12 standard, that can accommodate HIPAA code sets and is required for use as of 01/01/2012. Synonym: HIPAA 5010.

ACH. Automated clearinghouse. Entity that processes or facilitates the processing of information received from another entity in a nonstandard format or containing nonstandard data content into standard data elements or a standard transaction, or that receives a standard transaction from another entity and processes or facilitates the processing of that information into nonstandard format or nonstandard data content for a receiving entity.

actual charge. Charge a physician or supplier bills for a service rendered or a supply item.

actuarial assumptions. Characteristics used in calculating the risks and costs of a plan, including age, sex, and occupation of enrollees; location; utilization rates; and service costs.

additional development request. Formal request from a Medicare contractor for additional information needed to determine if a claim is covered and/or payable.

adjudication. Processing and review of a submitted claim resulting in payment, partial payment, or denial. In relationship to judicial hearings, it is the process of hearing and settling a case through an objective, judicial procedure.

adjusted average per capita cost. Estimated average cost of Medicare benefits for an individual, based upon criteria including age, sex, institutional status, Medicaid, disability, and end-stage renal failure.

administrative code sets. Code sets that characterize a general business situation, rather than a medical condition or service. Under HIPAA, these are sometimes referred to as nonclinical or nonmedical code sets.

administrative services only. Contractual agreement between a self-funded plan and an insurance company in which the insurance company assumes no risk and provides administrative services only.

administrative simplification. Title II, subtitle of HIPAA, that gives HHS the authority to mandate the use of standards for the electronic exchange of health care data; to specify what medical and administrative code sets should be used within those standards; to require the use of national identification systems for health care patients, providers, payers (or plans), and employers (or sponsors); and to specify the types of measures required to protect the security and privacy of personally identifiable health care information. This is also the name of Title II, subtitle F, part C of HIPAA.

advance beneficiary notice. Written communication with a Medicare beneficiary given before Part B services are rendered, informing the patient that the provider (including independent laboratories, physicians, practitioners, and/or suppliers) believes Medicare will not pay for some or all of the services to be rendered. Form CMS-R-131 (revised 03/2011) may be used for all situations where Medicare payment is expected to be denied.

AFEHCT. Association for Electronic Health Care Transactions. Organization that promotes the use of electronic data interchange (EDI) in the health care industry.

affiliation period. Alternative to preexisting condition exclusions. The length of time an HMO may require prior to issuing benefits. No premium may be charged during this waiting period and per HIPAA, the affiliation period may not last longer than two months (three months for late enrollees). The start date of the affiliation period must commence on your enrollment date under the GHP. If you switch to HMO coverage more than three months after your enrollment date, no affiliation period may be imposed.

age/sex rating. In health care contracting, structuring capitation payments based on members' ages and genders.

aggregate amount. Contracted maximum for which a member is insured for any single event in a health plan.

alternative delivery system. Any health care delivery system other than traditional fee-for-service.

American National Standards Institute. Organization that accredits various standards-setting committees and monitors their compliance with the open rule-making process that they must follow to qualify for ANSI accreditation. HIPAA prescribes that the standards mandated under it be developed by ANSI-accredited bodies whenever practical.

ARRA. American recovery and reinvestment act of 2009.

automated clearinghouse. Entity that processes or facilitates the processing of information received from another entity in a nonstandard format or containing nonstandard data content into standard data elements or a standard transaction, or that receives a standard transaction from another entity and processes or facilitates the processing of that information into nonstandard format or nonstandard data content for a receiving entity.

average length of stay. Average number of inpatient days within a given diagnosis-related group (DRG, the inpatient prospective payment system for Medicare patients). The average length of stay is based on factors such as geographical location and diagnosis and is also used to determine payment for outlier cases.

BA. Business associate. Person or organization that performs a function or activity on behalf of a covered entity but is not part of the covered entity's workforce. A business associate can also be a covered entity in its own right.

balance billing. Arrangement prohibited in Medicare regulations and some payer contracts whereby a provider bills the patient for charges not reimbursed by the payer.

basic health services. Defined set of benefits all federally qualified HMOs must offer enrollees.

BCBSA. Blue Cross and Blue Shield Association. Association that represents the common interests of Blue Cross and Blue Shield health plans. The BCBSA serves as the administrator for the Health Care Code Maintenance and also helps maintain the HCPCS Level II coding system.

beneficiary. Person entitled to receive Medicare or other payer benefits who maintains a health insurance policy claim number.

biller. Person who submits claims for services provided by a health care provider or supplier to payers.

billing agency. Company the applicant contracts with to prepare or edit the content of the claim.

carrier. Insurer or health plan that may underwrite, administer, or sell a range of health benefit programs.

CE. Covered entity. Under HIPAA, a health plan, a health care clearinghouse, or a health care provider who transmits any health information in electronic form in connection with a HIPAA transaction.

certificate of authority. State license to operate as an HMO.

Certificate of Coverage. Benefits included in an individual's health plan. State law requires all insured individuals and employers to receive a COC from the health plan providing coverage. Synonym: COC.

CHAMPUS. Civilian Health and Medical Program of the Uniformed Services. See Tricare.

CHAMPVA. Civilian Health and Medical Program of the Veteran's Administration.

charges. Dollar amount assigned to a service or procedure by a provider and reported to a payer.

charts. Compilation of documents maintained by the provider for each patient that includes treatment/progress notes, test orders and results, correspondence from other health care providers, and other documents pertinent to the patient's care.

CHIP. Children's Health Insurance Program.

church plan. Health plan established by and offered to employees of a church or other religious organization.

claim. Statement of services rendered requesting payment from an insurance company or a government entity.

claim adjustment reason codes. National administrative code set that identifies reasons for any differences or adjustments between the original provider charge for a claim or service and the payer's payment. This code set is used in the X12 835 claim payment and remittance advice and the X12 837 claim transactions, and is maintained by the Health Care Code Maintenance Committee. Synonym: CARC.

claim attachment. Any of a variety of hard copy documents or electronic records needed to process a claim in addition to the claim itself.

claim lag. Time elapsed between the date of a claim and its submission for payment.

claim manual. Administrative guidelines used by claims processors to adjudicate claims according to company policy and procedure.

claim rejection. Rejection of the entire claim. The provider may correct and resubmit the claim but may not appeal the claim.

claim status category codes. National administrative code set that indicates the general category of a health care claim's status. This code set is used in the X12 277 Claim Status Notification transaction, and is maintained by the Health Care Code Maintenance Committee.

claim status codes. National administrative code set that identifies the status of health care claims. This code set is used in the X12 277 claim status notification transaction and is maintained by the Health Care Code Maintenance Committee.

claims review. Examination of a submitted demand for payment by a Medicare contractor, insurer, or other group to determine payment liability, eligibility, reasonableness, or necessity of care provided.

clearinghouse. See health care clearinghouse.

CLIA. Clinical Laboratory Improvement Amendments. Requirements set in 1988, CLIA imposes varying levels of federal regulations on clinical procedures. Few laboratories, including those in physician offices, are exempt. Adopted by Medicare and Medicaid, CLIA regulations redefine laboratory testing in regard to laboratory certification and accreditation, proficiency testing, quality assurance, personnel standards, and program administration.

clinical reports. In the claims attachment proposed rule, reports, studies, or notes, including tests, procedures, and other clinical results, used to analyze and/or document an individual's medical condition.

closed claim. Claim for which all apparent benefits have been paid.

CMN. Certificate of medical necessity.

CMS. 1) Centers for Medicare and Medicaid Services. Federal agency that administers the public health programs. 2) Circulation motion sensation.

CMS manual system. Web-based manuals organized by functional area that contain all program instructions in the National Coverage Determinations Manual, the Medicare Benefit Policy Manual, Pub. 100, one-time notifications, and manual revision notices.

CMS manuals. Official government manuals prepared by CMS that detail procedures for processing and paying Medicare claims, preparing reimbursement forms, and billing procedures. These manuals were converted to web-based manuals (referred to as IOM, or Internet-only manuals) on October 1, 2003. At the time of the conversion, the manuals were streamlined, updated, and consolidated. Manuals may be accessed at http://www.cms.gov/manuals.

CMS-1450. Universal form used to file institutional claims.

CMS-1500. Universal form used to file professional claims.

COB. Coordination of benefits. In health care contracting, method of integrating benefits payable when there is more than one group insurance plan so that the insured's benefits and the payment of insurance benefits from all sources do not exceed 100 percent of the allowed medical expenses.

code set. Under HIPAA, any set of codes used to encode data elements, such as tables of terms, medical concepts, medical diagnosis codes, or medical procedure codes. This includes both the codes and their descriptions.

coder. Professional who translates documented, written diagnoses and procedures into numeric and alphanumeric codes.

coinsurance. Percentage of the allowed charges paid by a beneficiary toward the cost of care.

commercial carriers. For-profit insurance companies issuing health coverage.

commercial insurance carrier. See commercial carriers.

commercial plan. Health benefit coverage package offered by a commercial carrier.

common working file. System of local databases containing total beneficiary histories developed by CMS to improve Medicare claims processing. Medicare fiscal intermediaries, and/or carriers, interact with these databases to obtain data on eligibility, utilization, Medicare secondary payer (MSP), and other detailed claims information.

community rating. Methodology of state and federal governments that require qualified HMOs to request the same amount of money for each member in a plan.

comparative performance report. Report that provides an annual comparison of a physician's services and procedures with those of another physician in the same specialty and geographic area.

compliance date. Under HIPAA, date by which a covered entity must comply with a standard, implementation specification, or modification. This is usually 24 months after the effective date of the associated final rule for most entities but 36 months after the effective date for small health plans. For future changes in the standards, the compliance date would be at least 180 days after the effective date, but may be longer for small health plans and complex changes.

concurrent review. Review of services to determine medical necessity and appropriateness of care and occurring at the same time as the services are being provided.

conditional payment. Medicare reimbursement requested by the provider or supplier when worker's compensation, no-fault, or liability insurance will not pay or will not pay promptly. Such payments are conditioned upon reimbursement to Medicare if the other insurer has or had the responsibility to make primary payment. Promptly is defined as within 120 days after the claim was filed with an insurer or a lien is filed against a potential liability settlement.

Consolidated Omnibus Budget Reconciliation Act. Federal law that allows and requires past employees to be covered under company health insurance plans for a set premium, allowing individuals to remain insured when their current plan or position has been terminated. Synonym: COBRA.

coordination of benefits. Agreement that prevents duplicate payment for services when the member is covered by two or more sources. The agreement dictates which organization is primarily and secondarily responsible for payment. Synonym: COB.

Coordination of Benefits Agreement. Program that establishes a national standard contract between CMS and other health insurance organizations that defines the criteria for transmitting enrollee eligibility data and Medicare adjudicated claim data. CMS has transferred the claims crossover functions from individual Medicare contractors to a national claims crossover contractor, the Coordination of Benefits Contractor (COBC). This consolidation allows for the establishment of unique identifiers (COBA IDs) to be associated with each contract and create a national repository for COBA information. Synonym: COBA.

Coordination of Benefits Contractor. Contractor who consolidates activities that support the collection, management, and reporting of other insurance coverage for Medicare beneficiaries. The purposes of the COB program are to identify the health benefits available to a Medicare beneficiary and to coordinate the payment process to prevent mistaken payment of Medicare benefits. The COBC does not process claims, nor does it handle any mistaken payment recoveries or claims -specific inquiries. The Medicare intermediaries and carriers are responsible for processing claims submitted for primary or secondary payment. Synonym: COBC.

covered entity. Under HIPAA, a health plan, a health care clearinghouse, or a health care provider that transmits any health information in electronic form in connection with a HIPAA transaction.

data condition. 1) Collection of factual information represented by numeric or alphanumeric characters. 2) Description of the circumstances in which certain data are required. Under HIPAA, all of the data elements and code sets inherent to a transaction and not related to the format of the transaction.

data council. Coordinating body within the Department of Health and Human Services that has high-level responsibility for overseeing the implementation of the A/S provisions of HIPAA.

data dictionary. Document or system that characterizes the data content of a system.

data elements. Smallest named unit of information in a transaction. Data elements are standardized throughout the transaction set (e.g., DTP03) and always consist of a date or time period. The information placed in the field depends on the loop that it occupies. For example, in loop 2300, DTP03 is the discharge hour. In loop 2400, it is the date of service.

data mapping. Process of matching one set of data elements or individual code values to their closest equivalents in another set. This is sometimes called a crosswalk.

data model. Conceptual model of the information needed to support a business function or process.

data segment. Block or set of related data elements that contain related information (e.g., other diagnoses). A data segment may be one of two types: an information segment used to convey information about the provider, payer, or the services rendered; or a control segment that carries information necessary to the transmission and reception of the transaction.

data content. Under HIPAA, all the data elements and code sets inherent in a transaction and not related to the format of the transaction.

data elements. Smallest named unit of information in a transaction. Data elements are standardized throughout the transaction set (e.g., DTP03) and always consist of a date or time period. But the information placed in the field depends on the loop that it occupies. For example, in loop 2300, DTP03 is the discharge hour. In loop 2400, it is the date of service.

Data Interchange Standards Association. Organization that provides administrative services to X12 and several other standards-related groups.

database. Electronic store of utilization information used by payers to pay claims, negotiate contracts, and track utilization and cost of services.

date of service. Day the encounter or procedure is performed or the day a supply is issued. Synonym: DOS.

Department of Health and Human Services. Cabinet department that oversees the operating divisions of the federal government responsible for health and welfare. HHS oversees the Centers for Medicare and Medicaid Services, Food and Drug Administration, Public Health Service, and other such entities.

Department of Justice. Attorneys from the DOJ and the United States Attorney's Office have, under the memorandum of understanding, the same direct access to contractor data and records as the OIG and the Federal Bureau of Investigation (FBI). DOJ is responsible for prosecution of fraud and civil or criminal cases presented.

descriptor. Text defining a code in a code set.

designated code set. Medical code set or an administrative code set that the Department of Health and Human Services (HHS) has designated for use in one or more of the HIPAA standards.

direct claim payment. Method where members deal directly with the payer rather than submitting claims through the employer.

disclosure. Release or divulgence of information by an entity to persons or organizations outside of that entity.

disclosure history. Under HIPAA, list of entities that have received personally identifiable health care information for uses unrelated to treatment and payment.

DOB. Date of birth.

documentation. Physician's written or transcribed notations about a patient encounter, including a detailed operative report or written notes about a routine encounter. Source documentation must be the treating provider's own account of the encounter and may be transcribed from dictation, dictated by the physician into voice recognition software, or be hand- or typewritten. A signature or authentication accompanies each entry.

duplicate coverage inquiry. Request made to insurance companies or medical providers to determine whether there is other medical coverage under another plan. Synonym: DCI.

durable medical equipment. Medical equipment that can withstand repeated use, is not disposable, is used to serve a medical purpose, is generally not useful to a person in the absence of a sickness or injury, and is appropriate for use in the home. Examples of durable medical equipment include hospital beds, wheelchairs, and oxygen equipment. Synonyms: DME, DMEPOS.

effective date. Under HIPAA, the date that a final rule is effective, which is usually 60 days after it is published in the Federal Register.

EFT. Electronic funds transfer.

EHR. Electronic health record.

EIN. Employer identification number.

electronic claim. Claim submitted by a provider or an electronic media claim (EMC) vendor via central processing unit (CPU) transmission, tape, diskette, direct data entry, direct wire, dial-in telephone, digital fax, or personal computer upload or download. Effective October 1, 1993, clean claims submitted to Medicare electronically are paid 13 days after the claim is received.

electronic data interchange. Transference of claims, certifications, quality assurance reviews, and utilization data via computer in X12 format. May refer to any electronic exchange of formatted data.

electronic health record. Electronic version of individual patients' health-related information that has the interoperability to be created, managed, and consulted by more than one health care organization's authorized staff and clinicians.

electronic media claim. Automated claims processing method that uses a data storage tool to transfer claims data to the payer. EMC has been replaced by electronic data interchange (EDI).

electronic remittance advice. Any of several electronic formats explaining the payments of health care claims.

eligibility. Individuals and services qualified for coverage under a specific health care plan.

Employee Retirement Income Security Act of 1974. Law mandating reporting, disclosure of grievance and appeals requirements, and fiduciary standards for group life and health plans that are sponsored by private (but not public) employers. Also preempts state benefit mandates and premium tax laws for self-funded group health plans and allows these plans to be exempt from local or state reimbursement systems. Synonyms: ERISA, Public Law 93-406.

enrollee. Person who subscribes to a specific health plan.

enrollment. Number of lives covered by the plan.

EOB. Explanation of benefits. Statement mailed to the member and provider explaining claim adjudication and payment.

EOMB. Explanation of Medicare benefits. Explanation of Medicaid benefits. Explanation of member benefits. Typically sent to the provider and the patient, an explanation of how Medicare, Medicaid, or member benefits were paid, that is, the allowable amount paid, the coinsurance due to the provider or payable by the patient, or the reason why a claim may have been rejected or paid less or more than the original amount charged.

EPO. Exclusive provider organization. In health care contracting, an organization similar to an HMO, but the member must remain within the provider network to receive benefits. EPOs are regulated under insurance statutes rather than HMO legislation.

ERISA. Employee Retirement Income Security Act of 1974, Public Law 93-406. Mandates reporting, disclosure of grievance and appeals requirements, fiduciary standards for private group life and health plans, and preempts state benefit mandates and premium tax laws for self-funded group health plans.

exclusions. Services excluded from a plan's coverage by the employer or payer because of risk or cost.

exclusive provider organization. Similar to an HMO, but the member must remain within the provider network to receive benefits. EPOs are regulated under insurance statutes rather than HMO legislation. Synonym: EPO.

experience rating. Designation of a group's previous claims history to help determine premium rates.

False Claims Act. Governs civil actions for filing false claims. Liability under this act pertains to any person who knowingly presents or causes to be presented a false or fraudulent claim to the government for payment or approval.

Federal Register. Government publication listing changes in regulations and federally mandated standards, including coding standards such as HCPCS Level II and ICD-9-CM.

federally qualified HMO. HMO that meets CMS guidelines for Medicare reimbursement.

fee for service. Payment for services, usually physician services, on a service-by-service basis rather than an alternative payment system like capitation. Fee-for-service arrangements may be discounted or undiscounted rates.

format. Under HIPAA, data elements that provide or control the enveloping or hierarchical structure or help identify data content of a transaction.

fraud and abuse. Method of obtaining unauthorized benefits. Fraud is an intentional deception, misrepresentation, or statement that is known to be false. Abuse is a practice that is inconsistent with accepted medical, business, or fiscal practices.

GAO. General accounting office.

government mandates. Services mandated by state or federal law.

grace period. Set number of days past the due date of a premium payment during which medical coverage may not be canceled and the premium payment may be made, or after employment termination. It varies by health plan contract and state law but is generally 30 to 60 days.

group health plan. Under HIPAA, employee welfare benefit plan that provides for medical care and either has 50 or more participants or is administered by another business entity.

group model. HMO that contracts with a group of providers.

group segment. One or more related transaction sets. The group segment begins with the header and ends with the trailer. One complete transmission of a batch of institutional 837 claims is a group segment.

Health and Human Services. Cabinet department that oversees the operating divisions of the federal government responsible for health and welfare. HHS oversees the Centers for Medicare and Medicaid Services, Food and Drug Administration, Public Health Service, and other such entities.

health care clearinghouse. Under HIPAA, entity that processes or facilitates the processing of information received from another entity in a nonstandard format or containing nonstandard data content into standard data elements or a standard transaction, or that receives a standard transaction from another entity and processes or facilitates the processing of that information into nonstandard format or nonstandard data content for a receiving entity.

Health Care Code Maintenance Committee. Organization administered by the Blue Cross and Blue Shield Association that maintains certain coding schemes used in the X12 transactions and elsewhere. These include the claim adjustment reason codes, the claim status category codes, and the claim status codes.

health care operations. Specific set of activities related to an entity's covered functions.

health care provider. Entity that administers diagnostic and therapeutic services.

Health Care Provider Taxonomy Committee. Organization administered by the NUCC responsible for maintaining the provider taxonomy coding scheme used in the X12 transactions. The detailed code maintenance is done in coordination with X12N/TG2/WG15.

Health Informatics Standards Board. Standards group accredited by the American National Standards Institute that has developed an inventory of candidate standards for consideration as possible HIPAA standards.

health information. Information, whether oral or recorded in any form or medium, that is created or received by a covered entity; relates to the past, present, or future physical or mental health or condition of an individual; the provision of health care to an individual; or for the past, present, or future payment for the provision of health care to an individual.

Health Insurance Association of America. Industry association that represents the interests of commercial health care insurers. The HIAA participates in the maintenance of some code sets, including the HCPCS Level II codes.

health insurance claim number. Number issued by the Social Security Administration to individuals or beneficiaries entitled to Medicare benefits. The HICN card provides the beneficiary information necessary for processing Medicare claims.

Health Insurance Portability and Accountability Act of 1996 (HIPAA). Federal law that allows persons to qualify immediately for comparable health insurance coverage when they change employment relationships. Title II, subtitle F, of HIPAA gives the Department of Health and Human Services the authority to mandate the use of standards for the electronic exchange of health care data; to specify what medical and administrative code sets should be used within those standards; to require the use of national identification systems for health care patients, providers, payers (or plans), and employers (or sponsors); and to specify the types of measures required to protect the security and privacy of personally identifiable health care information.

health maintenance organization (HMO). Medical health insurance coverage that pays claims based on provider cost, per diem, or charge basis. Hospitals contract with an HMO to provide care at a contractually reduced price. HMO members pay a set monthly amount for coverage and are treated without additional cost, except for a copayment or deductible amount. Like all managed care organizations, HMOs use a variety of mechanisms to control costs, including utilization management, discounted provider fee schedules, and financial incentives. HMOs use primary care physicians as gatekeepers and emphasize preventive care.

health plan. Program that provides or pays the cost of health care services.

health plan ID. System for uniquely identifying all organizations that pay for health care services. Formerly referred to as the payer ID. Synonyms: health plan ID, national payer ID, plan ID.

health reimbursement account. Health care coverage funded by the employer as an employee benefit, administered by a third-party administrator, and may include employee tax exempt contributions.

health savings account. Health care coverage plan with a high deductible provided as part of a qualified trust that includes tax exempt employee contributions equal to the deductible up to a maximum level set by law.

HIC number. Health insurance claim number or Medicare identification number.

HICN. Health insurance claim number. Number issued by the Social Security Administration to individuals or beneficiaries entitled to Medicare benefits. The HICN card provides the beneficiary information necessary for processing Medicare claims.

HITECH. Health information technology for economic and clinical health.

hold harmless. Contractual clause stating that if either party is held liable for malpractice, the other party is absolved.

HPAG. HIPAA Policy Advisory Group, a BCBSA subgroup.

HPID. Health Plan Identifier. A 10-digit data element for health plan organizations to use in transactions with other covered entities and is also a new requirement for those health care providers who did not need to obtain and disclose a national provider identifier (NPI) in 2013. HPIDs will only be required for electronic transactions at this time. Complaince date for health plans is November 5, 2014 except small health plans who have until November 5, 2015.

ICD-10. International Classification of Diseases, 10th Revision. Classification of diseases by alphanumeric code, used by the World Health Organization.

implementation guide. Document explaining the proper use of a standard for a specific business purpose. The X12N HIPAA implementation guides (IG) are the primary reference documents used by those implementing the associated transactions, and are incorporated into the HIPAA regulations by reference.

indemnification. Type of hold-harmless clause that requires the responsible party in a liability claim to compensate the second party should the responsible party's actions result in liability to the second party.

independent medical evaluation. Examination carried out by an impartial health care provider, generally board certified, to resolve a dispute related to the nature and extent of an illness or injury.

individual practice association. Organization made up of providers who, along with the rest of a group, contract with payers at a discounted fee-for-service or capitated rate.

internal control number. Unique, 15-digit identifying number assigned by a Medicare carrier to every claim for control and inventory purposes that indicates the claim type, region, year, Julian date, batch number, and sequence. Synonym: ICN.

internet-only manuals (IOM). Internet-only manuals replace instructions previously contained in paper-based manuals.

itemized statement. Detailed statement of each item or service the patient received from the physician, hospital, or other health care supplier or professional. The BBA of 1997 gives Medicare beneficiaries the right to submit a written request for an itemized statement from their provider or supplier for any Medicare item or service. Providers and suppliers are required to furnish the itemized statement within 30 days of the request or be subject to a civil monetary penalty of up to $100 for each offense. Recommended information to be included on the itemized statement includes date(s) of service, description of services provided, number of services provided, benefit days used, noncovered charges, deductible and coinsurance amounts, amount charged, beneficiary liability, total paid by Medicare, referring physician, provider/supplier submitting the claim, and the Medicare claim number.

late charge. In relation to facility billing, a charge posted to an account after the final bill has been produced.

LCD. Local coverage determination. Published decision by a Medicare contractor regarding coverage guidelines for a particular service and is valid only in the contractor's jurisdiction. LCDs replaced local medical review policies for CMS as of 2006.

length of stay. Number of inpatient bed days for a single patient during a single admission. Synonym: LOS.

length of stay outliers. Cases in which length of stay falls outside the norm for a given diagnosis, procedure, or DRG. The length of stay may be longer or shorter than is typical.

liability insurance. Insurance that protects against claims for negligence or inappropriate action or inaction that resulted in injury to a person or damage to property.

lifetime maximum. Maximum amount an insurance plan pays on behalf of the insured for covered services received while enrolled.

limiting charge. Maximum amount a nonparticipating physician or provider can charge for services rendered to a Medicare patient.

limits. In medical reimbursement, the ceiling for benefits payable under a plan.

line item. Specific service or item detail of claim.

line item denial. Fiscal intermediary's denial of a specific line item on a claim that may be otherwise processable. Rejected line items cannot be corrected by the provider but may be appealed.

line item rejection. Fiscal intermediary's rejection of a line item on a claim that may be otherwise processable for payment. These rejected line items may be corrected and resubmitted by the provider, but cannot be appealed.

line of business. Different health plans offered by a larger insurer or insurance broker as a product line.

lives. Unit of measurement used by plans to determine the number of people covered. Calculated by multiplying the number of members by 2.5.

local codes. Generic term for code values that are defined for a state or other political subdivision, or for a specific payer. This term most commonly describes HCPCS Level III codes, but also applies to state-assigned institutional revenue codes, condition codes, occurrence codes, value codes, etc.

loop. Set of related data. For example, all billing provider information is contained in loop 2000A.

loss ratio. Ratio between the cost to deliver medical care and the amount of money taken in by the plan.

MAC. Medicare administrative contractor. One of 15 jurisdictional organizations that contract with CMS to adjudicate professional claims under Part A and Part B, responsible for daily claims processing, utilization review, record maintenance, dissemination of information based on CMS regulations, and whether services are covered and payments are appropriate. Four of the jurisdictions also include home health services. There are four separate MAC jurisdictions for DME services.

managed care organization. Generic term for various health benefit plans that provide coverage for health care services in conjunction with management and review of services provided to ensure services are medically necessary and appropriate. Synonym: MCO.

managed health care. 1) Managing active cases to ensure care is the most appropriate, efficient, and effective. 2) System of health care meant to manage overall cost. 3) Method of health care whereby contracted physicians participate in managing health care costs.

mandated benefits. Services mandated by state or federal law such as child abuse or rape, not necessarily covered by insurers.

mandated providers. Providers of medical care, such as psychologists, optometrists, podiatrists, and chiropractors, whose licensed services must, under state or federal law, be included in coverage offered by a health plan.

maximum allowable actual charge. Former provision of the Medicare program that applied to nonparticipating physicians before January 1, 1991, and set a limit on charges for physicians' professional services and most services provided incident to the professional services.

maximum out-of-pocket costs. Limit on total patient payments including copayments, deductibles, and coinsurance under a benefit contract in a specified time period.

meaningful use. 1) Sets of guidelines that must be followed as part of the HITECH Act. Three main components are specified in the Act: use of certified EHR in a meaningful manner (i.e., e-prescribing), electronic exchange of health information to improve the quality of health care, and submission of clinical quality and other measures. 2) Use of certified electronic health technology in measurable ways of both quality and quantity.

medical and other health services. Any of the services provided to a patient to diagnose, treat, or maintain health status, including services of health care providers and professionals; rural, inpatient, outpatient, and diagnostic services; physical/occupational/speech/sports therapy; dialysis; immunization and vaccines; blood products; drugs; nutritional and diagnosis instruction; equipment; supplies; and ambulance services.

medical code sets. Codes that characterize a medical condition or treatment. These code sets are usually maintained by professional societies and public health organizations.

medical documentation. Patient care records, including operative notes; physical, occupational, and speech-language pathology notes; progress notes; physician certification and recertifications; and emergency room records; or the patient's medical record in its entirety.

medical loss ratio. Ratio between the cost to deliver medical care and the amount of money taken in by the plan.

medical necessity. Medically appropriate and necessary to meet basic health needs; consistent with the diagnosis or condition and national medical practice guidelines regarding type, frequency, and duration of treatment; rendered in a cost-effective manner.

Medicare administrative contractor. Uniform type of Medicare administrative entity that processes both institutional and professional claims in specified geographic jurisdictions of the country. There are 15 A/B MACs that are scheduled to be combined into a total of 10 A/B MACS, while maintaining four DME MACs, and four home health/hospice MACs.

Medicare carrier. Organization that contracts with CMS to adjudicate professional claims under Part B, the supplemental medical insurance program. Medicare carriers are responsible for daily claims processing, utilization review, record maintenance, dissemination of information based on CMS regulations, and determining whether services are covered and payments are appropriate. This organization has been replaced by Medicare administrative contractors.

Medicare Carriers Manual. Manual provided by the Centers for Medicare and Medicaid Services to Medicare carriers containing instructions for processing and paying Medicare claims, preparing reimbursement forms, billing procedures, and adhering to Medicare regulations. This has been replaced by the Medicare manual system. Synonym: MCM.

Medicare Claims Processing Manual. CMS Internet-only manual (Pub. 100-04) that consolidated and replaced the paper hospital, intermediary, and carrier manuals. The manual outlines billing and processing instructions for all claim types.

Medicare contractor. Medicare Part A fiscal intermediary, Medicare Part B carrier, Medicare administrative contractor (MAC), or a durable medical equipment Medicare administrative contractor (DME MAC).

Medicare fee schedule. Fee schedule based upon physician work, expense, and malpractice designed to slow the rise in cost for services and standardize payment to physicians regardless of specialty or location of service with geographic adjustments.

Medicare Part B. Supplemental medical insurance that includes outpatient hospital care and physician and other qualified professional care. Claims from providers or suppliers other than a hospital are submitted to carriers for reimbursement. Hospital outpatient claims are submitted to their FI/MAC.

Medicare physician fee schedule. List of payments Medicare allows by procedure or service. Payments may vary through geographic adjustments. The MPFS is based on the resource-based relative value scale (RBRVS). A national total relative value unit (RVU) is given to each procedure (HCPCS Level I CPT, Level II national codes). Each total RVU has three components: physician work, practice expense, and malpractice insurance. Synonym: MPFS.

Medicare remittance advice remark codes. National administrative code set for providing claim or service-level Medicare-related messages that cannot be expressed with a claim adjustment reason code. This code set is used in the X12 835 Claim Payment & Remittance Advice transaction, and is maintained by the Centers for Medicare and Medicaid Services.

Medicare secondary payer. Specified circumstance when other third-party payers have the primary responsibility for payment of services and Medicare is the secondary payer. Medicare is secondary to workers' compensation, automobile, medical no-fault and liability insurance, EGHPs, LGHPs, and certain employer health plans covering aged and disabled beneficiaries. The MSP program prohibits Medicare payment for items or services if payment has been made or can reasonably be expected to be made by another payer, as described above.

Medicare supplement. Private insurance coverage that pays the Medicare deductible and copayments and may also pay the costs of services not covered by Medicare.

Medigap. Individual health insurance offered by a private entity to those persons entitled to Medicare benefits and is specifically designed to supplement Medicare benefits. It fills in some of the gaps in Medicare coverage by providing payment for some of the charges, deductibles, coinsurance amounts, or other limitations imposed by Medicare.

member. Subscriber of a health plan.

member months. Total of months each member was covered.

member services. In health care contracting, the payer department that works as a patient advocate to solve problems and may take claims appeals to a final committee after all other processes have been exhausted.

midlevel practitioners. Professionals such as nurse practitioners, nurse midwives, physical therapists, physician assistants, and others who provide medical care but do so with physician input. Synonyms: MLP, nonphysician practitioners, NPP.

minimum scope of disclosure. Principal that individually identifiable health information should be disclosed only to the extent needed to support the purpose of the disclosure.

modify or modification. Under HIPAA, change adopted by the secretary, through regulation, to a standard or an implementation specification.

National Association of Insurance Commissioners. Organization of state insurance regulators. Synonym: NAIC.

National Center for Health Statistics. Division of the Centers for Disease Control and Prevention that compiles statistical information used to guide actions and policies to improve the public health of U.S. citizens. The NCHS maintains the ICD-9-CM coding system.

national employer ID. System for uniquely identifying all sponsors of health care benefits.

national patient ID. System for uniquely identifying all recipients of health care services.

national payer ID. System for uniquely identifying all organizations that pay for health care services.

national provider identifier. Identification system developed by CMS to designate types of providers in the health care industry, including physicians, suppliers, home health agencies, and hospitals. Synonym: NPI.

national standard format. Generically, this applies to any nationally standardized data format, but it is often used in a more limited way to designate the professional EMC NSF, a 320-byte flat file record format used to submit professional claims. Synonym: NSF.

National Supplier Clearinghouse. Entity that approves providers and medical equipment vendors as "suppliers" under the Medicare program, issuing an identification number to approved applicants.

National Uniform Claim Committee. Organization, chaired and hosted by the American Medical Association, that maintains the CMS-1500 claim form and a set of data element specifications for professional claims submission via the CMS-1500 claim form, the Professional EMC NSF, and the X12 837. NUCC also maintains the provider taxonomy codes and has a formal consultative role under HIPAA for all transactions affecting nondental, noninstitutional professional health care services. Synonym: NUCC.

NCCI. National correct coding initiative. Official list of codes from the Centers for Medicare and Medicaid Services' (CMS) National Correct Coding Policy Manual for Part B Medicare Carriers that identifies services considered an integral part of a comprehensive code or mutually exclusive of it. Synonyms: CCI, correct coding initiative.

NCD. National coverage determinations. National policy statements granting, eliminating, or excluding Medicare coverage for a service, item, or test and indicate CMS policy regarding the circumstances under which the service, item, or test is considered reasonable and necessary or otherwise not covered for Medicare purposes.

NHII. National Health Information Infrastructure.

nonclinical or nonmedical code sets. Code sets that characterize a general business situation, rather than a medical condition or service. Under HIPAA, these are sometimes referred to as nonclinical or nonmedical code sets.

noncovered services. Health care services that are not reimbursable according to provisions of a given insurance policy.

NPI. National provider identifier. Standard eight-digit alphanumeric provider identifier implemented under the Health Insurance Portability and Accountability Act of 1996 (HIPAA) requirements. The first seven digits identify the provider and the eighth position is a check digit. Providers are required to report their NPI number for electronic and paper billing.

NSF. National standard format.

NUCC. National Uniform Claim Committee. Organization, chaired and hosted by the American Medical Association, that maintains the CMS-1500 claim form and a set of data element specifications for professional claims submission via the CMS-1500 claim form, the Professional EMC NSF, and the X12 837. The NUCC also maintains the provider taxonomy codes and has a formal consultative role under HIPAA for all transactions affecting nondental, noninstitutional professional health care services.

OEID. Other entity identifier. Data element that identifies organizations and entities, other than health plans, providers, or patients, for tracking purposes when used in reporting standard transactions by health care plans, providers or others in the health care industry.

OESS. Office of E-Health Standards and Services.

Office for Civil Rights. Department of Health and Human Services entity responsible for enforcing the HIPAA privacy rules. Synonym: OCR.

Office of Inspector General. Agency within the Department of Health and Human Services ultimately responsible for investigating instances of fraud and abuse in the Medicare and Medicaid and other government health care programs. Synonym: OIG.

Office of Management and Budget. Federal government agency that plays a major role in reviewing proposed federal regulations. Synonym: OMB.

OMB. Office of Management and Budget. Federal government agency that plays a major role in reviewing proposed federal regulations.

ordering physician. Physician who orders nonphysician services (e.g., laboratory services, pharmaceutical services, imaging services, or durable medical equipment) for a patient.

out of area. Medical care received out of the geographic area that may or may not be covered depending on the plan.

paneled. In health care contracting, provider contracted with an HMO.

paper claim. Claim that is submitted on paper, including optical character recognition (OCR) claims and claims that are converted to electronic format by Medicare. Medicare will not pay clean paper claims until the 26th day after the claim is received.

par provider. Provider who is participating in a health plan or Medicare program.

partial payment. Payment to a provider or member with the expectation that other payments will be forthcoming before the claim is closed.

participating provider. Provider who has contracted with the health plan to deliver medical services to covered persons.

patient status. Patient's discharge status as of the "through" date (or discharge date) of the billing period. This information is required for both inpatient and outpatient claims for Medicare billing purposes. Patient status may be any of the following: routine discharge, discharged to another facility, still a patient, or expired.

PATOS. Payment (received) at the time of service.

payer. Entity that assumes the risk of paying for medical treatments. This can be an uninsured patient, a self-insured employer, a health plan, or an HMO.

PAYERID. Centers for Medicare and Medicaid Services' term for its pre-HIPAA national payer ID initiative.

payment floor. Minimum number of calendar days that must pass before Medicare can pay a claim, established by Omnibus Budget Reconciliation Act of 1987 for Medicare claims. Payment is made no earlier than 14 days after claim submission for electronic claims and no earlier than 27 days for paper claims submission.

payment rate. Amount paid to the provider for health care services rendered to a plan member.

peer review. Evaluation of the quality of the total health care provided by medical staff with equivalent training, such as a physician-to-physician or nurse-to-nurse evaluation.

peer review organization. Organization that contracts with CMS to conduct preadmission, preprocedure, and postdischarge medical reviews and determine medical necessity, appropriateness, and quality of certain inpatient and outpatient surgical procedures for which payment may be made in whole or in part under the Medicare program.

PHI. Protected health information.

physician services. Professional services performed by physicians, including surgery, consultations, and home, office, and institutional calls.

physician work. One of three components used to develop relative value units (RVU) under the resource-based relative value scale. Physician work represents the value of the skill and time required to perform a service.

plan ID. System for uniquely identifying all organizations that pay for health care services.

plan sponsor. Entity that sponsors a health plan. This can be an employer, a union, or some other entity.

POS. Point of service. Health benefit plan allowing the covered person to choose to receive a service from a participating or nonparticipating provider, with different benefit levels associated with the use of participating providers.

PPO. Preferred provider organization. Program that establishes contracts with providers of medical care. Usually the benefit contract provides significantly better benefits and lower member cost for services received from preferred providers, encouraging covered persons to use these providers, who may be reimbursed on a discounted basis.

protected health information. Information that identifies an individual and describes his or her health status, age, sex, ethnicity, or other demographic characteristics. Synonym: PHI.

provider taxonomy codes. Administrative code set for identifying the provider type and area of specialization for all health care providers. A given provider can have several provider taxonomy codes. This code set is used in the X12 278 Referral Certification and Authorization and the X12 837 Claim Transactions, and is maintained by the National Uniform Claim Committee.

QIC. Qualified independent contractor.

reasonable and customary. Fees charged for medical services that are considered normal, common, and in line with the prevailing fees in the provider's geographical area.

reasonable charge. Under Medicare, lowest of either the actual charge, the charge customarily billed to patients, or the prevailing charge for the service. The reasonable charge represents the charge determination made by a carrier on a covered Part B medical service or supply.

recoupment. Recovery by a payer of any debt by reducing present or future payments and applying the amount withheld to the indebtedness.

regulation. Directive, order, ruling, or law put forth by an executive authority granted such powers by law.

release of information. Authorization from the patient that allows the hospital to release to the insurer or other payer the medical and billing information for determining coverage eligibility, medical necessity, the final diagnosis, and any procedures performed or as needed to process a claim for reimbursement.

remittance advice. Statement, voucher, or notice received by the service provider from a payer reflecting the status of adjudicated claims, either paid or denied. Synonyms: EOB, ERA, RA.

reopening. Action taken, after all appeal rights are exhausted, to re-examine or question the correctness of a final determination, decision, or cost report.

resource-based relative value scale. Fee schedule introduced by the Centers for Medicare and Medicaid Services to reimburse physician Medicare fees based on the amount of time and resources expended in treating patients with adjustments for overhead costs and geographical differences. Synonym: RBRVS.

resubmitted claim. Claim that has been sent more than once to the payer for a response.

return to provider. Entire claim is returned to the provider for correction and resubmission. Synonym: RTP.

risk adjustment. Method of predicting and adjusting payment for expenditures related to health care services based upon patient diagnoses and certain demographic adjusters.

risk contract. Contract between Medicare and a payer or a payer and a provider in which the payer (in the case of Medicare) and the provider (in the case of the payer contracts) receive a set amount for care of a patient base. If costs exceed the amount the payer or provider was paid, the patients still receive care during the term of the contract.

risk factor reduction. Reduction of risk in the pool of health plan members.

risk pool. Pool of people who will be in the insured group, their medical and mental histories, other factors such as age, and their predicted health.

SCHIP. State Children's Health Insurance Program.

secondary insurer. In a COB arrangement, the insurer that reimburses for benefits pending after payment by the primary insurer.

secondary payer. Organization that pays, according to its coverage guidelines, any residual balance remaining after another insurer pays the claim.

segment. Group of related data elements in a transaction.

self-funded plan. Plan where the risk is assumed by the employer rather than the insurer. The employer generally pays claims directly from a general fund account that may be managed by a third party.

self-funding. Health care program in which employers fund benefit plans from their own resources without purchasing insurance. May be self-administered, or the employer may contract with an outside administrator.

self-insured. Individual or organization that assumes the financial risk of paying for health care.

self-pay patients. Patients who pay for medical care out-of-pocket.

service date. Date a charge is incurred for a service.

service plan. 1) Plan that has contracts with providers but is not a managed care plan. 2) Another name for Blue Cross/Blue Shield plans.

signature. Physician's signature acknowledges that he/she has performed or supervised the service or procedure and that the transcription has been read and corrections made before signing. Signed or initialed laboratory and x-ray results show auditors that the physician has reviewed the information.

small health plan. Under HIPAA, health plan with annual receipts of $5 million or less.

SSN. Social security number.

standard transaction. Under HIPAA, transaction that complies with the applicable HIPAA standard.

tax identification number. Number an individual or organization uses to report tax information to the Internal Revenue Service, such as a Social Security Number (SSN) or employer identification number. Synonyms: EIN, TIN.

taxonomy code. Ten-character, alphanumeric sequence code that identifies the area of specialty of a provider. CMS maintains and distributes these codes.

tertiary payer. Third party responsible for paying a health insurance claim after the primary and secondary insurers have satisfied their payment obligations.

third-party administrator. Firm that performs administrative functions for a self-funded plan but assumes no risk. Synonym: TPA.

third-party liability. Third-party payer liable for the cost of an illness or injury, such as an auto or homeowner's insurer.

third-party payer. Public or private organization that pays for or underwrites coverage for health care expenses for another entity, usually an employer (e.g., Blue Cross Blue Shield, Medicare, Medicaid, commercial insurers).

time limit. In health care contracting, a set number of days in which a claim can be filed according to the payer or state insurance commission.

trading partner agreement. Agreement between the provider and the receiver of the claim transmission detailing the electronic data interchange requirements between the parties. For purposes of HIPAA, a trading partner agreement may not include any agreement to use the codes, segments, or transactions published in an implementation guide in a manner differently from that prescribed in the applicable guide. The agreement does not need to be formal. It may take the form of a manual, bulletin, or memorandum.

transaction. Exchange or transfer of information between two parties to carry out financial or administrative activities related to health care.

TRICARE. Federal program that covers the health benefits for families of all uniformed service employees. Formerly called CHAMPUS.

underbilled services. Uncoded or undercoded services that are often the result of medical records that lack the detail necessary to code at full reimbursement levels.

underwriting. Evaluating and determining the financial risk a member or member group has on an insurer.

undocumented services. Billed service for which the supporting documentation has not been recorded or is unavailable to substantiate the service.

Uniform Claim Task Force. Organization that developed the initial CMS-1500 professional claim form. The maintenance responsibilities were later assumed by the National Uniform Claim Committee.

usual, customary, and reasonable. Fees charged for medical services that are considered normal, common, and in line with the prevailing fees in a given geographical area.

utilization review. Formal assessment of the medical necessity, efficiency, and/or appropriateness of health care services and treatment plans on a prospective, concurrent, or retrospective basis.

verification of eligibility. Process by which the payer or provider determines that the beneficiary is currently enrolled in a plan and that the requested services are covered by the plan.

violation. Disregard or abuse of the laws, rules, or guidelines, knowingly or unknowingly resulting in receipt of inappropriate reimbursement.

waiver of liability. Provision established by Medicare to protect beneficiaries and physicians from liability when services are denied as inappropriate or medically unnecessary. Under the provision, if the Medicare beneficiary knew or should have known that the services billed for were not covered, the beneficiary is liable for paying for the services. If neither the beneficiary nor the hospital knew or reasonably could have been expected to know that the services were not covered, Medicare is liable for paying the claim. If the provider should have known and the beneficiary is protected from liability, then liability falls with the provider, and the hospital cannot bill the beneficiary for services other than deductibles and coinsurance amounts, even though no Medicare payment has been made. Beneficiaries who do not know that services were noncovered are protected from liability when the services are not reasonable and/or necessary (including adverse level of care determinations) and when custodial care is involved.

Washington Publishing Company. Company that publishes the X12N HIPAA implementation guides and the X12N HIPAA Data Dictionary, developed the X12 Data Dictionary, and hosts the EHNAC STFCS testing program.

whistleblower. Individual who discloses misconduct by a provider and may be eligible for monetary returns if the misconduct involves financial misconduct as determined on a case-by-case basis.

withhold. Percentage of payment to providers held by an HMO until the cost of referral or services has been determined. If the provider goes over the amount determined appropriate, the HMO keeps that amount.

workers' compensation. State-governed system designated to administer and regulate the provision and cost of medical treatment and wage losses arising from a worker's job-related injury or disease, regardless of who is at fault. In exchange, the employer is protected from being sued.

working aged. Patient or spouse, older than age 65, eligible for group health insurance through employment or the employment of his or her spouse. Under these circumstances, Medicare would be the secondary payer.

X12. ANSI-accredited group that defines EDI standards for health care. Most of the electronic transactions standards mandated or proposed under HIPAA are X12 standards.

X12 837. X12 "Health Care Claim or Encounter" transaction. This transaction can be used for institutional, professional, dental, or drug claims. Version 4010 of this transaction has been included in the HIPAA mandates.

X12 Standard. X12 standard that has been approved since the most recent release of X12 American National Standards. Since a full set of X12 American National Standards is released only about once every five years, it is the X12 standards that are most likely to be in active use. These standards were previously called "draft standards for trial use."

YTD. Year to date.